THE FORMATIVE YEARS OF

# AUSTRALIAN

C·R·I·C·K·E·T · 1803-93

Recent books by Jack Pollard

*Australian Fishing* (ed., 1986)
*When Stumps Were Drawn* (ed., 1985)
*Australian Rugby Union: The Game and the Players* (1984)
*Tribute to Lillee and Chappell* (1984)
*The Pictorial History of Australian Cricket* (1983)
*Australian Cricket: The Game and the Players* (1982)

# THE FORMATIVE YEARS OF
# AUSTRALIAN
## C·R·I·C·K·E·T · 1803–93

### JACK POLLARD

ANGUS
& ROBERTSON
PUBLISHERS

# Contents

# Preface

This book covers the first 90 years of Australian cricket, from the initial matches between garrison troops and settlers in Sydney's Hyde Park — 15 years after settlement began — through the formation of the first clubs, the introduction of inter-colonial games, the first tours by England and Australia, the establishment of Test cricket, until the inauguration of the Sheffield Shield in 1892–93.

Few cricket books were published in Australia in this period, a hardship modern cricket lovers would find hard to bear. Followers of the game relied almost entirely on newspapers for more than 50 years, then handbooks and journals began to appear. Many of the early cricket reporters were as ignorant of finer points as the novice participants whose activities they covered, understandable in a period when the laws of cricket constantly changed.

When William Fairfax and H. Biers published the first *Australian cricketers' guide* in 1856–57 in Melbourne, they simply reviewed the previous season and the prospects for the approaching one, neglecting early history. This modest annual lasted for three summers. Similar handbooks by W. J. Hammersley (1861–62), W. O. Whitridge (1876–77), T. W. Wills (1870–71), John Conway (1876–77), Harry Boyle and David Scott (1879–80) and Goodfellow and Hele (1878–79) followed, but most had brief, erratic careers.

The first history of Australian cricket was South Australian Clarence P. Moody's slim 1894 paperback *Australian cricket and cricketers*, followed by his *Album of noted Australian cricketers*, issued in six monthly parts in 1898. Moody later published *The seventh Australian team in England* and

*South Australian cricket: reminiscences of fifty years*, but none was as important as his first book. In this Moody used the term Test match for the first time and suggested which matches should be granted Test status. He wrote:

> Most interesting and important of the hundreds of matches played in England and Australia by visiting elevens to one country or the other, were those which by common consent were aptly styled Test matches. Many of these matches excited transcendent interest. It is difficult to draw an arbitrary line between Test matches in the fullest sense of the word and those in which so-called weak Australian teams took part, but the delicate task must be undertaken.

Moody did the job so well that his list of the first 38 Test matches became universally accepted. It took a little longer before his use of the term "the Ashes" was accepted as a symbol of Anglo–Australian supremacy. The term originated as a joke following England's defeat at The Oval in 1882 and was then used in reference to the series that immediately followed when Ivo Bligh's 1882–83 team to Australia won two of the first three international matches. It was then forgotten until Pelham Warner, searching for a title for his book on how England won three of the five Tests in 1903–04, settled on *How we recovered the Ashes*.

Moody is believed to have been the ghost author of George Giffen's book *With bat and ball*, the first hardcover edition by an Australian cricketer, which discussed the early years of first-class cricket. This book ran into three editions when it first appeared in 1898 and was reprinted in a facsimile edition in 1982 as *The golden age of Australian cricket*.

Thankfully, there were many books published in England before World War I that provided absorbing accounts of Australian cricketers. These included William Caffyn's *Seventy-one not out*, Lillywhite's *Annuals* and *Cricketer's Companion*, Haygarth's *M.C.C. cricket scores and biographies*, Dr W. G. Grace's reminiscences titled *"W. G.":*

*Cricketing reminiscences, The Walkers of Southgate* by W. A. Bettesworth, *A few short runs* by Lord Harris, *A cricketer's log* by Gilbert Jessop, *Talks with old English cricketers* by A. W. Pullin ("Old Ebor"), *Cricket of today and yesterday* by Percy Cross Standing, *Cricket* by R. H. Lyttelton, Harry Altham's *A history of cricket*, Peter Wynne-Thomas's biography of Arthur Shrewsbury *"Give me Arthur"*, the annual editions of *Wisden's cricket almanack*, and all the books by F. S. Ashley-Cooper.

Of the books published in Australia, Johnny Moyes' *Australian cricket: a history*, published in 1959, remains a sound outline of our cricket past, and the work from which all Australian cricket historians begin. The book had minor imperfections (for example I found a reference to cricket in Queensland in 1844, whereas Moyes' first reference to the game there was in 1857), but in the three decades since it appeared very few important corrections have emerged, despite hundreds of hours of research. Overall his history remains valid and I referred to it extensively in preparing this book, particularly in the early chapters. Ray Robinson's *On top down under* and Richard Cashman's *'Ave a go, yer mug!* were enormously helpful, as was Chris Harte's *History of the Sheffield Shield*, researched by Ric Finlay. But the real treasure was Phillip Derriman's *True to the Blue*, an unsurpassed source book published in 1985 by Richard Smart in association with the New South Wales Cricket Association. It is to be hoped that other states will produce similar works.

All of these books provided valuable background on early Australian cricket, but the main record of matches and players, disputes and controversies in the colonies during the years before Federation was Australian newspapers. A few noted players kept albums in which they included clippings, menus and even steamship tickets. Regrettably, only a handful kept diaries or wrote down their tour experiences, although the 15 articles by Frank Allan on the first Australian tour of England remain invaluable. Fred Spofforth's articles and interviews after he retired were equally useful, as were the 38 pages of press cuttings on the first intercolonial matches between Victoria and New South Wales kept by George Marshall (Notts, MCC and Victoria) and presented to the Melbourne Cricket Club Museum by his granddaughter, Mrs A. Clarke.

Harry Hilliard's articles in *Old Times* on the first matches in Sydney's Hyde Park, James Scott's hand-written recollections of early Sydney cricket, Arthur Gregory's albums, the researches by officers of various branches of the Australian Cricket Society—including the late Radcliffe Grace and the librarians Cliff Winning and Rex Harcourt—all provide important sources. For the rest I relied on the now defunct journals like *Bell's Life, Lone Hand*, the *Moreton Bay Courier*, the *Sydney Gazette*, the *Queenslander*, the *Referee* and the *Sydney Mail*, all of them painstakingly filed by the Brisbane solicitor Pat Mullins in his famous Brisbane cricket library. All of the major sources consulted are listed in the Bibliography.

# A rough and uneven ground

## New South Wales 1803–50

Cricket had developed from a village green game played with a cric or curved staff into one of the most popular summer sports in England by the time Yorkshireman James Cook discovered eastern Australia in 1770. On a bare strip of Hampshire heathland known as Broadhalfpenny Down, the Hambledon Club had made the game famous. This unique team, formed in 1750, held its own against all comers until 1769, when for a time it was near extinction. But between 1771 and 1781, when the idea of Australia as a penal colony was first mooted, the Hambledon Club won 29 of its 51 matches.

All bowling at that time was underarm and bowlers chose the strips of turf on which matches were played. Fieldsmen smoked on the field and catches were sometimes spilled by players too slow in stowing away pipes. The teams wore coats, often with velvet collars, knee breeches, stockings and shoes with big buckles that could tear fields-

*Members of the Marylebone Cricket Club, founded in London in 1787, playing at Lord's before 1809 when the ground was moved to St John's Wood*

men's fingers. Billycock hats (an early form of the bowler hat) were still worn. Noblemen sponsored their own teams and often retained outstanding cricketers as gamekeepers or gardeners. Betting was an integral part of the game.

When Governor Arthur Phillip sailed from Portsmouth in May 1787 with his expeditionary fleet of 11 ships carrying over 1000 settlers, including 759 convicts, the Hambledon Club was in decline and had lost its supremacy to Surrey, Kent and the White Conduit Club, all of which were strong enough to fully extend an eleven of All England. A group of cricketers from these teams who formed the Star And Garter Club in Pall Mall was about to issue a formal set of cricket rules. The game was then 69 years old in America and had a foothold in India, Scotland, Canada and Holland, but was still struggling to recover in Ireland from Cromwell's 1656 order for all bats, stumps and balls to be burned. While white settlement in Australia was being established, the Hambledon Club died.

Cricket's written history dates from the first part of the sixteenth century, though there are many hints of its earlier existence. By the middle of the seventeenth century it enjoyed wide popularity among the Celts in Ireland and in England, but it was on Broadhalfpenny Down, a tiny village pitch miles from anywhere, that it became a broader passion. "Here cricket grew to man's estate," wrote E. D. R. Eagar, for 31 years secretary of Hampshire, and a noted cricket historian. Players like William Hogsflesh, John Small, John Wells, "Silver Billy" Beldham, batsmen Nyren called "those anointed clod-stampers", Harry and

Thomas Walker "of the scrag of mutton frame", Edward ("Lumpy") Stevens, Thomas ("Shock") White, Edward Budd and George ("Squire") Osbaldeston were often prominent in single-wicket matches for big wagers. In their time grubbers were replaced by balls that bounced on a good length, a change in delivery that led to the straightening of bats from the original hockey stick design. Since 1775, when "Lumpy" Stevens bowled a ball three times through the gap in the two-pronged wicket of John Small, a third stump had been in use.

Sydney, when the first settlement began, was the enforced home of sullen prisoners who were put to work building houses, roads and bridges and farming poor soil. They had no facilities for sport. The arrival of free settlers, at Phillip's suggestion, created a greater demand for recreation. Governor King took over in 1800, and on his authority the first Australian newspaper appeared, the *Sydney Gazette And New South Wales Advertiser.*

The first edition of the *Gazette* appeared on 5 March 1803, when the settlement was 15 years old and the population of New South Wales was

*RIGHT: William Beldham, known as "Silver Billy", was one of the great players on Broadhalfpenny Down. He was described as "the beau ideal of grace, animation and concentrated energy"*

*FAR RIGHT: An illustration from England that would have inspired early Australian cricketers. A third stump had been added but batsmen still played without pads or gloves*

PLAY!

Pub.<sup>d</sup> by S Knights Sweetings Alley, Cornhill.

W.Day Lith.<sup>r</sup> to the King 17 Gate S.<sup>t</sup>

little more than 6000. Most of the *Gazette*'s space had to be devoted to government notices and cases before magistrates, but occasionally the editor showed his fondness for poetry. One of the first issues contained a lengthy account of a cockfight that had been stopped by soldiers. In the summer of 1803–04 a scrub-covered area of Sydney known as Phillip's Common (now part of Hyde Park), was cleared for cricket and on 8 January 1804, the *Gazette* reported:

> *The late intense weather has been very favourable to the amateurs of cricket who scarce have lost a day for the past month. The frequent immoderate weather might have been considered inimical to the amusement, but was productive of the very opposite consequences, as the state of the atmosphere might always regulate the portions of exercise necessary to the ends that this laborious diversion was originally intended to answer.*

The infant *Gazette*, which was often just a single sheet, gave no scores for this first match recorded in Australia, but its report clearly shows that cricket was played in Sydney at least from 1803. The players were probably civilians and officers of the ship *Calcutta*. Scoring shots were called "notches" not runs: notches were cut into a stick, with a larger notch for every fifth or tenth run, a method later replaced by scoring runs on paper. Teams were distinguished by coloured sashes or ribbons around their necks. The first Australian cricket balls were made by shoemakers, who stitched leather around cork or other stuffing. The first bats were fashioned from cedar, ironbark or other local timbers that were so hard they made builders complain. From these humble beginnings and from players who had never heard of "Silver Billy" Beldham or "Lumpy" Stevens or the notorious gambling cricketer, Lord Frederick Beauclerk, Australia was to produce its own heroes in a short period.

From scratch matches between teams that dis-

*The cradle of Australian cricket, Sydney's Hyde Park, in the 1840s. St Mary's Cathedral, later rebuilt, is in the background, the fielding side's tent at the left*

persed after one outing, the game progressed: clubs were formed, equipment was ordered from England, and the need for practice sessions arose. But the cricketers seldom attracted the attention of the convict editor of the *Gazette*, George Howe, who was born in St Kitts, West Indies. Nevertheless by 1810 interest in cricket had become

strong enough for the *Gazette* to mention a cricket ground. This paragraph appeared on 28 April:

*Monday last being Easter Monday, a fair commenced on the Cricket Ground, to which a sort of popular acquiescence has given the appellation of St. George's Fields; the recreative pastimes of which were carried on with much decorum and no less festivity for these days, during which the merry dance was kept alive in every booth, and other fair costumes of the Mother Country closely imitated.*

The name St George's Field was apparently not used for long, and an official name for Phillip's Common, as it was also known, was discussed. On 13 October 1810 the *Gazette* carried an order from Governor Macquarie:

*The whole of the open ground yet unoccupied in the vicinity of the Town of Sydney, hitherto known and alternately called by the names of 'The Common,' 'Exercising Ground,' the 'Cricket Ground,' and 'Racecourse;' bounded by the Government Domain on the north; the*

*Town of Sydney on the west; the Brickfields on the south; and Mr. Palmer's premises on the east, being intended in future for the Recreation and Amusement of the inhabitants of the Town, and as a field of exercise for the Troops; the Governor has thought proper to name the ground thus described 'Hyde Park;' by which name it is henceforth to be called and denominated.*

On 5 October 1811 the *Gazette* published a similar order outlining the boundaries of what was originally called Sydney Common, which included the area that became Moore Park and most of Centennial Park. This land covered 1000 acres (405 hectares) and was set aside initially for the "common pasturage of cattle belonging to the inhabitants of Sydney". For cricketers the most important section of this Sydney Common was the part now occupied by Sydney Cricket Ground.

Lord's opened on its present site at St John's Wood, London, in 1814, and on 28 July of the same year Edward William Gregory arrived in Sydney with his wife Henrietta and his infant sons Edward, Charles and George. On 12 June 1815, six days before the Battle of Waterloo, the Duke of Wellington watched officers of the Brigade of Guards play cricket near Brussels. While England rejoiced over Napoleon's surrender and the 40,000 French casualties, Epsom made 476 runs against Middlesex at Lord's, the highest total in any first-class match for 44 years. When Henrietta Gregory died in Sydney in 1819, her three sons were admitted to the Male Orphan Institute there, and their father heartlessly returned to England.

The boys were subsequently discharged from the orphanage in the care of various tradesmen. Edward was apprenticed to a shoemaker, but about 1827 became a government schoolteacher. Born in London about 1805, he began playing cricket for the Australian Club soon after it was formed in 1826. He married Mary Ann Smith at the Scots Church in Elizabeth Street, Sydney, on 25 May 1835. They had 13 children, seven of them boys,

and five of the boys later played for New South Wales in international or intercolonial cricket: Edward ("Ned") James (1839–99), Walter John (1841–1917), David William (1845–1919), Charles Smith (1847–1935) and Arthur Herbert (1861–1929). David became Australia's first Test captain. Between 1877 and 1926 members of the Gregory family were to play in 88 Tests.

By the 1820s boys born in Australia were among those who played cricket at a Sydney school. In 1821 Governor Macquarie ordered some bats and balls from His Majesty's Lumber Yard for his son Lachlan, a pupil at the Reverend Thomas Reddall's school at Macquarie Fields near the subsequent site of Ingleburn Army Camp. Macquarie added to his order a note that read, "The above articles are to be considered to belong to Lachlan as long as he remains at the Reverend Reddall's school and afterwards to be left for the use of the school". The bats and balls were to be a gift of the Crown.

A group of enthusiasts from Sydney-based regiments formed the Military Cricket Club in 1826, and the same year saw the formation of a club exclusive to native-born players, the Australian Club. Another club appeared at Windsor on the outskirts of Sydney in 1827, but declined to play the Australian Club because of the restrictions placed on its membership. The Sydney Club began in 1829 in a government paddock "on the site of the turnpike", which was in the area of the present-day Central Station. The players were keen to get away from pitches dominated by soldiers or the aloof members of the Australian Club, but they were soon ejected from their ground and the club disbanded.

Edward William Gregory, who like his brothers had been virtually deserted by his father, was not an outstanding player but a cheerful character whose gifts lay in teaching the game. One of his friends was Henry Frederick Green, an Englishman who had served in the Coldstream Guards and had fought at Waterloo. "Toby" Green played for the original Amateur Club. He was a storekeeper in Hyde Park Barracks and later took over from Richard Tress the Cricketers' Arms Hotel on the south-west corner of Pitt and Market Streets, Sydney.

Throughout the 1820s cricketers in England became increasingly keen advocates of round-arm bowling. John Willes of Kent pioneered the style, but the fight to have it legalised was led by one of its finest exponents, William Lillywhite. In 1827, when Sussex met an England XI in three matches, Lillywhite and James Broadbridge, also a round-arm exponent, bowled Sussex to victory in the first two matches. England then introduced an amateur, G. T. Knight, who bowled round-arm well enough in the third match to give England victory. In 1828 the Marylebone Club at Lord's, by then the recognised arbiter on the laws of cricket, sanctioned round-arm bowling by permitting bowlers to raise their arms level with their elbows.

Two years later John Richard Hardy took his

BA at Cambridge and bowled round-arm when he played in the third annual Varsity match against Oxford. Hardy came to Australia in 1832 and demonstrated the round-arm style in his first match in Sydney on Boxing Day. The style was criticised by opposing players and some spectators as unfair and unsportsmanlike. Hardy taught the style to Robert and William Still, who are often wrongly credited with introducing round-arm to Australian cricket. Hardy worked first as a copying clerk for the Executive Council and later joined the staff of the original *Australian*, becoming its editor and proprietor in 1835. He devoted a lot of space to cricket, but after two years sold the newspaper and became police magistrate at Yass. He was later transferred to Parramatta and when the goldrushes began in the 1850s he was appointed chief gold commissioner. He died in Yass on 21 April 1858.

His pupils, the brothers Still, had earned awesome reputations meanwhile as exponents of a straight-arm bowling style that produced unprecedented pace and deliveries that bounced high and wide off rough pitches to elude wicket-keepers, increasing the importance of good long-stops. In one match in which Robert Still bowled there were 18 and 24 byes in innings of 49 and 71 respectively.

The first match for which team totals were recorded was played on a pitch in Hyde Park, in front of the present St Mary's Cathedral, in February 1830. The Sydney *Gazette* carried this report:

> *The game on the Racecourse on February 26th was played between the Military and native-born youths between eleven o'clock in the fore-noon and five o'clock in the evening. At two o'clock it was thought the natives had no chance, and that they must be beat. However, as the day's play advanced, the Australians*

*Edgar Willsher, generally regarded as the first round-arm bowler and the player who changed bowling from the original underarm style*

*recovered all they had lost in the morning, and at length won the game. A prettier day's play than this was certainly never witnessed in the colony. At four o'clock it is estimated that there were upwards of 100 spectators on the ground.*

The 57th Regiment made 101 and 87, the civilians 76 and 136, giving the civilians the match by 24 runs and the stakes of £20 a side. The *Australian*'s account of the match noted that one soldier received "an unlucky salute on the nose" and a civilian was "nearly deprived of respiration by a ball that took him in the middle". On 3 March 1830, the civilians won the return match by 35 runs, scoring 95 and 75 against 82 and 52 by the soldiers. Apart from the stake money, there was heavy betting on the match in amounts of sawn timber, fat pigs, dripstones, maize, butter, salt fish, boots and snakeskin shoes. The players celebrated after both matches at Toby Green's hotel.

On 7 May 1832 a match between the 17th and 39th Regiments for a stake of £300 attracted more than 2000 spectators to Hyde Park, still known to some as the Old Racecourse. The skill of two privates apparently swung the match: the 17th boasted Private Carnell, a stolid batsman who had previously scored 22, 36 and 33 in successive innings, and Private Stafford, who had scores of 42, 30 and 26 to his credit. Reports of the match provided no bowling figures and showed that in two innings all eleven batsmen were dismissed. Carnell was said to have been "stopped by Gambier" for six runs, which apparently meant Gambier ran him out.

The 4th Regiment also had its outstanding cricketers. Private Hyde was a bowler of above average quality who gave the ball "a bias to the right side" and in one match against the Australian Club his "twisters" were described as virtually unplayable. Hyde defeated Edward Flood in a single-wicket match for £5 in 1833. The 4th also had an outstanding batsman in Lieutenant Alured Tasker Faunce, who arrived in Sydney with his regiment in 1831. Faunce played several fine

knocks. He attained the rank of captain, but left the army and in 1837 became police magistrate at Queanbeyan. He died suddenly as he bent to pick up the ball while playing in a Married *v.* Single match, the first known fatality in an Australian cricket match.

The Sydney *Gazette* stated in 1832 that cricket was now the prevailing amusement of the colony and that no gentleman could expect to "dangle at a lady's apron strings" unless he could boast of his cricket prowess. Respectable females enlivened cricket audiences, the paper added.

The military, however, could only field a strong team when they disregarded rank and concentrated on playing skills. They had a thrilling three-match series against the Australians in the 1833–34 season, which the Australians won through the "best fielding ever seen in the colony" in the third match after showing "unpardonable laziness" in the second.

The Marylebone or Amateur Cricket Club began in 1832, the Union in 1837, Royal Victoria in 1839, Prince Albert in 1840, Currency and City in 1844. Most had short innings but some, like the Currency Club, flourished and played an important role in the development of early Australian cricket. The clubs usually met in hotels and publicans quickly realised that the promotion of cricket stimulated their business. Several publicans became prominent players and officials and often helped to finance visits to other clubs.

Before one match at Sydney in 1834 the Supreme Court adjourned an important case to permit lawyers involved to play in it. Judge Dowling agreed to the adjournment despite objections from a leading barrister, Dr Wardell, who interjected: "To play cricket, no doubt!" when told that the other legal men were required elsewhere. For Hyde Park games players

*Harry Hilliard, who played in Hyde Park matches when 40 was rated a brilliant score and drinkers urged batsmen to hit the ball over the street into Elizabeth Street bars*

used Mountford Clarkson's Spread Eagle Hotel in Elizabeth Street as the pavilion. As the day progressed spectators in the hotel on the synagogue side boisterously joshed players on the field opposite about their inability to hit the ball over the road into the hotel.

One batsman who claimed he had several hits that narrowly missed the drinkers was Harry Hilliard. His memoirs, published in the magazine *Old Times*, provide a valuable record of Australian cricket in the Victorian era. Hilliard claimed that he had broken windows in Elizabeth Street and recalled several others achieving the same feat. He also referred to players being refused permission to practise with their clubs for several days and a fieldsman who received a punch for dropping a catch. Hilliard looked like a Mormon preacher, with a shiny bald head, short dark beard, and un-smiling lap-dog eyes. He ended his cricket career among the native-born players of the Currency Club.

According to Hilliard, the Currency players made a practice ground by moving some of the headstones in an old cemetery in George Street, now the site of St Andrew's Cathedral. They were often chased away by the police, who sometimes confiscated their bats. The lure of a cricket match was so strong that Hilliard frequently went absent from his job without leave. Although this habit landed him in court for breaking his indentures—he was apprenticed to a cabinet-maker in Pitt Street—he later wrote that it was worth it.

Hilliard played in numerous single-wicket matches with reasonable success. He was a stubborn batsman who could hold up an innings but seldom made high scores. New South Wales selectors appreciated his value and picked him for the state's initial first-class matches; on one occasion he kept wicket for the state. He took 2 for 27 with his right-arm fast underarmers. Hilliard died in 1914 in his eighty-eighth year.

One of the surprising traits in old-timers like Hilliard was their ability to stay well informed about cricket in England despite the huge distance that separated them from events there. They read voraciously about the game at home and kept albums of press clippings on English cricket. They knew all about the antics of the great gamesman Lord Frederick Beauclerk and how he made £600 a year betting on cricket. They knew, too, of Nicholas Wanostrocht, who, as "Felix", wrote a famous instructional work on the game, *Felix On The Bat*, and they followed the achievements of Alfred Mynn and Fuller Pilch and other great players of the early Victorian days. When copies of Nyren's *Young Cricketer's Tutor* (1835) or James Pycroft's *The Cricket Field* (1851) reached Australia they were sold within a few hours, and English publications like the *Gentleman's Magazine* were carefully combed for cricket articles.

In May 1834 a match was played between "eleven natives and eleven officers and immigrants". On the morning of the match the cornstalk flag was accidentally reversed—a handy excuse seized on by the superstitious for the natives' loss; the more likely reason was that the native-born players had failed to practise. There was animated applause when William Still became the first player in Australian cricket to go out to bat wearing pads and gloves. They were primitive garments that offered little protection, but they represented progress. Initially any form of protection had been ridiculed. Had not Nyren written about Tom Walker with "skin like the rind of an old oak and as sapless"? Nyren also wrote, "I have seen his knuckles knocked handsomely about, from Harris's bowling, but never saw any blood on his hands". These were exciting words for cricketers who rated manliness above all virtues. Only the increasing speed of the round-arm bowlers convinced players of the wisdom of Still's pads and gloves.

Players usually wore top hats or cabbage tree

*An inspiring illustration for early cricketers from* Felix On The Bat, *showing a daintily slippered batsman taking a full swing at the ball*

LEFT: *Alfred Mynn (left) and Nicholas Felix, at Lord's just before they played for the Single Wicket Championship of England in 1846*
ABOVE: *The Surrey Cricketers in 1852, one of the first illustrations showing batting gloves. Julius Caesar (second from left) wore both gloves, while William Caffyn (holding bat) preferred a glove only on his bottom hand*

hats during matches, while spectators appeared in their Sunday best, turning out as if for a wedding. The men promenaded with their ladies between innings or during breaks in play. The governor and leading members of the public service in-variably attended big matches. For a succession of governors—New South Wales had 13 of them in its first 50 years—horseracing and cricket in Hyde Park offered welcome diversion in a colony with limited facilities for amusement. Moreover, fraternising at the cricket was the fashionable thing to do back in England, where matches involving Winchester, Eton, Harrow and the universities had become outings for the rich and titled. Hadn't Lord Byron played for Harrow in 1805?

Civil servants who played cricket were doubly popular with the governors' intimates. Such a man was Henry Fysche Gisborne, second son of a member of the House of Commons, who arrived in New South Wales in the early 1830s and played in several matches between 1834 and 1837 with the "Immigrants". He was appointed the third police magistrate in 1836, and was subsequently Minister for Lands for the District of Port Phillip. "It was a pity," the *Sydney Morning Herald* commented, "to witness Gisborne outraging decorum by continually wearing his hat while administering justice on the Bench." The Immigrants also included a batsman named George Cavenagh, who had come to them from the Australian Club. Cavenagh became joint editor, with C. H. Jenkins, of the Sydney *Gazette* in September 1836. When Jenkins died the following year, Cavenagh became the sole editor. His best scores were 30 and 29; he also won a verdict for £225 in an action for libel against W. C. Wentworth. Cavenagh later became a stalwart of the Melbourne Cricket Club.

The *Commercial Journal*'s report of a match between the Australian and Union clubs on 7 February 1838, complained about what is now known as "sledging". "We have no objection to a little humorous chaff, either on the field or off it, but we certainly object to that low slang and insulting remarks so often resorted to by the Australians."

The pride of the public service was a long-serving batsman named Michael Fitzpatrick, one of the few early Australian cricketers whose career extended over a period of 20 years. Fitzpatrick was born in 1816 at Parramatta, then a farming district. He was a steady type of batsman and a useful slow bowler, with a top score of 70 not out made for the Victoria Club against the Australian Club in 1844. He had a brilliant career, starting as a clerk in the Lands Department and advancing rapidly, in between appearances in Hyde Park and Domain matches. He was clerk of the Executive Council, Under-Secretary of Lands and Works in the first responsible government (1856), member for Yass Plains in the Legislative Assembly, and at one time Colonial Secretary.

An intriguing bowler of the period was John Horner, one of the original members of the Currency Club, founded in 1843–44. He carried off the bowling honours with John Sly in almost every match in which he appeared over three seasons. The *Sydney Monitor* commented of Horner's bowling that "It was the best ever exhibited in the colony, nearly the whole of his balls ricocheting in such a way that a batsman could not stop them". Horner defeated Mountford Clarkson in a single-wicket match in February 1845. Playing for the Currency Club in a four-man match against the Victoria Club, he scored most runs and took seven of the eight Victoria Club wickets that fell in the two innings.

Despite the success of the Still brothers with round-arm bowling, underarm bowling lingered on for many seasons. (A Balmain club bowler, Ted Sherwood, bowled underarm leg-breaks in Sydney third grade matches as late as the 1930s.) John Rickards, a native of Sydney, had such success with his fast underarmers between 1832 and 1835 that he was nicknamed the "Australian Lillywhite". After one match the *Sydney Monitor* referred to Rickards as "Lillywhite" and players were recorded as "bowled Lillywhite" instead of "bowled Rickards" in the scores. The *Monitor* stated that "without exception Rickards was the best treat that the amateurs have had in years". Rickards' 57 not out for Single against Married in May 1833, was hailed as "an amazing number". The record lasted only 20 months; in January 1835, Edward Dormer O'Reilly, a British-born attorney, scored 69 for the Australian Club against a Military XI. Corporal Pearce, of the 4th Regiment, lifted the record to 84 not out in October 1836, and this remained the colony's highest score until John Tunks came up with the first century nine years later.

Another prominent underarm bowler in the Domain was Thomas Rowley, grandson of an officer in the New South Wales Corps, which had come to Sydney with the Second Fleet in 1790. His father, also Thomas Rowley, settled near Liverpool and married Catherine Clarkson, a sister of the leading cricketer Mountford Clarkson. Rowley junior, born in 1820, attracted consistent praise from his first appearance in club cricket at 17 until he retired from competitive cricket 20 years later. Rowley was Robert Still's team-mate in the Liverpool and Australian clubs, and they often shared the bowling honours. The *Commercial Journal* claimed in the 1840s that Rowley was "unrivalled in the list of Australian cricketers".

Despite its elitism, the Australian Club was the first Sydney club to welcome country teams. Maitland, an active club with 44 members, travelled to Sydney to play the Australian Club in 1845. Applauding this venture the *Maitland Mercury* stated that the Australian Club was so strong that Sydney teams would meet them only if they left out one or two of their best players. "The challenge of the Maitland men was unconditional, which of itself spoke well for the spirit and confidence of the men," said the *Mercury*. On a saturated pitch, Maitland were out for 44. Rain held up play for a day. On the resumption the Australian scored 120 and then routed Maitland for 19.

Unperturbed by this disaster, Maitland invited the Australian Club to a return match in Maitland. On a dry pitch Maitland were out for 34 notches, a result the *Mercury* attributed to the very effective bowling of Still and Rowley and to the Australian Club's fielding. "We do not remember seeing anything to equal their fielding," noted the *Mercury*. "There was no confusion or waste of running, but the instant the ball left the bat, there was someone ready to lay hold of it, and it was thrown in instantaneously."

The match was played on a field that had a slope at one side and when Hatfield, Ritchie, Still and Clarkson hit balls down this incline they had no trouble pushing along the scoring. One of Clarkson's hits rolled down the slope for six. The Australian Club were all out for 103 notches. Left to score 69 notches to make the Australian bat again, Maitland made 56, giving the Australian Club victory by an innings and 13 runs. The

players then competed at single-wicket cricket for varying side bets for the rest of the week.

In 1846 Maitland played a combined team from the nearby towns of Morpeth, Raymond Terrace and Paterson. The Morpeth ground for this match was "found to answer the purpose except that the grass was too high for the bowlers". The *Maitland Mercury* reported that when one of the Morpeth players insisted the stumps had to be 22 inches high, the Maitland players had to agree, although this forced their best bowler, Honeysett, to discard his round-arm bowling and revert to underarm. Maitland won, scoring 106 to 50 and 53.

Big-hitter John Mountford Clarkson, born in Sydney in 1812, played with the Amateur Club in the first fully recorded Australian cricket match in 1832. In 1842, when he also became proprietor of the Spread Eagle Hotel, Clarkson transferred to the Australian Club, probably to underline that he was Australian-born, and he played for that club throughout his 10 years as a publican. He played in more than 50 eleven-a-side matches, a high total considering the limited number of clubs and grounds on which they could play. His highest score was 70 not out against the Victoria Club in 1843. When he retired from his pub and from cricket he became an orchardist at Fiddens Wharf Road, Lane Cove, on land that is now part of Killara Golf Club. He was credited with hitting a ball out of Hyde Park clean over St Mary's Cathedral and was clearly one of the most powerful hitters in Australia's early cricket. His tombstone at the family vault in St Stephen's Cemetery, Newtown, bore the simple inscription, "One of the Old Cricketers".

Headquarters of the prestigious Australian Club, which dominated all Hyde Park cricket, was the Three Tuns Hotel, owned by Richard Driver senior, who was noted for his knowledge of the laws of cricket and much sought after as an umpire. Driver was the son of John Driver, who kept a hotel on the west side of Castlereagh Street, between what is now Martin Place and Hunter

Street. His son, Richard Driver junior, born near Liverpool in 1829, became one of the most influential figures in early Australian cricket. Driver Avenue, which leads up to the Moore Park entrance of Sydney Cricket Ground beside Kippax Lake, was named after him.

The younger Driver was admitted as an attorney and solicitor of the Supreme Court in 1856. His first important match was for the Union Club in 1847–48. He joined the Fitz Roy Club in the following season and played for the Australian Club from 1850 to 1856. Driver was one of the trustees of the Hyde Park Cricket Ground and of the Domain Cricket Ground, and played for New South Wales in the first intercolonial match against Victoria. He was secretary to the Corporation of Sydney for several years and held a seat in the New South Wales Parliament for 20 years, serving as Minister of Lands in the Parkes ministry in 1877.

One of the original members of the Australian Club was Edward Flood, a forceful batsman and splendid bowler. Flood's best batting performance, achieved in an era of low scoring, was 41 in each innings against the 4th Regiment on 26 December 1836. This was the match in which Mountford Clarkson made 51 and 32. Flood did not play after 1837 but sometimes stood as an umpire. He was an alderman in the City Council and a member of the Legislative Assembly.

Yet another outstanding publican cricketer was the former carpenter William Tunks, who kept the Currier's Arms Hotel on the corner of Bathurst and Castlereagh Streets for many years. His brother John scored the first century in Sydney cricket when he made 112 not out for the Currency Club against the Victoria Club in January 1845. William Tunks, born at Parramatta in 1816, also played for the Currency Club, but his importance was as a cricket administrator. He was one of the trustees of the Domain Cricket Ground, and helped to build up the New South Wales Cricket Association in the 1860s. Both Tunkses were friends of former Hobart publican

*The 1852 United England XI, forerunner of the teams that toured Australia: (L to R) Hunt, Wright, Adams, Mortlock, Lockyer, Wisden, F. Lillywhite, John Lillywhite, Dean, Caffyn, Grundy, Martingell, Sherman and Sampson*

Vernon Puzey, proprietor of the Crooked Billet

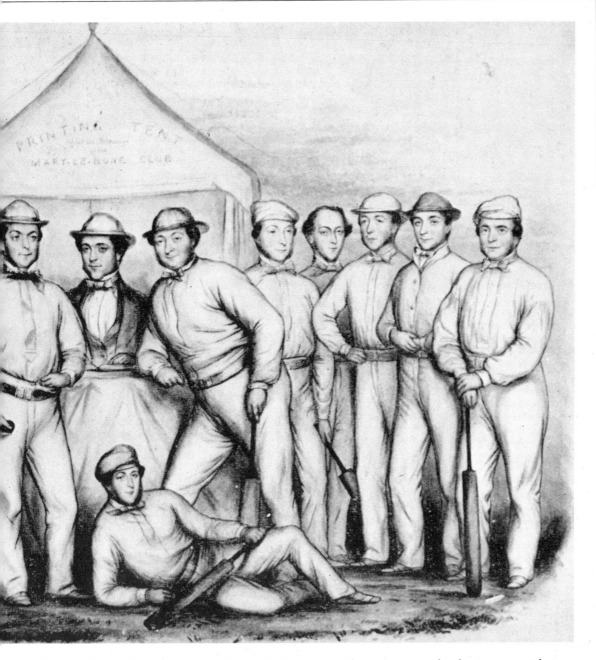

Hotel in George Street, who starred for the Union Club as a bowler of destructive pace between 1836 and 1840. Tunks Park, in the Sydney suburb of Cammeray, where dozens of matches are played every summer weekend, was named after William Tunks.

From the first matches, locally born players were always more popular than migrant cricketers, who were often heckled. One of the few English-born players to whom the "natives" took kindly was "silvertail" Francis Stephens, son of Judge John Stephens, Solicitor-General, and brother of Sir Alfred Stephens, Chief Justice of New South Wales from 1844 to 1873. Francis Stephens's

*From Hyde Park cricket moved to The Domain, where cows fouled the outfield and held up play. Although spectators could not be charged admission, cricket clubs built small stands and installed seats*

acceptance at the colony's highest social levels, coupled with his ability to mix freely with commoners, gave him such wide appeal that his early death in 1837 was mourned by all.

A player who did not enjoy Francis Stephens's popularity was J. C. R. (Charles) Wood, of whom it was contemptuously said, "he learned his cricket entirely in England". Wood, secretary of the Victoria Club in the 1840s, was Deputy-Assistant Commissary-General. He played four tense single-wicket matches against clubmates, twice defeating Michael Fitzpatrick and sharing honours with William Still.

One of the colony's first exponents of round-arm bowling was Captain Edward Ward, deputy master of the Mint, later Major-General Sir Wolstoneholme Ward, a rare character in all he did. When cows strayed on to the Domain and interrupted play, Ward solved the problem by borrowing some hurdles from a struggling athletic club with which he fenced the ground. Ward wore a monocle when batting and took guard with his buttocks facing the bowler, at whom he peered from behind his left shoulder. He took 27 wickets for New South Wales in four matches with his round-armers, average 7.6, advancing with a peculiar hop to the wicket and letting the ball go with a decidedly jerky action.

Another curious player was Tom Lewis, a batsman who felt he had to hit every ball and hated one to get past him. Lewis chased the ball wherever it pitched and even threw his bat at wide balls. The crowds' favourite, however, was the outstanding exponent of what became known as Sydney grubbers, underarmer John James McKone. The *Cricketers' Guide* considered that McKone's bowling had a "subterranean touch".

When he batted, McKone upset opposing bowlers by playing metres forward to every ball.

From the beginnings in Sydney's Hyde Park, Australian cricket spread to the Domain, cow pats permitting, and out to the colony's country areas, and in turn to Tasmania (where the first matches reported were in 1825), Victoria (1834), Western Australia (1835), South Australia (1839) and Queensland (1846). But first class cricket began in Tasmania, just 48 years after the matches in Hyde Park when "the amateurs of cricket scarce lost a day".

Very few of the early clubs endured for long. The most durable were the Derwent Club, founded at Hobart in 1835, which lasted until 1905 when it disappeared to make way for district cricket, and the Australian Club, formed in Sydney in 1826 and still a force in the 1850s. Generally clubs came and went before they had time to establish a following. Competition was casual, without trophies or regular fixtures. Even the strongest clubs often went for months without a game.

Pitches were crude and virtually unprepared and were frequently changed midway through matches. Cows, horses and other animals were a constant problem and even after more than four decades of cricket a correspondent in the *Sydney Morning Herald* in 1851 described the Hyde Park ground as "a piece of rough and uneven ground, as bare as a well-travelled road in parts, with alternate hillocks of earth and pebbles, long grass, ridges, holes and drains innumerable". Cricketers tried to prevent the public taking shortcuts across their fields by covering casually erected rail fences with tar.

Despite all the pitfalls, however, cricket was firmly established by the 1850s as a game for all Australians: the gentry, the services, ladies, teenagers and the ordinary working man.

# A letter mislaid

## Tasmania 1825–60

Throughout the first half of the nineteenth century Tasmania played a valuable pioneering role in Australian cricket. Tasmania, then known as Van Diemen's Land, became the second Australian colony in September 1803, when Lieutenant John Bowen, sent from Sydney by Governor King, established a settlement at Risdon Cove on the Derwent River with a party of 49, including 35 convicts. One object of the settlement was to forestall French interest in the island. Further support came in February 1804 when Lieutenant-Governor David Collins arrived with another 262 people, 178 of them convicts. Collins moved the settlement downstream to the present site of Hobart. Eight months later Governor King sent Lieutenant-Colonel William Paterson to establish a settlement at Port Dalrymple at the mouth of the Tamar River in the north. This party of 181, including 74 convicts, landed at what was to become George Town.

Governor Macquarie visited the island in 1811, endorsing the layout of Hobart Town, and unlike New South Wales, these settlements

*Some of the Tasmanian team that played Victoria in 1867: (L to R) (standing) T. Dalley, W. A. Collins, W. Cowle, H. R. G. Dumaresq, J. L. A. Arthur; (seated) D. Burke, D. Barclay; (in front) T. Whitesides and W. H. Walker, the team's captain. Tasmania's victory helped bring a return to 11-a-side matches*

quickly prospered; by 1818 they were exporting wheat to Sydney. Amid reports of French landings on the island and problems with unruly convicts, there was little time for official planning of sporting facilities, but some free settlers soon began building playing fields, often using convict labour to do so.

One of the first to recognise the need for recreation was publican Joseph Bowden, who built the Lamb Inn in Hobart Town after he arrived in 1824. The following year he organised the island's first cricket match between a team of free settlers and a side picked from garrison troops. The soldiers won the match, of which no scores are recorded, by 15 runs. The game proved such a boost to trade that Bowden staged a second at Easter 1826, for a stake of 50 guineas, a sum he could well afford as he had landed with more than £4000. His advertisement for the match announced that free colonists from the English counties of Kent and Sussex, "impregnated with cricket lore", would do battle with the choice of the whole island. The only known result of this match was the arrest of a convict who was posing as a casual spectator.

Governor Arthur granted Hobart Town Cricket Club tenancy of its own ground, on the site of the present Australian Broadcasting Corporation building, when the club was formed in October 1832. The first match was played there on 1 January 1833. In these formative years the growth of Tasmanian cricket was hampered by the island's wild, mountainous terrain and the lack of a regular coach service to Launceston, founded in 1824, 120 miles to the north at the point where the North and South Esk Rivers form the Tamar estuary. The Launceston Cricket Club, formed in 1843, is the third oldest surviving cricket club in Australia, following the Melbourne and Brighton clubs.

On 14 December 1832, the Launceston *Independent* reported that a match would be played on 26 December between 22 commoners on what was known as Government Green, for a stake of 50 guineas. "We heartily recommend to the support of every well-wisher of the colony this manly game," stated the *Independent*.

On 11 May 1833, a further match at Launceston was well attended despite bad weather. The *Independent* commented, "We congratulate our fellow townsmen on the formation of a club, composed as it is of the most respectable inhabitants of the country and founded upon the regulations of the first cricket clubs in England". Culturally and commercially Launceston made steady progress despite losses of manpower to the Californian goldrush in 1849, and to the Victorian goldfields in the early 1850s.

On 19 January 1835 the Hobart Town Club played a team from HMS *Hyacinth*, whose officers expressed themselves keen for some cricket immediately the ship docked. They were assisted by officers of the 21st Regiment, but there was no betting on the match at the special request of the officers, who said the honour of playing was enough. Two bands played throughout the five hours that the four innings occupied. Colourful marquees ringed the playing area. The hero was John Marshall, who by his display that day became known as the "Champion Cricketer of Hobart Town", a role he filled for the next 20 years.

Marshall, a pugnacious, heavily bearded allrounder with a blacksmith's arms, is believed to have been born in 1795, but this cannot be confirmed. He remains Australia's oldest representative cricketer, and he did not relinquish the captaincy of his state until he was fifty-eight. The oldest mainland cricketer to play in a first-class match was George Moore of Maitland, who played for New South Wales against Victoria in 1872–73 at the age of 52 years, 325 days.

Marshall, whose father worked for one of the first Tasmanian garrison regiments, batted for 105 minutes to score 13 runs in Hobart Town's first innings of 83, and scored 10 out of 84 in the second innings. He both bowled and kept wicket at different times during the match, and as captain he showed impressive tactical acumen.

# Hobart Town *v.* United Services

*Played at Hobart, 19 January 1835*

## Hobart Town Cricket Club

| First Innings | | Second Innings | |
|---|---|---|---|
| Roper, *b.* Blackwood | 0 | Roper, *c.* Munday | 46 |
| Walters, *b.* Blackwood | 9 | Walters, *run out* | 6 |
| Marshall, *b.* Blackwood | 13 | Marshall, *c.* Rideout | 10 |
| Smith, *c.* Rideout | 21 | Smith, *c.* Rideout | 4 |
| Wise, *b.* Blackwood | 4 | Wise, *c.* Ainslie | 0 |
| Deane, *b.* Blackwood | 1 | Deane, *b.* Blackwood | 0 |
| Gardiner, *b.* Blackwood | 12 | Gardiner, *b.* Lamotte | 0 |
| Hind, *c.* Blackwood | 0 | Hind, *c.* Ainslie | 7 |
| O'Donohoo, *b.* Ainslie | 4 | O'Donohoo, *lbw* | 7 |
| Emmett, *b.* Ainslie | 14 | Emmett, *b.* Blackwood | 0 |
| Hobson, *not out* | 0 | Hobson, *not out* | 0 |
| Byes | 5 | Byes | 4 |
| Total | 83 | Total | 84 |

## United Services

| First Innings | | Second Innings | |
|---|---|---|---|
| Rideout, *b.* Marshall | 5 | Rideout, *hit wicket* | 0 |
| Somerville, *b.* Marshall | 3 | Somerville, *b.* Marshall | 0 |
| Arthur, *hit wicket* | 6 | Arthur, *c.* Walters | 0 |
| Blackwood, *st.* Marshall | 0 | Blackwood, *b.* Marshall | 2 |
| Lamotte, *run out* | 2 | Lamotte, *c.* Marshall | 1 |
| Munday, *c.* Marshall | 2 | Munday, *hit wicket* | 1 |
| Ainslie, *b.* Marshall | 0 | Ainslie, *b.* Roper | 6 |
| Roy, *b.* Roper | 9 | Roy, *b.* Roper | 5 |
| Jupp, *b.* Roper | 6 | Jupp, *hit wicket* | 2 |
| Mortimer, *not out* | 0 | Mortimer, *b.* Roper | 0 |
| Collins, *hit wicket* | 0 | Collins, *not out* | 1 |
| Byes | 6 | Byes | 3 |
| Total | 39 | Total | 21 |

*Hobart Town won by 107 runs*

*John Marshall captained Tasmania in the first three matches against Victoria—the initial contests in our first-class history. He played until he was 58 and remains Australia's oldest first-class player*

Despite improvement in Tasmania's cricket strength, there was among the wealthy, genteel population an antagonistic attitude towards professional players in both the northern and southern strongholds of the colony. This prevented improvement in standards at a time when other states were eagerly signing professional coaches and groundsmen, and affected the staging of intercolonial matches between Tasmania and mainland states. Victoria believed the public would only watch matches in which the best players appeared, regardless of their status, and scoffed at the Tasmanian argument that the inclusion of professionals increased the costs of holding these games. Victoria also argued that if Tasmania wanted matches against the odds in which

Tasmanian sixteens opposed Victorian elevens, then Tasmania should not be surprised if Victoria included professionals.

Mainland coaches who offered to go to Tasmania were curtly rebuffed. When the great English all-rounder, William Caffyn, wrote from Sydney in 1869 exploring a possible engagement with the Hobart Association, the secretary replied that Hobart had no intention whatsoever of employing a professional. Only a few months later, however, the same association began negotiations with the Victorian professional Sam Cosstick but decided his terms of "six notes a week" were too high. The prejudice was reinforced when the Launceston Club engaged the Victorian professional T. B. Huddlestone and he disappeared after only one match.

Meanwhile John Marshall, a resourceful, obdurate personality, used his cricket success to further his business and social life. Roger Page, in his *History of Tasmanian Cricket*, relates how Marshall formed a closely knit group of players in which social position counted more than talent. Marshall's clique was drawn from a landed gentry that had quickly established itself in Tasmania, where free settlers often acquired vast areas of land at bargain prices. Landowners and businessmen formed, under Marshall's direction, teams which excluded the more lowly shopkeepers, publicans and small farmers.

Marshall worked for the Bank of Van Diemen's Land as an accountant and for many years lived at Lyndhurst, later the home of Enid and Joe Lyons, the brilliantly successful political duo. Marshall's long career was a striking testimony to his skills. His captaincy was crafty, and he had the ability of exploiting whatever assets he was offered. He could bat in any position in the order, keep wicket, and bowl to a plan.

The victory over the United Services team brought further challenges, which the Hobart Town Club left unanswered. Instead the club played two games against the Carlton Club, whose players lived a dozen miles from town; one game was eleven-a-side and the other a single-wicket affair. A player called Shiney made three ducks in succession for Carlton, in the first recorded appearance by an Aborigine in Australian cricket. Back in Hobart a quarrelsome meeting of the Hobart Town Club resulted in several members, including Marshall, resigning and forming the Derwent Cricket Club. The following day the Derwent defeated Hobart in a single-wicket grudge match. Marshall was the main reason Derwent were seldom beaten over the next 20 years, and as the club members included the Honourable J. H. Elliott, nephew of Governor Franklin, the club was also assured of government backing.

The Derwent Club had a keen rival in the Sorell team, which had to travel 40 kilometres for their away games. Derwent also arranged Married *v.* Singles and Natives *v.* Europeans contests. In one of these matches Henry Wade scored what was long thought to be the first century recorded in Hobart, a feat he accomplished despite the bowling of Marshall, who had been too hostile for the Services. There are no records of Wade's boundaries or the time he was at the wicket. Tasmanian historian Ric Finlay has recently discovered that a century was scored in Launceston a few days before this by E. Emmett, who made 137 not out for South Esk against Launceston in the north of the colony. Over the next three years the Derwent Club travelled to country areas such as Clarence Plains, Green Ponds, New Norfolk and Richmond, all of them within 65 kilometres of Hobart Town.

In 1844 the 96th Regiment took up station in Hobart for a five-year stint and formed the Garrison Club, which played regularly. Sergeants Miller and Windibank were the Garrison's strength. Meanwhile cricket had won support in rural areas in the north, with active clubs at Longford, Perth, not far out from Launceston and at Campbell Town in the Macquarie River Valley. Enthusiasm within the Launceston Club often waned, but when Adye Douglas and George

*Adye Douglas, the "father of cricket" in Launceston. The Launceston Cricket Club, founded in 1843, ranks third among Australia's oldest clubs*

Maddox took control it began to boom. They quickly won the support of Launceston's leading citizens and by 1850 had 50 young men on their books.

By then Melbourne had become a flourishing settlement thanks to the enterprise of Launceston men, John Batman and John Pascoe Fawkner. To discover fresh pastures they had crossed Bass Strait in 1834–35 and explored the lower reaches of the River Yarra, where Melbourne now stands. Aware of the affinity between the two cities, a group of Port Phillip cricketers challenged the Launceston Club to organise a Tasmanian team for a match. The offer was accepted, and it led to a request from the Launceston Club to Governor Denison to allot them land near Launceston racecourse for a cricket ground. The Launceston officials then asked the Derwent Club to nominate players so that a fully representative Tasmanian team could be fielded for the contest. The southerners were not overjoyed by this Launceston coup, but had no choice but to co-operate and send some players north.

Early in June 1850 a group of enthusiastic cricketers went down to the wharf to greet the Victorians. Some hired a rowing boat and went out to shout their welcome. When the steamer *Shamrock* berthed, the assembled cricketers were dismayed to discover that the Victorian players were not on board. The *Examiner* dubbed it a mis-understanding, but when the Launceston Club investigated the muddle, it was discovered that the official responsible had not posted the letter of acceptance in time for the Victorians to catch the *Shamrock*.

The Launceston Club had already challenged the Derwent Club, and the contest was broadened to enable the first North *v.* South match to be played at Oatlands, halfway between Hobart and Launceston, on 20 April 1850. The North won by 12 runs, but the South won the return at Campbell Town by one wicket. The longest inter-ruption to the North *v.* South matches was between 1852 and 1858, and the contests remained the proving ground for aspiring Tasmanian cricketers for more than a century. There was widespread regret at the decision in 1977–78, when Tasmania entered the Sheffield Shield, that a wider intrastate competition would provide a better preparation for Shield matches.

The advent of the North *v.* South matches not only linked Tasmania's two major settlements, but convinced administrators of the existing clubs that they could no longer tolerate well-heeled native-born aristocrats who could not play the game. Slowly the "passengers" were weeded out, pitches improved, and younger men encouraged to join the clubs. Roger Page records the case of a Launceston hotel keeper of suspected convict ancestry who had acquired wealth through dubious means. Although his cricket skills were limited,

he was never thrown out of the Launceston Club, but a team-mate said he had "no pretensions to be a gentleman".

Tasmanian cricket quickly won the support of prominent schools. Hutchins School, founded in Hobart in 1846, produced an impressive array of players who represented the state. Launceston Church Grammar School, also founded in 1846, developed a long list of fine players. The teachers at these schools were frequently people with ex-perience in English county cricket, who brought bats and other gear with them to replace the crude implements that had been fashioned from local materials.

Just as important as the Derwent and Launces-ton clubs were the country clubs patronised by Tasmanian landowners, who slavishly followed the conduct of traditional English squires. Families like the Arthurs and the Dumaresqs backed the game financially and had members of their staff and most of their relatives play. One of the most influential clubs was the Longford Union Club, which comprised property owners from surrounding districts.

A major problem was to secure quality pitches, particularly in Hobart, where the Derwent and other clubs found that their leases did not prevent their grounds being used to facilitate government expansion plans. The Derwent Club took over the Railway ground in 1832. After five years trying to improve the ground and its pitch the club asked Governor Franklin for permission to put a fence around the field to keep out cattle. This was granted and in 1838 the club fenced and turfed the ground at their own expense. Only two years later they had to leave because the ground was required as a drilling field for the 53rd Regi-ment. The government lent the club a horse-drawn roller when it moved to the nearby Battery ground, which, however, was too uneven for much improvement to be made. Finally the club returned to their old ground in 1843, only to find it damaged by carriage wheels. The club members made annual requests for help in the form of convict labour but these were not always granted.

Tasmanian cricket before 1850 was crude, backward and sedate. Round-arm bowling, which the Marylebone Cricket Club at Lord's had declared legal in 1828, was unheard of on the island. Wicket-keepers wore no protection on their hands or legs, nor did batsmen. Long-stops were the busiest men on the field. Apart from Wade's and Emmett's centuries, few innings before 1850 exceeded 50 runs, and John Marshall, admitted to be Tasmania's best batsman of his day, had a career top score of only 75. Any team which reached a total of 70 runs could count itself safe from defeat, although the Launceston Club did record a two-innings aggregate of 283 (141 and 142) in April 1850.

Cricket on the island was dominated by single-wicket matches, sometimes played with only five men on each side. The crease was marked on only one end of the pitch and the balls in an over were not counted. Bowlers could continue indefinitely. Sometimes wides and no-balls were counted as runs for the batsmen and leg byes were occasionally ignored. Batsmen kept running as long as they liked when they hit a ball into the outfield—when one blow by W. H. Westbrook sailed out of the Hobart ground and sped off downhill, 17 runs were taken. Batsmen had to stand inside the crease when they struck the ball and when it was returned or be run out.

Betting was a major feature of single-wicket matches, and conditions were often varied to accommodate gamblers. One match was staged with William Brown using a broom, and his opponent, a Mr Farrell, using a bat, with £5 and a bottle of wine for the winner, which was Brown. John Marshall was unbeaten in single-wicket games, although he frequently knocked down his own stumps deliberately after reaching a good score. This enabled him to get a bowl at his adversary when rain or bad light was threatening to prevent a result.

Unaware that they could bowl round-arm, Tasmanians persisted with lob bowling long after that style had disappeared from the rest of the cricket world. The idea was to beat the batsman by tossing the ball up in a high wide arc so as to hit the stumps on the full. Hobart bowler William Brown and Launceston's William Henty won big reputations as lob bowlers.

The introduction of regular North *v.* South matches, the five intercolonial contests between 1851 and 1858, and the visit of the All England team to Hobart in 1862 transformed Tasmanian cricket. Sadly, their superiority over Victorian cricketers only lasted until the discovery of gold in that colony and the rush of immigrants, many of them cricketers, to the goldfields. Tasmania had been ahead in agricultural production and general affluence, as well as cricket skills, but the gold strikes changed this almost overnight.

The matches against Victoria brought reforms in clothing, behaviour, equipment and playing techniques. Tasmanians started to field teams in uniform dress—in the south, for example, scarlet jackets, white trousers, white sweaters edged in blue and white caps. Spring-handled bats, leg guards, English-made balls, and gloves for both batsmen and wicket-keepers appeared. Round-arm bowlers began to emerge all over the island.

From a game dominated by the landed gentry, Tasmanian cricket changed dramatically to one where teams boasted that their success stemmed from the convict element. It must have come as a shock when in 1854 Victoria objected to the inclusion of a player in the Tasmanian side on the grounds that he was not a gentleman: the bewildered Tasmanians dropped the player named without further discussion. Back home the rivalry between north and south that had been simmering for years resurfaced and "North and South clashed bitterly on any and every issue, with the press as their major battleground," as Roger Page notes.

Transportation of convicts to Tasmania ended in 1853, a new constitution was introduced and the first responsible election was held in 1856, the year after the name Van Diemen's Land was

*The Entally ground during a match in November 1859 between Entally and Westbury. The Governor of Tasmania, Charles Du Cane, is third from the left amongst the spectators in the foreground*

changed to Tasmania. But the bitter argument between cricketers in the north and south still persisted.

Finally, the good sense of William Holden Walker prevailed. He persuaded Tasmanians to recognise the futility of bickering when they could field teams capable of providing mainland states and touring England teams with hard matches. Walker, who arrived in Tasmania in 1859, played for the Islington Albion Club in London before emigrating and was described in the 1859 *Lillywhite's Annual* as one of the "Gentlemen" of Middlesex County. He was a cool-headed man, whose big hitting could be awesome. On the Rail-

way Ground in Hobart he hit a ball into the Derwent River and at Launceston he hit a ball out of the ground across a wide road into a potato patch. Playing for North in 1860, he hit the southern bowling all over the ground, as well as taking ten wickets. In 1861 he hit a century against the Evandale club, whom he defeated off his own bat.

By 1866 Walker was rated the finest hitter in Australia, but he was appointed council clerk that year at the inland town of Fingal, where opportunities were limited and leave hard to get. Transferred to Hobart in 1873, he quickly regained all his old glory playing for the Derwent Club. The Hobart *Mercury* claimed he was as good as W. G. Grace, an obvious exaggeration but evidence of his revered status. He brought to the Tasmanian captaincy a tactical flair, impressing on his players the need for sound fielding and belligerent batting. Walker was one of the last under-arm bowlers seen in Tasmania, pitching the ball to a full length and always on the stumps. He could also keep wicket effectively.

The Southern Tasmanian Cricket Association was formed in 1866, the Northern Tasmanian Cricket Association in 1886, but for years the Launceston Club virtually controlled Tasmanian cricket and, under the guidance of Walker, arranged most intercolonial and other important matches. The Launceston Club's home ground was improved over a ten-year period to become one of Australia's most attractive sites, due largely to the efforts of W. A. Collins from 1863.

Collins, a stepson of Adye Douglas, was one of those dedicated aficionados cricket regularly produces. He collected funds from the public to spend on the ground and donated £300 himself. Most days he toiled at the ground before and after work. He was an excitable, edgy personality, who wrote frequently on cricket for newspapers and entered freely into whatever disputes were current. He took pride in arranging North *v.* South contests and in promoting matches on the Launceston ground. He scored 83 against a Ballarat XI there in 1872. Four years later he took a fatal dose of strychnine.

The loveliest ground in Tasmania was developed at Entally, 13 kilometres from Launceston, a field of exceptional natural beauty rimmed by oaks and elms. The field was originally part of an estate owned by noted Tasmanian cleric and later premier, Thomas Reibey, who presented the ground to the Entally Cricket Club. In this idyllic setting batsmen such as H. R. G. Dumaresq, R. J. Featherstone, and G. H. and Charles (C. R.) Arthur junior devoted themselves to graceful, fluent stroke-play. The Entally school reached its peak in the batting of John Lake Allen Arthur, acknowledged one of the most appealing stroke-makers in early Australian cricket. John Arthur's father, Charles, played for Tasmania in 1851 in the first intercolonial match, and his brothers, Charles junior, Alfred, Thomas and George,

*George Herbert Bailey, Tasmania's first Test cricketer. Born in Colombo and educated in England, he spent most of his life as a banker in Launceston and Hobart. He was a fine right-hand batsman and field*

were all fine cricketers. Charles kept wicket at Oxford University, but did not win a Blue.

John Arthur made his debut for Tasmania in 1866 aged 19 during a prolific season that included an innings of 151 in local cricket; two years later he captained the state in the absence of W. H. Walker. He scored 117 in a North *v.* South game in 1875 but won recognition on the mainland with his 39 in 1867 and 43 in 1869, both for Tasmania against Victoria at Melbourne. He was a lovable, much admired character but he died just before the first white Australian team toured England in 1877, leaving Tasmanians to argue over whether he or Herbert ("Bunker") Bailey was Tasmania's

best early cricketer.

Bailey, who spent his working life in banking, was born at Colombo in 1853 and educated in England at Lichfield Grammar School and at Elizabeth College, Guernsey. He was a free, wristy batsman and right-arm round-arm bowler, who was regarded as a cricketer of spirit. He was out of the state for 13 months on the 1877 Australian tour to England and for some years was posted at a bank in Albany, Western Australia. At the age of 40 he figured in a memorable stand with Claude Rock. Set to score 307 to win in the last innings against the South, the North won by eight wickets when Bailey (139) and Rock (113) scored 256 for the first wicket. Bailey also scored 227 not out for Derwent against Break-O'-Day in 1880–81 and 156 for New Town at the age of fifty-four.

Tasmanian cricket undoubtedly suffered in the early years from the dominance of the Derwent and Launceston clubs and from the north–south antagonism, but assistance came from various quarters. The Tasmanian Steam Navigation Company several times provided reduced fares to help Tasmanian cricketers play on the mainland. In 1861 the Melbourne Cricket Club offered to pay the expenses of players who might not be "sufficiently affluent" to afford the trip to Melbourne. Later Sir John George Davies, a former Speaker in the Tasmanian Parliament and one-time Mayor of Hobart, was a generous benefactor of Tasmanian cricket.

Davies, whose family founded the Hobart *Mercury*, played for Tasmania against four England touring teams between 1873–74 and 1887–88. He set an endurance record by appearing in 24 South *v.* North matches from 1865 to 1889, but as he failed to score ten times in these matches and averaged only 12.05 in 37 completed innings for the South, his cricketing ability may not have been the sole reason for his selection. He was a willing contributor when funds were short, an eloquent speaker in committee rooms and Tasmania's best-known cricket writer, as well as manager of an Australian shooting team at Bisley.

There were not enough businessmen like Davies ready to support Tasmania's cricketers when intercolonial cricket began and there was barely a voice raised against Tasmania's exclusion from the initial Sheffield Shield competition in 1892–93, an attitude difficult to reconcile with Tasmanian enterprise in staging Australia's initial first-class match. The Australian Board of Control and the Victorian Cricket Association took the initiative in 1907 by suggesting the formation of the Executive Cricket Council of Tasmania in an effort to overcome north–south jealousies and properly represent the island on the national body—but with little discernible effect.

Tasmanian cricket, however, never lacked characters. One of the most colourful was the fiery pace bowler Tom Hogg, who in 1863 in his first senior match was no-balled for lifting his arm above the shoulder. Hogg, one of 11 children whose father died in his thirties, said the umpire was ignorant of the rules of cricket and stalked from the field. He was in good company, for in England in 1822 John Willes, of Kent, had been no-balled for bowling round-arm against MCC, and in 1862 Edgar Willsher had been no-balled for bowling overarm for England against Surrey. Although Hogg had to restrict himself to round-armers, he made dramatic progress. He took 5 for 13 and 5 for 4 against Victoria in 1866, and remained Tasmania's best bowler for more than a decade. Hogg was also a skilled oarsman and rowed for Tasmania in the first intercolonial regatta on the Derwent. He was a teacher at the

*LEFT: Sir John George Davies, one-time Speaker of the Tasmanian Parliament and Mayor of Hobart, represented Tasmania 15 times at cricket and led the Tasmanian team to New Zealand in 1884*
*OVER PAGE: The successful Gloucestershire side of 1886 included six amateurs: (L to R) J. A. Bush, A. D. Greene, H. Hale, D. D. Radcliffe, G. Francis and (front) W. G. Grace. Hale toured New Zealand with Tasmania in 1883–84, before going to England*

*Claude William Rock, an outstanding Tasmanian-born all-rounder who turned in some brilliant displays for Cambridge University*

Reverend R. O. Powlett Harris's High School in Hobart and became the first Australian bowler to clean-bowl W. G. Grace. In the 1872 Colonies match Hogg baffled the best batsmen in Australia.

Hogg's enforced modifications to his bowling produced an action that defied erudite description. He strolled casually to the crease and, in the words of the Melbourne *Telegraph*, "seemed to take the ball from behind his right ear and go through a little legerdemain with it behind his back before launching it". His most destructive ball was a fast full toss which curled in the air, and it was this delivery that defeated W. G. Grace and sundry other notable players. Batsmen felt hemmed in against Hogg, who pitched the ball right up on the stumps every time and regularly destroyed the batting of Hobart teams. After he moved to

Launceston, increasing weight forced him to reduce his pace and to jog slowly between wickets. Hogg then compensated as a batsman by producing some enormous hits back over the bowlers' heads, making his batting in his later years almost as awesome as his bowling of earlier times.

Subdued by the batting of Arthur and Bailey, southern Tasmanian cricket revived briefly between 1870 and 1872, and was also helped by encouragement from Governor Charles Du Cane, who often joined them in the Hobart nets. Du Cane had learned to bat at Charterhouse and Exeter College while he took his master's degree at Oxford. His support gave Tasmanian cricket prestige but it could not overcome what one commentator called its "illustrious isolation", uplifted only by the graceful strokes seen on pretty fields such as Entally.

The absence of a single Tasmanian from the initial international matches—they were not described as Tests until 38 matches had been played between teams from England and Australia—puzzled and irked all Tasmanians. They recalled that Tasmanians had usually done well against mainland teams and in mainland games. When Victoria played the Rest of Australia in 1872, four Tasmanians, John Arthur, Richard Barnes, John Davies and Tom Hogg, were chosen. Davies fell over a roller and injured a knee at practice, which prevented him from playing, but Barnes (3 for 10 and 1 for 11) and Hogg (2 for 27 and 1 for 13) bowled well, and Arthur scored more runs than anyone in the match, with 49 and a match-winning 34 not out in the last innings. Eleven of Victoria met Thirteen of the Rest of Australia in this match, odds that the Rest—who represented the best players in Australia at the time—should never have accepted. Strangely, the match has been sanctioned as "first-class" by cricket statisticians because of the calibre of the players involved. The Combined Thirteen won by five wickets in Melbourne.

For a long time Tasmanian cricket followers took satisfaction mainly from the feats of their

*Dr Roland ("Rowley") Pope, who learned all his cricket from Tom Kendall at Hutchin's School, Hobart.*

players overseas. E. H. Butler played for the Gentlemen against the Players in 1877 and in eight matches for the United South of England XI that included W. G. and G. F. Grace, W. R. Gilbert, and W. Midwinter. His brother, C. W. Butler, was called on to help the 1877 Australian team when they were short during their England tour, and W. G. Grace named his fourth son Charles Butler in his honour.

Claude William Rock, son of a Deloraine doctor, took 6 for 39 at the age of 15 for North against South, became a valued player in the Cambridge team, and was rated the best bowler at an English university by *Lillywhite's Annual.* Harold Hale, born in Western Australia in 1867, learned the game at St Peter's, Adelaide, and at Hutchins School in Hobart, where he was enrolled in 1880 and received instruction from Test bowler Tom Kendall. Hale toured New Zealand with a Tasmanian team while still at school and took 7

for 42 against Canterbury. He played for Gloucestershire in 1886–89, practising in W. G. Grace's backyard, and for the Gentlemen in 1886. He was in the Cambridge University side from 1887 to 1890. He took 99 wickets at 23.18 in 57 first-class matches and scored 1067 runs at 12.12. Hale's cricket captain at Hutchins School was the tireless traveller Roland James Pope, who filled in for Australian teams on tour in 1886, 1888 and 1890. Another nomad was the Tasmanian batsman Vere Harris, who played for East Melbourne, for the Albert Club in Sydney, for the New South Wales "Practice Squad", and for Western Australia against South Australia in 1898.

Despite the undoubted talent on the island, Tasmanians were compelled to accept that they were part of Australia but separated from it by Bass Strait, a rough, unpredictable stretch of water no cricketers — and certainly no selectors — enjoyed crossing. One of Billy Walker's team-mates recalled that Walker was eating breakfast on a trip across the Strait when a huge wave burst into the cabin and washed his steak and coffee from the table. Walker calmly called for another steak and a fresh cup of coffee. "You know, I wouldn't have missed this trip for £100," he said as another huge wave hit the boat. The remark won Walker the respect of his team, but at that instant most would have taken the £100 for their team spot.

In an era in which many Australians endured isolation, however, Tasmanian cricket was hampered most by the strange reluctance of the strong, prestigious clubs in Hobart and Launceston to hire professional players to coach and strengthen their teams. This attitude of gentlemanly disdain towards professionalism, which apparently stemmed from the comparative affluence of Tasmanian land-holders compared with the harsher, less sophisticated life on the mainland, undid the promising early start Tasmania made in cricket. It was in direct contrast to the approach of the leading Sydney and Melbourne clubs in building their playing strength and mastering the game's skills.

# Cricket on the goldfields

### Victoria 1838-60

Two official attempts to found convict and military settlements in the region now known as Victoria failed before a permanent, unofficial colony was begun by free settlers. Edward Henty, who with his father and brothers had reached Tasmania too late to secure free land grants, formed a pastoral headquarters on the shores of Portland Bay in November 1834. The following year John Batman did a deal with a local Aboriginal tribe and set up a depot at Indented Head on the western shore of Port Phillip. In England that year J. H. Kirwan caused a sensation by taking all 10 wickets for Eton in a match against the MCC at Eton.

Waves of settlers from the north closely followed the invasion from Tasmania and soon occupied the northern and western plains. By 1838 it was estimated that there were 31,000 Europeans south of the Murray River. Almost naked Aborigines wandered about a town that consisted of wattle and daub houses roofed with sheets of

*The Melbourne Cricket Club XI of 1865 was a powerful outfit studded with notable players. Dick Wardill (fifth from the left) scored the first century in Victoria and later called the meeting that formed the Victorian Cricket Association*

bark and coarse shingles. The Yarra River and its swamps were thick with pelicans and ducks, and John Batman described the quail that flew past in shimmering clouds, a thousand at a time.

Horseracing was Victoria's first sport, the initial meeting being staged close to Batman's Hill, on what is now Spencer Street Station, in March 1838. On 15 November that year five gentlemen settlers sat down and drew up a document to form the "Melbourne Cricket Club" with a subscription of one guinea. The five signatories—F. A. Powlett, R. Russell, Arthur Mundy, C. F. Mundy and George B. Smyth—each paid their guinea and on the same day D. G. McArthur, first secretary of the club, bought two bats, balls and stumps for £2 0s 3d.

The founders of Australia's most venerable cricket club were all influential figures in the new colony. Powlett, the first president, was Crown Land Commissioner of the Western Division of Port Phillip Settlement and the first police magistrate. Russell was a surveyor, who had drawn up plans for Melbourne under the orders of Governor Bourke the previous year, and a first-class rifleman who shot ducks and kangaroos on the river bank; he also raced a horse in Melbourne's first race meeting. Arthur and C. F. Mundy worked for the Melbourne Insurance Company, while George Smyth, then a captain of the 80th Regiment, later became captain of Melbourne's Mounted Police.

The best cricketer among the Melbourne Cricket Club's founders was Powlett, a descendant of the Reverend Charles Powlett, who had helped found the Hambledon Club on Broadhalfpenny Down. He took the first hat-trick and made the first century recorded in Victoria, and is one of only two presidents of the Melbourne Cricket Club to play for his state (the other was T. F. Hamilton).

Two days after its formation the Melbourne Cricket Club played its first game—on 22 November 1838 against the Military, on a ground located where the Royal Mint now stands in William Street, between Latrobe and Little Lonsdale Streets. The *Port Phillip Gazette*, in its description of this match, reported that it was played on one of the most "beautiful pleasure grounds around this fast rising town". The *Gazette* added:

> *During the week arrangements had been made by the gentlemen civilians of the district to play a match of cricket against The Military... It was a heart-enlivening sight to witness from an adjacent hill the ground as it was laid out— camps pitched, banners tastily arranged, and the all-enlivening smiles of beauty that would have graced a far-famed tournament of olden times... At 12 precisely a signal called the players to their post, when the game commenced, The Military taking first innings. We have not the particulars of the game before us and can therefore but briefly notice those who distinguished themselves. After a duration of some hours the match resulted in a triumph for the Civilians. Mr Powlett's and Mr Donald Macarthur's bowling and Mr Russell's batting attracted universal applause. On the whole the game was played with esprit de corps, a judgement and activity that a first-rate club in England might not be ashamed to boast of.*

Powlett was one of two early members of the Melbourne Cricket Club to fight in a duel and the only president to do so. In his duel with a merchant, Mr Hogue, on Flemington Hill in 1842, two shots were fired. Hogue missed, but Powlett sent a bullet through Hogue's clothing. The other MCC duellist was Peter Snodgrass, whose father was a lieutenant-colonel. Snodgrass shot off one of his own toenails in his first duel, against a grazier named William Ryrie. In his second, against the young barrister Redmond

---

*The letter that led to the formation of the Melbourne Cricket Club in November 1838. The five men whose names are listed at the top paid the one guinea subscription in advance—the rest paid later*

It is proposed to form a Cricket club,
with half a ~~guinea~~ one Guinea Subscription

A. Powlett.        Paid
R. Russell         Paid
A W Mundy          Paid
C F N Mundy        Paid
Geo N Smyth        Paid

Smith              Jamieson
Donald McArthur    webster
P. Snodgrass       Sims
William Ryre       Brock
Highett            Bacchus
Williams           Allen
Meek               Pitman
                   Hind       &c &c

{ The above is a copy of the original List of the Melbourne
  Cricket club, in the possession of the undersigned; the first five
  names us signed, the remainder merely proposed
                                    Robert Russell
                                     Octr 26 1859

copy {

                        Melbourne 15th Nov 1838

        Mr Arthur Esq.

                        Jo. H. Davis Dr

Jo. 2 Batts balls & Stumps          £ 2 = 3

            Recd paymt          for H Davis
                                  J Barnet

Barry, he again discharged his pistol before the signal, this time without inflicting any damage. Barry did the gentlemanly thing and fired his pistol in the air. Redmond Barry later became Victoria's first solicitor-general and as a Supreme Court judge was to pass sentence on the bushranger Ned Kelly. Snodgrass became a member of parliament and, according to a newspaper of the time, a "voluble if not eloquent" chairman of committees in the Legislative Assembly.

Apart from the founders, perhaps the most influential early member of the MCC was David Charteris Macarthur, born in Gloucestershire in 1808, and a dedicated cricket buff. He travelled from Sydney to open Melbourne's first bank in a two-roomed brick cottage on the north side of Little Collins Street, between Queen and Elizabeth Streets. An armed sentry and two mastiffs formed the guard. Macarthur worked so diligently to promote cricket in the colony that he became known as "the father of Victorian cricket", but he was past his prime by the time first-class cricket was introduced and had to be content with the presidency of the MCC from 1868 to 1877.

Shortly after the formation of the Melbourne Cricket Club, the Melbourne Union Cricket Club was founded, with a membership of retailers, tradesmen and artisans. On 12 January 1839 the MCC played the Union Club, which won handsomely. A return match followed on 17 January and this time the MCC won easily, with Powlett scoring 120, the first century in the colony. The Union Club's star was a tradesman named Thomas Halfpenny, who kept wicket and clobbered the ball hard and often as a batsman. In a later match between Benedicts and Bachelors, Powlett scored 101 runs in the Bachelors' two innings total of 180. Other matches included Civil v. Military, the first half of the alphabet versus the second half, and Whiskers v. Clean-shaven. The beards won by seven wickets, a notable victory since most men in the colony were clean-shaven until the goldrush of 1851.

George Cavenagh had by then given up the editorship of the *Sydney Gazette* and become sole owner of the *Port Phillip Herald*, which began on 3 January 1840. He was president of the Melbourne Cricket Club from 1846 to 1854 and won the batting average in 1846–47. Cavenagh imported staff and an editor, William Kerr, from England, and in 1849 his newspaper became the Melbourne *Herald*.

The Brighton Cricket Club began in 1842 and played its matches on a stretch of turf that had been an Aboriginal camping ground a few years earlier. Brighton had two outstanding round-arm bowlers, Coldham and Brown, whose presence gave the club real standing in Victorian cricket. Brighton played its first match against the Melbourne club on Easter Monday 1845 before "a great turn out of the fashionable world". Melbourne made 70 in its first innings, Brighton 62. After a half-hour spell they resumed, but Melbourne could not cope with the opposition bowling and Brighton won comfortably.

After that match the Melbourne player John Highett, whose "purse never ran below the low-water mark", discovered that he had been robbed of his coat and £500 that he had left in its pockets. At a time when £1 was a good wage this was an extraordinary theft, accomplished after Highett left his jacket in the dressing-room to go out and play. The coat was later found by the chief constable, but without the money. The Melbourne columnist "Garryowen" commented that "there can be little doubt that the paper money was promptly placed in the melting pot of the publicans and thus put into speedy liquidation".

The 1840s brought difficulties for the Melbourne Cricket Club, the shortage of funds preventing all but the most essential work on the club's pitch. Committee men often had to dip into their wallets for the club to remain solvent. Although the club struggled for survival, the entrance fee remained at one guinea, and by 1847 there were 127 members, including W. C. Haines, who became Victoria's first premier when responsible government began. Another member was

Dr Patrick Cussen, who performed the first surgical operation in the colony, successfully removing the arm of a soldier who had blown off his fingers firing a salute to Lady Franklin with a blunderbuss in 1839.

When the Melbourne Club played at Geelong in 1847, the trip there on the steamer *Asphrasia* took eight hours. The Geelong players also travelled by boat to Melbourne for the return match, arriving the night before at the Shakespeare Hotel, on the corner of Collins and Market Streets, where they met the Melbourne team.

The Melbourne Cricket Club moved to a site on the south bank of the Yarra, opposite the southern end of Spencer Street, in 1848. The pitch was laid down where John Pascoe Fawkner had raised the colony's first wheat crop in 1836, in the area now known as South Melbourne. Club secretary George Cavenagh lobbied skilfully for the Emerald Hill site. When he applied to Superintendent La Trobe to use the land, he pointed out that Sir George Gipps had granted a similar request for land from the Australian Club in Sydney and had supplied a team of convicts to help turf the pitch. La Trobe gave the Melbourne Cricket Club 10 acres (4 hectares) but no convict labourers. The club immediately erected a wooden booth, an improvement on the tent used at Batmans Hill, and enclosed the playing field with a four-rail "pig-proof" fence, at a cost of £30 13s 4d. Turfing the wicket area cost £24 13s 6d.

On 1 August 1850 the House of Commons passed the Colonies Bill, which separated the Port Phillip settlement from New South Wales and created the State of Victoria. When the official news reached Melbourne on 11 November, there were days of celebration in which fireworks and rockets illuminated Emerald Hill and most of Melbourne. Throughout the colony bonfires blazed, tar barrels burned in the streets, publicans served free beer and shopkeepers displayed "Welcome to Separation" banners. The celebrations lasted a fortnight, culminating in a procession watched by 10,000 people to mark the opening of the new Princes Bridge.

As its part of the celebrations, the Melbourne Cricket Club agreed to the first intercolonial match in Launceston against Tasmania. A special meeting of all members decided that the Victorian players should have their own colours for this event and adopted red, white and blue, which have remained the MCC's colours. The match in Launceston in February 1851 was a notable success, but before the return could be organised in Melbourne, gold was discovered, totally disrupting not only cricket but the entire life of the colony.

The first strike was at Clunes in July 1851, followed quickly by strikes at Warrandyte and Ballarat, which became one of the world's richest surface goldfields. Within three weeks Melbourne, Geelong and Williamstown were emptied of most of their male populations. Streets that had been crowded by drays were deserted. Farmers left their properties, professional men walked out of their rooms, and teachers abandoned their schools, which had to close. Ships in Port Phillip Bay were left without crews, even their masters heading for the goldfields.

Somehow the Melbourne Cricket Club rounded up a team and played the return match against Van Diemen's Land on 29 and 30 March 1852, in the presence of the governor and several thousand spectators. Play began at noon and a champagne lunch was taken in the wooden shed at Emerald Hill at half past one. Spectators lunched in a special marquee at tables loaded with a variety of meats and champagne provided by Melbourne's seven breweries. After the toasts the players resumed the game.

On the goldfields some former Oxford and Cambridge men argued about the cricket prowess of the two universities. The result was a challenge match in 1853 between teams called the Light Blues and the Dark Blues. The 1880–81 edition of Boyle and Scott's *Australian Cricketers' Guide* included an article on this match, which described how the bats were made of ironbark and the ball,

*A lithograph by H. Deutsch of a match in 1864 between the United Victorian XI and Eighteen of Ballarat. Mining towns like Ballarat fielded several strong teams*

borrowed from a miner, of indiarubber. The Dark Blues batted first and lost two wickets without scoring but were rescued by a stand of 20 runs. The writer of the article reported:

*One of the batsmen, a fellow named Barney, looked more like a bandit than a cricketer in his huge boots, broad-brimmed hat, and jet-black flowing beard, but he was a tremendous slogger and created a sensation. Our innings closed for 43, with a chap named Johnson heading the list with 19. During lunch the wagering was heavy, with quite a few nuggets put down.*

*The Light Blues soon had 10 on the score sheet, and they went to 15 without loss. I tried underhand lobs, and the first was hit for five, but then a wicket fell, and indeed two more at the same score. An old Cantab, by as correct play as could be shown on the peculiar pitch, increased the score to 35, and the other batsman—not a Cantab—overshot the mark in backing up before the ball was delivered, and I turned and knocked the stumps flying. The umpire gave him out, and the batsman made tracks for the tent, but the crowd shouted 'Swindle,' and told him to go back. The hum of voices swelled into a deafening roar, but after a long argument it was admitted that he was out and harmony was restored. The last two were now in and when only three short of our score, one of the batsmen made a good hit. They ran one and the fieldsman fumbled the ball. 'Go again,' yelled the crowd, which they did, and the fielder, recovering the ball took a shot at the wicket and knocked a stump out of the ground. He was carried from the field in triumph.*

The Dark Blues had defeated the Light Blues by two runs.

Goldfields cricket was raucous, argumentative, but without a hint of bitterness. The players may have been grimy and their clothes flecked with stains and dust, but their muscles were hard and they chased the ball keenly right to the end of the day. The audiences invariably exhibited the Australian love of gambling. Losses or wins were taken in good heart and the combatants usually ended the day toasting each other in the refreshment area.

The *Argus* reported in 1852 that a match between 11 Melbourne gentlemen and 11 gentlemen of Adelaide had been held at the Emerald Hill ground:

> *That the match was not finished, when time was called, was a godsend to the Adelaidians, who would in all probability have been soundly beaten if it had been played out, the scores of the Melbournites for two innings being so large as almost to preclude hope for the other side, even had they played their second innings. We may mention that Mr Fook's wicket-keeping was clever and that the fielding of Messrs Cary and Dicker was very much admired.*

An Australian Cricket Club was formed in Melbourne in October 1850, and on Boxing Day that year the annual sports were held in front of the White Hart Hotel at the top of Bourke Street, facing the present Parliament House. One of the features of the sports was a race for a dozen billy goats. On Emerald Hill, some of the best cricketers in action were from Tasmania, including A. H. Park, who was born at Oatlands in 1840 and later played for New South Wales.

Williamstown, founded in 1852, proved an active club, with Sir John Taverner, Sir George Verdon and Richard Seddon, later Prime Minister of New Zealand, among its founders. The club's funds were so low that every member was required to spend half an hour each week pushing the roller because there was no groundsman. The settlement at Gellibrand Point had been officially named Williamstown in 1837; the cricket ground was on a site adjoining Fort Gellibrand and the basalt

road built by convicts passed behind it.

The South Melbourne Club began in 1853, and a month later the Bendigo Cricket Club was founded. Richmond, oldest of Melbourne's present district clubs, began in 1854. The most exciting cricket, however, was on the goldfields at places like Wood's Point, near Ballarat, where rough ground did not restrict the players' enthusiasm.

The Melbourne Cricket Club members liked the ground at Emerald Hill, although it was low-lying and the Yarra flooded once and washed away the players' shed. The club had spent several thousand pounds on grading, turfing, fencing and on a small pavilion and members were justifiably proud of their work.

On 12 September 1854 the first railway train in Australia ran from Melbourne to Sandridge, which is now Port Melbourne. The engine was a six-wheeled tubular boiler of 30 horse-power. Melbourne newspapers talked with pride of this iron horse, which achieved speeds of 25 miles an hour (40 kilometres per hour). The train pulled three carriages on its inaugural run, and in the third was the band of the 40th Regiment. All the notable citizens of Melbourne travelled in the front two carriages and when the train reached Sandridge they attended a banquet. There were 20 speeches but nobody mentioned that the new railway line passed through the middle of the Melbourne Cricket Club's ground.

Governor La Trobe offered the club two alternative sites and the committee chose a plot 228 metres in diameter in the hollow of Richmond Paddock, where billy goats grazed. The secretary of the MCC wrote to the superintendent on 15 August 1853, asking for permission to remove such trees as might be necessary to convert the new site into a cricket ground and to build a cottage. On 23 September the governor granted permission for the club to enclose four hectares of Richmond Paddock and erect whatever buildings were deemed necessary. The ground was to be used for cricket only.

Melbourne was then suffering from goldrush

fever. When a performance finished at Queen's Theatre, actors were showered with nuggets, some more than 30 grams in weight, instead of the customary flowers. Immigrants arrived at the rate of 3000 every week, and alongside the Melbourne Club's original ground at Emerald Hill a tent city sprang up. Melbourne was "clamorous with drunken revels, which now and again culminated in crimes of audacious violence". There were good fish in the Yarra, and it was often alive with ducks. A tribe of Aborigines camped not far from Princes Bridge and both sides of the river boasted wallabies and kangaroos. The Richmond end of the Melbourne Club's new home was thick with timber and thieves were known to hide there, ready to pounce on travellers walking down to the boat at Punt Road Hill.

Melbourne Cricket Club members shrugged off the inconvenience the railway had caused them and set about converting their new site at Richmond Paddock into one of the world's best cricket grounds. In November 1854 the members played their first match on the new pitch. They put up an iron fence to keep out non-paying spectators and a wooden pavilion and staged a Married *v.* Singles contest. The move brought an immediate change in luck and in four months in 1855 the club's membership increased by 200, most of them men who had prospered in the goldrush.

Two months after the Melbourne Club occupied its new ground, the Sydney Cricket Club challenged Geelong to a match. Geelong was the main port for those *en route* to the goldfields. The challenge caused wide speculation, for the Sydney club offered to pay £75 towards the Geelong team's expenses to sail to Sydney and play the match. Just after Geelong declined the invitation, the Melbourne Cricket Club inserted an advertisement in the *Argus* challenging any team in Australia to a match with stakes of up to £1000. This led to the first match between Victoria and New South Wales in March 1856.

George Marshall, one of the outstanding early wicket-keepers, travelled from his birthplace in

*An illustration of the match between Victoria and New South Wales in Melbourne in January 1858. Victoria won by 171 runs*

Nottingham in the late 1850s to take up residence in Melbourne's Spencer Street. He signed an agreement with the Melbourne Cricket Club, which provided him with 15 shillings a day to bowl to members and one pound a day for playing in the club's matches. About the same time the MCC's

secretary, Dick Wardill, arranged for Rowland Newberry to receive £10 a month to reside in the Melbourne Cricket Ground pavilion and take care of the club's property. One of Newberry's jobs was to eject non-members from the ground. Marshall proved a hard-working model migrant, who rose from this humble start to become a shopkeeper, then hotel keeper and finally a sponsor of an England cricket tour of Australia. He was a stubborn, ethical man, who followed the highest standards of behaviour.

There was argument in Melbourne at the time over who was the city's outstanding cricketer. James "Jerry" Bryant, a right-hand batsman and right-hand round-arm bowler, who had played for Surrey and for Victoria against New South Wales in the first intercolonial match against that state, challenged any man in the colony to a game of single-wicket cricket. A comparatively unknown right-hand batsman and left-arm bowler named

John Mace responded and defeated Bryant by 24 runs. It turned out that Mace had played for Bedale in Yorkshire alongside the All England players Ron Iddison and George Anderson. Mace and his brothers had been lured to Victoria to search for gold. Both John and Christopher Mace later went to the Otago goldfields in New Zealand. They represented both Victoria and Otago.

Before he left Australia John Mace met Thomas Wentworth Wills in a single-wicket match before "an immense crowd of spectators" on the Melbourne Club's ground. Mace was out for four after 25 balls and Wills then scored 57 runs off 257 balls. Both Mace and Wills played for the Richmond club, which won the first club competition in Melbourne in 1860–61. The city's clubs at that time included Collingwood, St Kilda, South Melbourne, and the all-powerful East Melbourne side, which had been founded by Tom and Charley Dight with the help of Fred and Joseph Moody.

East Melbourne practised on a variety of grounds, including one at Clarendon Street. The club changed its name from the original Abbotsford Cricket Club when permission was sought for a permanent home on a field known as Captain Lonsdale's cow paddock. East Melbourne and Melbourne shared the honours in the Melbourne premiership until 1872–73, when South Melbourne won for the first time.

There was also a Challenge Cup for the Coppin Trophy, presented by the Hon. G. S. Coppin, president of the Richmond Club. The trophy was at stake on a match-by-match basis and any club that held it for two years without defeat had the right of permanent ownership. Richmond at one stage held it for 22 months and appeared certain to take permanent possession, but were beaten by East Melbourne. The *Argus* described it as "the glittering illusion, always to be played for, but never won. From the little

*ABOVE: The first Melbourne Cricket Ground pavilion, built for the international match in 1862*
*RIGHT: A fieldsman chases a ball to the boundary during a match between teams from Sydney and Melbourne at Richmond, Melbourne, in 1855. Notable families in the colony, including Commissary-General Cotsworthy's brood, are depicted in the foreground*

differences the Coppin Trophy has already given rise to, it promises to be the very apple of discord among cricketers".

The star of the Richmond team, Tom Wills, was a comparative rarity in the goldrush days of the 1850s and 1860s — a third-generation Australian. His grandfather, Edward Spencer Wills, had been the youngest son of an English county family, who married in Britain and emigrated to Australia about 1799 to make his fortune. He built up a prosperous merchant's business in Sydney very quickly but died in 1811, aged 32, leaving a widow with six young children. A year later Mrs Wills married George Howe, publisher of the Sydney *Gazette*. Her youngest son, Horatio, ran away to sea at 15 and was shipwrecked in the Marquesas, where it was said he owed his life to the romantic intervention of a local princess, and finally managed to escape, returning to his family long after they thought him dead. He worked in the Sydney office of the *Gazette* and at 21 married Elizabeth Wyre and squatted at Molonglo, between Canberra and Queanbeyan. There, on 19 August 1835, T. W. Wills was born.

Four years later the family crossed the Murray into Victoria with 5000 sheep and 500 cattle, investigated the western pasture, and settled in 1840 at Ararat — so named by the devout Horatio Wills for the resting place of the Ark. Here Horatio won the respect of local Aborigines, and Tom spent a happy childhood that included regular cricket matches. His cousin and future brother-in-law H. C. A. Harrison was a frequent visitor. Shortage of labour caused by the goldrush forced Horatio to sell the Ararat property and settle in Geelong, where he became the member for Grant in the first Victorian Legislative Assembly.

Meanwhile Tom Wills was sent to Rugby School in England from 1852 to 1855. He became the school Rugby and cricket captain and played against MCC and I Zingari; he also received

*Thomas Wentworth Wills, Australia's first outstanding cricketer, not long after he returned to Australia after playing for Rugby School, Kent, MCC and Cambridge University*

his school matches with appearances in 1856 for Kent and the MCC, and for Cambridge in the varsity match against Oxford, although he was not strictly eligible. He had enrolled at Cambridge but did not take up residence and at the end of that year he returned home.

The lack of fitness among the colony's leading cricketers appalled Wills, who blamed it on their inactivity during winter. When the season ended he looked for some form of exercise for his cricketers and decided that Rugby was too rough. With H. C. A. Harrison he invented Australian Rules football as the alternative. Wills was unquestionably the first outstanding Australian-born cricketer, a bold, gifted ball-player of courage and enterprise, but he was destined for a life of tragedy.

Several cricket clubs functioned briefly in the 1850s, despite losing many players to the gold-fields. But this migration to the country at least had the benefit of promoting the game in outlying districts. The first match at Colac, 160 kilometres south-west of Melbourne, was played in 1853; bats had to be made by the local wheelwright, the ball by the shoemaker. Despite the lack of a paper to circulate news of the match, a large crowd gathered near the blacksmith's shop. There, according to Isaac Webb's *History Of Colac and District*, "we wielded the willow and trundled the leather to the wonder and astonishment of all". At intervals the players stopped the game and pressed fiddlers to work and "the gentlemen and ladies present indulged vigorously in dancing on the pitch".

The Melbourne cricket historian David Roylance recorded that the St Kilda Club shocked "the most glacial upholders of royal protocol" by applying in 1857–58 for Royal patronage. The club's petition, supported by Sir George Stephens, requested the right to use title, "The Royal Cricket Club of Victoria". Queen Victoria's private secretary, Sir G. Phipps, considered the application "entirely inadmissable". Lord Carnarvon, as Colonial Secretary, asked Sir Edward Lytton to reply, saying, "I think a civil letter be

regular coaching from John Lillywhite. He was an outstanding round-arm bowler, and an excellent field, but had a peculiar, if successful, batting style in which he "scarcely moved the bat at all unless the ball was well pitched up to him". He followed

the Royal accolade. Stephens proved ahead of his time in advocating a national control authority. The question of national control and the rights of players was to become a dominant issue for more than a century.

T. W. Wills took 181 wickets for the Melbourne Cricket Club in 1857–58, and in 1860–61 a club cricket competition began in Melbourne, with Richmond the first premiers. Early in 1857 word came from England that the Reverend W. Fellows had driven a ball 175 yards (159 metres), the longest authenticated hit in cricket. Two years later there was news that a hat had been awarded for the first time to a bowler who took wickets with three successive balls, thus introducing the "hat-trick" into the lore of the game. (First to perform the hat-trick in Victoria was F. A. Powlett, foundation president of the Melbourne Cricket Club, in a club match; the date is unknown.)

*Bell's Life In Victoria* boasted on 11 February 1860, that "The world-astounding excitement of the Victorian goldfield has caused a flow of emigration to these shores which our neighbours could not acquire with their staid inducements, and as cricketers are neither mindful of rank nor class we have had our nick from 'broadcloth to fustian' as to make us very strong indeed". *Bell's* undoubtedly intended this as a jibe at New South Wales's cricket strength, but the cricket clubs of South Australia must have been just as envious of the playing talent the goldrushes had attracted to Victoria.

*Cricket in the Victorian bush was often played under extremely primitive conditions. This pitch had to be cut out of a heavily timbered area*

drafted declining". A year later Sir George Stephens represented St Kilda at a meeting of all the city's cricket clubs called by Melbourne. He tried to introduce the question of "a cricket congress of the Australian Colonies", but was ruled out of order. St Kilda never reapplied for

# Amateurs and gentlemen
## South Australia 1836–75

Twenty-three months after the colony of South Australia was proclaimed on 28 December 1836, an advertisement for a cricket match appeared in local newspapers. It is therefore likely that cricket began in South Australia before it was played in Victoria, or at least in the same month. The advertisement was directed to "gentlemen cricket players" and announced that a meeting of patrons of "that old English and manly game of cricket" would take place at the London Tavern, opposite Gilles Arcade, with the aim of forming a club. Gentlemen wishing to join were urged to attend.

The advertisement appeared in both the *South Australian Register* and the *South Australia Gazette*, on 3 November 1838, whereas the meeting that founded the Melbourne Cricket Club was held on 15 November. Both colonies differed from others in Australia in that they were founded by free settlers. Victoria was first populated by frustrated Tasmanian settlers, while South Australia emerged from a hybrid system that created neither a Crown Colony nor a chartered company, but required all

*Cricket was often played under the most difficult conditions. This pitch at Strathalbyn, South Australia, was cleared from a rocky strip of ground beside the river*

land-holders to buy their land at 20 shillings an acre. On 24 November 1838, three weeks after the first advertisement, another appeared in both papers, advising that two members of the London Tavern Cricket Club were ready to play any two gentlemen at single-wicket cricket for £10 or £20.

This initiative, from a publican keen to boost his business, inspired a further long announcement boasting of the facilities offered by the Royal Admiral Hotel, in Hindley Street, Adelaide. The proprietor announced that he expected a supply of bats, balls, and stumps of the very best quality to arrive any day in the *Prince George* and that he proposed to form a club for cricket lovers to promote that healthy game.

Not to be outdone, John Bristow, owner of the Great Tom of Lincoln Hotel, in the Adelaide suburb of Thebarton, inserted an advertisement on 19 October 1839, in the *Register* and the *Gazette*, which read:

CRICKET
*A grand match will be played on Monday, October 28, on the Thebarton Cricket Ground between Eleven Gentlemen of Royal Victoria Independent Club, and Eleven Gentlemen of Adelaide, for Twenty-two guineas a side. Wickets to be pitched at 10 o'clock. Refreshments will be provided, and everything done that can add to the pleasure of the public.*
*By their obedient servant,*
*John Bristow.*

Added attractions on the day of the match included a greasy pole, juggling acts and foot races. The Gentlemen of the Royal Victoria Independent Club won by 11 runs.

The ten commissioners who first administered the colony laid Adelaide out with ample space for parks and gardens. Cricketers found, however, that they had to compete for the best space with the colony's fast-growing population of cows. Some of the ground most suited to cricket became instead staging camps for new settlers, and what space remained was bumpy. The gear was primi-

*From its earliest days cricket in South Australia attracted entire families. This shot of the crowd at Adelaide Oval underlines how well-dressed audiences were for big cricket*

tive, usually handmade by its owners, and refinements like pads and gloves were unknown until a player named Smith arrived in 1847 and joined the Adelaide Cricket Club. He became famous as the owner of the first pads seen in the colony, but when he donned them for the first time he was bowled first ball. Thereafter he was known as "Pads and Gloves" Smith.

South Australia's first outstanding cricketer

assured everyone that the style was now accepted by the MCC at Lord's. He informed his critics that when he had played against the Rest of England in 1842 almost every bowler favoured the round-arm technique.

South Australia was fortunate to have a writer who fully documented the state's early cricket. This was Clarence P. Moody, who wrote under the pseudonym "Point" in the *Register*. Moody wrote four books, one of which had a major influence on all international cricket by defining what comprised a Test match, and turned out hundreds of match reports and articles. He also wrote on football. His honesty and thorough knowledge of cricket were well recognised and he did a great deal to boost the game in South Australia.

Moody wrote about a player named Colman, who rode 77 kilometres from his home at Strathalbyn to play cricket in Adelaide, played all day, and then rode home again in the dark. He also recounted the unhappy experience of a sailor named Wilkins who challenged any player in South Australia to a single-wicket match. W. B. T. Andrews, then secretary of the Adelaide Cricket Club, took Joe Cocker to the Halfway House Inn on the Port Road to accept Wilkins' challenge. A match was arranged for £10 a side. Wilkins insisted that each man do all his own fielding. Cocker won the toss and selected his own pitch at the bottom of Stanley Street, North Adelaide. Several hundred people gathered for the contest.

was John Collard ("Joe") Cocker, who had played for Kent in 1842 with Alfred Mynn and Fuller Pilch. Cocker arrived in Adelaide in 1846 and quickly proved the best underarm bowler in the colony. He was also a batsman of quality. Cocker became publican of the Kentish Arms in North Adelaide and formed a club called Kent and Sussex, which later was strong enough to play the Adelaide Club, which had its ground across the river near the bridge over the Torrens.

Cocker's team included the brothers Bill and Tom Botten. Tom was the first round-arm bowler in South Australia. His bowling was viewed with suspicion by opponents and spectators, but Cocker

Cocker hammered the first ball from Wilkins for four and then proceeded to hit Wilkins' bowling all over the field. The crowd tired of the slaughter and shouted to Cocker to end it, but he carried on remorselessly until he reached 109, when he permitted a ball from Wilkins to strike his stumps. Some consider this the first recorded century in South Australia; Judge Bundey's century is the other possibility, but the dates of both are unknown. Wilkins could only score seven runs in two innings and did not enforce the agreement which gave the loser the right to a return match.

An admirer wrote that Cocker could play cricket all day in the fiercest heat on the ground in front of his hotel. When he could not find adults to play with him, he collected young boys whom he instructed in the arts of the game.

*Nothing delighted Cocker more than to be bowled by one of his protégés. Then in the evenings he would entertain us with his fiddle in the parlour of the hotel, and many's the pleasant evening we spent there listening to his music and his yarns about Alfred Mynn, Fuller Pilch and the other identities whom he played with in Old England.*

Cocker drifted away to the goldfields in Victoria but eventually returned to establish his own business in Adelaide.

Cocker's only challenger for the right to the first century in South Australia was Judge W. H. **Bundey,** who as a boy at Woodside, in the Adelaide Hills, had scored a 100 with a bat he and his father fashioned from the limb of a cherry tree. Judge Bundey was an ardent cricketer who in 1852 called the meeting that formed the Union Cricket Club, a name taken from the hotel at Marryatville where the meeting was held. On 11 January 1854 this advertisement appeared in the *South Australian Register*:

*I, on behalf of the Union Cricket Club, do hereby challenge the Province of South Australia to play a friendly match upon the Park Lands between North and South Adelaide. This challenge to remain open for ten days from the date hereof. The said game to be played from day to day until completed.*
— *W. H. Bundey, secretary.*

Even the great Joe Cocker could not prevent the Union Club defeating the Rest of South Australia when the challenge was accepted. The Union Cricket Club scored 96 and 134, of which a player named Baker scored 51. Cocker scored 20 not out and 10. Tom Botten took 7 wickets for the Rest,

Cocker 3, Coleman 6, but the bowling hero of the match was Dobson, who took 10 wickets in all for Union, strongly supported by Hall, who took 9.

Judge Bundey later recalled that this victory ruined the Union Club, for it demonstrated a strength other clubs could not match. Interest declined through lack of challenges, members refused to practise and only a year later the Adelaide Club defeated the Union by an innings. Cocker and Tom Botten bowled out man after man. The Adelaide Club players were known as the "Toffs" because of their advertisement seeking "gentlemen" cricketers. North Adelaide were called the "Pig And Whistles" for a time when they held their meetings at the pub of that name. When they switched to the Reverend Dr Jeffries' church hall, they became known as the "Holy Boys".

South Australian-born cricket historian Johnnie Moyes later reflected:

*It was a great pity that Union should have died so soon, for it was clearly a fine club, and Judge Bundey was a great cricket lover, and extremely popular with the younger generation because he consistently advocated time off from work for cricket practice, telling the business men that they would benefit beyond measure if they adopted this idea. Apparently they did not believe him, and the Judge in his advocacy of "more leisure" seems to have been born a century too soon.*

The newly formed South Australian Cricket Club dominated the state's cricket in the 1860s, largely because it leased 2.5 hectares of the North Adelaide parkland where Adelaide Oval now stands. Another strong club of the period was the United Tradesmen, founded in 1861 by William

*An early sketch of the site for Adelaide Oval viewed from Montefiore Hill, showing the lush parklands for which the ground later became known*

Botten, brother of demon round-arm bowler Tom and licensee of the Lord Melbourne Hotel. This Botten was reported to have played in England with the leading players of Kent. He was assisted by Phillip Brown, who had played cricket regularly in Cambridgeshire.

Chief rivals of the United Tradesmen were the Eastern Suburban Club players, who were organised by a former Kapunda resident John Scandrett and included the brothers Wood and a noted early trio, Charlie, George and Jim Gooden. The Goodens were inspired players and when they switched to a new club, East Torrens, in 1865, they invested it with an enthusiasm that has enabled it to endure for more than 120 years. The Gooden brothers were strongly influenced by their English father, who was determined to re-capture the bucolic spirit of old England and nurture the view that a game of cricket was a

fitting reward for hard work for both gentleman and servant alike. Another advocate of this notion was Samuel Davenport, who organised a match at his property in Macclesfield solely to entertain his tenants and workmen.

A bowler named Cox took 15 wickets to enable the South Australian Cricket Club to over-whelm the Union in 1862. This immediately led to suggestions that a match be staged between British and colonial-born teams. The *Register*'s report of this affair on Thebarton racecourse reflected the interest colonial gentry took in cricket. The *Register* noted that among those present were

*the Lord Bishop of Adelaide, the Hon. Mr Foster, the Hon. Dr Davies, the Hon. Mr Morphett, Mr Tom Reynolds, M.P., the Reverend Mr Farr, who appeared to have given*

*his boys at St. Peter's College a half day's holiday, Mr Maturin, Dr Woodforde, and other gentlemen of standing and influence in the colony.*

*There was a dearth of ladies, at which we felt some surprise, recollecting the interest they take in matches in general, and remembering how their presence used to adorn matches at Marylebone and in the counties of England. As they may be intending to grace the scene by their presence today, we refrain from harsh censure, and content ourselves with assuring them that with the striking instances of adroitness and agility of the players, the cheers of spectators at every instance of remarkable cleverness and success, the circling concourse of observers, the flaunting of flags, the music swelling and falling with the breeze, the treat they lose by keeping away is not less than the disappointment their absence creates.*

The Colonials led by 22 runs on the first innings and left the British-born players 146 runs to win. After the British had slumped to 7 for 41, they claimed it was too dark to continue. The umpires did not agree and when no further British-born batsmen appeared they awarded the match to the Colonials, a decision that caused bitterness.

By 1846 cricket clubs had been formed in suburban areas and villages on the outskirts of Adelaide. Two of the most prominent were the Walkerville and Thebarton clubs. When these clubs played a challenge match on 30 November 1846, the fee for participation was announced at "a guinea a bat", a price that was beyond the means of all but the wealthy gentlemen of the colony.

Cricket in the 1850s was regarded by some in Adelaide as an activity that reinforced British Imperial virtues and helped compensate for isolation from the Motherland. The *South Australian Register* of 28 February 1850, reported a speech where there was reference to hard-fought contests "with bats for swords, balls thrown almost with the force of artillery". The *Register* remarked that the player judged the best batsman in this match,

The South Australian XI that lost by seven wickets to Victoria in November 1880 on the East Melbourne Ground: (L to R) (back) J. Chittleborough, J. Noel, H. Gooden, J. Hide; (centre) T. Richards, W. Bullough, J. Gooden (captain), A. Slight, A. Pettinger; (front) J. King, G. Giffen, W. Slight, J. Goodfellow

Mr Mortimer, called his bat "Lucknow" after the battle of the same name.

The game soon came to be played at two distinct social levels. The powerful South Australian Club included H. Yorke Sparks, Major J. A. Fergusson, and several of the Ayers family among its members, influential figures in the colony who were determined to have cricket played in the best English tradition, with all the trappings of good breeding and gentility. The

same year. Kapunda in their initial game defeated Hamilton on Baker's Flat by an innings, and later George Davey scored 71 not out for Kapunda against Barossa Valley. In 1864 matches were played at Clare, Clarendon, Guichen Bay and Rapid Bay. Angaston lost both their first two encounters with Nuriootpa. Most of the cricket in the state's south-east was played on dirt until the 1880s, the players only occasionally enjoying games on grass.

One of the organisers of cricket outside Adelaide was James Chittleborough, who played at Morphett Vale and was one of the founders of the Universal Club. After a lively game between British and Colonials, he presented all the players with a portrait of himself in cricket gear and afterwards entertained them to "a grand old spree" at the back of the Shades, a hotel kept by a Mr Aldridge. "Our matches were right royal affairs and there was genuine fun to be had from them," one player wrote. Chittleborough later joined the Hindmarsh Club, which was founded in 1862, and with King and Howlett played against Norwood, who were represented by Jim Gooden, Morcom and Cole, whom they beat by one run.

The Kent Club was formed in 1866 and produced several outstanding players, including Arthur Malcolm who became recognised as Adelaide's champion cricketer. The St Peter's College XI, which had already begun to develop its splendid ground, was very strong at that time. The Alberts, who were virtually unbeatable for three seasons, were absorbed into the Kent Club. Not long after he switched to the South Australian Club, Arthur Malcolm met James Gooden in a well-publicised contest in which each man was allowed three fieldsmen. Malcolm won by scoring 3 and 6 in his two innings, compared with Gooden's 4 and 1.

The small amount of work that went into preparing fields was devoted entirely to the pitch. Fielding areas were rough and lumpy, and heavy drives often shot over a fieldsman's head or thudded into his shins. Most bats and stumps were

other level was the cricket conducted by publicans, which was "tainted" by professionalism, heavy gambling, payment of incentives to the best players, and, in the opinion of some, excessive drinking.

Throughout the 1860s clubs sprang up in South Australian country towns, with new settlers taking to the cricket fields at Jamestown, Caltowie, Gawler, Gladstone and Orroroo. The first recorded intertown game in the south-east was between Penola and Mosquito Plains (Naracoorte) on 13 July 1860. In January 1862 Penola managed only eight runs, five of them byes, in their first innings against Mount Gambier, on a flat piece of ground near the National School, just off Sturt Street. Kadina first played in February 1862, the Mount Pleasant Club in March of the

made from local she-oak, the bat all one piece without springs. Balls lacked rubber or cork cores and seldom bounced. When gloves first appeared for wicket-keepers they were flimsy mittens, not unlike modern gardening gloves.

Following the centuries by Judge Bundey and Joe Cocker, the next century recorded in South Australia was scored by F. D. Harris, of St Peter's College, who knocked down his own stumps after reaching 101 out of 163 against the Young Cricketers Club in 1870. Sir Charles Du Cane, Governor of Tasmania, and a former prominent cricketer in England, led a team against St Peter's later the same year. This time Harris scored 82 and was presented with a bat for his effort. Harris appears to have been the first of the long list of outstanding players developed at St Peter's.

South Australian followers knew that cricket between colonies had begun in Launceston, Melbourne, Hobart and Sydney, and scoresheets survive of a match between the Gentlemen of Adelaide and the Gentlemen of Melbourne in the 1850s. In February 1871, the secretary of the Norwood Club, John Hill, wrote to the Melbourne Cricket Club inviting them to send a team

for a match in Adelaide. Hill, five of whose sons played for South Australia, was told that his suggestion was too late for the current season and was asked to repeat the invitation the following September. The Melbourne Club asked for a guarantee that the South Australians would pay all expenses for the trip and also bonuses for two professionals.

The chance to stage this event was hindered by the lack of a suitable ground in Adelaide, so H. Yorke Sparks, of the South Australian Cricket Club, paid his own fare to Melbourne to discover what was required to establish and maintain a first-rate ground. Sparks carefully examined issues such as the role of ground staff and the finances of a major arena. When he returned he persuaded the South Australian Club to take the initiative. The club sent a circular to other clubs signed by Sparks:

*I beg to inform you that an effort is being made to form a Central Cricket Ground similar to those existing at present in the sister colonies, the want of which has hitherto acted very prejudicially against the success of the game here, and as the Corporation of Adelaide has*

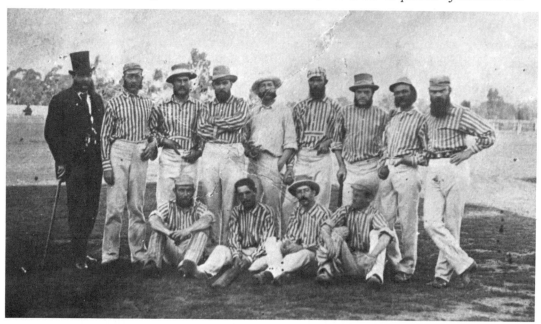

*granted a suitable piece of ground, it is proposed to have it grassed, fenced, levelled, and surrounded by a belt of trees, shrubs, etc., so as to render it both serviceable and ornamental, and a place of pleasant resort. As the achievement of this objective must necessarily incur a large expenditure, the committee have thought it desirable to appeal to the admirers and patrons of manly sports for assistance. May I have the pleasure of including your name in the list of subscribers?*

Sparks supported the circular with a letter to the *Register* stressing that the proposed ground could be used for a variety of sports. His efforts raised £150, and work on the pitch began, on what is now Adelaide Oval. The total cost was £200 which left a shortfall of £50. A bigger problem was that the Adelaide Corporation would not permit any charge for admission on the land it had leased to the South Australian Cricket Club. Undaunted, Sparks and his followers decided to try and form a controlling body for cricket throughout the state.

The secretary of the Norwood Club was instructed to write to the South Australian, Kent, North Adelaide, Norwood and South Adelaide clubs, inviting them to a meeting to form a South Australian Cricket Association. The secretary's letter also went to influential gentlemen of the colony. The fact that many well-established clubs, most of them associated with hotels, were omitted from the invitation list, which included only people of high repute, effectively snubbed professional cricketers and ensured that only the Adelaide cricket aristocracy attended.

Scotsman Major J. A. Fergusson, ADC to the governor, and a member of the South Australian Club, was in the chair, and among those present were Mr Justice Gwynne, Sir John Morphett and several members of parliament. The meeting on 31 May 1871, at the Prince Alfred Hotel, learned that the cost of establishing an association ground would be £300, but this caused no surprise to wealthy men. On the motion of John S. Bellhouse, seconded by E. M. Ashwin, they founded the South Australian Cricket Association and appointed a committee, with John Pickering as foundation secretary. The governor, Sir James Fergusson, accepted nomination as president and was succeeded by successive governors until 1897, when governors became the SACA patrons and Sir Edwin Smith the first of a succession of active presidents. One early president was Frank Grey Smith, later president of the Melbourne Cricket Club, whose name is perpetuated by a grandstand at the MCG.

After members pledged their financial support to the new association, the South Australian Club offered the SACA the land on the North Park Lands, to be leased on a peppercorn rental. The sole condition was that the association pay the club's £50 debt for work done on the pitch. The association set its initial subscriptions at a guinea for non-playing members and half a guinea for players, but it quickly became apparent that the costs of preparing the ground and paying for visiting teams from other colonies would not be raised unless the association charged gate admission.

The association accepted a tender from H. Copas to level, plough and plant fresh grass on the outfield. G. W. Gooden, knowledgeable in both cricket and gardening, was appointed the first curator. Copas's quotation proved unrealistic, and he eventually charged twice as much for his work. He had to secure judgment in the Supreme Court, however, before he was paid.

Merchant-farmer John Darling, whose son Joe (his sixth child) was then only 10 months old, introduced a Bill in the Legislative Council in September 1871, which granted the SACA a lease on 12 acres (nearly 5 hectares) of the Park Lands. During the debate on the Bill, the association's influential friends proved very useful. One MP

*The Jolimonters, an East Melbourne team, photographed in their colourful striped shirts during a visit to Adelaide in the 1880s*

*Adelaide Oval, not long after it was first fenced. The ground was founded after a long fight between cricket lovers and citizens outraged by what they regarded as a theft of public parklands*

claimed that the association consisted of "a number of moneyed men of the city" well capable of raising the funds needed for a grandstand on the Park Lands without asking the government to pay for this. The Bill was passed with only one dissenter and a long struggle began with the City Council over the proposal for paid admission to the ground. A newly elected mayor of Adelaide announced that he would not allow parkland to be taken from the public and defended the right of all sporting bodies to use the ground.

Eventually the association promised that it had no objection to the public making the parkland "a promenade" when cricket was not being played there, which swayed some opponents of the association's lease. But the council further delayed work at the ground by demanding £20 a year rent

for it, a large sum for a new control body. After protracted debate the rent was reduced to £7 a year for the first seven years and £14 for the following seven years. This was carried only on the casting vote of the mayor. The lease was granted to Mr Justice Gwynne, E. T. Smith and H. Ayers, the association's trustees. The newly acquired ground was dubbed "The Oval", in a resolution legend says was framed by a Surrey man. It was later thought by some SACA officials to have been James Edward Goodfellow, who played for South Australia in 1880–81. But Goodfellow was born in Surrey in 1850 and, aged 21, would have been too young to have influenced the naming of the ground in 1871. It is the only major ground in Australia with this name.

Not long after winning the struggle for the ground, the SACA adopted a code of rules which banned gambling at The Oval and restricted its use solely to clubs affiliated with the association. The code embodied the principles of manliness, discipline, fair play and subservience to the team. Not long after the code's adoption, the fence and dry grass inside the ground caught fire. Considering the precarious bank balance after this setback, it was surprising that the association continued to exclude certain clubs from its membership. Those who enjoyed betting on the cricket and drinking during matches continued to play on unprepared pitches on any available open ground without the prestige of membership in the SACA, which remained a small, elite organisation for a number of years.

Gooden plunged into his duties at The Oval with enthusiasm, fencing the playing area and planting trees, but he had plenty of problems. Water was not laid on and had to be carried from a single tap near the entrance gate. The ground was very rough, with only a few patches of couch studded among the thistles and weeds, and the surface was an uncompromising clay that made cultivation difficult. Gooden had to plant rye grass to cover patches of earth around the edges of the playing area.

The first match organised by the South Australian Cricket Association, between British and colonial-born teams, had to be played at St Peter's College on 11 November 1872, because The Oval was not ready for use. Although steady rain was falling when play began at noon, the match continued until six o'clock, by which time the Britishers had scored 70 and 2 for 32, the Colonials 35 and 106. A recent immigrant named Lungley took 7 for 18 in the Colonials' first innings and a further six wickets in the second innings with his left-arm deliveries and was 17 not out when play ended. Davenport took 5 for 15 for the Colonials and made 27 in the best innings of the day.

At the end of 1872 the Melbourne Cricket Club organised play between a Combined XIII from the other colonies and a Melbourne XI. Sydney supplied seven players, Tasmania supplied three and South Australia sent S. Morcom, J. E. Gooden and J. F. King. The Combined team won by five wickets. Newspapers commented that the three South Australians lacked the skill of the other players and added that their batting demonstrated that cricket in South Australia had not advanced as much as in the other colonies. Morcom was praised for his fielding in this first appearance by South Australians outside their own colony.

At the first annual meeting of the SACA on 28 October 1872, the secretary announced that the association had 107 honorary members and 48 playing members, and had received £160 in fees. Public donations had lifted the total to £313, but the SACA still needed £250 to meet its debts. Soon afterwards Judge Bundey persuaded the state parliament to set aside £300 in the 1873 estimates to boost the funds of the SACA to build a pavilion at The Oval. Bundey pointed out that the Assembly gave considerable support to agricultural societies. "If the House provides advantages for animals without brains, it ought to do the same for animals with brains," Bundey argued.

H. Yorke Sparks succeeded John Pickering as SACA secretary in 1873, and immediately announced a campaign to raise £1500 for improvements to The Oval. A public appeal failed, and the association had to borrow the money by issuing debentures to its own committeemen. Gooden had to be relieved of his duties as landscape gardener and was sent out to collect subscriptions on a percentage basis. Through the winter the SACA could not afford to keep a curator at the ground, and thistles and weeds grew undisturbed. In the spring Sparks bought 150 iron posts at an auction sale and offered them to the association at cost. One member claimed that "such independent action by the secretary was reprehensible", but Sparks' offer was accepted.

The SACA took four years to organise local cricket into a competitive system and 20 years to set up a competition based on electoral districts. The association's early efforts were almost entirely devoted to improving The Oval, tightening its membership structure to keep out undesirables, and attracting the support of important citizens. This influence was strong enough for public holidays to be declared for major matches at The

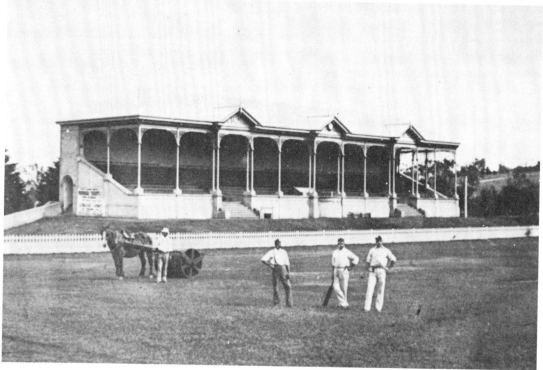

LEFT: *A group of South Australian cricketers during a club match at Adelaide Oval in the late 1870s*
BELOW LEFT: *The first grandstand at Adelaide Oval was opened in November 1882 and enlarged 20 years later. The ground's entire staff is shown here, with the only piece of equipment, a horse-drawn roller*

Oval, the dimensions of which followed those of its namesake in London. There was a disturbance at the ground in 1874 when a player who was not affiliated to the SACA was discovered in one of the competing teams — affiliation to the SACA and prompt payment of fees to member clubs were regarded as socially essential conduct.

Two club games at The Oval were usually played simultaneously at the northern and southern ends of the ground. The 1874–75 season witnessed 38 contests on The Oval in its first summer under SACA management. Apart from club matches, the programme included a series of special games involving Marrieds *v.* Singles, British against colonial-born, and a match against the enterprising Kadina Club. J. E. Gooden won a special trophy for the best batting average in these games. The highlight of the season was South Australia's biggest intercolonial duel in which a virtual Victorian Second XI played Eighteen of Adelaide. The pitch was uneven and during the lunch break on the second day half a dozen players got between the shafts of the roller and flattened the worst bumps. Some citizens of Adelaide grumbled over the 2 shillings admission charge, but takings for the three days were £285 and spelt salvation for the Australian Cricket Association's finances.

The association's right to prevent the poorer members of the community from watching cricket at The Oval caused long, often bitter, debate in the South Australian parliament. One MP accused it of adopting tactics designed to stop people "peeping through the fences". The SACA was well aware that its ground was on public land and never prosecuted small boys who eluded the barbed wire. Another MP proposed a change in the association's lease to ensure that part of The Oval was set aside for free admission to those who could not afford the entrance money. Segregation of crowds based on the English habit invariably meant that patrons in the Outer had to wait longer for improvements than those who patronised the grandstands. From the time they opened, Australia's first-class grounds included smokers' stands, governors' boxes, ladies' reserves, mounds known as hills, and later, members' pavilions.

Through its control of The Oval, the SACA performed the role of entrepreneur to football, cycling, tennis, lawn bowling and even lacrosse, and stage-managed all early major sport in South Australia. From its offices at The Oval it fashioned close links with councils, parliament, leading merchants and the law, sustaining an elitism unknown in other states. Cricket remained the main sport conducted at The Oval, but the money from football and other sports enormously strengthened the SACA power and purse, enabling it to pursue the amateur ideals that typified the middle class of Victorian England.

Amateurism was the official ideology of those who ran the SACA. Proper conduct, rather more than heredity, was the mark of an amateur gentleman. Across Australia a handful of the best-known professionals contributed to their relegation in status with a series of well-publicised misdemeanours, most of them caused by alcohol. But Australian cricket never suffered from the formal division between amateur and professional apparent in English cricket. On the field Australian teams have always had players ready to tell captains and members with wealthy backgrounds where they could deposit their money. From the earliest days the players were shrewd enough to see the benefit of being regarded simply as cricketers.

# A wide field and fair play

## Western Australia 1835–96

The governor of New South Wales, Sir Ralph Darling, acting on instructions from London, sent a small contingent of soldiers and convicts to Western Australia late in 1823, when suspicion was aroused about the motives of French ships in the area. A garrison commanded by Major Edmund Lockyer formally proclaimed the site part of Australia when they arrived at King George Sound on Christmas Day 1826. Three years later, after Captain Charles Fremantle had landed at the mouth of the Swan River and confirmed British claims to the west coast, the first free settlers arrived from England. The capital was founded at Perth on 12 August 1829.

An advertisement appeared in a Perth newspaper on 5 April 1835 with a challenge from builders working on the new Government House to their counterparts on the Commissariat building to one or more cricket matches. No scores have survived but the *Perth Gazette and Western Australian Journal* of 13 April 1835 applauded the originators of cricket in Western Australia.

*This manly exercise has been started with some spirit within the last fortnight in Perth, and we*

*The original Kalgoorlie Miners' XI. The captain (front row, centre) was the only man in town who owned a full set of whites. The umpire (back row, left) did his job carrying a rifle, an accessory later umpires no doubt envied*

understand that a club is also likely to be formed at Guildford. The Perth club consists at present of 22 members. They meet each Saturday afternoon at the Flats. The ground is not well adapted for the purpose, but it is expected that the Governor will grant a suitable piece of ground adjacent to the town for the purpose, from which opinion we are reluctantly compelled to dissent. The revival of the sports of our native country in a distant land forms a connection which it should be our pride to encourage.

The Perth club does not number very many efficient hands. There are, however, some gentlemen among whom are two men of Kent who play an excellent game both in batting and bowling. An amusing private match at single wicket came off on Wednesday last between Mr L. Samson and Mr J. Leake. The former beat the latter by one run. A very handsome dejeuner was provided on the ground, of which several ladies and gentlemen partook. The day passed off with great glee.

A week later the *Journal* reported:

The lads who started a cricket match on Good Friday and again on Easter Monday have felt themselves aggrieved that we have not noticed them. The fact was we were not aware that it was a regular organised club such as by its regulations and the conduct of its members made it worthy of such notice. If they will abstain from playing on Sundays and on such days as are set apart for religious observances, we shall be happy to hear of their progress.

The members of the Perth Cricket Club were annoyed by this report and replied on 27 April:

The Perth Club are very much surprised at the paragraph in the Perth Journal on 13th instant stating a direct falsehood, as not one of the members of the club played in the match reported. It is a fact known to most of their townsmen that on Easter Eve they played the

Guildford Club at Perth and beat them by 40 odd runs, the major part of them being youths who feel proud in laying the foundation of English sports in this flourishing colony. They therefore consider it their duty to contradict the statement of a few experimental amateurs... as all we wish is a wide field, fair play, a good umpire, and no favour.

In May 1846, when the population of Perth was under 5000, the Tradesmen of Perth played the Perth Club in the first match in Western Australia for which scores were kept. The *Perth Gazette and Western Australian Journal* published a lengthy report.

We have seldom seen any of our public amusements so well attended. In fact, everyone was there. The day was cool, but the ground horribly dusty and a brisk breeze having set in from the north-west, the clouds of dust were stifling. At 9½ the umpires commenced to pitch the wickets and at 20 minutes after 10, the first ball was bowled. Throughout the innings the bowling was admirable, chiefly being of the 'slow school,' but not less dangerous than the rapid play of some modern artists. As the scores show the incautious or hasty player had no chance, but so wary were the strikers in most cases that sometimes three overs were called without a notch.

In general the batting was good. There was a visible want of practice in most of the men on both sides, but there was sometimes some exquisite play. In fielding the Club men had it hollow. In short, on reconsidering the whole matter, we think the Tradesmen showed the best bowlers, the Club the best fielders, and if there be any difference in the batting—if anything, it is very slight—we think it is in favour of the Club. It is worthy of note that throughout the match not a wide ball was scored.

The newspaper's scores did not credit bowlers

# Tradesmen v. Perth Cricket Club

*Played at Perth, May 1846*

## Tradesmen

| First Innings | | | Second Innings | | |
|---|---|---|---|---|---|
| Leonard, *b.* Harris | | 2 | Leonard, *b.* Harris | | 2 |
| E. King, *not out* | | 18 | E. King, *b.* Harris | | 4 |
| C. King, *b.* Steele | | 5 | C. King, *b.* Harris | | 11 |
| Foster, *b.* Harris | | 4 | Foster, *c.* Vigors | | 1 |
| Brown, *c.* Singleton | | 0 | Brown, *c.* Brown | | 0 |
| Allpike, *b.* Harris | | 0 | Allpike, *c.* Stone | | 0 |
| Hall, *b.* Harris | | 0 | Hall, *touched the ball* | | 2 |
| Hailes, *b.* Steele | | 0 | Hailes, *b.* Harris | | 1 |
| Nairne, *run out* | | 0 | Nairne, *not out* | | 1 |
| Hokin, *b.* Steele | | 0 | Hokin, *b.* Steele | | 1 |
| Chipper, *b.* Harris | | 2 | Chipper, *b.* Steele | | 0 |
| *Byes* 6, *no ball* 1 | | 7 | *Byes* 2, *no ball* 1 | | 3 |
| | Total | 38 | | Total | 26 |

## Perth Cricket Club

| First Innings | | | Second Innings | | |
|---|---|---|---|---|---|
| Stone, *b.* C. King | | 0 | Stone, *b.* Leonard | | 0 |
| Vigors, *b.* C. King | | 8 | Vigors, *b.* C. King | | 4 |
| Steele, *b.* C. King | | 10 | Steele, *not out* | | 9 |
| Irby, *b.* C. King | | 0 | Irby, *b.* C. King | | 1 |
| Andrews, *c.* Brown | | 1 | Andrews, *c.* Leonard | | 6 |
| Harris, *b.* C. King | | 2 | Harris, *b.* C. King | | 0 |
| Singleton, *run out* | | 1 | *Byes* 1 | | 1 |
| Tamsitt, *b.* C. King | | 4 | | | |
| Meikleham, *c.* Nairne | | 1 | | | |
| Broun, *not out* | | 7 | | | |
| Suxpence, *b.* C. King | | 1 | | | |
| *Byes* 10 | | 10 | | | |
| | Total | 45 | | Total (for 5 wickets) | 21 |

*The Perth Club won by 5 wickets*

Note: These scores, as published, do not group no-balls, wides, byes, leg-byes
and so on as sundries, but list them in each category.

when batsmen were dismissed by catches. Hall was undoubtedly the first in Western Australia to be out for handling the ball.

The same teams played a return match on the following Thursday, when it was reported that the Tradesmen did not display their usual adroitness. The Tradesmen scored 18 runs in reply to 84 in the first innings, but despite misgivings about the second innings they managed 88, falling only 26 short of the Perth Club's aggregate of 132, a commendable recovery.

The Tradesmen demonstrated their enthusiasm for cricket by offering to clear the ground allotted for public recreation, fence it and install drains, so that it could be played on throughout the year. For this they were unanimously praised and one newspaper said their effort "redounds highly to the credit of our community".

On 23 May 1846 the *Perth Gazette and Western Australian Journal* launched an attack on critics of recreation.

*It has been attempted to cast a slur upon these amusements. All we have to observe on this point is we pity the narrow-minded individuals who entertain such opinions, we sincerely hope their hours of seclusion from what they term 'the vanities of the world' may be as innocently spent as in the instance of our present remarks. There was no rioting, drunkenness, or unseemly conduct evinced, either on this or previous occasions; a number of persons met together to enjoy a manly sport, in which one and all participated. That all parties may long continue this unanimity of feeling is our earnest desire.*

During the 1840s and 1850s cricket began in most settled regions of the state. Matches were reported at Bunbury, York and Toodyay, 70 kilometres from Perth and 14 kilometres, on a rough road, from Northam. York challenged any team in Western Australia to play for a stake not exceeding £40 on the day of the York races. Towards the end of March 1850, Bunbury fielded two teams, Marrieds and Singles, against a district

*An illustration from the English magazine,* Tatler, *showing Australian settlers setting out for an up-country match. The magazine said Australians in the west regularly rode long distances to play cricket, and townships combined to form teams*

then known as the Vasse, later Busselton.

Perth cricketers had their first real test of strength in two games against the newly formed Fremantle club in November 1852. The *Independent Journal of Politics and News* in its report of the first match in Perth stated that the boundaries were marked by small red flags. A marquee was erected for the ladies' lunch, a pastrycook "constantly perambulated the ground", and the band played throughout the day. Fremantle believed their hopes rested on dismissing the Perth crack, Dr Jones, cheaply, but even though Jones made a "pair", Perth still won. Fremantle scored 62 and 42, and

Perth, 61 and 7 for 45, winning by three wickets.

Newspapers gave only brief coverage of the day's play, preferring to devote more space to the prominent citizens present, the quality of the refreshments, the large attendance from Fremantle and the ladies' hats. This annoyed one reader, who, signing himself "An Old Cricketer", wrote lengthy letters painstakingly analysing the performance of each player. He talked of "cross hits" (presumably hooks or pulls) and "sharp bowlers" (who were either round-armers or quicks), and praised stonewallers, whose batting "flurried the bowlers and so benefited the harder hitters". He blamed Dr Jones's failure to score in the second innings on his mistake in "taking a left-handed bat which caused his being caught out the first hit". Finally "Old Cricketer" summed up:

*I trust the Perth men see their want of practising together, and will make every preparation for the return match, for they must bear in mind that they are to play on a ground to which they are unaccustomed, and unless they are well up in their fielding, they may expect to be beaten; and they must recollect that heavy bets are dependent on their exertions, so that their friends' purses are equally concerned with their own credit and renown.*

The Perth players failed to learn from the warning of "Old Cricketer" and Fremantle won the return encounter by seven wickets on a sandy pitch in scrubland on the shores of the estuary, a short distance from Fremantle. The *Independent Journal of Politics and News* commented that the ball generally stopped where it fell, a "circumstance that greatly favoured the Fremantle players, they being the hardest hitters". The paper praised the Fremantle folk for keeping their visitors well supplied with champagne and refreshments. "Dr Jones' fine bowling, Corporal Taylor's and Mr C. King's judicious batting, and Mr Weldman's fielding, were universally admired," the report added. Perth scored 48 and 37, Fremantle 40 and 3 for 46.

Perth and Fremantle met for the third time in February 1853, on a day ruined by rain. The papers agreed that conditions prevented good cricket, but play began with the Perth team "resolved to retrieve the honour they had lost in Fremantle". Again the reports focused more on the lively display of tents and the champagne and other beverages, which flowed in abundance, than on the game. Some of those present did not watch the play because of the threatening weather, preferring the comfort of the refreshment tents. Reporters poked their heads out of the tents long enough to discover that Perth had won by scoring 58 and 37 against Fremantle's 25 and 24, but everyone agreed the game was an unsatisfactory test of strength.

This led to a "decider" on the Perth ground in March 1853, but the *Inquirer*'s cricket reporter was unimpressed, claiming that the teams proved little because there was no marked difference in their play and that "the public have had enough of Cricket of late".

*We may mention that Dr Jones shone during this match as a batter as well as a bowler, as may be seen by reference to the score. An unfortunate accident occurred to one of the Fremantle Eleven, Mr Dighton, who broke his arm while in the act of throwing up the ball, an unusual but not, we are informed, an unheard-of occurrence. This accident somewhat delayed the sports and when the sun went down, there were two of the Fremantle side to go in, but with the score against them, it was deemed unnecessary further to contest the game.*

Perth made 70 and 88, and Fremantle made 30 and 8 for 29.

Despite this curt rebuff from the *Inquirer*, regular contests between Fremantle and Perth cricketers continued until 1862, when Fremantle broke the pattern and sailed to Bunbury—in a vessel called the *West Wave*—to play the local eleven. The voyage took two and a half days and although several of the Fremantle players were badly seasick, they recovered to beat the Bunbury side by an innings in a low-scoring game. On New Year's Day 1863 Perth met Fremantle, and it was reported that "as usual the Perth players were defeated". Two months later Bunbury travelled to Fremantle for a return match and they were beaten again, this time by 115 runs. Cooper's 52 in Fremantle's second innings was the highest individual score in the colony to that time.

The Perth club was "remodelled" in March 1863, and, to the surprise of all cricket followers, defeated Fremantle. The margin was a mere two runs, but it reversed the long sequence of Fremantle victories. George Knight was Perth's hero with an innings of 29 runs.

Geraldton and Beverley formed cricket clubs in about 1866, and regular play began between

Beverley and York. Before matches against other colonies were considered, the major goal of cricketers in the west was a trip to another town. Perth began to send teams to Northam and York. The practice of the best players in the colony appearing for either the Perth or the Fremantle club was altered when the 51st Regiment formed a team that included several skilled cricketers who had played regularly in England.

The best ground in the colony, however, was at Bunbury, on a large open plain between the town and the sea. Bunbury staged a memorable event in April 1865, against a team from Busselton, 44 kilometres further down the coast. Heavy ran fell on the day of the match. Players and spectators hung about gloomily, aware that the hospitality provided for the visitors at the Wellington Hotel might be wasted. Suddenly their Busselton opponents appeared, riding in an excited group through the town, their bats over their shoulders, showing "in the most unmistakable manner their contempt at such trifling inconvenience as wind and rain". Bunbury won the game by 64 runs and the celebrations that followed remained vivid in the minds of the townsfolk for years afterwards.

The need for a better cricket ground in Perth was raised regularly in the newspapers. Some believed that new facilities might lead to a revival of good behaviour among players and spectators. The Perth club appeared to have made progress when it secured government permission to clear a swamp and establish a cricket field there, but the scheme foundered when one convict working at the site attacked another with a pickaxe. The undrained swamp was abandoned. There was rejoicing, too, when the Bishop of Perth allowed the playground belonging to the Bishop's School to be partially ploughed up with the view to

*This Aboriginal side from New Norcia Mission, coached and captained by H. B. Lefroy (centre, with ball), was a leading cricket team in Western Australia's early years. Missionaries encouraged the Aboriginals to play the best white sides*

adapting it for cricket. By the time this plan fell through two English teams had toured Australia (in 1862 and 1864) without playing in the west.

In the 1865 match between Fremantle and Perth, Edward Ashton scored 79 not out for Fremantle, which won by an innings. In 1867, after Fremantle had inflicted a further defeat on Perth, the Perth newspapers condemned the "Fremantle larrikins" for showering Perth players with stones as they left the ground. Fremantle papers took a light-hearted view of the hooliganism.

*A rather amusing scene occurred on the departure of the Perth cricketers. Several of the unruly juveniles with no knowledge of the correct way to let the Perth cricketers depart, poured a volley of stones into the van, dislodging the passengers and the cricketers, who, however, soon put the young urchins to flight, but not before one or two of them had received a good boxing on the ears, which they richly deserved.*

Fremantle boasted a splendid cricket ground, "prepared and levelled by the government" by the end of 1867, and there was great delight in 1869 when the officers and crew of HMS *Galatea* played there in the presence of HRH the Duke of Edinburgh, after which the Duke "partook of refreshments at the residence of the Harbour Master, Lieutenant Croak, R.N.". But when the third England team captained by W. G. Grace arrived in Western Australia is the summer of 1873–74, Perth was still struggling to find a suitable ground.

One newspaper blamed Perth's regular defeat by Fremantle on the attitude of Perth youths to any form of exertion. "Exhausted by the fatigue of clerical labour, the well-fed youth seeks the muscular exercise of Napoleon or the intellectual and varied recreation of crabbing, while the more robust ventures on a walk with the young ladies at young ladies' pace," the report said. "Hence the flaccid visage and pallid cheeks familiar to visitors to the city."

Perth's continual failure against teams from

Fremantle was also attributed to the poor standard of the Perth ground and to the overambitious attempt to run two clubs in the city. Thus in March 1878, the Perth Union and Perth clubs amalgamated to form the Metropolitan Club, which it was hoped would consolidate the best available talent. The Metropolitan had as its first captain a player bred in the purple. John Charles Horsey James, son of the Reverend J. H. James, was born in Rome in 1841 and educated at Rugby and Oxford, where he played in the First XI. He later became Commissioner of Titles in Western Australia.

James had R. A. Sholl as "sub-captain", a combination that brought an immediate improvement to the fielding of the Perth side when they played Fremantle only one week after the Metropolitan was formed. One commentator at this match praised a bowler named Randell for adopting the round-arm style and said that a catch by Parker "would have brought down the house at Lord's or The Oval".

The most notable achievement of the Metropolitan Club was the formation of the Western Australian Cricket Association. At the club's annual meeting on 2 October 1885, a motion was carried instructing its officers to consider forming a state association. This in turn resulted in a meeting of cricket clubs at the United Services Hotel on 12 November, which agreed to form a body "subject to the Municipal Council letting an adequate portion of the Recreation Ground for the exclusive right to playing matches thereon by the said association".

The council received a deputation eight days later, and James and Stephen Henry Parker of the Metropolitan Club presented their case for a three-year lease. They had a good reception, the council's legal experts agreed and the lease was granted on 25 November 1885. The association was formed immediately, with the Perth, City Temperance, Union and Metropolitan clubs as foundation members. Executives of the new body included prominent lawyers and businessmen and several men who were or became members of the Legislative Council. The following year I Zingari and the Fremantle Club were admitted to the association.

The formation of the Western Australian Cricket Association owed everything to the expertise and diligence of J. C. H. James. In the meeting with the city council he had stressed that the WACA did not seek exclusive rights to all the recreation ground, only to part of it, and that they had no objection to footballers using the ground in winter. In this way he outwitted football officials, who did not want fencing at the ground. One councillor wondered where volunteer militiamen would drill if the lease was approved. James's homework paid off and the lease was approved by eight votes to two with two abstentions. The approval carried the proviso that no admission charge would be made in this public park.

Officials of the WACA did not have long to savour their success because they had to confront the problem of the poor maintenance of the ground. After a load of sand was laid in October 1886, the *West Australian* commented that "if the ground was rough last season then this season it will bear close resemblance to the tumbling ocean on a rockbound shore". A concrete pitch was laid but it was found to be so variable that it "obviated the necessity for covering it with matting".

Despite the successful use of the concrete pitch by the Perth and I Zingari clubs from the opening date of 25 March 1886, it was soon obvious that the association needed a turf pitch it could call its own, a place reserved exclusively for cricket.

The 1885 goldrush to the Kimberley district brought many new settlers to Perth, many of them with a cricket background. They were drafted into whatever clubs the WACA believed they could strengthen. An interesting arrival was B. V. ("Bernie") Scrymgour, a leading South Australian junior who later gave invaluable service to his home state and to Australian cricket. At this stage of his life, however, he was more determined to

*Two administrators who played a major role in building Western Australia's cricket strength: (above) Frederick Dudley North, WACA secretary from 1890 to 1896 and (below) J. C. H. James, WACA president for the Association's first twelve years*

even though five English teams had by 1885 toured Australia without visiting the west. At a time when Test cricket was established in the east, the WACA still found itself struggling to secure an adequate supply of water, which they reminded the Perth Council was necessary for "the preservation of pitches and trees". The first annual report of the WACA recorded that the association had obtained a water barrel with handles attached, as if it were a major coup.

James was a tough, able and hard-working president, who could look beyond the problems of the local organisation. He convened a meeting in March 1887, which explored the possibility of Western Australia sending a team to sister colonies in the east. The meeting decided that such a tour should be organised as soon as possible and called for subscriptions. A month later James reported that letters had been sent to all the other colonies and that the WACA had about £550 in kitty to pay for the proposed tour.

On 10 October 1887 the *West Australian* announced that after discussions with Harry Boyle and Dr Henry ("Tup") Scott, of Melbourne, the Metropolitan Club had agreed to engage a professional coach, W. V. Duffy, for £100 a season. Duffy left Melbourne for Perth on 15 October 1887 to become the first professional coach in Western Australia, an appointment that brought Western Australia into line with long-established cricketing practice in eastern Australia.

The hiring of Duffy was part of an effort to improve playing standards in Perth and to send a team to play the eastern colonies. But when Duffy arrived he found the association had cast aside thoughts of an eastern tour to concentrate on solving the problem of securing a central ground.

In fact Derby, a township on the north-west coast of the west Kimberley district, produced the first team to travel out of the colony. In May 1889 Derby's team went to Darwin, then part of South Australia, where they were defeated soundly by an innings and 223 runs.

get rich quickly in Western Australia.

While officials and newspapers lamented the lack of a reasonable ground, the Perth City Council remained ignorant of cricketers' needs,

On 9 December 1889 a deputation from the Western Australian Cricket Association met Governor Sir Frederick Broome, and asked him to set aside a plot of land on the foreshore of the Swan River that was at the time under water and a nuisance to the city. The association said that with a government loan of £3000 to £4000 at 5 per cent interest, and with the help of a dredge and prison labour, a cricket ground could be established. They added that this would be of wide benefit to all sports. Sir Frederick, in one of his last acts before retiring, acceded to this request, setting aside 11 hectares of swampland on a 999-year lease, and pronounced, "I am glad as almost the last official act of my long administration of this Colony's government to serve so good a cause as cricket".

The WACA trustees issued debentures, which they personally guaranteed, erected a fence, let a contract to raise the entire ground half a metre, took levels, planted trees, erected a pavilion, laid down a bicycle track and tennis courts, and imported some Merri Creek soil from Melbourne for turf pitches. All cricket in the west had until then been played on ill-prepared turf or coconut matting pitches. There was temporary dismay when it was discovered the Board of Health planned a sewerage farm next door to the ground, but a letter to the Administrator stressing that this would destroy all the WACA's hard work, as well as its big plans for the future, resulted in the removal of the farm to another site.

The association then went through an agonising period of trying to raise money for essential work on their project. All their funds went into it and they repeatedly had to ask the government and the public for help. One citizen who wrote to the *West Australian* suggested floating 100 £5 shares in the ground, which would secure the buyers lifelong admission rights; each share would admit one gentleman and two ladies. More debentures were issued. One concerned Western Australian offered a loan of £1000 at 7 per cent interest. Slowly the work proceeded.

*This was the first Western Australian team to venture east, visiting Adelaide and Melbourne in 1893. The side was coached by William Duffy (back row, third from left), a professional, and the trip was the brainchild of Frederick North (front row, centre)*

Association secretary F. D. North reported in 1891 that £350 had been spent on fencing and an iron

shed. Clearing, grubbing and levelling had cost £15.

In November that year a representative of the WACA interviewed Alfred Shaw, manager of Lord Sheffield's touring English team, in Adelaide about the prospects of a West Australian tour. The required guarantee to bring Shaw's team to Perth was so far beyond the WACA's means that negotiations ceased after a few days.

Cricketers in the west frequently dropped their axes and gold pans or stopped milking long enough to play cricket. In the Gnowangerup and Denmark areas near Albany, most teams included characters who milked their cows before dawn, rode 50 kilometres to the cricket and arrived home in the dark, with the cows waiting to be milked

*The Western Australian Cricket Association Ground at East Perth soon after it was opened, with the Swan River in the background. The original tiny stand was soon replaced*

again. They were tough, sunburnt men, often with huge hands. Once converted to the joys of the game, many kept playing for half a century.

The major drawback for cricket in the west

was the vast distance that separated it from the rest of the world. In London it had been found that sending convicts to Western Australia was expensive and ineffective in relieving the pressure on British gaols, and transportation ceased in 1868. By the 1870s the colonists had begun to feel the results of declining imperial expenditure. The colony had been linked by telegraph to the eastern states in 1877 and the first major railway had been built from Geraldton to the mining district of

Northampton in 1874–79. But the sole contact with eastern Australia was by small coastal ships that provided passengers with such a buffeting as they crossed the Great Australian Bight that no sane cricketer would contemplate the journey.

The turning point came early in the 1890s with the discovery of gold at Coolgardie and Kalgoorlie. Prospectors flocked to the towns by camel train and wagons, but eventually the gold pro-vided the money to build railway links with Fremantle and finally, in 1917, with the eastern states. Even then the trains took such a long time to travel to Perth that passengers needed several days to recover, and it was not until the advent of the aeroplane that the isolation of Western Australian cricketers ended. They were to make an impact on all Australian cricket with remarkable speed from then on.

# Such a manly pastime

## Queensland 1844–95

Queensland, established in 1823 as a penal colony which was then part of New South Wales, did not become a separate state until 1859. Long before that cricketers were active in the Moreton Bay area and on the rich lands to the west of Brisbane at Ipswich and across the Darling Downs. Governor Brisbane, after whom the state capital was named, saw Queensland as a northern prison, which would relieve pressure on the convict settlement established at Port Macquarie in 1821. This was a place for intractable prisoners, particularly those who committed further offences after arriving in Australia. Nearly all of these convicts were returned to Sydney in 1839 because of the high cost of maintaining the settlement, and the suitability of Port Arthur in Tasmania as a prison for the worst offenders. Moreton Bay was opened for free settlement in 1842.

When cricket arrived in Queensland in the early 1840s the game was taken up by free settlers, but conditions were still very primitive. On 18 April 1844 the *Sydney Morning Herald* published this item from its Moreton Bay correspondent:

> *The lovers of the manly and exhilarating game of cricket, will soon have an opportunity of*

*The ladies joined the men in this match at Cooroy Showground on Queensland's Darling Downs in the 1870s*

*displaying their prowess, a club having been formed at South Brisbane, designated as the 'Albion' cricket club, Mr D. Bunten, of the Woolpack Inn, acting as treasurer, and Mr John Payne, secretary, and Messrs Hopkins, Smith, Mather, and Love, as a committee, for carrying the arrangements into effect. Parties are admitted members by paying a small fee to the secretary, and the field operations will commence so soon as the bats, ball and stumps are received from Sydney.*

This, the first recorded reference to cricket in Queensland, was followed on 27 June 1846 by an account in the *Moreton Bay Courier* of a match in Brisbane between an eleven of working men and an equal number of gentlemen, for a stake of £5 10s 0d a side. The match was played as a climax to race week on the terrace leading to the government gardens. The gentlemen won easily, the workers promptly handed over the stakes, and arrangements were made for a similar match at the following year's race week.

Even before free settlement began, the squatters could not be contained, and by 1842 the best Darling Downs land had been claimed. On 18 October 1848 the *Courier* reported that a cricket club had been started at Ipswich and the first game played there on 13 October. The club had 20 members who intended to challenge Brisbane's cricketers. "Such a manly pastime as this ought to meet with encouragement, as it certainly tends to the preservation of health," the *Courier* added.

The races at Drayton, on the outskirts of Toowoomba, ended earlier than expected in May 1850, so a cricket match between a Drayton XI and a Squatters XI was organised. The *Moreton Bay Courier* reported that the Squatters scored 40 and 48 to easily beat Drayton, who managed only 24 and 21. This impromptu event aroused such interest that the Ipswich Cricket Club insisted on playing the Squatters at Ipswich on 14 June.

A tense struggle ensued, with Ipswich winning by six runs. The Ipswich XI, comprising Carbery, Wilkinson, Hanran, Goode, Snedden, Jones, Warren, Mullen, Costin, Carling and Byrnes, scored 65 and 69, a total of 134. The Squatters team of Thewell, Fairholme, F. Bigge, Burgoyne, Collins, Bell, Davidson, Horton, Bowerman, H. Thewell and Walker, scored 69 and 59, a total of 128.

Cricket had to compete for newspaper space with horseracing and rowing, both of which were very popular. The *Courier* of 17 December 1850, in an account of the Christmas sports at Drayton, said: "Besides the races already advertised, and which would appear to show a great march of fashion amongst the shearers, there is a hurling match, for which it is expected a few 'Tipperary Boys, Corkonians and Dubbos' will contend. The Squatters are to have a cricket match . . . and a pigeon race."

Queensland cricket received a big boost on 14 January 1857 when William Gilbert Rees was invited to travel from his home on the Darling Downs to play for New South Wales in an intercolonial match against Victoria on the Sydney Domain. The New South Wales captain George Gilbert, who had played for Middlesex and the Gentlemen in 1851, knew that Rees was a "crack bat who combined a strong defence with brilliant hits all round!" Rees, a cousin of W. G. Grace, had played for Gloucestershire and was related to Gilbert and also to William Lee Rees, then a prominent figure in the Melbourne Cricket Club and the Victorian XI. W. G. Rees made a useful 28 for New South Wales and also played in seven matches that summer for the Sydney Garrison Club, scoring 257 runs in 12 innings and taking 30 wickets for 173 runs. He had managed Stonehenge and later Goomburra on the Downs for Richard Tooth, of the brewing family.

Rees's presence in Queensland began a trend for wealthy, well-bred Englishmen to work and play cricket on newly established properties. By 1876–77 Conway's *Australian Cricketers' Annual* reported that in the Mackay district alone there were no fewer than seven sugar planters who had played for Oxford or Cambridge. Some of them stayed only a year or two, others spent their lives in Queensland, but their inclusion in local teams was a substantial boost for Queensland cricket.

Rees's cricket credentials were impeccable. His mother, the former Mary Pocock, was a sister of W. G. Grace's mother, Martha. His school, the Royal Naval School at Camberwell, occupied a house rented to the Navy by Nicholas Wanostrocht, who wrote famous cricket tutorials under the name "Felix", because he feared parents of his pupils might look down on a cricketing schoolmaster. As a boy Rees played against teams from Alfred House coached by "Felix". Rees, born in 1827, was 21 years older than W. G. Grace, but they were both part of an unsurpassed cricket nursery which included at least ten second generation cousins—five Graces, two Reeses, at least two Gilberts, and Willy Pocock. Rees played for Mangotsfield club in Bristol, where W. G. Grace learned cricket, and in W. G.'s words, "the club was much strengthened by the appearance of two nephews of my mother, William Rees and George Gilbert, who stayed with us during the holidays".

William Rees was a beguiling mixture of adventurer and artist—a sensitive man with a battered nose, as quick with his fists as with his sketching pencil. He returned to England in 1858 to marry his 19-year-old cousin, Frances Gilbert, and during this visit was so pleased with the 10-year-old W. G.'s progress that he presented him with a bat. W. G. later recalled that the bat was not full size, because Rees had agreed with Grace's parents that bats should match the height and strength of the users. "But it had what I always wanted—a cane handle," wrote W. G. Rees and his bride settled in New Zealand's South Island, where he played an important role in opening up the province of Otago and founding the city of Queenstown.

When Rees left, Queensland soon found other cricket heroes. Many new clubs appeared regularly and the game became more organised. Sparked by the redoubtable Captain George Maughan, who had been involved earlier in Tasmanian cricket, Ipswich outclassed Brisbane from 1843 to 1859. Ipswich adopted the name North Australian Cricket Club, and asked members to pay their one guinea annual subscription six months in advance. They preferred to challenge other clubs through the newspapers rather than by means of formal letters.

Nehemiah Bartley, in *Australian Pioneers And Reminiscences*, attributed Ipswich's dominance to the diabolical habit of local banks who imported their tellers, ledger-keepers and accountants from "the classic cricket recruiting grounds in the south—Launceston and Maitland". Ipswich's North Australian Cricket Club and Brisbane's Moreton Bay Club played two notable games in July and November 1859, just before Queensland became a separate state, when the Ipswich money men finally got their comeuppance.

For the first match, at Brisbane, the Moreton Bay Club took in a team sprinkled with doctors, solicitors and professional men, plus cobbler James Bolger, an underarm bowler also highly regarded for his wicket-keeping, who hailed originally from Kilkenny. They found themselves confronted by the formidable Captain Maughan of the Australasia, with his long black pirate's beard, red cap and shirt, a miniature W. G. Grace; by Harry Logan of the Bank of New South Wales; by the 185 centimetre F. O. Bryant of Joint Stock; by Harry Gilchrist, of Gilchrist, Watts and Co., who were all prime bats; and by an artful bowler named Coulson, from one of the Maitland banks. Nehemiah Bartley wrote that Coulson had the advantage of "an extra joint in his shoulder" and could, "like a railway semaphore, send his arm up with the ball, till it stood all but perpendicular. Then, like lightning, his arm would be flat at his side, the ball impelled, each time swift and true, straight at the middle stump".

The *North Australian* reported that the town was deserted for the two days of the cricket. Ipswich won the toss and sent Brisbane in. At the end of the first day Brisbane had scored 97, to which Ipswich had replied with 118. Brisbane used Bolger as a bowler and his deputy wicket-keeper allowed 28 byes, which more than accounted for Ipswich's lead. The game resumed next morning after a boisterous evening at McAdam's Hotel and immediately runs began to flow. The *Moreton Bay Courier* described the game thus:

> *The people of Brisbane made a holiday of the occasion and it was quite cheery to witness the interest manifested. A tent was erected for the comfort of lady patrons and each team was nationally picturesque, the Brisbane players sporting white shirts and blue caps, the Ipswich players red shirts containing colours so popular in the Crimean War, red, white and blue.*

Bryant of Joint Stock had taken four wickets when Bolger went to the crease, and for the next three-and-a-half hours Bolger "stood in the hot sun" to score 118, the first century recorded in Queensland, before he succumbed to fatigue and was bowled by Bryant. Spectators surrounded Bolger as he walked from the field and carried him to the tent "where he might refresh himself and gain some repose". His team continued to a score of 204, an unheard of total in those days.

When Ipswich began their second innings, Bolger was unfit to field. Brisbane players believed that the wily Captain Maughan had agreed that Master Coley, a young spectator, would replace Bolger until he was fit to take the field, but when Bolger recovered Maughan refused to let him rejoin the game. At stumps the North Australian Club was 4 for 112, needing 71 runs with six wickets in hand.

The match was to have concluded the next day, a Monday, but only one Ipswich player arrived—the rest were required at their ledgers. They managed to secure leave to finish the game on the following Thursday, when Bolger took his place on the field. The last six North Australian batsmen managed only another 22 runs, giving

Moreton Bay victory by 51 runs. A single-innings match between mixed teams of spectators and players from both sides was played to fill in the rest of the day. Despite his absence from the early part of the North Australian Cricket Club's innings, Bolger took 3 for 10, giving him a match total of six wickets for 54 runs along with his memorable century.

A return match was arranged four months later as part of the celebrations to welcome Queensland's first governor, Sir George Ferguson Bowen. This time the Moreton Bay Club scored 87 and 91 to defeat the North Australian Club, 64 and 81, by 33 runs. Bolger topscored for Moreton Bay with 47 not out in the second innings. Captain Maughan was the best of the North Australian batsmen with 34 in the second innings, and he was the only batsman to hold up an attack spearheaded by Bolger, who took nine wickets. Ten days later Queensland became a separate colony, with a population of about 23,520, having lost a fight to have part of the New South Wales northern rivers district included.

At this time there was intense interest in cricket on the Darling Downs. The Drayton Cricket and Gun Club was founded on 15 April 1859 at a meeting at the Downs Hotel, and funds were raised to purchase bats, balls and stumps. Before the end of that year the Drayton club played Toowoomba, where the Cricket Club was founded, officers appointed, and subscriptions collected at Witham's Hotel late in October. On 10 November 1859 the *Darling Downs Gazette* reported that a contest between teams of schoolboys from Drayton and Toowoomba had produced a win for the Drayton boys, whose innings yielded 69, ten more than their rivals' score. The boys had a return game in November 1860, which Drayton again won. The Darling Downs thus pioneered junior development.

In Brisbane, the clubs were hard pressed to find land suitable for cricket. When South Brisbane played North Brisbane in the presence of Governor and Lady Bowen on 13 March 1861, the pitch at Green Hills, near the Reservoir, was studded with crab holes. The *Courier* commented that it would have liked to have seen Cowlishaw's "round hand" bowling on a better field. Cowlishaw took 5 for 30 off 90 deliveries in North Brisbane's first innings. This match between the main Brisbane clubs, following the demise of the Moreton Bay Club, finished with a four-wicket win for North Brisbane. In a return game on 20 April Cowlishaw took nine wickets and Bolger ten as South Brisbane reversed the result and won by seven wickets.

The first Australian tour by an England team in 1861–62 led to public meetings in Brisbane to discuss the prospects of the All England XI playing Twenty-Two of Queensland at Brisbane. Captain Maughan complained at one of these meetings that the committee appointed to arrange the England team's visit included only Brisbane men. His comment demonstrated the need for a control body that would balance the wishes of cricketers throughout the state. But when an association was set up it was called the Brisbane Cricket Club, probably modelled on the all-powerful Melbourne Cricket Club.

The Brisbane Cricket Club's first promotion was a grand challenge match on 11 January 1862, between three-man teams captained by G. Plank and J. Bolger. Originally, stakes for this event were £10 a side, but when it was found that Bolger had included George Cowlishaw, a "crack from Sydney" and the brother of the prominent Brisbane Cowlishaw, the stake was waived and the teams played solely for honour. Plank's team, which included D. Jacobs and J. Meades, had innings totals of 9 and 5. Bolger's team, in which J. Birley joined G. Cowlishaw, scored 46 in their only innings. After this match it was announced that the governor would be patron, and the colony secretary, R. G. W. Herbert, president of the Brisbane Cricket Club.

When the attempts to attract the 1861–62 England team to Brisbane failed, the *Moreton Bay Courier* commented that although this would be a major disappointment the "licking Queensland

would have taken would have been very sore indeed" and would have diminished rather than aroused interest in cricket. Far better for Queensland to try and build up her cricket strength through matches with southern colonies, said the *Courier*, urging the newly formed Brisbane Cricket Club to establish a strong administration, lack of which had caused many Queensland teams to disappear, their members dispirited.

The Brisbane Cricket Club began by staging a game between Marrieds and Singles, which the Singles won by 10 wickets. Next a single-wicket competition was held between a Mr Launder and a Mr Putnam, but this ended abruptly when Mr Putnam was given out for handling the ball. Then came a meeting of an All Brisbane side and a "hot eleven" from the migrant ship *Flying Cloud*, whose team was said to comprise experienced Kentish players. For this match, Mrs Ahern of St Patrick's Tavern had a large marquee erected, and the pitch at Green Hills was properly marked out. The men from the *Flying Cloud* showed they could bat well, but the fielding of the Brisbane side was markedly superior. All Brisbane made 93 and 1 for 19, *Flying Cloud* 62 and 47.

The 1861–62 summer ended with the arrival in the *Jessie Munn* of one Joseph Offley, who claimed he had been a professional bowler in England. A special meeting of the Brisbane Cricket Club was held to consider Offley's offer to become the club's first professional coach. The committee decided to organise a scratch game the following Saturday to assess his skills. Offley made a poor impression but maintained he was suffering from the effects of the voyage. He then proposed playing eleven members of the club single-handed, but the club settled for just two matches, the first between Offley and Bolger, the second between Offley and Cowlishaw.

*OVER PAGE: "The Grand Cricket Match", a watercolour attributed to S. T. Gill, showing the first All England XI playing Twenty-Two of New South Wales in the Outer Domain, Sydney, in 1862*

THE AUSTRALIAN CRICKET PRINT 1981.
LIMITED EDITION No. 424 OF 850.
PUBLISHED BY INTERNATIONAL PRINTMAKERS HOUSE.

OKET MATCH
ELEVEN

UTER DOMAIN

Offley was ignominiously defeated in both games, scoring only three runs in two innings against Bolger and then failing to score in two innings against Cowlishaw, whose only innings produced 13 runs. The *Moreton Bay Courier* said it was hoped that the results would teach Offley, a round-arm bowler, a lesson in humility. This was a far different result to that at Beechworth, Victoria, the previous summer when George Griffith, the big hitter from Surrey in Stephenson's England team, defeated an entire eleven on his own. Griffith scored eight in his innings and then dismissed Beechworth for one run. Offley disappeared from Brisbane after failing to emulate Griffith, leaving challenges from Brisbane schoolboys unanswered.

By 1862 cricket was being played at Bowen and in the following year at Gayndah, Biggenden and Nanango. Meanwhile in Brisbane the Sheriff of Queensland rejected a request from the Brisbane Cricket Club for prisoners to work on the cricket field at Green Hills "when their services are not otherwise required". Toowoomba managed only 21 runs in an innings against Dalby in April 1864, but star bowlers Hull and Crane routed Dalby for nine. Toowoomba's second innings produced 37 to set up an exciting finish when Dalby, 9 for 50, won narrowly. This event provoked arguments galore and at the dinner afterwards further squabbling ended with the Dalby team walking out.

To improve its team for the approaching intercolonial match in 1863–64 between XXII of Queensland and XI of New South Wales, the Brisbane Club sent a strong side by coach to play an Ipswich XI. With the building of the Western Railway in progress, the Ipswich Club had secured the services of a 127-kilogram navvy named Joe Meads, who proved a champion underarm bowler. Ipswich scored 56, Brisbane 4. The humiliated Brisbane players pleaded that their form had been affected by the 40-kilometre coach trip—the frequent stops for refreshment that did the damage. George Cowlishaw scored two, there were two

byes, and ten batsmen recorded ducks. T. B. Foden took 4 for 2 for Ipswich, a performance which won him a place in the Queensland team against New South Wales.

There was a nasty dispute in the return meeting a week later at Brisbane when Somerset was caught off the glove from the bowling of the giant Meads. The Brisbane umpire, Mr K. Newman, refused to give Somerset out, although the Ipswich umpire, Mr G. Thorne, had already done so. The Ipswich team refused to continue unless the umpires were changed, the players left the field and only returned when new umpires were appointed. Somerset's 12 runs enabled Brisbane to tie Ipswich's score of 42.

Cricket began in tropical Queensland when clubs were formed at Maryborough (1860), Gladstone (1868) and Rockhampton (1862). At Clermont a local side played regular matches.

Clermont was the site of the controversial throw by "Billy the Blackboy", which has appeared in *Wisden* for many years as a world record. A newspaper called *The Peak Downs Telegram* first reported his prowess on 16 February 1872, noting that spectators were much impressed by the throwing of Billy, an Aborigine who worked for Jack Thorn, proprietor of the Clermont Hotel and backer of the local cricket team. A contest was arranged between innings during which Billy threw a cricket ball 142½ yards (130 metres), the "2½ yards being for deviation in measurement" by people who did the measuring. Allegations that the throw had not been properly measured followed, and in March 1873, the *Telegram* commented: "We have not the slightest doubt over the accuracy of the throw, which was witnessed by several gentlemen still in Clermont. Everyone who saw it said it surpassed anything they deemed possible". The newspaper nominated a former Cambridge cricketer and oarsman C. J. Graham, MLA for Clermont, as one of the witnesses. A long correspondence in *Lillywhite's Scores And Biographies* disclosed that several tapes were used to measure the throw. All the measurements confirmed a throw of at least 128 metres.

Many of the north Queensland towns in which cricket was played could only be reached by boat. Entire towns turned out to welcome the boats which arrived with visiting teams. At Bowen, which is credited with staging the first match in north Queensland, the local club played a team from the crew of the survey ship *Pioneer* in 1862. The *Port Denison Times* reported a game in November 1863, between the locals and the crew of the survey ship *Salamander*. The teams were given some grandiose titles: when the Central Queensland Club played its first game on 24 May 1862, at Rockhampton, it named the competing teams "The World" and "Australia".

A group of Victorians who had migrated to Queensland formed the Victoria Cricket Club in Brisbane in 1863 and challenged the Ipswich and Brisbane clubs. After accepting the challenge, Brisbane Cricket Club found that the Victorians had been bolstered by a new arrival who was far above the standard of other Queensland players. He was W. G. ("Willie") McNish, a former team-mate of the Gregory brothers in the Nationals side in Sydney. McNish could not prevent the Brisbane Club winning by eight wickets, although he scored 48 not out and 17 not out. The Victoria Club scored 113 and 61 but ruined their chances by conceding 61 sundries, including 50 byes, in the Brisbane Cricket Club's first innings of 154. McNish played in Brisbane from 1863 to 1868, during which period he was a mainstay of the Victoria Cricket Club and founder of the Legal Cricket Club.

The ease with which McNish handled the bowling of hitherto successful bowlers like the Cowlishaws and Joe Bolger was a clear warning that Queensland cricketers were below the standards of the best southern states. The major problem was the lack of a first-rate ground. Before the first intercolonial match in Brisbane, New South Wales players suggested that the only solution was for the Brisbane Club players to attend to "picking and rolling" themselves. The Brisbane Club could not follow this advice because they held no lease on their land, making it open to all. The Brisbane Council even cut off the water supply when those who used the fields at Queen's Park and the Green Hills site did not pay the water rates.

The shortcomings in administration inhibited the Queenslanders in the first games against another colony in 1864 and 1865. The Ipswich players in the Queensland XXII arrived by steamer only the day before they faced the New South Wales XI at Green Hills. It was reported then that other players from Dalby were still on the way. Some players, unknown quantities to the selectors, were not even considered. The ground was in poor condition, with deep pools of water all over the outfield when the visitors—including Charles Lawrence, the England professional, Nat Thompson and Edward Gregory—inspected it.

Architects who examined the specially erected grandstand on the night before the match ordered further reinforcement to the structure. The organisers did not have the right to enforce admission charges. They were peeved that some spectators were mean enough to refuse the "trifling charge exacted". The New South Wales XI won easily, scoring 32 and 145 against 45 and 46. Several publicans who had erected booths at the ground complained they were out of pocket because of poor attendance.

Queensland's main gain from this venture was the engagement of the state's first professional coach, James ("Jemmy") Moore, for £2 a week. Moore hailed from West Maitland and was the brother of George Moore, grandfather of Charlie Macartney. Both Moores played in the Combined Australian team, which in February 1862 defeated the All England XI. "Jemmy" Moore remained on the payroll of the Brisbane Cricket Club for only a year, but he did valuable work in his short stay.

New South Wales and Queensland did not meet again for ten years. Meanwhile new clubs appeared all over Queensland and standards gradually improved. Sports stores opened in Brisbane and locals no longer had to send to Charles Lawrence in Sydney for equipment. Most ships that arrived from England with migrant passengers were immediately challenged to a game of cricket. Ipswich, Gympie, Gayndah and Toowoomba all had enthusiastic teams prepared to travel, and at Warwick, W. G. Slade started an I Zingari XI.

Cricket boomed in Maryborough with the formation of another club, the Maryborough United Cricket Club, in 1864 at a meeting in a tobacconist's shop. A tent was erected for a dressing room on the town's reserve, where groups of supporters set to work removing dozens of old trees. The *Maryborough Chronicle* stated:

*Many an evening was spent burning the debris; tough yarns, tarpaulin musters, and ginger beer etcetera from the Southern Cross Hotel filling in the intervals. The volunteers had hosts of inspectors and advisors whose comments they did not appreciate. A silken flag—white with a four-inch border of blue and 'M.U.C.C.' embroidered in the centre—was worked and presented by Mrs Culmsee. It fluttered gaily on Boxing Day when the first Marrieds versus Singles match was played.*

Maryborough made their first visit to Rockhampton in 1865, the captain of the steamer that took them north acting as one of the umpires. Maryborough found the hospitality too much—everything from the steamship company to its captain was toasted in a raucous manner—and scored only 29 and 43, compared with Rockhampton's 54 and 83. J. R. Warner topscored for Maryborough with 13. Later James Mahoney and John Blanchard formed the Yengarie Club in Maryborough. The Mahoney family remained prominent Queensland cricketers for years, and one member was a Rhodes scholar.

In Brisbane, the Victoria Club became the dominant side after the Brisbane Cricket Club collapsed. United often pushed Victoria hard, and

the Albert Club had a decade of success before it, too, disappeared. A generation of young cricketers suffered through the lack of both a state control body and a coach. They had no Caffyn, Lawrence, Wills or Kendall to instruct them.

In 1875, solicitor James Beal, whose nephew Charles later managed Australian teams on tour in England, arranged another visit to Queensland by a New South Wales side, which included stars such as Alick Bannerman and Tom Garrett. Before the first game against Eighteen of Queensland, each New South Wales player had to address his team-mates on how the match should be run. A player named Coulter gave the most entertaining speech and was made captain. The Queenslanders outdressed their opponents, wearing white flannels and a straw hat bearing the word "Queensland" on the bands. The Sydney men simply wore the colours of their clubs. Coulter's eloquence did not help, as Queensland won by 69 runs, scoring 121 and 47 against 48 and 51.

Attendance was more than 3000 on the first day and because of inadequate planning everything drinkable soon ran out. Even water could not be bought on a day of fierce heat and spectators went thirsty until someone found a Chinaman's well (12.19 metres deep) under Sutherland Hill, near the Hamilton Ground.

New South Wales defeated Eighteen of I Zingari at Warwick and Eighteen of Brisbane at Queen's Park, both by an innings, in the other matches of the tour.

Mismanagement of the first Brisbane match led to a meeting at Brisbane's Royal Hotel in mid-March 1876, which resulted in the formation of the Queensland Cricket Association. The foundation clubs were the Albert, Stanley, Milton, Eagle Farm, Shaws, Police and GPO; Sir Maurice O'Connell, a grandson of Governor William Bligh, was the first president. Country clubs soon

*Sir Maurice O'Connell, first president of the Queensland Cricket Association, a position he held from 1867 to 1879*

*George Down, secretary of the Queensland Cricket Association in 1878 and 1881 and president in 1901–02*

*Percy Stanislaus McDonnell played in 19 Tests. He began his career with Victoria in 1877–78, moved to New South Wales and finally Queensland*

joined and within two years delegates from Toowoomba, Ipswich, Blackall and Warwick attended QCA meetings.

In a colony with an area of 1,073,600 square kilometres, a major problem for the infant association was to secure reliable information on the form of players in outlying areas. In Rockhampton, H. S. Finch-Hatton and John Ewan Davidson were reported to be outstanding among the promising up-country cricketers. Players such as J. W. Haygarth, a cousin of Arthur Haygarth (author of the famous books, *Scores and Biographies*), R. C. and M. F. Ramsay—all well known in England—and one of the seven Lyttelton brothers were working on the Darling Downs. But before railways and adequate roads were built their ambitions

and fitness for big cricket were unknown. Cricket buffs argued that Queensland seldom fielded its best teams when the state lost to sides from the south.

Early Queensland cricket was also burdened by a lack of discipline on days of extreme heat. The *Queenslander*, in an account of an 1879 match, said: "Spectators were astonished that some of the players kept on their legs, let alone played cricket. The sooner cricket authorities put down this demoralising habit of drinking to excess the better". The paper added that several matches that year had been conspicuous for the players' thirsts.

Teams short of key players often advertised for help. A typical newspaper advertisement inserted by the Graziers' Club read: "Wanted at once, two clerks for a butchering establishment; previous experience not necessary; must however be first-class bowlers".

Cairns defeated Herberton in 1883 and in the late 1880s played Port Douglas to decide which town was to have first use of the government dredge. By 1889 Cairns went by boat to play at Geraldton (later Innisfail) and Townsville. Cricket was played at Mareeba, Gladstone, Roma, Mitchell, Bundaberg, Gympie and Maryborough. In 1883, the first match was played at Charters Towers on a matting wicket, while the first concrete pitch was laid at Townsville by the Rooney brothers in 1886.

Cricket was well established in Townsville in the 1880s and by the end of the decade a strong club competition was in progress in the district. Townsville players went by ship to Bowen and Ingham on the Herbert River, in November 1884. By 1886 Charters Towers and Townsville met regularly. British naval ships called at Cooktown and played local elevens. There was cricket, too, at Tamborine, Beenleigh, the Logan River area, Goodna, Esk, Waterford and Beaudesert. Brisbane's Stanley Club played at Rockhampton at Easter 1883. By the 1890s cricket was played at Croydon and on Thursday Island.

As in the south, betting was often a problem. The Queensland Cricket Association resolved in 1879 that it "views with regret the increasing baneful influence of betting in connection with the game of cricket". Pitches were so rough, three-figure scores were "as rare as a four-leaved shamrock".

The biggest problem of all, however, was in finding a ground for big matches in Brisbane, and for many years players visiting Queensland had to endure the most primitive conditions. Matches were held at Eagle Farm, Queen's Park, the Albert Ground, Breakfast Creek, Bowen Bridge Road, the Exhibition Ground and other inferior sites. Merri Creek soil was imported from Victoria to improve several Brisbane pitches, but it was not until 1895, when 5 hectares of ground at Woolloongabba were dedicated as the Brisbane Cricket Ground, that the QCA found a home. And before the 'Gabba was converted into a first-class arena thousands of tonnes of soil had to be deposited there, grandstands built, pitches laid and the outfield levelled.

# For love or money

## Controversy and intercolonial cricket 1851–64

Intercolonial cricket began in Australia 50 years before Federation and the official designation of the colonies as states, 41 years before the Sheffield Shield competition started, 26 years before the first Test matches and 126 years before Kerry Packer introduced his "Pyjama Game". These first games between the colonies were colourfully staged, eventful, and seldom free of controversy. They sharpened rivalry between the colonies, set a pattern for the conduct of all first-class cricket in Australia and helped a number of players make the jump from club to international cricket.

Altogether 75 intercolonial matches were played on level terms between 1851 and 1892. The players, who originally appeared in coloured clothing, were rewarded only by the fame that accompanied success. This often proved costly, as they usually paid their own expenses and were not compensated for the loss of wages. For a select few, outstanding displays in intercolonial cricket paved the way for tours of England, which were generally lucrative.

Tasmania, one of the strongest cricket colonies before the discovery of gold on the mainland,

*A drawing on stone, by Henry S. Glover, of the intercolonial match between Victoria and New South Wales at Melbourne in January 1858*

INTERCOLONIAL CRICKET MATCH.
PLAYED BETWEEN THE VICTORIA & N.S. WALES CLUBS.
on the Melbourne Ground. Jan.y 12. 13. & 14. 1858.
DICATED TO THE LOVERS OF ENGLISH SPORTS BY THEIR OBD.T SERV.T F.L. ROBINSON.

staged the first intercolonial match at Launceston when it accepted a challenge from the cricketers of Port Phillip in February 1850. Frustrated by the lack of a ground, the Launceston players approached Governor Denison and persuaded him to allot them a piece of the land near Launceston racecourse. They then sent news of the challenge to Hobart and the Derwent Club agreed to send players north for the contest. After the failure of the Victorians to arrive, leaving players and officials waiting in vain at the wharf, play finally began early in 1851. This time the Tasmanians took the precaution of asking the captain of the SS *Shamrock* to confirm by telegraph that the Victorians were on board as soon as the ship cleared Melbourne.

The Victorian visitors were given an uproarious welcome and after two days of strenuous entertainment the match began on Wednesday, 11 February. Slow bowler W. Henty sent down the first delivery in Australian first-class cricket, bowling a darkish red ball bearing the inscription "Dark, Lord's Ground 5½ in.". The Tasmanian team comprised three players from Hobart, one each from Longford, Perth and Westbury, and five from Launceston. John Marshall, the Tasmanian captain, then in his fifty-sixth year, stood erect and fit and handled his bowlers and fieldsmen skilfully after sending the Victorians in to bat.

Victoria scored 82 in their first innings, thanks to a stylish 17 by their captain W. Philpott and some heavy hits by later batsmen. Marshall opened the Tasmanian innings with G. B. Du Croz and they scored 25 in an hour before the lunch bell rang. After the break Tasmania took a lead of 22 runs when their first innings total reached 104 in 160 minutes. The Victorians had difficulty with Henty's high-pitched slows in their second innings, apparently preferring faster bowling. Marshall added to Victoria's problems by splendidly stumping Philpott, and Victoria were all out for 57. Set to score 36 to win, Tasmania had lost 6 for 15 in poor light when stumps were drawn.

Next morning Tabart clinched a win for Tasmania by three wickets with some bright

hitting for 15 not out after being dropped off the second ball. The Victorians could have blamed the stormy crossing of Bass Strait, spectators who overflowed on to the field or the lavish hospitality, but they graciously said they had been "well entertained and well beaten". The next day they won more friends by travelling to Bishopsbourne to play a one-innings match against boys of the College. With the *Shamrock*'s departure delayed until 17 February, they had time for a weekend in Hobart, where they collected £30 for charity. At the wharf 1000 people gathered to give the Victorians a joyous send-off, and Philpott's farewell speech was drowned by the band.

The Launceston Club wrote to Melbourne in October 1851 suggesting a return intercolonial match, and found the Victorians keen to accept. The match began on 29 March 1852 on a pitch on the south side of the Yarra roughly opposite the present World Trade Centre. (The Melbourne & Hobson's Bay Railway Co. took over this land a year or so later for the Melbourne to Port Melbourne railway line.) Most of Melbourne's leading citizens attended.

By stumps on the first day Victoria was in a winning position. Hamilton, who had looked menacing in the first match, this time found Henty's slows to his liking and there were several big hits in his 42, more than half the Victorian total of 80. Tasmania began disastrously, losing five wickets for only nine runs before Tabart and Maddox made a stand. Cox succeeded with some hefty swings, but then Maddox took a crushing blow on the shins and had to retire lbw, leaving Tasmania with a first innings total of 65. Victoria pressed their advantage by scoring 127 in the second innings and at stumps had taken four Tasmanian wickets for 41. Tasmania were all out for 81 on the second morning when their last six wickets fell cheaply, giving Victoria a 61-run victory.

The *Sydney Morning Herald* commented on 10 April 1852 that the "conquering" Tasmania versus Victoria match would be played next year and

# Victoria *v.* Tasmania

*Played at Launceston, 11–12 February 1851*

## Victoria

| First Innings | | |
|---|---|---|
| J. Cooper, *b.* McDowall | | 4 |
| W. Philpott, *c.* Maddox *b.* McDowall | | 17 |
| T. Hamilton, *b.* McDowall | | 10 |
| C. Lister, *run out* | | 10 |
| A. Thomson, *b.* McDowall | | 1 |
| R. Philpott, *b.* Henty | | 12 |
| T. Antill, *st.* Marshall *b.* Henty | | 0 |
| J. Brodie, *c.* Henty *b.* McDowall | | 17 |
| F. Marsden, *b.* Henty | | 2 |
| M. Hall, *not out* | | 6 |
| M. Hervey, *b.* Henty | | 0 |
| *Sundries* | | 3 |
| | Total | 82 |

| Second Innings | | |
|---|---|---|
| J. Cooper, *b.* Henty | | 0 |
| W. Philpott, *run out* | | 3 |
| T. Hamilton, *lbw b.* McDowall | | 35 |
| C. Lister, *c.* Maddox *b.* Field | | 3 |
| A. Thomson, *b.* Henty | | 0 |
| R. Philpott, *c.* Westbrook *b.* Henty | | 1 |
| T. Antill, *not out* | | 0 |
| J. Brodie, *c.* Tabart *b.* Henty | | 5 |
| F. Marsden, *b.* McDowall | | 2 |
| M. Hall, *lbw b.* McDowall | | 6 |
| M. Hervey, *c.* McDowall *b.* Henty | | 1 |
| *Sundries* | | 1 |
| | Total | 57 |

## Tasmania

| First Innings | | |
|---|---|---|
| G. DuCroz, *b.* Antill | | 27 |
| J. Marshall, *c.* Lister *b.* Antill | | 13 |
| W. Field, *b.* Antil | | 0 |
| G. Maddox, *b.* Antill | | 1 |
| G. Gibson, *b.* Hamilton | | 8 |
| W. Westbrook, *b.* Antill | | 10 |
| C. Arthur, *b.* Antill | | 1 |
| J. Tabart, *b.* Hamilton | | 2 |
| V. Giblin, *not out* | | 7 |
| W. Henty, *b.* Antill | | 0 |
| R. McDowall *c.* Antill *b.* Hamilton | | 11 |
| *Sundries* | | 24 |
| | Total | 104 |

| Second Innings | | |
|---|---|---|
| G. DuCroz, *b.* Antill | | 6 |
| J. Marshall, *c. and b.* Antill | | 0 |
| W. Field, *c.* Thomson *b.* Brodie | | 1 |
| G. Gibson, *b.* Antill | | 4 |
| W. Westbrook, *c.* Cooper *b.* Antill | | 4 |
| C. Arthur *c.* Hervey *b.* Antill | | 0 |
| J. Tabart, *not out* | | 15 |
| V. Giblin, *b.* Antill | | 1 |
| R. McDowall, *not out* | | 4 |
| *Sundries* | | 5 |
| | Total (7 for) | 37 |

*Tasmania won by 3 wickets*

hoped that "Sydney cricketers will show their pluck by challenging the winners". By the time the third match was played at Launceston in March 1854, however, the friendly relations between the teams had cooled. The Tasmanians objected to professionals in the Victorian team, believing also that it was unsportsmanlike for the Victorians to practise with professional ground bowlers. The Victorians in turn said it was a hardship to leave their jobs for a fortnight and regretted that they could include only two players from the first two matches in their team.

Marshall won the toss for the third time in succession and sent Victoria in to bat. Hostile bowling by McDowall and newcomer Robert Still, who bowled fast underarmers, compensated for the absence of Henty. Victoria's first innings ended at 80 after three hours' dogged batting. Tasmania began cautiously but established a lead of 17 runs through some confident hitting towards the end of the innings. Victoria's second knock yielded only 50 runs, and Tasmania lost only two wickets in scoring the 33 runs needed for victory. Still, 23 not out, was prominent again.

John Marshall's control of proceedings from behind the stumps gave Tasmania a decided advantage, for he allowed very few unnecessary runs and sustained pressure on every batsman. His placement of fieldsmen and his alertness helped produce sparkling displays from his players. Melbourne newspapers were generous in their praise of his skill. One paper considered that his wicket-keeping was "seldom surpassed in England—almost perfect; as sharp as a needle". But it was his last big match, for after 30 years of playing cricket in Tasmania he retired at the age of 58. He remains Australia's oldest ever first-class cricketer, and is regarded as the "Father of Tasmanian Cricket", his name appearing more often than any other in accounts of the early matches in Tasmania. Only George Moore, born in 1820, who played for New South Wales in 1873–74 for the last time in his 53rd year, approaches Marshall's record.

Conflict between the Launceston Cricket Club and the Southern Tasmania Cricket Association prevented further matches between Victoria and Tasmania until 1858. The Victorian team that summer included several fast round-arm bowlers, a style barred in Tasmania where it was regarded as foul play. Tasmanians, with heavier rainfall, had years of lush crops, the mainlanders occasional drought. Prosperity perhaps gave room for loftier ethical standards.

Victoria won the first encounter in February at Launceston when Gideon Elliott returned some of the most astounding figures in the entire history of cricket. Elliott, a former Surrey professional lured to Australia by the goldrushes, finished with nine wickets for two runs. Seventeen of his 19 overs were maidens.

Faced with this onslaught from a bowler whose style they considered a form of treachery, Tasmania were all out for 33. The Tasmanian bowlers did well to restrict to 115 Victoria, who adopted swashbuckling tactics to pass Tasmania's small total. Although Elliott did not bowl, Tasmania fared only slightly better in the second innings with 62, giving Victoria victory by an innings and 20 runs.

Despite this debacle, more than 5000 people were present a week later for the start of the next Tasmania *v.* Victoria match, the first first-class match held in Hobart. Claims that the Victorians were the equal of the best English county teams were immediately shown to be exaggerated as Victoria slumped to a first innings total of 78. W. Brown in his sole appearance for Tasmania took 7 for 42. Elliott and Wills bowled fast and straight when Tasmania struggled to 51, 27 runs behind. Not one batsman reached double figures. High drama followed as Brown ripped through Victoria's batting with his underarmers. Brown finished with 8 for 31, and with two run-outs, Victoria were out for 67. In the excitement of three completed innings in a single day, nobody counted the number of overs Brown bowled.

The task of scoring 95 runs on the second day did not appear to be beyond Tasmania: they

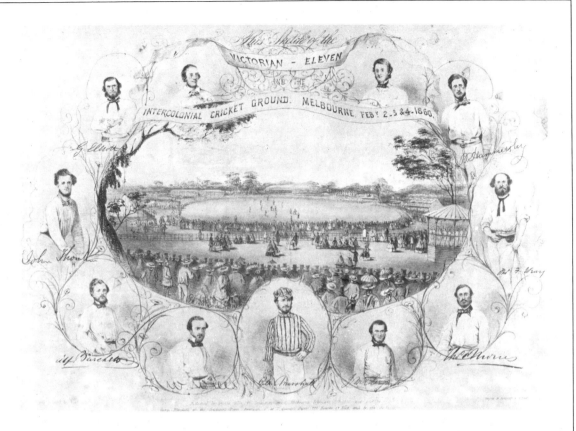

*A sketch of the Victorian XI, at the Melbourne venue for the February 1860 match with the New South Wales XI, including players' signatures. Gideon Elliott (top left) was one of Australia's first demon bowlers*

not only failed miserably, but also took a fearful battering. Wills and Elliott peppered them with deliveries that must have seemed like cannon-shot. Tasmania managed only 25 runs. Elliott took 4 for 6, giving him 7 for 25 in the match, and Wills 5 for 10, with match figures of 11 for 35.

Newspapers accused the Tasmanian batsmen of cowardice, but they had bruises all over their shins and arms to prove they had resisted manfully on a horrid pitch. The truth was that round-arm bowling had been regarded in Tasmania as unsportsmanlike and the players had had no practice against it.

Elliott's destructive bowling feats were not uncommon. Against New South Wales he took 7 for 27 and 3 for 7 in 1855–56, 5 for 17 in 1857–58, and 2 for 13 followed by 6 for 23 in 1859–60. He had learned his peculiar skills in Surrey, where he was born in 1828, and in an intercolonial career that spanned the years 1855 to 1861 he took 48 wickets at 4.93 apiece for Victoria. His speciality was a grubber that hit batsmen around the ankles, of which the *Australian Cricketer* said, "Batsmen required a sharp eye to dispose of these shooters".

Stunned by the severity of these defeats Tasmania did not risk their cricket reputation against Victoria for a further seven years. In the interval round-armers were encouraged in club cricket and a few appeared when the North *v*. South matches resumed. Lacking experience, they were inclined to bowl wides, contributing to a high number of sundries.

Meanwhile first-class cricket began on the mainland when New South Wales played Victoria

*Richard Driver, politician and cricket administrator, made the first Victoria–New South Wales match possible by making up the shortfall in the fund to send a team south from Sydney*

*William Tunks who, with Richard Driver, was a leading figure in the moves to get a New South Wales team to Melbourne. The Sydney side refused to play for a side stake, claiming honour was enough*

in 1856. The Melbourne Cricket Club placed an advertisement in the *Argus* challenging all comers to play them for a stake of £500. A Sydney group calling themselves the "Inter-Colonial Committee" were gathered together by William Tunks and accepted the challenge. Tunks collected donations towards expenses, added about £16 of his own, and persuaded barrister Richard Driver to accompany the team to Melbourne as umpire.

New South Wales allegedly won a moral victory by refusing to play for cash. The *Argus* praised this move: "Of late years cricket, like chess, has been invariably a game of love, money being a thing unmentionable. The stake is now for the supremacy of local play respectively, and the broader grounds upon which the contest is placed are decidedly more calculated to produce the better sport."

This was misdirected idealism, for the truth was that the Sydney players had no chance of raising betting money. They only raised the £181 to pay for the trip south because Driver put in £60 of his own money when the trip was in jeopardy a few days before they left Sydney. The lack of stake money did not inhibit bookmakers from appearing at the game, where bets of 2 to 1 against New South Wales were freely taken.

Before a ball was bowled there were arguments about the toss, who should bat first, whether different pitches should be used for each innings and what the umpires should wear. After Victoria won the toss, the New South Wales captain George Gilbert told the Victorian captain William Philpott that convention gave the visiting team the choice of who should bat first. Gilbert won the point and New South Wales sent Victoria in to bat. A scorer, equipped at the ground with a printing machine, promised updated scorecards at the fall of each wicket.

Victoria opened with Mather and Sargeant, who hit the first ball of the match for two. Sargeant reached seven before an underhand "trimmer" from McKone lowered his stumps and he departed, his runs having been "obtained in the most gallant manner". Coulstock scored four and then "caught the ball on his bat, but in the most unaccountable manner as far as spectators were concerned was given out leg-before-wicket". Morres "assumed the vacant timber" and Mather was run out trying for a fifth run. Morres was "compelled to lower his flag" to the wily Gilbert, Cumberland left for two, and Captain Hotham, "declared a vacant wicket after he received a ball from McKone which rattled among his bails, with no doubt to him a discordant note". Philpott was bowled for five. Lowe found McKone's bowling too straight and "his stumps became unsettled to such an extent that the air of the pavilion was considered best for him". Gilbert bowled the last man with a shooter, and Victoria were all out for 63.

When Murray and Tunks opened for New South Wales, Murray edged the first ball to slip and was caught. Bradridge left for two, Gideon Elliott again being "the assailant", then Elliott had Hilliard leg-before-wicket. After New South Wales had lost 8 for 19, including the wicket of Gilbert, bookmakers had Victoria at 3 to 1 on, but Driver and McKone "completely retrieved the position for their side, scoring 36 runs, exclusive of wide balls", before they were separated. Morres replaced Coulstock in the attack but immediately bowled a series of wides. Driver, who had only gone into the New South Wales team at the last minute when Joseph Rutter failed to turn up, managed 18 before he was bowled, and Howell scraped together 11 invaluable runs, giving New South Wales 76, a lead of 13 runs. Gate takings for the day were £60 5s 0d.

Both teams fielded without their boots, either barefooted or in stockings, for the pitch was a dust bowl that summer. (The Melbourne Cricket Ground also served as grazing pasture in the 1850s, and cattle and goats were to be found there between matches.) The *Argus* used "Mr" before each player's name in its account of the proceedings, and commented that the New South Wales players had a "homely appearance", apparently a jibe at the Sydneyites' white drill trousers, guernseys and socks. The Victorians wore white flannels.

McKone, who had topscored with Richard Driver with 18 in New South Wales's first innings, teased the Victorians out for only 28 on the second morning. He finished with 5 for 11. Set to score 16 to win, New South Wales lost 5 for 5 to hostile bowling by Elliott and Lowe, but a few good blows by Gilbert won the match. Gilbert's handling of the New South Wales team and their superior fielding and throwing proved the difference between the contestants, although the winning margin was only three wickets. There was great excitement when the *City of Sydney* sailed up Sydney Harbour several days later with the news that New South Wales had won.

At a subsequent meeting of New South Wales's first representative team on 21 October 1856, the following resolution was passed: "That Mr Richard Driver be requested to give up the ball which he received from the Melbourne players, as secretary of the New South Wales team, for the purpose of depositing the same, with a suitable inscription in some public place in this colony".

# Victoria *v.* New South Wales

*Played at Melbourne, 26–27 March 1856*

## Victoria

| First Innings | | |
|---|---|---|
| D. M. Sargeant, *b.* McKone | | 7 |
| J. Mather, *run out* | | 16 |
| R. Coulstock, *lbw, b.* McKone | | 4 |
| T. Morres, *b.* Gilbert | | 2 |
| Capt. A. Hotham, *b.* McKone | | 0 |
| C. Cumberland, *c.* Bradridge *b.* Gilbert | | 2 |
| W. Philpott (Capt.), *b.* McKone | | 5 |
| P. Kingston, *not out* | | 12 |
| F. Lowe, *b.* McKone | | 2 |
| A. Lewis, *c.* and *b.* Gilbert | | 8 |
| G. Elliott, *b.* Gilbert | | 1 |
| *Sundries* | | 4 |
| | Total | 63 |

| Second Innings | | |
|---|---|---|
| D. M. Sargeant, *b.* McKone | | 5 |
| J. Mather, *b.* McKone | | 0 |
| R. Coulstock, *c.* McKone *b.* Murray | | 2 |
| T. Morres, *c.* Howell *b.* Murray | | 1 |
| Capt. A. Hotham, *b.* Murray | | 0 |
| C. Cumberland, *run out* | | 1 |
| W. Philpott, *run out* | | 11 |
| P. Kingston, *b.* McKone | | 0 |
| F. Lowe, *not out* | | 1 |
| A. Lewis, *b.* McKone | | 5 |
| G. Elliott, *b.* McKone | | 1 |
| *Sundries* | | 1 |
| | Total | 28 |

| Bowling | Balls | Maidens | Runs | Wickets |
|---|---|---|---|---|
| Gilbert | 68 | 3 | 34 | 4 |
| McKone | 68 | 3 | 25 | 5 |

| Bowling | Balls | Maidens | Runs | Wickets |
|---|---|---|---|---|
| McKone | 52 | 4 | 11 | 5 |
| Murray | 40 | 2 | 16 | 3 |

*Note: This scorecard, as published in Sydney and Melbourne newspapers and since repeated in various cricket histories, is notable for the inclusion for the first time in Australia of bowling analysis. But the bowling figures for the New South Wales first innings do not add up when 13 sundries are included.*

Although present at the meeting, Driver did not comply with the request. His niece Beatrice sent the ball to the New South Wales Cricket Association, which has it still, several years after Driver died.

The wide public interest in the New South Wales victory in their first game against Victoria, helped create a demand for a new Sydney pitch, which was marked out at the Domain the same year. The *Sydney Mail* recounted that when Tunks and Hilliard were measuring a field at the southern end, Governor Sir William Denison (not long transferred from Tasmania) passed by and asked why they had not chosen the northern end. Tunks and Hilliard replied that the northern end was reserved for soldiers. Sir William told them to forget the military and lay the pitch down in the best place. Even with such viceregal licence they had trouble finding an area that was not bumpy or fouled by grazing cattle. The Victorian *Cricketers' Guide* stated in 1861 that "Twenty runs on the Domain are equal to 30 or 35 in Melbourne." Long-stops had particular problems dodging cow pats, a hazard even for spectators

## New South Wales

| First Innings | | |
|---|---|---|
| R. Murray, *c.* Morres *b.* Elliott | 0 | |
| W. Tunks, *b.* Elliott | 1 | |
| J. S. Bradridge, *b.* Elliott | 2 | |
| H. Hilliard, *lbw b.* Elliott | 0 | |
| G. H. Gilbert (Capt.) *c.* Morres *b.* Coulstock | 6 | |
| J. McKone, *not out* | 18 | |
| R. Vaughan, *b.* Elliott | 0 | |
| E. Saddler, *b.* Coulstock | 7 | |
| J. Beal, *st.* Lowe *b.* Coulstock | 0 | |
| R. Driver, *b.* Elliott | 18 | |
| G. Howell, *b.* Elliott | 11 | |
| *Sundries* | 13 | |
| | Total | 76 |

| Second Innings | | |
|---|---|---|
| R. Murray, *b.* Elliott | 5 | |
| W. Tunks, *b.* Elliott | 0 | |
| J. S. Bradridge, *b.* Lowe | 2 | |
| H. Hilliard, *not out* | 1 | |
| G. H. Gilbert *b.* Lowe | 7 | |
| J. McKone, *b.* Lowe | 0 | |
| R. Vaughan, *not out* | 1 | |
| R. Driver, *b.* Lowe | 0 | |
| G. Howell, *b.* Elliott | 0 | |
| *Sundries* | 0 | |
| | Total (for 7 wickets) | 16 |

| Bowling | Balls | Maidens | Runs | Wickets |
|---|---|---|---|---|
| Elliott | 104 | 16 | 28 | 7 |
| Coulstock | 80 | 9 | 31 | 3 |
| Morres | 24 | 1 | 13 | — |

| Bowling | Balls | Maidens | Runs | Wickets |
|---|---|---|---|---|
| Elliott | 44 | 4 | 7 | 3 |
| Lowe | 36 | 3 | 9 | 4 |

*New South Wales won by three wickets*

on footpaths.

On Saturday 6 December 1856 the first ball was bowled on the Domain pitch in a match between the Garrison Club and Royal Victoria. A few months later the so-called Grand National Cricket Match, the return between New South Wales and Victoria, was played there. A committee formed to stage this match selected the Domain as the best available pitch despite protests from the curator of the Botanical Gardens. The City Corporation lent carts to help move soil to level the ground. The governor paid half the £10 cost to prepare the pitch, Mr A. L. Park the other half.

William Tunks played a major role in overcoming strong objections to this use of the Domain by citizens who regarded it as a public park. He wrote to cricketers urging them to subscribe match funds and attend the game. One man wrote back: "I have taken a wife and cannot come", but he enclosed a cheque. The match committee met regularly in James Cunningham's hotel, accepting advice from team captain George Gilbert and Captain Ward.

*An old lithograph of the first intercolonial match in Sydney's Domain in January 1857. Victoria won by two wickets*

By then William Tunks had forsaken hotel keeping to become a contractor. He supplied blue metal for Sydney streets and also erected the first telegraph lines to country centres as well as the first from Sydney to Melbourne. He became Mayor of St Leonards when he moved across the Harbour and was re-elected 15 times. Several of the letters Tunks wrote urging acceptance of the Domain as a place for major matches, as opposed to a park in which people strolled, are preserved by the New South Wales Cricket Association.

The first day of the match in January 1857 attracted 10,000 spectators, and when the game reached a climax on the third day 15,000 were present. The 11th Regiment's band entertained Governor Denison and his guests during breaks in play. *Bell's Life* described the "Fair ladies mustered in such force to illuminate with their sunny smiles and bright eyes the sombre 'phisogs' of the nobler sex" and chastised spectators who refused to move from in front of the scorers' tent for shouting "absurd applause with stentorian lungs".

Although George Gilbert had not long before received great praise for scoring 118 not out for the Albert Club against the Nationals, he had his critics as a captain. W. J. Hammersley wrote: "His batting is effective but wanting in finish. His fielding is good and would be elegant if he curbed his too exuberant spirits for the gratification of the cabbage tree mob. He is wont to keep spectators in good humour". The critics condemned Gilbert for not using a wicket-keeper and contrasted this with the Victorian tactics of using both

There was no scoreboard but the *Sydney Morning Herald* reported that spectators were able to follow the scores thanks to the enterprise of Mr Taylor, of *Bradshaw's Guide*, who issued cards from his printing press on the ground. The bowlers were restricted to four-ball overs and only round-arm and underarm bowling were permitted. Approach runs were short.

Set to score 104 to win, Victoria were all out on the third day for 38, giving New South Wales a win by 65 runs. Wills took 6 for 26 and 4 for 40 for Victoria, Ward 2 for 23 and 5 for 15. Gilbert's 31 was the top score for the match.

Victoria's captain in this match was William Joseph Hammersley. Born in Surrey in 1828, he had played for Cambridge University, Surrey and MCC, and later became editor of the *Cricketers' Register For Australia*. Thirty years later Hammersley wrote in the *Sydney Mail*:

> I thought it the queerest match I had ever taken part in, as some of the Sydney men played without shoes, in their stockinged feet, and one or two even discarded those necessary articles. We had a grand dinner somewhere, at which Sir W. Denison was present and lots of officers in gaudy uniforms. What with dinners, picnics, oysters on the harbour, we were a very limp lot when we returned to Melbourne.

a wicket-keeper (George Marshall) and a long-stop (Butterworth). Bearing in mind the flimsy gear wicket-keepers used at the time when long-stops were the second most important fieldsmen, Gilbert's ploy was akin to Mike Brearley's in one-day cricket.

Betting favoured Victoria who were 5 to 4 on before the match. Victoria were reported to have been backed in Sydney and Melbourne for £4000 to £5000 and, incredibly enough, the *Sydney Morning Herald* reported one bet of £1600 to £1000 on. The odds eased at the end of the first day when New South Wales had scored 80 against Victoria's first innings of 63. One supporter of the New South Wales team was reported to have laid £100 on them in four different places. New South Wales's trump card proved to be Captain Ward, then in control of the State Mint, for the Victorians could do little with his round-armers.

The success of the Grand National match led to moves to form a New South Wales Cricket Association, but it was three years before this was achieved. Country cricket had boomed with the discovery of gold west of the Divide and in 1857 *Bell's Life* said there were 24 country clubs in New South Wales. Indeed the need to bring tearaway Bathurst bowler George Biggs Richardson across the mountains to strengthen the state side accelerated the formation of the New South Wales Cricket Association. (Richardson took 15 wickets at 7.00 in two seasons for New South Wales, including 6 for 42 *v.* Victoria in 1859–60.)

New South Wales's supremacy did not last long. Victoria won five successive matches after

their defeat in the Domain. The third match, in January 1858, gave Victoria an overwhelming win by 171 runs. This game was memorable for a hat-trick by George Gilbert, the first in Australian first-class cricket. Gilbert's initial victim fell lbw, his second was caught, and Gilbert completed the feat with a catch off his own bowling. Despite the hat-trick Victoria scored 238, a huge total for those times. New South Wales managed only 57 and 69. Not long afterwards Gilbert became a swagman, begging for his keep along the way. Later he even wrote to the struggling NSWCA for handouts.

*ABOVE: George Gilbert, one of W. G. Grace's cousins, captained New South Wales in early intercolonial matches. He had played for Middlesex and The Gentlemen a few years earlier*
*RIGHT: The first intercolonial match played at Sydney in 1859 was won by Victoria, whose team included outstanding players like George Marshall, Tom Wills, William Hammersley and Gideon Elliott*

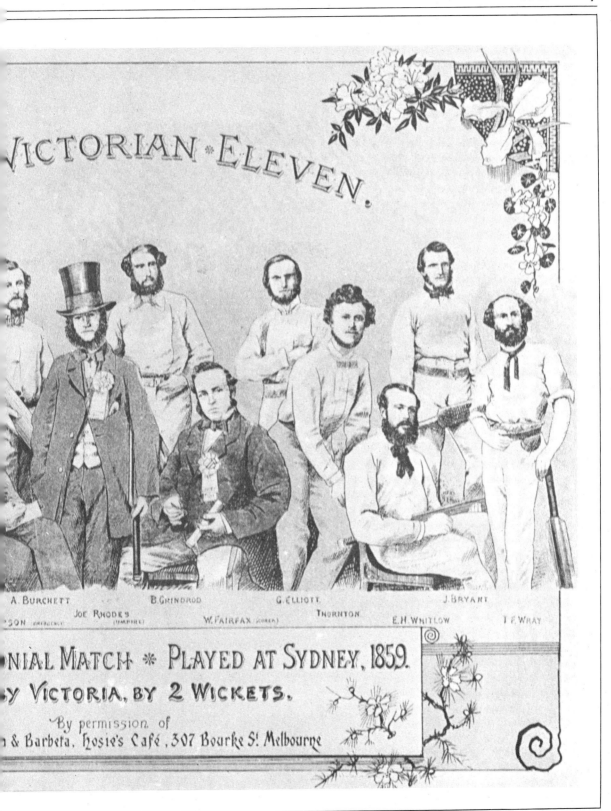

VICTORIAN ＊ ELEVEN.

A. BURCHETT   B. GRINDROD   G. ELLIOTT   J. BRYANT
..SON (EMERGENCY)   JOE RHODES (UMPIRE)   W. FAIRFAX (SCORER)   THORNTON   E. H. WHITLOW   T. F. WRAY

..NIAL MATCH ＊ PLAYED AT SYDNEY, 1859.
..Y VICTORIA, BY 2 WICKETS.
By permission of
..n & Barbeta, Hosie's Café, 307 Bourke St. Melbourne

*Teams for the 1866 Victoria v. New South Wales match. Tom Wills is the bald-headed figure holding the ball in the centre of the sketch. He later suicided by stabbing himself with scissors*

George Marshall, who by then had sold his outfitters shop to become a hotelier in Melbourne, added venom to Victoria's bowling. Tom Wills took 5 for 25 in New South Wales's first innings, Gideon Elliott 5 for 17 in the second. Wills also made 49 not out. Wills was in his prime in a career that yielded 130 first-class wickets at about 10 apiece and 602 runs at 12.28. In 1859 he took 11 for 90 in the New South Wales match, and in 1860, 9 for 39. His 1859 coup was remarkable as he broke the middle finger of his right hand early in the match. His skills remained for years but Elliott's were short-lived. Indeed Elliott's sad decline as a bowler dated from the time he took over the Royal Hotel in Punt Road.

When Queensland became a separate colony in 1859, Wills's father was so impressed by the

children, including the elder Wills. Tom only missed the massacre because his dray had broken down some distance from the station and he had stayed behind to repair it. After the tragedy he gave up the Victorian captaincy to manage his father's station.

Years later Tom Horan wrote in the *Australasian* under the pseudonym "Felix" that Wills was "the W. G. Grace of Australia, as well known for his good nature and kind heart as he was famous for his skill as a player". Wills, tall and elegant of bearing, also won high praise as a captain, and Lillywhite said after watching him swing his 1.36 kilogram bat, "He hits terrific".

The three-pronged attack of Wills, Elliott and the wily professional Sam Cosstick was supported by Marshall's craftsmanlike wicket-keeping, the all-round expertise of John Conway and the belligerent batting of Dick Wardill. The only doubt about this fine Victorian team centred on Wills's bowling action. At a time when half the population was illiterate, some profound prose was devoted to his alleged "chucking". A Sydney critic summed up: "His bowling is difficult to play, though at times its fairness is debatable, but as anything short of an absolute throw is now allowed, it would require a very strong umpire to 'call him'. He bowls with his head, varies his pace with as much speed as wisdom, and soon finds a batsman's weak spots."

The first meeting of the New South Wales Cricket Association was held in the open on Sydney Domain on 13 December 1859. The main advocates of the association's foundation, William Tunks and Richard Driver, did not turn up, but the 25 people who did elected Joe Clayton as treasurer and Tunks and Driver as co-secretaries. Nine months later the *Sydney Morning Herald* published the association's constitution and named lawyer–businessman J. B. Darvall as first president.

After the initial England tour of Australia in 1862, New South Wales was strengthened for the February 1863 match against Victoria by the inclusion of Charles Lawrence, the England, Surrey

opportunities there that he sold his property in Geelong and moved north with his relatives, staff and stock. The full party of 25 people reached Cullingaringo Station at Nogoa, 322 kilometres from Rockhampton on 3 October 1861. Aborigines began pestering them immediately. Wills senior had been on such friendly terms with Aborigines around Geelong that he did not consider they would menace his entourage. They were resting on 17 October when the Aborigines took them by surprise and killed 19 men, women and

and Middlesex all-rounder. Edward Gregory also appeared that season. Crowd support had increased every year and by the time the teams took the field in Sydney the tradition of Victoria *v.* New South Wales grudge matches was well established. Only the undisciplined cows grazing at one end of the Domain did not feel the tension.

Conway struck the New South Wales batsman Sydney Jones a nasty blow on the leg with a very fast delivery. Jones required a runner, but he continued to hobble about in pain. When Jones wandered out of his crease, Marshall whipped off the bails and appealed. The New South Wales umpire at the bowler's end rejected the appeal, saying that he had already called "over", but the Victorian umpire ruled that Jones was out. Intense argument followed and amid uproar the Victorian players walked off the ground and drove back to their hotel.

Next day all except two Victorians waived the appeal against Jones and agreed to continue the contest. George Marshall and the English-born all-rounder William Greaves, the two dissenters, caught the next ship back to Melbourne. New South Wales won by 84 runs—scoring 108 and 97 to 76 and 45—and Sydney newspapers said the defection of Marshall and Greaves did not affect the result. Marshall had other ideas. Back in Melbourne he gave his version of events in a letter to the *Argus*:

*The ball went through to the longstop and was returned to me. Jones, in attempting to regain his equilibrium, drew one foot over the crease and I put down the wicket and threw the ball up. While the ball was in the air, the Sydney umpire called "Over", and on my appealing to our umpire, Jones was given out.*

*The consequence was that a scene ensued which I am happy to say is never witnessed out of Sydney. The mob refused to let Jones retire, or Thompson to come in, although the Sydney captain, Lawrence, ordered it, and we were all compelled to leave the ground. Wills was struck*

*Joe Clayton, secretary of the New South Wales Cricket Association from 1857 to 1864, played a major role in organising the early intercolonial matches*

*a severe blow in the face by a cowardly vagabond, and Huddlestone and Hope were both struck by heavy sticks from behind.*

*I was bullied and threatened not only at the ground but even at my hotel, where a deputation waited on me with the avowed purpose of assaulting me.*

Marshall added that he had withdrawn from the match to keep faith with those who had subscribed money to send the Victorian team to Sydney. While he could make allowances for the behaviour of the rowdy mob of 10,000, he could not excuse the New South Wales committeemen who, with badges of office on their coats, joined in the hooting and groaning. Tom Wills in turn wrote a letter to the *Sydney Morning Herald* in which he said that the real culprit in the whole affair was the former New South Wales captain George

Gilbert. Wills argued that when Jones had been about to accept the umpire's decision and leave the field, Gilbert came forward from the New South Wales tent and shouted, "Go back, go back!", which aroused the mob "to hoot and yell like demons" and eventually stone the Victorians as they left the field. The team left the Domain under close police escort. Wills added that he had "never played here yet without there being a row, and in every case Victoria has given way, but on this occasion I am determined to make my stand, for although we have been defeated we have not been conquered in a fair field".

Thus began the first of hundreds of controversies that have enlivened Australian cricket. Melbourne newspapers urged their cricketers to boycott any Sydney intercolonial match. The *Empire* condemned the Sydney rowdies who shouted "Hit Marshall on the nose!" and spoke of "the ruffianly assault on Huddlestone on his way from the wickets to the Victorian tent". The Melbourne *Evening News* blamed the row on the Sydney players' convict ancestry:

*Scratch a Russian and you will find a Tartar underneath. Scratch a New South Wales man and you discover the evidence of convictism. He may not be a convict himself, but his father was, and it will take many generations to obliterate the taint. Sydney is based on convictism, built up with it, supported by it. Convictism is the nature and the essence of the community inhabiting the shores of Port Jackson. It is no wonder, therefore, that that very respectable man and excellent cricketer George Marshall left the city in disgust.*

The recriminations that followed prevented a match being played in 1864, and New South Wales Cricket Association members were bitterly resentful of the charges made against them. One constructive result of the affair was the formation of the Victorian Cricketers' Association, in October 1864, player members paying an annual subscription of half a guinea. The main aim of this association was to restore intercolonial matches so that truly representative teams could be chosen to play against visiting English teams. But for years afterwards the trip to Sydney was perilous for Victorian cricketers, who, according to the *Australasian*, came to dread the cry: "There's a Victorian cricketer — 'eave a brick at 'im!"

# A junket around the colonies

## England in Australia 1861–64

The All England XI was formed in 1846 through the efforts of one man, the former bricklayer William Clarke. He was married to the widow Chapman, who kept the Trent Bridge Inn, at the back of which Clarke developed the riverside ground into one of the most famous cricket sites in the world. The Eleven quickly gained in strength and popularity, the side being reinforced by the addition of players like Alfred Mynn and Felix from Kent, and Lillywhite and Dean from Sussex. The team played in nearly 40 country districts in its first three years. Clarke, a slow underarm bowler, was the captain and business manager.

Between 1850 and 1860 the All England XI was so successful that a second team, known as the United England XI was formed. Clarke ran the original All England XI like a dictator and resisted change. Many players in the United England XI had quarrelled with Clarke. Both elevens flourished, for they were full of striking

*The Domain, Sydney, during the match between George Parr's team and Twenty-Two of New South Wales in March 1864. The Englishmen won by four wickets*

*The All England XI, formed in 1846, included strong players such as Mynn, Felix, Lillywhite, and Clarke, whose efforts saw the famous ground at Trent Bridge developed*

personalities like Julius Caesar, who always demanded that his full name be used in the score-books, "Ducky" Diver, whose nickname derived from his dapper appearance, and John Wisden, founder of the famous almanack. William Clarke took 2385 wickets between 1846 and 1853, averaging 340 wickets a season. Although many of his victims were village novices, this was a rich haul for a man who had lost an eye in a child-hood accident and who had discovered cricket late in life.

When Clarke died in 1855 at the age of 57, another Nottinghamshire man, jovial George Parr, took over the team. In 1859 he took the side on a tour of Canada. The success of this tour and of the American tour by a team led by Notting-hamshire professional Richard Daft (acclaimed as

the finest batsman then on view in England), in 1861, impressed a Mr Devlin, an Australian on a visit to London. Devlin discussed the idea of an England team making a similar tour of Australia with Heathfield Harman Stephenson, captain of Surrey, and began writing to leading English players seeking their reaction to an Australian tour. Devlin did not pursue this scheme further when he learned of the players' demands, and handed over his project and correspondence to Melbourne hoteliers Felix Spiers and Christopher Pond. Spiers

owned the Royal Hotel and Cafe de Paris in Bourke Street, and Pond was host of the Piazza Hotel, at the corner of Bourke and King Streets.

Spiers and Pond originally wanted to bring author Charles Dickens to Australia for a lecture tour, but when Dickens failed to respond to their offer of £10,000, they discussed the idea of an English cricket tour with the impresario George Selth Coppin, who urged them to proceed. Coppin was the most active and successful entrepreneur of the Australian theatre in the mid-nineteenth century. He operated four Melbourne theatres, introduced camels, Turkish baths and roller skating to Australia, and was a member of Parliament and first Grand Master of the Masonic Lodge of Victoria.

Spiers and Pond estimated it would cost £7000 for a cricket tour, a figure calculated from a study of Devlin's letters. The sum included an estimated fee of £150 per player, plus fares and expenses. They soon realised that long-distance negotiations with the English cricketers were ineffectual, so they sent a Mr Mallam to England to finalise arrangements. He arrived in London to find that the All England and United England elevens had both split up and become Players of the North and Players of the South. He promptly went to Birmingham, where a match between these teams was scheduled. At a dinner given by Captain Frederick Marshall (later General Marshall) he outlined plans for the Australian tour.

Batsman Parr, speaking from the experience of England's Canadian tour in 1859, claimed that £150 per player was inadequate for a trip of some 50,000 kilometres. His northern team-mates agreed. The tour appeared to have collapsed, for without the northern players a representative touring team was not possible.

Mallam returned to London and with the help of Heathfield Stephenson and the Surrey Cricket Club secretary William Burrup, persuaded "Terrible Billy" Caffyn, Tom Sewell and the big-hitting George Griffith to join a side to be led by Stephenson. Mallam made a special trip to

Dublin to get Charles Lawrence's signature on a tour agreement. Later additions were William Mudie, so thin he was known as "the Surrey Shadow"; Tom Hearne, a member of the famous Middlesex cricket family; George "Farmer" Bennett, who made a success out of bowling high-tossed round-armers for Kent, after serving a gaol term for burglary; red-faced Yorkshireman Roger Iddison and his team-mate Edward Stephenson; and George ("Tiny") Wells, of Sussex. Mallam tried hard to add Richard Daft, acknowledged as the finest player in England, but failed.

Lawrence was an insatiable traveller who used cricket skill as a passport to the far corners of the world. He was born in Middlesex on 16 December 1828, and as a schoolboy at Merton often wagged school to travel to London and watch Fuller Pilch play at Lord's. Lawrence became a professional at the age of 17 and joined the Perth Club in Scotland, and in 1849 he took all ten wickets for Scotland against the All England XI, his victims including Felix, Box, Mynn, Pilch and Lillywhite.

Later he helped found the United Ireland XI and also served as its secretary. Playing for United Ireland he took 5 for 20 when the All England XI was dismissed for 55. He also appeared for Surrey in 1854 while he lived at Mitcham, and in 1861 played for Middlesex. His dismissal of Felix with a shooter that knocked over all three stumps was still remembered when he set sail for Australia.

The twelve-man, all-professional team, invited by Mallam and brought to Australia by Stephenson, comprised a good-humoured group of established players, but without cricketers like Parr and Daft it could not be considered the best available. Their experience was, however, enough to overwhelm naive and poorly disciplined opposition, even though the tour was run as a social junket by the promoters.

The team assembled in London for a farewell banquet, were photographed in the stable-yard of their Haymarket hotel, and left Liverpool for Australia in the six-masted steamship *Great Britain*, which weighed 2032 tonnes and had been specially refitted for the trip to Melbourne. There were only two larger steamers afloat at the time. As she pulled out from the wharf with 687 passengers on board the England team sang "Anchors Weighed" for those on the dock, and William Caffyn, the famous "Surrey Pet", gave them a solo on his cornet. For this he was punished by a plague of mosquitoes that tormented him throughout an otherwise pleasant journey.

More than 3000 people gathered at the

*ABOVE LEFT: Heathfield Harman Stephenson, captain of the first English team to tour Australia in 1862. The Englishmen toured for £150-a-man after novelist Charles Dickens failed to respond to the promoter's invitation to tour*
*RIGHT: The first English team to tour Australia: (L to R) (back) W. Mudie, H. H. Stephenson, Mr Mallam, T. Hearne; (centre) G. Bennett, W. Caffyn, G. Griffith, R. Iddison, E. Stephenson; (front) G. Wells, W. Mortlock, C. Lawrence*

*The scene outside sponsors Spiers and Pond's Melbourne restaurant when the first English team arrived on 24 December 1861*

Melbourne dockside to greet them on Christmas Eve 1861. Each player wore a white hat trimmed with a blue ribbon and as they drove through the streets to the Cafe de Paris they were applauded by wildly cheering crowds. They rode on the roof of a coach pulled by four magnificent greys and when they reached Bourke Street thousands more spectators blocked all traffic. The Melbourne *Herald* claimed that there had been no welcome like it since the Athenians arrived in Corinth.

The Englishmen discovered that there were 70 cricket clubs in Victoria alone, most of them

employees in a locality kept secret to prevent the players being mobbed. Melbourne Cricket Club members joined them for further practice a few days later at St Kilda. "Farmer" Bennett demonstrated a few of his prodigious hits, and for the rest of the tour was labelled "The Lion Hitter".

England's first match in Australia began at the Melbourne Cricket Ground on New Year's Day 1862. Two days beforehand Stephenson announced that England was still weary from the 67-day sea voyage and would not play unless the number of their opponents was reduced from 22 to 15. One paper contended that England had "shown the white feather". Spiers and Pond compromised by reducing England's opposition to 18, but the dispute helped add to the excitement that electrified the city from early morning. People flocked in from outlying districts in coaches, wagons and sulkies, on horseback, and in overflowing trains. The Melbourne *Herald* considered that more than 15,000 people were there for the start of play, but others thought the crowd was much larger. A Sydney cricket lover expressed dismay that Melbourne rather than Sydney was staging the first match against England.

The English players confessed they were astonished by the staging of the match. On a fiercely hot day each player was supplied with a helmet-type sun hat, and they all had coloured sashes around their waists and the same coloured ribbon on their hats. These colours were printed beside each man's name on the scorecard so that spectators could identify them. Bright marquees and awnings circled the ground along with a new stand with accommodation for 6000 that had just been completed. The area beneath the stand was reserved for publicans, who advertised that they had stocked 500 cases of beer for the occasion.

Bullock wagons were parked outside in the streets as the Eighteen of Victoria began their innings and the England players took the field to the playing of the national anthem. The crowd stood in silence but when the band finished "God Save the Queen" they burst into a tremendous roar.

only a few years old, with the Melbourne Cricket Club dominant. They were also surprised to find none of the social barriers that existed in England against professionals. Entertainment was lavish and scarcely a day passed without a champagne breakfast. The day after their arrival they had to be driven eleven kilometres into the bush to practise on a pitch specially prepared by Spiers and Pond

# Eighteen of Victoria *v.* H. H. Stephenson's XI

*Played at Melbourne, 1–4 January 1862*

## Eighteen of Victoria

| First Innings | | | Second Innings | | |
|---|---|---|---|---|---|
| J. M. Bryant, *lbw, b.* Bennett | | 11 | J. M. Bryant, *b.* Sewell | | 0 |
| G. Marshall, *c.* Iddison, *b.* Griffith | | 27 | G. Marshall, *c.*Mortlock, *b.* Sewell | | 0 |
| J. Sweeney, *lbw, b.* Griffith | | 16 | J. Sweeney, *c.* Lawrence, *b.* Sewell | | 0 |
| C. Mace, *st.* H. Stephenson, *b.* Griffith | | 5 | C. Mace, *b.* Sewell | | 21 |
| J. Huddleston, *c.* Sewell, *b.* Bennett | | 6 | J. Huddleston, *c.* Iddison, *b.* Sewell | | 18 |
| R. W. Wardill, *run out* | | 0 | R. W. Wardill, *c.* Lawrence, *b.* Griffith | | 18 |
| C. Makinson, *b.* Bennett | | 0 | C. Makinson, *run out* | | 0 |
| T. Morres, *b.* Bennett | | 0 | T. Morres, *run out* | | 0 |
| S. Costick, *c.* Mudie, *b.* Bennett | | 8 | S. Costick, *c.* Iddison, *b.* Griffith | | 11 |
| J. B. Thompson, *hit wicket, b.* Bennett | | 17 | J. B. Thompson, *run out* | | 0 |
| G. Elliott, *b.* Griffith | | 4 | G. Elliott, *c.* Iddison, *b.* Sewell | | 3 |
| T. F. Wray, *c. and b.* Griffith | | 3 | T. F. Wray, *c.* H. Stephenson, *b.* Iddison | 0 |
| S. S. Rennie, *lbw, b.* Bennett | | 9 | S. S. Rennie, *c.* Lawrence, *b.* Iddison | | 0 |
| J. Conway, *run out* | | 0 | J. Conway, *st.* H. Stephenson, *b.* Caffyn | 1 |
| J. Stewart, *b.* Griffith | | 1 | J. Stewart, *b.* Iddison | | 0 |
| S. Hopkinson, *run out* | | 0 | S. Hopkinson, *c.* Bennett, *b.* Caffyn | | 18 |
| G. O'Mullane, *not out* | | 0 | G. O'Mullane, *not out* | | 0 |
| B. Butterworth, *c. and b.* Griffith | | 0 | B. Butterworth, *c.* Iddison *b.* Sewell | | 0 |
| *Extras* | | 11 | *Extras* | | 2 |
| | Total | 118 | | Total | 92 |

| Bowling | Balls | Maidens | Runs | Wickets |
|---|---|---|---|---|
| Caffyn | 36 | 2 | 23 | — |
| Bennett | 148 | 10 | 53 | 7 |
| Griffith | 116 | 12 | 30 | 7 |

| Bowling | Balls | Maidens | Runs | Wickets |
|---|---|---|---|---|
| Caffyn | 28 | 5 | 5 | 2 |
| Griffith | 41 | 4 | 9 | 2 |
| Lawrence | 44 | 1 | 31 | — |
| Sewell | 104 | 16 | 20 | 7 |
| Iddison | 88 | 12 | 24 | 3 |

# H. H. Stephenson's XI

| *First Innings* | | |
| --- | --- | --- |
| G. Bennett, *c.* Butterworth *b.* Conway | 11 |
| E. Stephenson, *b.* Conway | 34 |
| W. Mudie, *b.* Elliott | 22 |
| G. Griffith, *c.* Butterworth, *b.* Cosstick | 61 |
| W. Caffyn, *c.* O'Mullane, *b.* Stewart | 79 |
| R. Iddison, *b.* Conway | 31 |
| H. H. Stephenson, *b.* Conway | 2 |
| C. Lawrence, *c.* Conway, *b.* Bryant | 20 |
| T. Sewell, *b.* Stewart | 3 |
| W. Mortlock, *not out* | 11 |
| T. Hearne, *b.* Stewart | 8 |
| *Extras* | 23 |
| Total | 305 |

| *Bowling* | | | | |
| --- | --- | --- | --- | --- |
| | *Balls* | *Maidens* | *Runs* | *Wickets* |
| Conway | 205 | 20 | 60 | 4 |
| Cosstick | 124 | 19 | 31 | 1 |
| Bryant | 195 | 18 | 33 | 1 |
| Stewart | 153 | 9 | 50 | 3 |
| Elliott | 101 | 7 | 48 | 1 |
| Morres | 25 | – | 9 | – |
| Marshall | 16 | – | 8 | – |
| Makinson | 60 | 1 | 43 | – |

Conway bowled five wides, Stewart 4, Cosstick, Elliott and Morres 1 each

*Stephenson's XI won by an innings and 96 runs*

---

Around the ground were shooting galleries, hurdygurdies, fruit and sweet stalls, and small boys selling scorecards and photographs of the players. A painter who brought his ladder did a thriving business helping spectators to take up vantage points in the trees. Billy Caffyn opened the bowling for England but had to come off because of pains in his arms, caused by infected mosquito bites. George Marshall gave his side a good start by scoring 27, but the Eighteen of Victoria were all out for 118, with 6 ducks. Of the England bowlers Griffith took 7 for 30, Bennett 7 for 53, with 3 run outs. Caffyn had the satisfaction of top scoring with 79 in an England first innings of 305, with "Ben" Griffith next best on 61.

In their second innings Victoria were all out for 92, including 10 ducks. Sewell took 7 for 20, and Stephenson's side won by an innings and 96 runs. Apart from Marshall, kindly Sam Cosstick,

a right-arm fast bowler born at Croydon in Surrey, was the best of the locals. A sweepstake for the highest scorer, with a first prize of £100, was held. The man who won it presented Caffyn with a brand new £10 note.

More than 45,000 people paid to see the contest, which finished early on the fourth day. The takings covered all Spiers and Pond's costs for the entire tour. To fill in the remaining time on the fourth day, the entrepreneurs arranged the first balloon ascent ever seen in Australia. The balloon was called "All England" and had pictures of Queen Victoria and the England players painted on the outside. It was aloft for 35 minutes, drifting all over Melbourne, before the balloonists, Mr and Mrs Brown, brought it down in Albert Street.

The second match of England's tour was against Twenty-Two of the Ovens district at Beechworth. To get there required a tiring 322

*A sketch of the scene at the Melbourne Cricket Ground during the first international match in Australia. England defeated Eighteen of Melbourne by an innings and 95 runs. The crowd was so large that the money collected for this match paid for the entire tour*

kilometre journey in a coach drawn by four horses, with a pair behind. Despite the trip, England scored 264 and disposed of the opposing Twenty-Two for 20 and 53. The English top-scorer Griffith then took on an eleven at single-wicket cricket. He won by dismissing them all for one run, scoring six himself.

A week later England returned to Melbourne to meet Twenty-Two of Victoria, who bundled them out for only 101. The only significant scores came from "Tiny" Wells, 32, and extras, 20. The Twenty-Two scored 153 and 144 but the match ended in a draw. It was a heartening result for the locals. Further huge attendances had Messrs Spiers and Pond congratulating young Mr Mallam. Sewell took no fewer than 15 wickets in the second innings of the fourth match against Twenty-Two of Geelong, which England won by nine wickets.

There was another joyous demonstration when the ship bringing the England players berthed in Sydney. More than 15,000 people assembled at Circular Quay, all of them cheering wildly. A capacity crowd filled the Domain and when Mortlock made a handsome 76 to take England's first innings to 175, a spontaneous collection among the spectators earned him an unexpected £20. The Twenty-Two of Sydney scored 127 and succeeded in dismissing England a second time for only 66. Needing 116 to win, the Twenty-Two managed only 65 and England won by 49 runs on the fourth day. The governor, Sir John Young, watched every ball bowled and attended the dinner for the England players afterwards.

Spiers and Pond next sent the English cricketers to Bathurst, the oldest settlement west of the Blue Mountains, 213 kilometres west of Sydney. Six kilometres from Bathurst their coach, drawn by six splendid greys, was met by a large cavalcade of officials, cricketers and a brass band. Several of the tourists admitted that they were "quite touched" by the welcome, but the match against the local Twenty-Two was curtailed by rain and declared a draw. England scored 211, with 45 sundries, more than anybody got with the bat. The Twenty-Two made 49 and were 6 for 25 when the violent storm struck.

The aura of invincibility that surrounded the English team vanished when they returned to Sydney to play a Combined Twenty-Two chosen from the best players of Victoria and New South Wales. Here they encountered one of Australian cricket's most memorable characters, George Moore. In his photographs Moore, who was born in Bedfordshire in 1820, looks a crusty, morose old man, but he lived until he was 96, fathered four children, and continued to play cricket in the Maitland district (where he ran a confectionery business) until he was 75. He made his debut in eleven-a-side matches for New South Wales against Victoria when just a few weeks short of his fifty-first birthday in 1871 and played his last match for the state against W. G. Grace's XI in 1873–74, when he was 52 years 325 days old. He remains mainland Australia's oldest active first-class cricketer.

The Moores rate second only to the Gregorys among New South Wales cricket families. Apart from George, whose father and grandfather were said to have played county cricket in England, his brother James and James's sons William and Leon all played for New South Wales. The most famous member of the family was George's grandson, Charlie Macartney, whom George introduced to the game by bowling green apples to him in Maitland.

George Moore took 4 for 22 off 83 balls against Stephenson's team, helping the Twenty-Two to win by 12 wickets. England scored 60 and 75, the Twenty-Two 101 and 8 for 35. Sydney feted the Englishmen throughout this visit, forcing unlimited champagne on them, clapping as soon as they were recognised in the streets, and staging a special programme at the Victoria Theatre. There was an emotional farewell dinner at Tattersall's Club punctuated with eloquent speeches. Another

*George Moore, the Maitland cricketer who continued playing for New South Wales until he was 52 years and 325 days old. He remains the oldest mainland first-class cricket player*

large crowd escorted them through the streets to
the Quay for the start of their voyage to Tasmania.
Rockets were fired as they sailed up the Harbour,
headed for a convict island that was to provide
a lesson in sports promotion.

Spiers and Pond inserted an advertisement in
Tasmanian newspapers inviting matches with "any
cricket club". A trustee of the Hobart cricket
ground, Thomas Westbrook, reputedly the best
point fieldsman in the country, replied. Spiers and
Pond informed him that Tasmania would have to
provide £1000 and pay all the English cricketers'
expenses. Westbrook was not happy with the
terms but when he called a public meeting in
Hobart to discuss the tour, a Mr Gardiner,
manager of the American Circus then touring the
island, offered to donate half the proceeds of one
night's performance at the Hippodrome. His
generosity led to a rash of donations that
guaranteed the England–Tasmania clash. The
conditions of the match were then announced by
Messrs Spiers and Pond:

*That we play a three-day match in your city,
and that we bring out a team to your ground
at our expense and we have the privilege of all
entrance fees at the gates, sub-letting sites for
booths for sale of liquors, printing, etcetera, and
every other benefit that may accrue from the
ground. The committee to provide a team of
Twenty-Two, free of expense to us, fence in
the ground, get it in proper order for play, and
provide a sufficient body of police to keep the
playing area free.*

The Englishmen arrived in Launceston on the
*Royal Shepherd* on 19 February 1862. After clearing
the docks they endured another boisterous welcome outside their hotel. To get some sleep for
his players, Stephenson went out on the hotel
balcony and, after introducing each man, asked
the crowd to disperse. His plan must have worked,
for when they went on to Hobart England beat
the Twenty-Two of Tasmania by four wickets.
When the match finished early another match was

arranged, one side captained by E. Stephenson,
the other by H. H. Stephenson.

At this point, Spiers and Pond, wallets
bulging, permitted the players to organise a match
in Melbourne between Surrey and the Rest of the
World. The six Surrey tourists had the help of
five local players born in Surrey and the remaining
six visitors teamed with five locals. The World
batted first and scored 211, Bennett playing
splendidly for 72. Surrey followed on after scoring
only 115 but made 179 in the second try, Caffyn
reaching 79. The World lost five wickets in
scoring the 83 needed to win. Caffyn and Bennett
received £10 each for their efforts.

Ballarat gave the English players a joyful
welcome and handed the tourists the proceeds of
a night at the local theatre. Twenty-Two of
Ballarat scored 122 and 107, England 155, and the
match ended in a draw. Ballarat organisers presented Tom Hearne with a prize bat for topscoring
with 37 not out. At Sandhurst, against Twenty-
Two of Bendigo, the Englishmen scored 257
against 81 and 103 to win by an innings. Caffyn
made 57 and Bennett 56. When the match finished
Charles Lawrence played a single-wicket game
against one of the Bendigo players, which he won
by scoring when his opponent bowled a wide.
Neither batsman scored in two innings. Twenty-
Two of Castlemaine ended the tourists' winning
run by defeating them by two wickets. They dismissed England for 80 and 68. Castlemaine scored
54 and 18 for 96. Then Griffith, Iddison and
Lawrence played eleven of the locals and beat
them.

The farewell match of the tour against
Twenty-Two of Victoria ended unsatisfactorily
when the Victorian captain insisted on drawing
stumps with England 12 runs short of outright
victory. The Victorian skipper claimed the original
agreement was that the match should not extend
beyond four days. England made 218 and 7 for
63, Caffyn again scoring freely for 45, Victoria
140 and 151. Spiers and Pond gave half the receipts
for the last match to the England players, who

*A lithograph, attributed to H. Deutsch, of the England XI batting against Twenty-Two of Ballarat at Ballarat in March 1862. This first English team played 11 of its 13 matches against sides of 22*

were also offered £1200 to stay a further month. The players refused because of commitments at home. After the match the English team planted 12 elm trees on the outskirts of the Melbourne ground.

Two of the Englishmen averaged more than 20 runs an innings. Caffyn totalled 419 at 23.27, including the tour's top score of 79, and Griffith scored 421 at 22.15. Iddison ran away with the bowling honours, taking 103 wickets at 6.61. No other England player reached 100 wickets, although some had a lower average. England lost only two of the 13 matches played. Of the matches against twenty-twos, 5 were won, 2 lost and 4 drawn. The match against an eighteen was won. Stephenson proved an admirable captain who could bat, bowl, keep wicket, make witty speeches and

hold his liquor. His fast round-armers had a pronounced break-back. He was regarded as one of England's best coaches and Australians benefited from his tuition. Caffyn and Iddison did most of the bowling, delivering more than 400 overs each.

Stephenson maintained that Australian bowlers were too predictable and needed to develop more variation. They also had to learn the science of attack, he said, mentioning how the great William Clarke walked around the practice nets on the morning of a game studying opponents and plotting their downfall without taking his coat off. He supported his argument by describing the wide range and subtlety of the bowling of William Lillywhite, which included the "tice", a yorker that Lillywhite could make drop at will.

Spiers and Pond made a profit of £11,000 from the tour, which the partners invested in fares to London, where they opened a refreshment room at the old Bishopsgate Station on the Metropolitan railway. They opened similar rooms at other railways and in 1873 pulled down an old inn and built the Criterion Hotel near Piccadilly Circus. Later they added more restaurants to their empire. The England team all received tour bonuses of 100 sovereigns.

The tour produced great improvement in the technique of Australia's best players. There was also a major coup when Charles Lawrence chose to remain in Sydney, accepting an offer of £200 a year to coach for the Albert Club. The English players had a pleasant voyage home; passengers were entertained by Caffyn on his cornet and the ship's cook on the trombone. (On one occasion the cricketers stuffed a towel down the trombone to render it pianissimo.) Asked his opinion of Australian players he had met on the tour, Roger Iddison exclaimed, "Well, oi doan' think mooch of their play, but they're a wonderful lot of drinkin' men!"

Word quickly spread among the cricketers of England about the lavish hospitality and warmth of the Australians' welcome to Stephenson's team. By then the major counties—Surrey, Yorkshire, Nottinghamshire, Lancashire, Kent and Middlesex—were all growing in strength, and county cricket had begun to overshadow matches involving the All England and United England teams. The Grace family had begun a marvellous tradition in Gloucestershire, E. M. Grace playing a series of wonderful knocks in 1862.

Umpire John Lillywhite took a historic step in August 1862, when he no-balled Edgar Willsher six times in succession for raising his arm above the shoulder when Willsher was playing for England against Surrey at The Oval. Willsher threw down the ball and stormed off, followed, with the exception of V. E. Walker and C. G. Lyttelton, by the other England players. Nobody believed Willsher's delivery was unfair but Lillywhite considered it his duty to no-ball him.

The Marylebone Cricket Club, which had been steadily growing in stature as arbiter of the laws of cricket, had had no control over the initial England tours to Canada and Australia. The club

became involved, however, when Lillywhite no-balled Willsher and two years later overarm bowling became legal. "Lillywhite was made the scapegoat; but he could console himself with the thought that by his firmness he had caused the lawmakers to act," wrote W. G. Grace.

Reports of the new bowling style took years to filter into all levels of the game in Australia, and indeed, when George Parr brought the second England team to Australia in 1864, the tourists as well as the locals still bowled underarm or round-arm. E. M. Grace, the sole amateur in Parr's team, preferred lob bowling. Once again the players enjoyed a round of banquets, champagne breakfasts and luncheons, interrupted spasmodically by a little cricket.

Parr's reputation had preceded him to Australia and the Australian cricket-loving public, seeing him play for the first time, soon realised

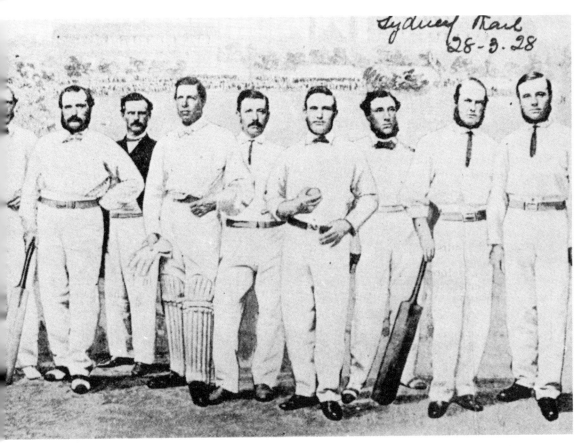

*Sydney Mail*
*28-3-28*

*The second All England team that toured Australia in 1864. George Parr (centre, holding bat), captain of the team, was known as "The Lion of the North". The only amateur in the side was E. M. Grace (second from left), a brother of W. G. and G. F. Grace*

why he was acknowledged as the finest leg-side hitter of all time, a batsman whose footwork had helped revolutionise batsmanship. He could play back and cut or hit square, or dance down the pitch to drive. He was a natural, uncoached player, his skills honed by years of practice. He was not much more than medium height, blue-eyed, of florid complexion with a thick chestnut moustache and whiskers. Australians did not encounter his legendary "queer temper". They saw instead a captain who allowed no slackness on the field and was held in awe by his men. One of his ancestors had been a noted batsman when the wicket was still formed by two stumps and a bail. In a colony where meals could be dependent on skill with a gun, George's marksmanship was widely admired.

Many have identified the Melbourne Cricket Club as sponsors of the second England tour, but there is no doubt it was organised and subsidised by Parr's old Nottinghamshire crony, George Marshall. Parr's terms are unknown. Marshall did receive support from the Melbourne Cricket Club, who helped stage the main tour matches on the Melbourne Cricket Ground. There was also a ready network of country centres within easy coach-ride of Melbourne, eager to put up guarantees for tour matches. The terms of the tour were set out in Parr's letter to Marshall, dated 21 February 1863, from Radcliffe on Trent:

*Your letter of 24th December last duly came to hand, and in reply I beg to say, on behalf of myself and other parties that we accept the proposals made by you to play a series of matches in Australia during the ensuing season, upon the terms named in your letters to me, for which purpose we propose to leave England in September next. The team will comprise some of the finest cricket talent in the world; amongst them are Dr E. M. Grace, T. Lockyer, R. Carpenter, T. Hayward, G. Anderson, J. Jackson, W. Caffyn, J. Caesar, G. Tarrant, and R. C. Tinley, who with myself and another to be selected will form the party. I am desired by all to express their wish that you provide us with free berths by the* Great Britain, *and advise me therefore that I may advise the other parties . . . We are glad to hear that the Melbourne Club have granted you the use of their ground and hope you will be equally successful in other localities.*

The last place in the England team was left to the players to decide. Parr wrote to Marshall that the controversial left-arm bowler Edgar Willsher was a certainty, but the place went instead to Andrew Clarke, of Nottingham, son of the founder of the All England Eleven, a useful cricketer renowned for his outfielding. Willsher's omission was left unexplained. Caffyn was the only member of the team who had toured with the first England team.

Parr received a letter from Charles Lawrence in Sydney offering terms for an alternative tour. Since arrangements had been completed with Marshall, Parr declined this offer and told Lawrence to contact Marshall if he wanted the English team to appear in Sydney. "Perhaps in a few months the feeling of displeasure against Mr Marshall in New South Wales may abate, or if not, you may be able to arrange terms with him as to our playing against you," Parr wrote. Tom Wills described Lawrence's bid to negotiate with Parr as vindictive and an insult to all Victorian players. Wills made the suggestion that Parr's team tour New Zealand and bypass the Sydney Domain and Maitland.

*The Melbourne Cricket Ground during the second England team's match against Twenty-Two of Victoria. A carpenter who brought a ladder charged spectators for help in securing vantage points in the trees*

At Liverpool, before they left, several members of the England team had difficulty in getting away from relatives who believed they would be attacked and eaten by blacks in Australia. Caffyn's cabinmate George Anderson became ill whenever the *Great Britain* struck even slightly rough weather and Caffyn spent most of the 61-day voyage nursing him. Tarrant had a jolly time fishing for seabirds with a piece of pork on a giant hook. E. M. Grace, a doctor of medicine

began before a crowd of 15,000 at the Melbourne Cricket Ground on 1 January 1864. The England team, pitted against Twenty-Two of Victoria, wore bow ties and white shirts flecked with red dots. There were no coloured ribbons on their helmets this time, and the cicadas in shrubs and trees around the ground rivalled the noise of the crowd. George Marshall faced the first ball, which went for two byes.

The Twenty-Two scored 145, England 176, with Tom Hayward and Bob Carpenter associated in a long stand. Hayward was a stylist, graceful and effective, who relished hitting the ball past midwicket and drove with a prominent flourish. Carpenter was the foremost exponent of his time of back foot play, quick on his feet and eager to lift the ball into vacant spaces. Hayward made 61, Carpenter 59.

The Twenty-Two made 143 in their second innings, leaving England 114 to win. The Englishmen moved the score along without fuss, expecting the match to be played out, but promptly at six o'clock, with England nine short of victory and six wickets left, the umpires drew stumps despite protests from spectators.

Marshall next sent England on a tour around Victorian country centres, Sandhurst (later renamed Bendigo), Ararat and Ballarat, where E. M. Grace defeated Tom Hayward in a 100-yard (91 metres) foot race. Tinley's high lobs confused all the country batsmen and caused several early finishes. Whilst there, E. M. Grace and George Tarrant played Eight of Ballarat at single-wicket cricket. The Englishmen scored 20, the locals 11. The coach trips were arduous affairs over barely discernible roads, every rut tossing players against each other. E. M. Grace provided a graphic description: "Driven by the coolest and ablest drivers that ever held the ribbons, the coaches dashed all night in and out of ruts and holes, over stones and mounds, round trees and logs, through creeks and gullies and waters that flow a foot deep into the coach itself."

The players took advantage of early finishes

like his brothers W. G. and A. Grace, found a diversion in extracting a troublesome tooth from Tarrant's upper jaw.

A carnival welcome awaited the Englishmen as their coach drove through Melbourne streets to Marshall's hotel, the Cricketers' Arms. During the two weeks they had to prepare for the first match, they went quail shooting and picnicking, were feted at dinners, and were guests at the Melbourne Cricket Ground when matches resumed between Victoria and New South Wales. From the outset there was criticism of several English players who attempted to profit from the sale of cricket equipment.

A tour described as a "continuous ovation"

to go off to the diggings. After good wins over Ararat, Maryborough and Castlemaine, they headed back to Melbourne where their captain had been recovering from an indisposition that had stopped him joining in the destruction of country bowlers and the fun of midnight sprints down main streets. By then the tourists had become used to bearded miners and squatters asking them about their old associates and masters at Eton, Harrow, Winchester, Rugby, Oxford or Cambridge.

Sydney newspapers published dozens of letters from their readers, arguing about the morality of charging spectators to watch the Englishmen on the Domain, a public park. There was still strong antagonism towards George Marshall because of his boycott of the latter part of the Sydney inter-colonial match of the previous year. Charles Lawrence wanted Parr's team to play several matches in New South Wales for a guarantee of £1600, plus expenses and 20 per cent of the takings, after deducting £2000 to cover his costs. Parr at first declined because of his obligation to George Marshall and instead took the Englishmen off to New Zealand.

They left Melbourne on 25 January, bound for Dunedin, where they were booked to play Twenty-Two of Otago on 2 February. The cricketers had a turbulent trip in their tiny ship, the *Alhambra*, and after being tossed about in their cabins for several days they anchored on 31 January at Port Chalmers, close to a Maori settlement. The players went ashore in a small boat and the Maori chief immediately took a fancy to George Parr. "Don't leave me, for goodness' sake," exclaimed Parr. "I don't like the look of this fellow." Poor Parr then had to go through the Maori ceremony of kissing all their women, which he felt certain would "make their men turn awkward".

Returning that night, Parr swore that he would never leave the *Alhambra* again, but next

*Two of the outstanding players in the second England team, Tom Hayward (left) and Robert Carpenter, in the uniform the players wore throughout the tour*

morning he was persuaded to join in a procession of boats in which the England team brought up the rear in a boat decked in flags. Guns were fired, bands played and a warm, noisy demonstration ushered the cricketers ashore. After lunch and speeches at the port's best hotel, they set off over the mountains for Dunedin, passing through superb scenery. Next day the Twenty-Two scored 71 and 83, England 99 and 1 for 58 on a very rough pitch. Tom Hayward took 15 wickets in the Twenty-Two's first innings and nine in the second. A match between a combined Twenty-Two of Canterbury was drawn.

Chris Tinley's lobs again routed the batsmen in the match at Christchurch, where England won by an innings and two runs; England scored 137, the Twenty-Two 30 and 105. There was a similar result in the return match at Dunedin, Tinley again bowling throughout, where the Twenty-Two of Otago scored 98 and 49, England 198. The Englishmen returned to Melbourne after planting memorial trees around the Dunedin ground. By the end of February details were finalised for matches in Sydney.

More than 20,000 people watched the first match against Twenty-Two of New South Wales, led by Charles Lawrence, which included "Ned" Gregory and his brother Walter, who later fathered three noted sportsmen. The Twenty-Two began with 137, then England scored 128. The locals were confident of victory, but heavy rain completely changed the situation and the Twenty-Two managed only 50 in conditions more familiar to the Englishmen. England lost six wickets in scoring the 60 needed to win. The return match, also on a wet pitch, ended in a draw; the Twenty-Two scored 102, and England 114.

The decisive third match was again affected by rain and the Twenty-Two made only 68 in their first innings. England headed this by only seven runs. Among the crowd was an eleven-year-old boy named Frederick Spofforth who admired George Tarrant as he strained every muscle to bowl faster than Australians believed possible. Tom

*Another of the elaborate newspaper layouts published during the second England team's visit, this one for the match against Twenty-Two of Victoria. The Victorian captain, George Marshall (centre), is the only local player in the layout*

a batsman who cut and pulled balls off the middle stump in defiance of style and purists. After he returned to England he became a coroner, noted for ordering post-mortems when he needed to get away to the cricket pitch. He fielded so close to batsmen that he inspired a quip that he wanted to have an inquest on himself. Overshadowed by his brother, W. G. Grace, he still scored 75,762 runs in all matches, with 122 centuries.

The excitement over the close England win in the Domain had barely subsided when the players boarded the steamer *Wonga Wonga* to return to Melbourne. A vast horde of people farewelled them at the wharf, but a few kilometres outside Sydney Harbour the ship collided with a small yacht, the *Viceroy*. The *Viceroy* sank almost immediately but a lifeboat from the *Wonga Wonga* saved all its passengers. Caffyn later recalled the event:

> *Poor George Parr was utterly dazed and paralysed with alarm. Tarrant quite lost his head. The first thing he did was to rush below to get a collection of curios given to him on the trip. Then when the boat was lowered he endeavoured to get into it, and was told by the sailors to keep out of the way in no very choice language. Julius Caesar, on the other hand, behaved in a manner worthy of his name, keeping very cool and collected, and doing all he could to assist the crew.*

Lockyer, England's wicket-keeper, was also admired as he gathered deliveries so wide of the stumps that most keepers would have left them to their long-stops. The Twenty-Two struggled to 83, leaving England 77 to win. Three England wickets fell quickly amid mounting tension as Caffyn and Hayward struggled for runs. They both made 17, but a rush of quick dismissals again had England in trouble. England's last pair managed to score the winning runs.

E. M. Grace was one of the team's most colourful characters, a brilliant point or long leg field who always wore a white handkerchief hanging from his belt. For years after this tour Sydney cricketers imitated him and newspapers often referred to fieldsmen who wore handkerchiefs "a la Grace". This was the cross-bat Grace,

While crewmen ascertained the damage in the dark, the players were very concerned about the women passengers on board. The *Wonga Wonga*, badly in need of repair, limped back to Sydney. Here it was discovered that John "Foghorn" Jackson, who had the habit of violently blowing his nose when he took a wicket, had failed to live up to his nickname, sleeping through the whole affair after "doing himself proud" at the farewell lunch.

The players boarded another ship for Melbourne two days later and immediately after arriving took a train to Geelong. Twenty-Two of Geelong scored 103 and 9 for 64; England replied with 135. Next they played a pick-up exhibition between "Tarrant's Eleven" and "Parr's Eleven" at Maryborough. After Parr's team had won by 50-odd runs Dr E. M. Grace challenged any six of the locals at single-wicket cricket. They accepted and the doctor batted for the rest of the day for 106 not out; the opposition were content just to say they had bowled at him.

In Ballarat, England scored 310, their highest score of the tour. Bob Carpenter made 121 of these—the first century by an English cricketer in Australia. George Parr's 65 included a liberal sprinkling of his famous leg-side hits. The match was drawn with the Twenty-Two of Ballarat scoring 127 and 15 for 48. The last fixture of the tour, against Twenty-Two of Victoria at Melbourne, was interrupted by rain and ended in a draw. The Twenty-Two made 150 and 17 for 83; England scored 131 in their only innings. Of the sixteen matches played, all against the odds, England won 10 and had 6 draws. Carpenter headed the batting averages with 399 runs at 22.11, thanks to his century in the second last match.

Throughout the tour George Parr was troubled by erysipelas (an inflammation of his skin), and although he was never as commanding a batsman as in England, his wit and modesty were very much admired by his opponents. England's fielding made a fine impression on every Australian cricketer.

The man who really made the tour for Parr's side, however, was Robert Crispin Tinley, a short-statured slow bowler of surprising skill from Nottingham. On ill-prepared pitches outside the major arenas he hoodwinked novice batsmen with ridiculous ease. His 171 wickets at 3.71 gave team-mates more leisure time than a side with only 12 players could have expected.

The tour also saw a touching transformation among the players towards their only amateur, E. M. Grace, who wrote:

> My position with the Eleven has been somewhat difficult. It required no great perception to see that any little occurrence might raise bad feeling. At first one or two had almost looked for chances to try and quarrel, but this had entirely passed. The Eleven had been attentive and kind to me, and now, when they were leaving me behind, two or three shook hands with me with tears glistening in their eyes.

Ten of the team sailed for Bombay on 26 April 1864, and E. M. Grace remained behind to visit friends. Each Englishman made £250 from the tour after expenses and went home laden with gifts and mementoes. William Caffyn stayed to take up a £300-a-year job as Melbourne Cricket Club professional. He had become engaged before he left England and when his fiancée joined him in Melbourne they were given a glittering wedding. Caffyn's seven-year stay in Australia was to have a profound effect on the development of Australian cricket.

# The Billy and Charlie Show

## The influence of English professionals

Australians coached by Englishman William Caffyn and Charles Lawrence developed contrasting batting styles. Lawrence, Australia's first paid coach, was a slightly-built man of medium height, regarded as a top-class all-rounder when he came to Australia at the age of 33. When he worked for the Albert Club, he stressed the value of playing back. Caffyn, on the other hand, never tried to make batsmen bat alike. If a man was a hitter, he encouraged him to hit; if he preferred stonewalling, Caffyn let him play naturally. Overall Caffyn liked his pupils to play forward.

William Caffyn was happy at the Melbourne Cricket Club where he could make suggestions to players about their technique and demonstrate the soundness of his ideas for hours in the nets. "The chief difficulty I had was in teaching them to keep the ball down when cutting, and for a long time they were at a loss to understand how I did this so successfully," he wrote. "I tried to

*Charles Lawrence, fourth from the left in this shot of Stephenson's team in Australia, was responsible, with Caffyn, for a dramatic improvement in Australian cricket standards*

impress upon them that the essential of cutting was in timing the ball accurately."

Caffyn made his highest score in Australia, 121 for the Melbourne Club against Richmond, but he never played for Victoria. After only a year in Melbourne he heard of a chance to return to his old trade as a barber in Sydney, and generously the Melbourne Club recognised his desire to set himself up for when his cricketing days were over and released him from his contract. His wife's skill in styling women's hair helped them prosper in Sydney, and Caffyn also got part-time work with the Warwick Club. Mrs Caffyn was very delicate, however, and doctors' calls were frequent. The Caffyns had numerous children—three sons and a daughter were born in Australia—but two sons died here.

Caffyn set high standards for his pupils but higher ones for himself. A reporter in *Cricket*, a weekly published in 1898, captured this search for excellence best after a Caffyn failure: "As Caffyn neared the dressing tent he flung first his bat from a distance of perhaps ten to fifteen yards. Next would follow a glove, then another, and finally Billy himself, stamping his feet, and telling us he ought to be horsewhipped for getting out".

Hairdressing in Sydney paid well and after a year Caffyn persuaded the Warwick Club to allow Edward ("Ned") Gregory, who belonged to the Albert Club, to share his coaching, each man working for three days a week. Caffyn continued to play regularly for the Warwick Club and for New South Wales and his presence undoubtedly intensified Victoria's desire to beat New South Wales. He returned somewhat reluctantly to England after seven years in Australia, after failing to secure a coaching job in Tasmania that would have aided his wife's health. Six years later his outstanding pupil, Charles Bannerman, scored Test cricket's first century.

Between them perfectionist Caffyn and gregarious Charlie Lawrence closed the gap between English and Australian cricket standards, lucky though they were to coach so many gifted young players. Both taught by example, demonstrating strokes in the nets. Often they took away the nets on one side of the field to show their pupils where to pitch the ball and how to field to it.

After he returned to England Caffyn reflected

ABOVE: *William Caffyn in the days when he was one of the finest players in the All England XI and known as "Terrible Billy". He had an important influence on Australian cricket as a coach*
RIGHT: *A photograph of William Caffyn after his wife's ill health forced him to return to England. He delighted in each success by an Australian team, knowing that he had laid the foundations for their exciting progress in the game*

John Coffey
1828 — 1912

on his charges in his book *Seventy-one Not Out*.

*Australians were delightful pupils, always willing to be shown a new stroke, quick to do their best to retrieve an error, never taking offence at having faults pointed out, never jealous of one another. It is not a matter of great surprise to me that Australian cricket has become what it has.*

*Their bowlers of forty years ago were undoubtedly in front of their batsman. Even at that time some of their bowling was very tricky in regards to variety of pace and break, although some seemed to lose confidence to attempt this 'head work' in a match, at which time they were usually content to bowl straight and keep a good length. Still, even at that time one could perceive the germs from which the present perfection in Australian bowling has sprung.*

He was also unstinting in his praise for Lawrence and his skill as a communicator. He was proud that Surrey had helped save the first England tour to Australia when the project seemed to be foundering: "It is very pleasant for me as a Surrey man to remember that my native county has been so closely connected with Australian cricket in its infancy".

Australian cricket was transformed during the ten years between the visit of the second team under George Parr in 1864 and the arrival of the third team in 1873. This was due to the perseverance of Caffyn and Lawrence and the migration of skilful English amateurs and a group of professionals from English county teams. Some of their fellow English professionals were not as decorous as others, but their influence added to Australia's growing expertise.

Sam Cosstick, a professional enticed to

*Sam Cosstick, for many years the Melbourne Cricket Club's main ground bowler. He played for Victoria and New South Wales in the first big matches against England after migrating from Surrey*

Australia by gold fever, joined the Melbourne Cricket Club when he left Surrey. There, wearing a white trilby, he was ready to bowl for hours at the nets to the members for a salary of £150 a year. But on the voyage to Sydney for the match against New South Wales at Christmas 1866, he and fellow migrant William Greaves were charged with being drunk. Before the match at the Albert Ground the organisers staged a 183-metre race between the Victorian and New South Wales cricketers. During the race Greaves fell down and, by blocking the path of other runners, enabled Cosstick to win the race by some 18 metres. Greaves claimed that he had fallen by accident, but in view of his close friendship with Cosstick cricketers found this hard to believe. Both performed badly in the cricket match, which led to Victoria's suggestion to the New South Wales intercolonial committee that professionals be excluded from future matches in the series. The Sydney match that year was a shambles from the outset, when the welcoming committee went down to the wharf to greet the Victorians, only to find they had arrived the day before.

Greaves was hired as a professional bowler at the Melbourne Cricket Club for the sum of ten shillings a day for four days a week. By the start of the 1867–68 season, however, the Melbourne Cricket Club committee had tired of the behaviour of both Cosstick and Greaves, and sacked them both. Tom Wills was brought in as the club's "tutor" at £3 10s 0d a week. Following an appeal Cosstick was reinstated and his term extended until the end of April 1868. Meanwhile Melbourne Cricket Club committeeman I. D. Kelly reported the disgraceful behaviour of players Conway and Hardcastle on a return journey from Ballarat on 11 April. Hardcastle admitted he was drunk during the trip and resigned from the club.

The Melbourne Cricket Club was always generous in its appreciation of outstanding cricket by its members. Cosstick and Wills both had their share of £5 bonuses when they performed well. Another who benefited from the club's magnanimity was Gideon Elliott, who was given Rowland Newbury's job as "pavilion keeper" when Newbury resigned to promote Aboriginal cricket.

The Albert Club was a powerful force in Sydney cricket under Charles Lawrence. It had the best ground, and several of the best players, and when matches between New South Wales and Victoria were discontinued in 1864, because of the controversial 1863 game, the Albert Club stepped in and arranged matches against the Melbourne Club, whose team included William Caffyn. The Albert Ground at Redfern was opened on 29 October 1864, with a match between "Eleven Players of the World" and Eleven of New South Wales. Lawrence led the World XI to victory. C. P. Moody, writing on the early intercolonial matches, commented on the role of Lawrence: "It was not so much with his bowling as with his correct batting, the feature of which was his back play, that Lawrence moulded and vastly improved the style of Sydney batsmen."

When intercolonial matches resumed in 1865 at Melbourne, the New South Wales team had abandoned "grubbing" bowling for the overarm style. Its members included four professionals: Lawrence, Caffyn, Ned Gregory and the Birmingham-born Nathaniel Thompson. Despite this, Victoria won by an innings and 20 runs. Wills scored 58 of the Victorian total of 285. New South Wales managed 123 and 143 in reply.

Careful levelling and regular rolling, which had been advocated by the first two English touring teams, led to better pitches which brought dramatic improvements in batting technique. The evolution from underhand to round-arm bowling created big improvements, too, in Australian bowling standards, although some observers found difficulty in deciding the difference between bowling and throwing. Harry Hilliard claimed that Wills threw for Victoria and Twopenny threw for New South Wales. Umpires began to watch the delivery style of all bowlers. Lawrence, the trendsetter, bowled with a high round-arm action, his arm swinging round level with the point of his shoulder. His style was a frequent topic of conversation at his "cricketing depot" in George Street near Circular Quay, where the struggling NSWCA held its meetings for several years.

At a crucial stage of a Melbourne game Wills deliberately overstepped the crease when he bowled. He then made a mark with his foot to which he called the umpire's attention. The umpire, who had already no-balled Wills twice for throwing, fixed his eyes on the mark. The cunning Wills then scattered the stumps with a deliberate throw without being called.

From the start of his coaching in New South Wales Lawrence realised that his pupils needed much wider experience, so he welcomed a challenge from Queensland in 1864. He advertised for cricketers willing to make the trip, and when 26 candidates turned up at his Sydney home suggested that they play three practice games to enable him to choose the best players. When Lawrence announced his team—Thompson, Foulis, Jones, Moore, Curtis, Crampton, Readet, Aylward, Clark, Ned Gregory and himself, with J. H. Neal twelfth man, Clayton as scorer and Richard Driver as umpire—the *Sydney Morning Herald* critic predicted disaster. He said few of the team would reach double figures and Queensland would win easily.

The captain of the steamer the *Telegraph*, which took the team north, refused to take shelter as heavy seas and gales battered the ship and the cricketers reached Brisbane a sick and sorry lot. Cheering crowds lined the Brisbane River and rockets lit up the sky as the cricketers disembarked, however, and their discomfort was soon forgotten. The *Telegraph*'s captain opened a crate of champagne to welcome the Brisbane officials aboard and at the team's hotel further celebrations continued far into the night.

June rains had flooded the ground and the Green Hills pitch at Countess Street, making play impossible on the day appointed. The next day, 3 June, Lawrence managed to find a dry space for the wicket to be pitched, with both ends covered in sawdust. There were still pools of water on the field when the Governor and Lady Bowen arrived but play began. The *Brisbane Courier* commented that:

> *The whole of the cricketers turned out and greeted the vice-regal party with three hearty cheers. As the day advanced the number of spectators increased; and here we may say to those who preferred to stay outside the fence and a bad view of the ground to paying one shilling for entrance that their conduct savours somewhat of meanness.*

The ball proved difficult to get away on the rain-soaked field and the New South Wales Eleven were bundled out for 32. The Twenty-Two of Queensland, chosen after weeks of trial matches, fielded admirably. T. B. Foden took 6 for 6, including the wickets of Gregory, Thompson and Lawrence. The Twenty-Two of Queensland had lost 7 for 16 by the end of the first day. The wicket-keeping of Joe Foulis, who stumped three and caught one batsman, was a revelation to the Queenslanders. One of his victims expressed amazement when he arrived back at the tent: "Thought the ball had passed the beggar".

Lawrence took 14 for 25 in Queensland's first innings of 45, Thompson 7 for 9. Although they had trailed by 13 runs, New South Wales took their score to 7 for 145 in the second innings and then dismissed the Twenty-Two for 49, to win by 83 runs. The Maitland all-rounder James Moore took 11 for 14 in Queensland's second innings. Thompson finished the match with a total of 28 (four-ball) maiden overs. The *Courier* summed up:

> *The very bad state of the ground could not but militate against the display of first-rate cricket;*

*Seven cricketers who played major roles in establishing Australia in international cricket: (L to R) (back) George Bonnor, Nat Thompson, Claude Beal, Harry Boyle; (front) Charles Lawrence, George Moore, Harry Hilliard*

*but in spite of frequent slips and capsizes, jumping after the ball into water holes, and other unavoidable mishaps, an amount of good play was exhibited by both sides.*

After the game there was further excitement when thirty uninvited guests had to be ejected from a players' banquet at the Victoria Hotel, presided over by the Colonial Secretary, the Hon. R. G. W. Herbert. The party continued until it was time for the interstate visitors to board the *Telegraph* for the return voyage to Sydney.

For three days the steamer ploughed through huge seas, which left other ships stranded on the beach. Waves sweeping over the vessel extinguished the galley fires and the cricketers and crew had nothing to eat. When the coal ran out the captain began burning deck fittings for fuel. Richard Driver pleaded with the captain to put him ashore, claiming that his presence was urgently needed in the New South Wales Parliament and he could travel more quickly by road. The captain complied only when the *Telegraph* reached the shelter of Broken Bay. With their belongings still on board the battered ship, the cricketers straggled along the road to Sydney, where debris from wharves and jetties swirled around the harbour and waves burst over Pinchgut.

Queensland played nine practice games before a team was selected to visit Sydney for their second intercolonial match in 1865. The Queenslanders had been strengthened by the decision of the Maitland professional bowler James Moore to play a season in Brisbane, but the lack of a control body still hampered development. This was clearly demonstrated by the unfortunate omission of T. B. Foden, one of the successes of the first intercolonial match. The team's travel and general expenses were raised by public subscription in Brisbane.

The Brisbane organising committee objected to the inclusion of Caffyn in the New South Wales team as they considered him "a Melbourne man".

Their fears proved justified when the Twenty-Two of Queensland were out for 50 and Caffyn proceeded to hit the Queensland bowlers all over the Domain. His 55 enabled New South Wales to reach 198. Lawrence took 12 for 24 in Queensland's second innings of 41, giving New South Wales victory by an innings and 107. Ten summers were to pass before a Queensland intercolonial match produced any surprises.

Matches between Victoria and Tasmania resumed in 1865 and continued until 1873. For the 1866 matches in Tasmania, the locals fielded teams of sixteen. The East Melbourne right-hand underarm bowler Daniel Wilkie mesmerised the Tasmanians in the first match in Launceston, taking 6 for 15 and 11 for 12, but in the second match at Hobart the Tasmanians produced an astonishing reversal. Tom Hogg bowled his shooters at will to help dismiss Victoria for 30 and 32. Victoria were handicapped when two players left for home after the first day, leaving nine to play sixteen.

At Sydney in 1866 New South Wales recovered from the previous season's slump, scoring 145 and dismissing Victoria for 74 and 58.

In December 1867, Dick Wardill returned to the Victorian team for the Melbourne match against New South Wales. After three wickets fell for 60 in this game, he shared a fourth wicket stand of 113 with the former Oxford University batsman George Robertson, the first century partnership in Australian first-class cricket. Wardill then went on to score 110, the first century in Australian first-class matches. When in form, Wardill hit the ball very hard, but he was an erratic character easily depressed by failure. In this match he batted with great confidence, and although Nat Thompson batted soundly to score 35 and 60, New South Wales made only 158 and 173 in reply to Victoria's 252. Wardill again dominated with 45 not out in Victoria's second innings of 3 for 82.

Dick Wardill was born at Liverpool, England, in 1835. He served at various times as secretary of the Melbourne Cricket Club and of the short-lived Victorian Cricketers' Association, and was a member of the intercolonial match committee. He made 383 runs in 10 first-class matches at 25.53. Off the field, however, he gambled heavily at cards and over a period absconded with £7000 from the Victoria Sugar Company, who employed him as a clerk. When his crime was discovered, Wardill confessed to the directors of the company. Before he could be charged, he ducked out of the back of his house in Punt Road, South Yarra, and drowned himself in the river. His body was not recovered for three days and it was reported that unscrupulous rivermen tried to extract £10 for the body from Wardill's relatives.

The sad death of Australia's initial first-class century-maker at the age of 38 was deeply felt by his brother — younger by seven years — Benjamin Johnson Wardill, who was also a migrant from Liverpool. The Wardills had played together in Victorian teams. Ben also worked for the Victoria Sugar Company until he became the first paid secretary of the Melbourne Cricket Club in 1878. He played against Parr's team in Melbourne, managed three Australian teams to England (1886, 1899 and 1902), and when he retired after 32 years, Melbourne Cricket Club's membership had grown from 400 to 6000.

The 1867 Victoria *v.* Tasmania match on the Melbourne Cricket Ground was one of the most thrilling of all intercolonial fixtures. Victoria, weakened by the absence of the Irish-born batsman Tom Kelly and the reliable Sam Cosstick, included for the first time Aboriginal players, Cuzens and Bullocky. All the Victorian fieldsmen had difficulty hitting the ball past 16 fieldsmen, and four run outs helped limit their first innings to 99. After Whitesides and Dumaresq began with a stand of 38, John Arthur made 39 and Tasmania reached 108. Hogg then bowled with great hostility to take 6 for 52. Only Dick Wardill was at ease against him, scoring 42 of the Victorian total of 96. Set 88 to win, the Tasmanian Sixteen went confidently to 30 before Whitesides was run out

and Dumaresq fell to a brilliant catch at point by Cuzens, who fell on his face but held the ball millimetres from the turf.

Every run scored now brought cheers as Tasmania edged closer to the target. Wills was at his exciting best in taking five wickets cheaply, but Walker got Tasmania home with an innings of 19 in which he was dropped several times. With eight runs needed, Bullocky dropped a simple catch at square leg. Tasmania took three runs from an overthrow. The winning run came from a cheeky bye after ten Tasmanian wickets had fallen. Tasmania won by five wickets, the precise start the Melbourne Club organisers had given them in each innings to try and produce a close match. In the grandstand Ben Wardill fumed behind his bristly moustache but as befitted a soldier with the rank of major in the East Melbourne Volunteer Artillery, he resisted commenting on the Victorians' sloppy fielding under pressure or the big advantage the MCC had mistakenly given the Tasmanians.

Tasmania's victory led to a stern warning from Ben Wardill that "If you are still desirous of playing odds against us, you are not to be surprised at the introduction of professional players. Otherwise we should have an exceedingly weak team." Tasmania repeated the dose at Hobart in 1868. After Tasmania scored 105, Victoria was again curbed by brilliant fielding and made only 62. Tasmania's second innings produced 146 and Glynn, Stewart and Daly then clinched a win by taking three wickets apiece. Tasmanian sixteens had thus defeated Victoria in three successive matches.

Pressure for a return to eleven-a-side matches emanated from southern Tasmania, but Victoria was not interested in the proposal unless professionals could be included in the teams. The Victorians argued that spectators would not attend cricket unless the best players were on view and that southern Tasmanians' suggestion would result in a loss of revenue. Faced with an "amateurs only" plea from Tasmania, the Melbourne Cricket Club decided, on the casting vote of the chairman, to reject the level terms proposal. The Southern Tasmanian Cricket Association responded with an ultimatum that the joint Tasmanian team for the next match would include only eleven players. The Northern Tasmanian officials had always argued that there was no honour in defeating inferior Victorian Elevens, but for the 1869 match they agreed to concede the point.

Victoria scored 409, the highest total ever on the Melbourne Cricket Ground, with Joe Phillips contributing 115, the second intercolonial century. Tasmania replied with 18 and 131, the brothers Arthur batting well in the second innings. Shocked by the one-sided and humiliating defeat, the Launceston Club informed the Southern Tasmanian Association in January 1870, that "as Victoria declines to play without professionals, Tasmania should play with 16 men". The south telegraphed its answer: "Prefer eleven. Professionals should not play". There were no Hobart players in the next match, and a Northern Sixteen was heavily defeated.

Cricket's reputation for good manners also suffered in a 1869–70 match between Sydney's Warwick and Albert Clubs when Alfred Park and Charlie Oliver had a punch-up in the centre of the field. Oliver was useful with the bat as well as with his fists and later that season set a record for an opening stand in Sydney by adding 155 with Dave Gregory for the Alberts against Sydney University, a stand that was unbeaten for six years until Alick and Charles Bannerman put on 285 for Warwick against East Sydney.

Victoria played an amateurs-only match against Tasmania in 1870 with unfortunate results. Tasmania began with 163 to which Victoria replied with 197. Harry Barrett, coming on late in the Victorian innings, took 5 for 8. Tasmania then collapsed for 36 in the second innings on a soggy pitch. Victoria lost interest in playing Tasmania for a further three years, concentrating instead on matches against New South Wales. Between 1867 and 1873, Victoria defeated New South Wales in seven consecutive matches, which

made play against Tasmania seem unimportant. Victoria and Tasmania met again in March 1873 but this was the last time for 16 years.

George Marshall died of "softening of the brain" attributed to sunstroke in 1868. The following year Tom Wills, already drinking heavily following the massacre of his family, retired from the Victorian team. Victoria found adequate replacements in Frank Allan, a fast-medium left-arm bowler who could make the ball swing disconcertingly, and an influx of English visitors. The Reverend (later Canon) Edwin Sardison Carter demonstrated his Yorkshire expertise with an innings of 63 in 1868, playing the strokes that had got him into Oxford University and I Zingari teams. (One commentator remained unimpressed with Carter, saying Victoria could easily raise an eleven capable of beating eleven amateurs like him.) Lieutenant Charles Gordon, of the Buckinghamshire Regiment, made 121 in his sole appearance. Bransby Beauchamp Cooper, the Indian-born former Middlesex, Kent and Gentlemen batsman, played 11 intercolonial matches, with a top score of 45.

Allan's 8 for 102 and 8 for 20 in his first appearance on the Sydney Domain in 1870 won rapturous reviews. The Sydney match in 1871 was moved from the Domain to the superior Albert Ground pitch where batsmen immediately benefited. Most Sydney clubs were delighted by the change, as it ended the dominance of the Australian Club based at the Domain, and gave all clubs a financial boost. All spectators had to pay at the Albert Ground whereas many had watched cricket free at the Domain.

The 1871–72 season produced the historic "lost ball match" between Melbourne and East Melbourne. There was a dispute over the number of runs scored before a fieldsman called "lost ball". The two runs involved represented the difference between a tie and an East Melbourne victory. At the end of play the East Melbourne scorer, Charlie Hipwell, could not balance his books. Both teams' scorebooks were then locked up over the weekend.

*The Victoria v. New South Wales match held at Melbourne in 1870, and won by Victoria. By this time intercolonial matches had become highly fashionable affairs and were frequently used as meeting places for politicians, judges and soldiers*

The following Monday Melbourne had the two runs disallowed and East Melbourne were declared the winners. The dispute was made worse by lack of a central control body which could have dealt with it.

New South Wales and Victoria had plenty of talented batsmen in the early 1870s, but New South Wales had only one efficient bowler for the two seasons following the departure of Caffyn and Lawrence. This was Joseph Coates, a left-arm medium pacer who had learned swing and cut in Huddersfield. Coates narrowed the margin between the states to 21 runs in 1873 by taking 6 for 21. Finally, after four wins in 12 matches, New South Wales broke through in 1874 when Coates found a menacing partner in Frederick Robert Spofforth, the Balmain-born son of a Yorkshire migrant. Spofforth began bowling underarm as a schoolboy at Hokianga in New Zealand but switched to overarm when he returned to Australia and was inspired by the bowling of Englishman George Tarrant. Spofforth confessed that when he switched styles, learning swing and change of pace, he found it difficult not to throw.

Spofforth and Coates ended the Victorian stranglehold on intercolonial cricket with the assistance of Caffyn's best pupil, Charles Bannerman. He first took the field for New South Wales in 1870–71 but did nothing exciting until he played innings of 81 and 32 not out in 1874. Tom Kelly made 86 for Victoria but it was not enough and New South Wales began a sequence of seven straight wins. This match also saw the first appearance of Victorian Tom Horan, and right-handed Jack Blackham, who became known as "the prince of wicket-keepers".

Australia's bowlers reached a high standard in the 1870s. This was demonstrated by the wins of both Victorian and New South Wales sides over Dr W. G. Grace's tourists in 1873, although both local sides did have extra men. The switch to two matches each summer between Victoria and New

South Wales undoubtedly lifted the standard. At Sydney in 1875, newcomer Edwin Evans and Joe Coates for New South Wales and Cosstick and Billy Midwinter for Victoria bowled superbly. New South Wales won by 71 runs.

Evans's talent had first been recognised at Newington College. He was hailed as the successor to Wills as Australia's best all-rounder and justified this in a sensational debut at Melbourne in December 1875. Victoria began with 136, of which the consistent Kelly scored 71. Charles Bannerman matched it with 83 out of 171. Trailing by 35 runs in the first innings, the Victorians remained confident as the opposition had last use of the pitch. Bowling unchanged, Evans and Coates removed them for 34, giving New South Wales victory by an innings and one run. Evans's accuracy overpowered Victoria, and he finished with an analysis of 17.3 overs, 13 maidens, 16 runs and seven wickets.

New South Wales were in the happy position of having four top-class bowlers—Coates, Evans, Spofforth and Tindall. If any one of the leading trio failed, Edwin Tindall, a highly competent medium-pacer from the Albert Club, could be relied upon. William Lloyd Murdoch, born at Sandhurst, Victoria, in 1854, joined the New South Wales team in 1876, highly recommended by his mentor Charles Lawrence. Hugh Hamon Massie first played in 1877 and Tom Garrett and Alick Bannerman in 1878, when Percy McDonnell and "Joey" Palmer joined the Victorian team.

The Sydney record for the highest innings total was lifted to 500 in March 1878, when Harry Moses and a batsman named Cape both hit centuries and enabled the Commercial Bank to beat the Joint Stock Bank by 435 runs. Three weeks later The King's School improved on this with 532 against Oaklands, who scored only 65 in reply; W. S. Brown, J. Hillas and E. Pell all made centuries for the school. The record for the lowest score went to a Marlborough junior team, who failed to score at all against the Undaunteds.

South Australia, ignored by the first two

*Tom Garrett, one of Caffyn's keenest pupils, was a right-hand batsman of rare quality even in his school days. He later became Australia's youngest ever Test cricketer*

English teams to Australia, played its first inter-colonial match in 1874 when a strong Victorian eleven went to Adelaide and defeated Eighteen of Adelaide by 15 runs. On their new oval South Australia made a dramatic improvement and in 1876 a South Australian Eighteen dismissed a Victorian Eleven for 29 and 51; W. O. Whitridge took 8 for 10 in the first Victorian innings.

South Australian administrators regarded professionals as necessary to improve standards, but dispensable if they misbehaved. The minutes of the South Australian Cricket Association for 1874 recorded an offer by a Mr Cole to play for the Eighteen of Adelaide against Victoria. "It was resolved that Cole's offer to play for £5 be declined but that the match committee be authorised to pay Cole a sum not exceeding two guineas to reimburse him for actual loss." Another request was made by J. E. Goodfellow who asked for a match fee of a guinea a day to play against Lord Harris's English tourists in 1878. The South Australian Cricket Association, not acting very consistently, refused Goodfellow's offer and barred him from all association matches in that season. In the minutes of the association, professionals were always referred to without the prefix Mr or their initials, although amateurs received these courtesies.

Jesse Hide's appointment as the South Australian Cricket Association's coach brought major improvements but it was not until 1880 that South Australia again played Victoria, this time on level terms at the East Melbourne ground. Victoria piled up 329, Horan making 113, and Fred Baker 83. The South Australians failed to handle William Cooper's big leg breaks in their first innings, scoring only 77. Following on, they recovered splendidly, reaching 314. Will Slight made 70, George Giffen 63, H. Gooden 49 and Hide 48. The South Australian seven-wicket defeat away from home was creditable. Victoria and South Australia met annually after that for a further 16 intercolonial competitions.

Aborigines had taken so readily to cricket in the early years of white settlement that several settlers saw big possibilities in exploiting their skills. They seemed to have a natural aptitude for the game, for they were quick-footed, had strength and whip in their shoulders and arms and easily mastered fundamentals. Initially they were used to make up numbers, batting last and rarely securing a bowl. They quickly proved worthy of better treatment.

When the pastoral lands around Harrow and Edenhope in western Victoria were taken up in the 1840s, two Aborigines, Peter and Bullocky, became regular members of teams raised on the properties. By 1865 there were records of Aboriginal teams defeating white teams. In 1869

*The Sussex all-rounder Jesse Hide spent several seasons (from 1878 to 1883) in South Australia as curator of the Adelaide Oval. His coaching vastly improved standards throughout the State, helping South Australia win intercolonial matches*

Johnny Taylor caused a minor sensation in the Canberra region when he scored 35 runs from a four-ball over at a time when all hits were run out. Only in Tasmania, where Aborigines had been systematically slaughtered in the 1830s and 1840s, were there no Aboriginal cricketers.

William Hayman was so enthralled with Aboriginal players at Edenhope that he sent pictures of them in action to a man named Rowley, a partner with a Mr Bryant in the firm which ran a large refreshment tent at Melbourne Cricket Ground. Hayman suggested a match at the ground, mainly in the interests of raising funds for Aboriginal welfare. This action led to the first tour of England by an Australian team, an Aboriginal side led by Charles Lawrence, which played 47 matches in 15 English counties between May and October 1868.

# Boomerangs at Lord's

### The Aboriginal tour of England 1868

The tour by 13 Australian Aborigines ten years before a white Australian team was a venture that failed to yield big profits, but it put spear-throwing tribesmen who occasionally dressed in possum skins onto 40 English cricket fields. The Aborigines, all full bloods, were a curiosity in a world still debating Darwin's *Origin of Species.* They were a colourful group who avoided liquor as best they could and won as many matches as they lost at a time when Australia's white cricketers were simply not up to touring standard.

Their trip had its origins in the Lake Wallace region of western Victoria. The Aboriginal cricketers were chiefly from two tribes, the Madimadi and the Wutjubaluk, who ranged over land in the vicinity of the towns of Bringalbert, Apsley, Harrow and Edenhope. Most of them worked on properties where they were fed and clothed in return for labour and taught to play cricket by the sons of pastoral pioneers.

D. J. Mulvaney, in his excellent book on the 1868 tour, suggests that cricket's communal team

*Some of the Aboriginal team that visited England photographed, before they left, in Melbourne. Tarpot, coach Tom Wills and Mullagh are at the rear. At the front: (L to R) Rose, Bullocky, Cuzens, Peter, Paddy, Dick-a-Dick, Watty and Twopenny. Wills dropped out of the venture before the side sailed*

organisation and the accompanying barracking provided the Aborigines with a substitute for the lost rituals of ceremonial life. To William Hayman, who ran the Edenhope cricket team, they were just darned good cricketers who might bring some publicity to the district.

Initially Hayman had no thought of financial gain when he sent pictures of the Aboriginal cricketers to Rowley and Bryant, suggesting a sponsored match. Rowley and Bryant accepted the idea and arranged for Tom Wills to go to Edenhope to coach the team. Wills must surely have pondered the irony of accepting such a job—it was only five years since the massacre of his family in Queensland—but he spent seven months coaching the black cricketers.

On Boxing Day 1866 Wills and Hayman took the team to the Melbourne Cricket Ground. Playing before 10,000 spectators produced extreme nervousness in the players and seven of them were out for ducks. Johnny Mullagh's 16 and Bullocky's 14 enabled them to scrape 39 together. Mullagh dismissed both Melbourne Cricket Club openers cheaply but Dick Wardill made 45 before the club were all out for 100. Mullagh scored 33 in the second innings and Wills 25 not out, but the MCC won the match early on the second day by nine wickets. At a sports meeting, an integral part of early cricket matches, organised on the third day, the Aborigines gave a display of boomerang- and spear-throwing. Tarpot also ran 91.5 metres backwards in 14 seconds, Mullagh cleared 2.2 metres in the high jump, and also threw a cricket ball almost 101 metres.

The Melbourne *Herald* praised the team.

*That they have been thoroughly acquainted with various points of the game was manifestly evident by the manner in which they conducted themselves on the field. Mullagh and Bullocky showed themselves to be no mean batsmen. They not only stopped balls, but hit them, showing good direction and strong defence. Their fielding was very fair.*

*The Aboriginal team that went from Western Victoria to Melbourne to play the Melbourne Cricket Club XI on Boxing Day 1866: (L to R) Mr Hayman, Captain, Sugar, Jellico, Cuzens, Needy, Mullagh, Bullocky, Tarpot, Sundown, Tom Wills, who umpired, with Officer and Peter seated in front*

Three weeks later Mullagh and Cuzens were included in the Victorian XI to play Sixteen of Tasmania, the first of their race chosen for inter-colonial cricket. On the day of the match Mullagh was ill and Bullocky took his place. Tasmania won by five wickets, and the *Age* claimed that Victoria's defeat was due to Mullagh's absence.

One of the spectators at the Aborigines' Melbourne display was a mysterious Englishman,

"Captain" W. E. B. Gurnett, who offered Wills and Hayman a year-long contract for a tour by the team around the colonies and to England. Hayman returned to Edenhope at this point to recruit more players. (It is interesting to note that before enlisting a player he asked permission of the owner of the property where the man worked, although the Aborigines were not legally bound to the whites.) When Wills took the team to matches at Geelong, Bendigo and Ballarat, the first suggestions that he and Hayman were exploiting the Aborigines were made, the first of several controversies about the team and the tour.

Advertisements appeared in Melbourne newspapers on 2 February 1867 announcing that the Aborigines would play a second match a week later on the Melbourne Cricket Ground as a prelude to their departure for England via Panama. On the morning of the match only two members of the Melbourne Cricket Club turned up before a small crowd, but a scratch game between the Aborigines and a side called the "County of Bourke" was arranged. Although the *Age* had reported that some of the cheques issued by Gurnett to pay for expenses in Bendigo had been dishonoured, Gurnett arrived at the ground to introduce the Aborigines to the governor. After the day's play the governor presented Cuzens with a bat, a prize for the best batting in the game, despite the efforts of a newcomer described as "Paddy the slogger" who was reported to have hit hard and often.

Following the *Age*'s disclosures, R. Brough Smyth, secretary of the Central Board for the Protection of Aborigines, wrote to the Victorian Chief Secretary expressing concern that the Aboriginal team might be abandoned and left destitute in England. Smyth argued that the promoters of the tour should lodge a guarantee with the government to ensure the team's safe return; otherwise the government should cancel the tour. The Chief Secretary replied that the government had no legal right to interfere.

Amid suggestions that they would perish from disease in England, the Aborigines moved on to a two-day match against the Albert Club in Sydney. The governor of New South Wales watched the Sydney team defeat the Aborigines by 132 runs. Caffyn thought so little of their play that he challenged the entire team to play him at single-wicket cricket, but the challenge was not accepted.

Before the Aborigines took the field Captain Gurnett attempted to have Wills and Hayman arrested for breach of contract and play only proceeded when Charles Lawrence agreed to act as guarantor. Mulvaney believes that Gurnett was the one who defaulted and that this action was merely a subterfuge. Nevertheless, the team was left stranded in Sydney after the match and it fell

*The Aboriginal team practising at the Melbourne Cricket Ground before their tour of England in 1868*

to Hayman to hastily arrange games and raise enough money to get the players home. They returned to Melbourne, penniless, at the beginning of May. The local Lake Wallace paper, the *Hamilton Spectator*, concluded: "It is evident that Hayman and his blacks entrusted themselves into hands which were not quite trustworthy".

The black players returned to Edenhope and dispersed, all hope of a tour of England apparently gone. Hayman said he had lost £400 on the venture, Gurnett had not been seen since the last Sydney match and Wills had terminated his association with the team in Melbourne. The cost to the Aborigines had also been high. Sugar had died before the first match at the Melbourne Cricket Ground, although he appears in photographs of the "Aborigine Cricket Club" taken before the game. His replacement Watty died on the road home, Jellico and Paddy never regained

their health and died of pneumonia after they returned, while Tarpot and Dick-a-Dick were both seriously ill.

The inquest into Watty's death revealed that he and other members of the team had been continually drunk and that the majority of the players had been completely unable to cope with the living conditions encountered on their trip. The survivors would be permanently affected by their exposure to the white man's city life.

Within three months, however, the team was reconstituted, its members practising daily around the shores of Lake Wallace. Charles Lawrence, who at that time mixed coaching with hotel keeping in Sydney, arrived in the district with George Smith, a former Mayor of Sydney, and a G. W. Graham, and they expressed themselves keen to back a tour of England. Lawrence took over the captaincy, supervised practice and designed striking uniforms that were to become a major feature of the team's subsequent appearances.

Lawrence had learnt from his experience with

the All England Eleven and produced separate uniforms for cricket and athletics. For cricket the team wore red shirts, known as Garibaldis, with white linen collars, white flannel trousers, blue belts and neckties, and blue and white diagonally striped flannel sashes, with merino undershirts for warmth. The outfit was topped off with coloured peaked caps, each player having his own colour. For athletics they wore coloured caps and trunks and long white tights, and for displays of spear and boomerang throwing and other warrior-like pursuits, they wore possum or kangaroo skins across their loins and shoulders.

Lawrence wore a white cap; Red Cap, a black cap; Mullagh, red; Cuzens, purple; Dick-a-Dick, yellow; Mosquito, dark blue; Peter, green; Jim Crow ("Neddy"), pink; Bullocky, chocolate; King Cole, magenta; Sundown, checks; Harry Rose, Victoria plaid; and Twopenny, the player Lawrence brought with him from New South Wales, wore a McGregor plaid. The players sometimes exchanged caps or wore sashes that were individually coloured but there is no doubt they were strikingly garbed.

Despite the debacle of the first tour Lawrence persuaded Victorian newspapers that the Aborigines would prove worthy representatives of the colony in England. Good crowds watched a series of matches to raise funds for the trip and newspapers declared that Lawrence's association with the team was "sufficient guarantee that on this occasion the whole affair is genuine".

The team departed from Edenhope on 16 September 1867, in a wagon so crowded that Cuzens was thrown out on his head when the wagon hit a rut. Luckily he was not seriously hurt, and was able to continue the journey with the other 12 players, a cook, Lawrence, Hayman, all their gear and the coachman. Charley Dumas replaced Harry Rose, who returned home to Geelong, where Tarpot also joined the party. Two of the players, Dick-a-Dick and Red Cap, were the trackers who had won Australia-wide admiration in 1864 when they found Isaac, Frank

and Jane Duff, the children who went missing from Spring Hill station, north of Apsley, for nine days.

At Warrnambool the team posed for special individual photographs. Only Johnny Mullagh, Cuzens, Red Cap and Bullocky wore their cricket ensembles, and by chance it was these three that proved the team's most reliable and consistent players in England. The rest wore animal skins or their athletic uniforms and were photographed with clubs, spears or parrying shields. They also played a match at Warrnambool, dismissing a local sixteen for 19 and 24 and scoring 140 to win comfortably. Mullagh made 48 not out and then took 10 wickets. Lawrence maintained firm control over his players in this match, which proved invaluable in discounting rumours that the majority of the team had been drunk when they left Lake Wallace.

The Aborigines next played a draw at Geelong and while the newspapers and the Central Board for the Protection of Aborigines debated claims that they were being exploited, the team slipped aboard the *Rangatira* off Port Phillip Heads and moved on to Sydney. Almost unanimously newspapers applauded what Mulvaney calls "a shrewd and contemptuous gesture", and said that in smuggling the Aborigines onto the ship Hayman and Lawrence had been too smart for the Board.

After matches at Wollongong, West Maitland, Singleton and Newcastle, the team played two final matches at the Albert Ground. Big crowds turned out for the second match against an Army and Navy team which included William Caffyn. Almost 5000 people saw the home team dismissed for 64, with Cuzens taking 8 for 23. The Aborigines then scored 237, of which Cuzens made 86. It ended in a draw after the second day with Army and Navy 2 for 51, before 9000 spectators. Lawrence's team appeared in a display after the game. The highlight was a mock battle between two sides of six men, wearing possum skins and multicoloured headdresses made up of broad plaited bands of cabbage tree leaves and a crest of lyrebird plumage.

*Tom Wills (far left) with the Aboriginal players after a practice session in Melbourne. The players had to be shipped out of Victoria in secrecy so as to dodge opponents of the English tour*

Tarpot went on board the *Parramatta*, which was to take the team to England, but became ill and had to stay in Australia. Lawrence, then in his fortieth year, accompanied the team with Hayman and Smith, who acted as business manager. After a voyage of three months, which included a stop in Hong Kong, the team reached

Tiger played in all 47, Twopenny in 46, Dick-a-Dick and Mullagh in 45. William Shepherd, an old Surrey professional who travelled as the team's umpire, had to play in seven matches and captained them when Lawrence rested. Hayman was an enthusiastic scorer throughout.

They played mostly on rough fields. Only the main grounds employed groundsmen and even at Lord's a flock of sheep was left to graze for two or three days before games to keep the grass down. Just four years earlier the Sussex team had refused to play at Lord's because of the poor condition of the ground. Underarm and round-arm bowling coexisted with the overarm style that had become legal when the laws of cricket had been revised in 1864.

Cricket historian Arthur Haygarth wrote that the Aborigines played their matches either for £200 a game, or for the entire match proceeds less £20 paid to the host clubs. Haygarth described the tour as "very lucrative". Other writers of the time stated that although the tour was financially successful, expenses were so high that the profit was small. Nevertheless one of the sponsors, George Smith, profited sufficiently to buy several stallions which he sent back to Australia. Despite the fondness for grog they shared with white men, the team arrived on time for all its matches, and alcohol proved a problem only at Lord's, where Bullocky failed to complete the game.

"Nothing of interest comes from Australia except gold and black cricketers," commented the London *Daily Telegraph* when the team reached Gravesend and began practising for their first game on 25 May. Between then and the last match on 15 October, the Aborigines exhibited immense stamina. Travelling frequently in uncomfortable conditions over rough roads they overcame major setbacks, especially King Cole's death of tuberculosis in Guy's Hospital, London, on 24 June, and the illnesses which forced Sundown and Jim Crow to be sent home in August. Down to 11 plus their white leaders, the side overcame fatigue in a manner which one sportswriter considered

England for a tour that was to see them on the field for 99 days out of a possible 126. They faced a programme of only 10 matches when they arrived, but proved so popular they played an additional 37. Lawrence, who captained the side, took part in more than forty matches. Redcap and

incredible. They played 11 matches in September and six in October, in cold conditions far more unpleasant than any encountered later by white Australian teams.

English newspapers found them a novelty at first and focused on their gait and their physical shape, but largely lost interest after the first few matches. *The Times* sent a reporter to the first game at The Oval and another to Lord's, but he wrote that the Aborigines' play was a "travestie upon cricket". After that the paper ignored them. But, in a cold summer, they regularly attracted crowds of 5000. The *Sheffield Telegraph* dubbed their opening game "decidedly the event of the century". The *Rochdale Observer* called them "stalwart men, of manly, dignified and confident gait and bearing". Other papers expressed surprise at their "gentle and by no means unintellectual appearance".

There were no tea breaks in their matches and lunch occupied just 35 minutes between 2 p.m. and 3 p.m. They were not provided with lunch and had to compete with spectators who crowded the refreshment tents. At York they were barred from the luncheon tent. This snub upset Johnny Mullagh but was treated as a joke by his team-mates. Most centres looked after them well and the Surrey club entertained the whole side to dinner. A Surrey man, Julius Caesar, who had toured Australia with Parr's team in 1864, also acted as an umpire in one of their matches at The Oval.

Lawrence's skill in public relations served the team well. His informative press notes were quoted directly so that rival newspapers often used identical phrases. *Sporting Life*, for instance, was given a list of the players' tribal names and the common names by which white people knew them:

| | |
|---|---|
| Dick-a-Dick | Jungunjinanuke |
| Peter | Arrahmunijarrimun |
| Johnny Mullagh | Unaarrimin |
| Cuzens | Zellanach |
| Sundown | Ballrinjarrimin |
| King Cole | Brippokei |
| Tiger | Bonmbarngeet |
| Red Cap | Brimbunyah |
| Bullocky | Bullchanach |
| Mosquito | Grougarrong |
| Jim Crow | Jallachmurrimin |
| Twopenny | Murrumgunarriman |
| Charley Dumas | Pripumuarraman |

*Sporting Life* noted that no arrival since "the ingenious George Martin brought Deerfoot from America to contend with English pedestrians" had been anticipated with such curiosity as that of the black Australians. The paper added that it should not be inferred that the Aborigines were savages— "they are perfectly civilised, having been brought up in the bush to agricultural pursuits as assistants to Europeans".

The Marylebone Cricket Club committee initially voted against staging a match at Lord's but later reversed their decision. They prohibited a sports display or an exhibition of warrior skills. Despite this the Aborigines recognised the crowd's wish to see their tricks and demonstrated their use of weapons. This historic match, the first by Australians at the game's headquarters, saw the men from Edenhope opposed to a Marylebone team which included an earl, a viscount, a captain, and a lieutenant-colonel who was out twice without scoring to Cuzens' bowling. Cuzens bowled 60 overs and took 10 wickets for 117 runs. MCC won with scores of 164 and 120, compared with 185 and 45. The Australians were hampered by Bullocky's absence in the second innings. W. G. Grace said the Aborigines played well and showed conspicuous skill at the game.

Only a handful of the players had real cricket talent but others, such as Charley Dumas, made

*A photograph at Lord's of the Aboriginals who toured England ten years before the first visit by white Australians. George Smith (top, centre) financed the tour and William Hayman (bottom) managed the team*

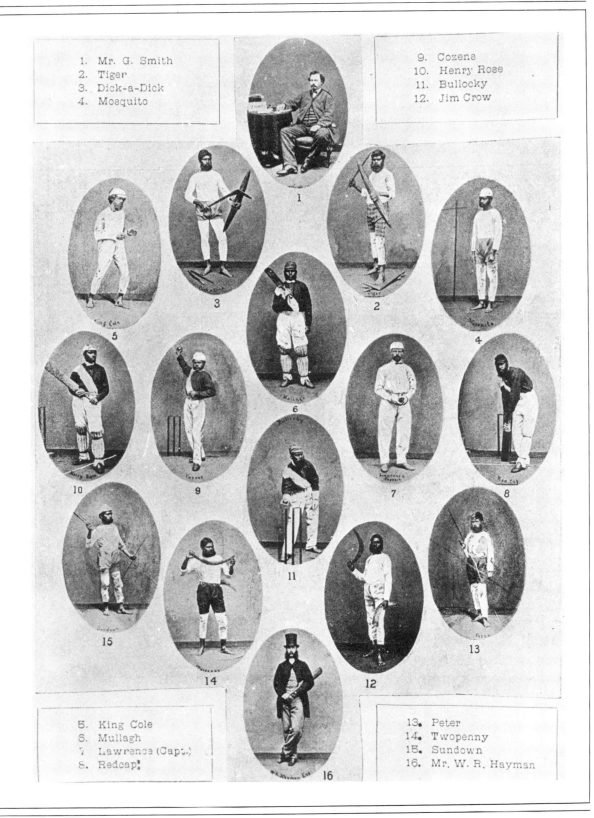

1. Mr. G. Smith
2. Tiger
3. Dick-a-Dick
4. Mosquito

9. Cozens
10. Henry Rose
11. Bullocky
12. Jim Crow

5. King Cole
6. Mullagh
7. Lawrence (Capt.)
8. Redcap.

13. Peter
14. Twopenny
15. Sundown
16. Mr. W. R. Hayman

up for this with their skilful demonstrations of native weapons.

At Bramall Lane, Sheffield, Twopenny drove a ball past mid-on which the fieldsman at first refused to chase, and then only at a sullen jog. Meanwhile Twopenny and his partner ran nine. The Surrey club presented a talent award of a sovereign to Mullagh when he scored 33, and then 73 in 130 minutes. Mullagh achieved the highest score of the tour at Reading, where he made 94. Mullagh, Cuzens and Lawrence dominated the side's bowling, sending down 4324 of the 4983 four-ball overs bowled. These three bowlers took 609 wickets, compared with 105 by the rest of the team. The wicket-keeping was shared among Twopenny, Mullagh, Cuzens and Lawrence. Dick-a-Dick occasionally took brilliant catches but the rest of the fielding was ordinary. Their running between wickets was poor, and there were some 60 run outs on the tour.

There were frequent accusations that Twopenny and to a lesser extent Cuzens were "chuckers", partly because few umpires could differentiate a legitimate delivery from a throw. The bowlers did well to limit their opponents to only three centuries in the 47 matches played: A. N. Hornby scored 117 for East Lancashire, J. C. Gregory 121 not out for Gentlemen of Surrey, and G. M. Royle 100 not out for Nottinghamshire Commercial Club. Perhaps the outstanding feat against the Aborigines was by J. Smith, whose 6 for 28 for South Derbyshire included four wickets in one four-ball over.

Boomerang and spear-throwing delighted spectators everywhere, although at Bootle one of Mullagh's boomerangs veered off-course in a high wind and sliced through a spectator's hat, gashing his head open. Dick-a-Dick was one of the great attractions of these exhibitions, running backwards at speed and deflecting balls thrown at him from metres away with a parrying shield. Hundreds of balls were thrown at him in these displays but none ever struck him.

A big crowd-pleaser was the cricket ball throwing segment of their displays. Dick-a-Dick or Mullagh usually resisted challenges comfortably with throws varying between 87 and 100 metres. They were outthrown only at Nottinghamshire by a player named Hardcastle, and by a 20-year-old W. G. Grace, who had throws of 106, 107 and 108 metres.

The Aborigines' uncanny accuracy at hurling spears with the assistance of wooden spear-throwers amazed students of weaponry in their audiences. In a display at Trent Bridge three spearmen were completely hemmed in by spears thrown from up to 73 metres away. A spear from a throwing stick cut a dog in half at The Oval. One of Lawrence's best tricks was to catch a ball thrown hard and high at him from across the field on the blade of his bat.

Late in October 1868 the team boarded the 1118-tonne *Dunbar Castle* for the voyage home. They arrived in February 1869, almost exactly one year after they left, but were required almost immediately for a match in Sydney, which fortunately was washed out. A three-day match in Victoria was drawn and their tour ended in a spate of runs, the Aborigines scoring 9 for 331, and the Duke of Edinburgh's ship, HMS *Galatea*, 5 for 293. Proceeds were donated to the Aborigines but small crowds meant poor pay. The players did not receive any tour bonus but neither did they travel steerage on the voyage home or fall victim to disease, as opponents of the tour had predicted.

They were reported back in Hamilton in March, 17 months after they had left. Most of them died prematurely and in obscurity. Only Johnny Mullagh achieved any fame and he remains a legendary figure in the region where the team was recruited. A quiet, peaceful man of some tenderness, he never married because he could not bring himself to marry one of the black women of the district and no white woman would have him.

Mullagh never appeared in intercolonial cricket but he did play for the Victorian team against Lord Harris's touring England party in

# Tour Averages

*All overs were four-ball*

|  | Batting | | | | | |
|---|---|---|---|---|---|---|
| *Name* | *Matches Played* | *Completed Innings* | *Times Not Out* | *Total* | *Highest Score* | *Average* |
| Mullagh | 45 | 71 | 4 | 1,698 | 94 | 23.65 |
| Lawrence | 40 | 57 | 12 | 1,156 | 63 | 20.16 |
| Cuzens | 46 | 72 | 8 | 1,358 | 87 | 19.9 |
| Bullocky | 39 | 61 | 3 | 579 | 64 | 9.33 |
| Red Cap | 47 | 73 | 3 | 630 | 56 | 8.46 |
| Twopenny | 46 | 70 | 6 | 589 | 35 | 8.29 |
| King Cole | 7 | 10 | 2 | 75 | 18 | 7.5 |
| Tiger | 47 | 69 | 5 | 431 | 32 | 6.17 |
| Shepherd | 7 | 11 | 0 | 66 | 11 | 6.0 |
| Dick-a-Dick | 45 | 66 | 5 | 356 | 42 | 5.26 |
| Peter | 42 | 59 | 7 | 284 | 30 | 4.48 |
| Charley | 44 | 53 | 13 | 218 | 17 | 4.6 |
| Mosquito | 34 | 20 | 26 | 77 | 8 | 3.17 |
| Jim Crow | 13 | 15 | 4 | 37 | 12 | 2.7 |
| Sundown | 2 | 3 | 0 | 1 | 1 | — |

|  | Bowling | | | |
|---|---|---|---|---|
| *Name* | *Overs* | *Maidens* | *Runs* | *Wickets* | *Average* |
| Twopenny | 176 | 78 | 242 | 35 | 6.9 |
| Mullagh* | 1,877 | 831 | 2,489 | 245 | 10.0 |
| Red Cap | 366 | 141 | 576 | 54 | 10.7 |
| Cuzens | 868 | 361 | 1,296 | 114 | 11.3 |
| Bullocky | 22 | 7 | 46 | 4 | 11.5 |
| Lawrence* | 1,579 | 451 | 3,022 | 250 | 12.1 |
| Dick-a-Dick | 35 | 6 | 96 | 5 | 19.2 |
| Shepherd | 56 | 14 | 124 | 6 | 20.7 |
| King Cole | 14 | 4 | 34 | 1 | — |

* This analysis does not include figures for the first innings against Rochdale, and the second innings against Tynemouth (North Shields), when Lawrence apparently took 7 wickets and Mullagh 12. Both bowlers would have taken 257 wickets in this case.

*Source:* Adapted from *Sporting Life*, 28 October 1868

*Johnny Mullagh, the outstanding player on the Aboriginals' tour of England, was a sensitive, proud man who preferred to sleep in the open than endure insults from white men in hotels*

which took part in the Murray Cup competition until the 1890 season. He sometimes played against old tour mates like Tarpot.

Johnny Mullagh remained sensitive to racial indignities all his life. Johnnie Moyes recorded that Mullagh once travelled with the Harrow team to Apsley, where the local captain suggested that Mullagh could eat in the hotel kitchen instead of joining the players in the dining room. Mullagh left the premises and spent the night in the open. Moyes also recounted the story of a match in which Mullagh deliberately hit a catch rather than continue batting against Apsley after their captain called him "a nigger". When asked why he deliberately sacrificed his wicket, Mullagh replied: "Oh, anything is good enough for a nigger".

Mullagh went to Sydney one year with the Victorian team but a poisoned hand prevented him playing. On the first night some Victorian players complained of a gas leak in their hotel. The players traced it to the ground floor where Mullagh had a small room. They had to break the lock to get into a room which they found full of gas. The players threw open the window and roused Mullagh with difficulty. He told them he had *blown* the gas out hours ago. For the rest of the stay, Mullagh's room was lit by a candle.

In August 1891, James Edgar discovered Mullagh's body at his camp in the scrub. His bat and stumps were buried with him in Harrow cemetery and each Harrovian cricketer present threw a sprig of blackberries and yellow flowers on to his grave, a symbol of the club's colours. A memorial was erected on the local sports ground, later named Mullagh Oval. The *Hamilton Spectator* collected money for the memorial. His headstone was inscribed on one side with his England tour average, 23.65, and on the other side with his Murray Cup average, 45.70.

Of the other English tourists, probably only Red Cap and Tarpot survived Mullagh. Twopenny returned to Sydney and played for New South Wales against Victoria in an 1870 intercolonial match, the only other member of the team

1879. He bowled 12 overs without success, scored 4 in Victoria's first innings, and topscored with 36 in the second innings. He lived in Melbourne for a time as a professional at the Melbourne Cricket Club but preferred life alone as a rabbiter on James Edgar's Pine Hills property. He was a superb horseman and enjoyed breaking in horses and riding round the sheds at shearing time. He remained a member of the Harrow Club team, to appear again in big cricket. Twopenny could not reproduce the form which gave him nine wickets for nine runs against Hampshire from 10.2 overs. Eight of his victims that day were bowled and he caught the tenth batsman. But he was dropped after only one match for New South Wales and later appeared in court on alcohol-related charges.

The first systematic count of full-blooded Aborigines in Victoria in 1877 disclosed that this group had dwindled to 774. Several of the cricketers who had made the first abortive tour to Sydney in 1867 or the full tour of England a year later were among those who could not be counted, although Dick-a-Dick was reported at a race meeting at Mount Elgin station in 1884. There are no records of what happened to Jim Crow and Sundown, sent home ill from England, but a Jim Crow was reported to have been murdered some years later at Euston in the Murray River region.

At the local school on the foreshores of Lake Wallace, where the Aborigines practised with Wills and Lawrence, there is a monument to the team, erected largely through the efforts of school-teacher H. G. Martindale, who raised the money and had former Test captain Vic Richardson unveil it in 1951. It consists of two plaques. One carries the names of the team; the other reads simply, "In this vicinity, the first Aboriginal cricket team to tour England trained prior to departure in 1868. Matches won 14, matches lost 14, matches drawn 19".

The Aboriginal tour had little lasting impact on Australian cricket but it undoubtedly influenced English ideas about Australian cricketers. When the great fast bowler Fred Spofforth sat at Lord's with the England player A. G. Steel during the first white Australian tour under Dave Gregory in 1878, Steel was approached by the Reverend Arthur Ward, who commented, "I hear you're going to play against the niggers on Monday". Steel thereupon introduced Spofforth as the "demon nigger bowler".

# The first year of Grace

### W. G. Grace's tour of Australia 1873–74

By 1873 William Gilbert Grace, still only 25, had come out of the family orchard to dominate cricket in a manner unmatched by any other player. His consistently high scores and round-arm wicket-taking were impressive, but it was the style of this tall, athletic, broad-shouldered man with the black beard and imperious manner that set him apart. His success was soundly based on a wonderful eye, copybook technique and brilliant athleticism, but it depended as much on his lusty, assertive, almost cocksure approach. Unquestionably he overawed many of his opponents, a master cricketer renowned from his teens for his gamesmanship.

He was an extraordinary performer on rough, low scoring pitches; he was adaptable and fearless and combined good health with strength of character; he was willing to accept injury; and he was willing to take risks which could reverse an apparently hopeless situation. Newspapers talked about him as a symbol of the British Empire, and he was the best-known Englishman of his time.

*The third English team that toured Australia in 1873–74: (L to R) (back) G. A. Bush, W. Oscroft, R. Humphrey, J. Southerton, W. McIntyre, F. H. Boult, A. Greenwood, W. R. Gilbert; (middle) W. G. Grace, G. F. Grace; (front) J. Lillywhite, H. Jupp. The team lost three matches*

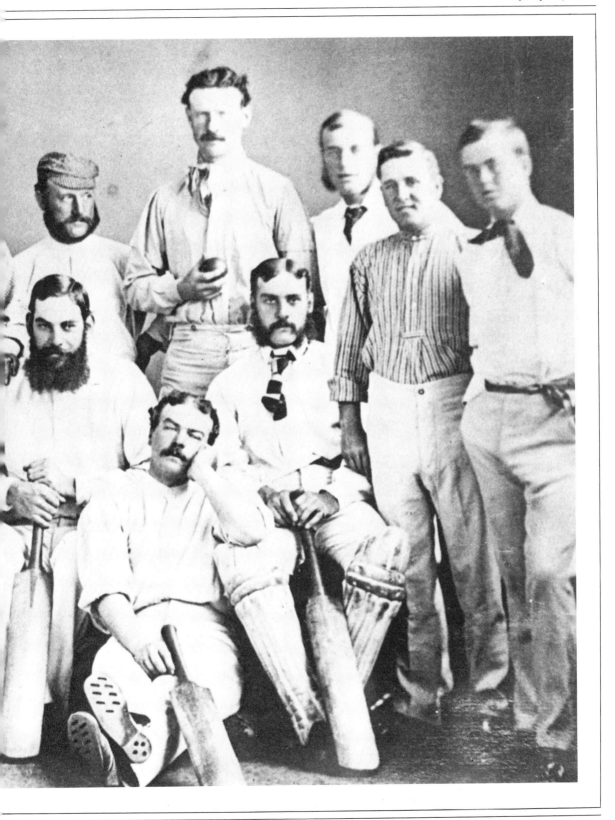

Grace scored his initial first-class century at the age of 15, with an innings of 170 for South Wales against the Gentlemen of Sussex. Despite his youth he was picked the following year to play for both the Gentlemen and All England. In 1871 he scored 2739 runs in 35 completed innings, a prodigious feat on good pitches, but on the chipped, broken, dusty or sodden strips of this time a quite astonishing effort. In 1873, when he became the first cricketer to achieve the double of 2139 runs and 106 wickets, a syndicate of East Melbourne, South Melbourne and Melbourne Cricket Clubs, at the suggestion of Dick Wardill, invited Grace to choose a team to visit Australia. The East Melbourne and South Melbourne Clubs put up £1750 between them, the Melbourne Club a further £2000, with Thomas Ferris Hamilton, former president of the Melbourne Club and an MCG Trustee, holding the guarantee. Grace, ostensibly an amateur, accepted for a personal fee of £1500, plus all expenses for his wife and himself. Professionals in his team received £170 each. Wardill's suicide sadly came four months before the tour began.

The Melbourne syndicate soon found that they had snared one of cricket's smartest bowlers, as well as a great batsman. Although a round-armer of ungainly style he was adept at exposing batsmen's faults. Grace's bowling looked commonplace until batsmen tried to hit it. This was the man who got batsmen out by directing their attention to the sun or a flock of birds, with what one of his contemporaries called "a curious rotary action before delivery from a large hand in which the ball was well concealed and seemed to leave by the back door".

All nine Grace children learned their cricket in happy family games. Their father, Dr Henry Mills Grace, was coach, and W. G.'s four sisters urged their dogs to chase long hits. W. G. later practised the batting skills he had learned with a broom handle in front of stumps chalked on a wall. Richard Daft wrote that the Graces' mother knew more about cricket than any woman he ever

*A sketch of a cricket match at the Melbourne Cricket Ground between Victoria and the third English team that toured Australia during the 1873–74 season. This tour of Australia was W. G. Grace's first*

met, was a better player than her husband and most of her offspring, and could throw a cricket ball 65 metres. To the day she died her sons telegraphed match scores to her at the end of each day's play. W. G.'s achievements unfortunately denied his brothers, three of them also doctors, proper recognition of their rare talents. Between them W. G., Edward Miller (1841–1911), George Frederick (1850–80), Henry (1833–95) and Alfred (1840–1916) Grace lifted Gloucestershire to a level where it could take on the best professional teams in England.

W. G.'s doctorate was never a courtesy title as has been suggested. He completed his medical

studies despite a dislike for scholarship, and fulfilled the demands of a country doctor each winter. He hired a locum to fill in for him in the cricket season.

For the first of his two Australian tours, W. G. put together a more balanced lineup than either of the two earlier England touring teams, although Hornby, Emmett, Yardley, Shaw and the wicket-keepers Pinder and Pooley were unavailable. W. G. married a few weeks before the steamer *Mirzapore* left for Australia in October 1873 and he treated the tour as an extended honeymoon. The team comprised W. G. Grace, J. A. Bush, F. H. Boult, W. R. Gilbert, A. Greenwood, R. Humphrey, H. Jupp, J. Lillywhite, M. McIntyre, W. Oscroft, J. Southerton, and G. F. Grace, the fifth and youngest brother. Oscroft, Greenwood, Southerton and McIntyre brought a large supply of bats and photographs to sell

during the tour. Oscroft refused to share with the others in this venture as he considered they would be too proud to demand the highest prices for the goods. (Southerton, playing in 1870 for Surrey against MCC at Lord's, went into cricket folklore by walking off when he skied a ball into the air. The catch was dropped but Southerton did not return and he went into the record books as "retired, thinking he was caught".)

The tour was badly organised from the start. The professionals travelled second-class to and from Australia, and were lodged in hotels inferior to those provided for the amateurs. W. G. quarrelled frequently with reporters, who compared him unfavourably with his charming brother George Frederick Grace. The *Australasian* called W. G. "a bumptious and overbearing" captain. His literary collaborator, Arthur Porritt, was probably more accurate when he described Grace as a "big grown-up boy, just what a man who only lived when he was in the open air might be expected to be".

The *Mirzapore* ran aground in the Suez and the team had to transfer to the *Nubia* at Colombo, but 52 days after leaving England they arrived at King George Sound in Western Australia. Aborigines gave the Englishmen a demonstration of boomerang throwing and W. G. tried his hand at it, almost beheading one of his men. "Another foot, would have needed an inquest," W. G. wrote later in his biography.

In Melbourne a big contingent of cricket-lovers greeted the team. The president of the Melbourne Cricket Club placed his carriage at the disposal of the Graces. When the Englishmen arrived at a match at South Melbourne that afternoon, 7000 spectators burst into applause. One of their hosts commented, "We never experience any unpleasantness at Australian grounds". Fifteen minutes later an umpire's decision sparked a demonstration. A large section of the crowd rushed onto the field and play had to be abandoned, a foretaste, wrote W. G., of "experiences which fell to our lot".

There was simply not enough important cricket in Australia to develop umpires who could be relied on at a time of constant changes in the law. England had already begun using professional umpires, a procedure still a long way off for Australia. Grace was not above taking advantage of this weakness in Australian umpiring and later boasted that when one of his players, Bush, was bowled first ball, he replaced the bails, informing the umpire that the batsman always had a trial ball. The umpire accepted this and Bush continued batting. A fieldsman who caught a W. G. skier in another match fell over the boundary chains. The umpire gave England one for the shot, which was all the batsmen had run. "I did not complain about not getting five for a hit over the chains as I was fairly certain I had been caught," Grace wrote.

Three days before England's first match W. G. asked the Melbourne groundsman how work on the pitch was progressing. The groundsman explained that the pitch would be selected on the morning and have a roller on it for an hour or so before play began. W. G. went to the sponsors and stressed that the pitch for such a match required much more than a brief preparation.

*This incident rather put me in mind of the MCC at home, for at that time the powers that be at Lord's thought a few hours' preparation was enough for any pitch. I take upon myself the credit of having shown Australians how to prepare a pitch, and of disabusing their minds of the idea that a good pitch can be obtained without special attention.*

Play was delayed while the Victorian players held an election for captain, the organisers not wanting to choose between George Robertson of the Melbourne Cricket Club and John Conway of South Melbourne. When the players went into committee they appeared to the *Argus* like a solemn conclave of cardinals. Robertson got the job by 12 votes to six.

But the hero of the match was Bransby Beauchamp Cooper, born in India and educated at Rugby. He had played for the school against the Marylebone Cricket Club. Cooper had at one time partnered W. G. in a stand of 283 for the Gentlemen of the South against Players of the South, Cooper scoring 101, W. G. 180. Cooper made 84 in a total of 266 for Eighteen of Victoria. Conway, 32, and Harry Boyle, 30, kept England chasing the leather.

Allan and Boyle shared the bowling for the Victorians with likable old Sam Cosstick. Between them they had England out for 110. Forced to follow on, England managed only 132, losing by an innings—an ignominious start to their tour. W. G. Grace made 23 and 51. A crowd of 40,000 watched, each person having paid half a crown admission. England's regular bowlers failed and W. G. blamed himself for not taking the ball earlier. He took 10 for 49, his brother G. F. Grace 4 for 35. A correspondent wrote in the *Australasian* that unorthodox spinner Cooper had been responsible for England's defeat but "any numbskulls who talk about Eleven Victorian natives playing this Eleven of England are prattling about that they don't understand".

The Englishmen travelled 161 kilometres over hot and dusty roads for their second match at Ballarat where they found Wills, Cosstick, Gaggin and Allan among the opposing Twenty-Two. On a well-rolled pitch W. G. and G. F. Grace scored the first centuries of the tour, W. G. 126, G. F. 112. Oscroft might have scored the third

*RIGHT: The Victorian Eighteen that defeated Grace's team by an innings and 23 runs. Play was held up while they had an election for the captaincy, with George Robertson winning the job over John Conway OVER PAGE: Two shots of the great W. G. Grace in action. His bowling action (left) was decidedly round-arm but he had deceptive flight, while he always batted with immense concentration (right)*

century but on 65 skied a ball and ran. When the catch was dropped, Oscroft found himself at the same end as G. F. Grace, who had not moved, and was run out. Twenty-Two of Ballarat made 276 on a day W. G. described as the hottest on which he had ever played, and the match was drawn. The seats at the ground were so hot that some spectators could not sit down. A Ballarat reporter summed up: "The sun shone infernally, the Eleven scored tremendously, Ballarat fielded abominably, and we all drank excessively". Also that summer in Ballarat, the first women's cricket match in Australia was played, between teams made up of miners' daughters.

The 119 kilometres to the next match at Stawell had to be covered by Cobb & Co coach along a bush track "quite undeserving of the name road". Initially some of the team objected to travelling in such discomfort, but after prolonged argument they left Ballarat, four hours late. The first 24 kilometres were bearable but the final 95 kilometres were agonising, the horses labouring up to their hocks in dust. To relieve their boredom two English players took pot shots at birds through the coach windows.

The secretary of the Stawell Cricket Club and many townsfolk greeted the Englishmen 32 kilometres from town. Cheering crowds lined the last 5 kilometres to Stawell. Two brass bands struck up welcoming tunes so enthusiastically that the horses on one coach took fright and overturned the vehicle. The tourists finally reached Stawell at 8.30 p.m. The warmth of their reception quickly made them forget the nightmare 12-hour trip.

After inspecting a goldmine and shooting with his cousin W. R. Gilbert, W. G. Grace opened the batting with Jupp on the following day on a pitch he described as "execrable".

*The cricket was shockingly poor, and the match a ludicrous farce. One ball actually stuck in the dust and did not reach the batsman. It was ludicrous to play on such a pitch but we were in for it and we went through with it. The result was that we were all out in 70 minutes for 43. If all the catches we gave had been held our total would have been smaller still. It is scarcely worthwhile recording the progress of the play, though it should be stated that we were beaten by 10 wickets. A plague of flies which swept over the field added to our discomforts in this remarkable match.*

While the *Australasian* charged that the match had been rigged, Grace gave his men a stern warning about drinking during games, and then went off into the bush for some more shooting, since the match had ended in two days. When W. G. returned he was not surprised to learn that the third day had seen Twelve of Stawell beat the six English professionals. The locals made 29, the professionals 2—both to McIntyre off one hit.

The trip to Warrnambool had to be made in two stages, with an overnight stop on the way. Torrential rain fell overnight and when the Englishmen emerged to board their coaches at 4.30 a.m. they found that the bush tracks had been transformed to muddy bogs. The coach wheels sank to their axles, the players were soaked to the skin, and despite frequent changes of horses the first 50 kilometres took more than five hours. Five players were left behind at Hexham to lighten the load and the remainder reached Warrnambool at 7.30 p.m., after a journey of 19 hours.

The Twenty-Two of Warrnambool included B. B. Cooper, Allan, Wills, Conway and Irish-born William Gaggin, all of whom, Grace said, "seemed prepared to regard themselves as representatives of any district in the Australian continent". This time the pitch was sodden and slow but the cricket less of a burlesque than it had been at Stawell. James Southerton took a hat-trick to help dismiss the Twenty-Two for 68 and Jupp scored 58 not out in a splendid innings to give England an advantage. They pressed home to win by nine wickets, their first tour success. This pleasure was marred, however, by the gamblers

*The Irish-born right-hand batsman William Gaggin, one of the Victorians Grace's bowlers found difficult to remove*

*received. Several steamers crowded with people came out to meet us, and gave us ringing cheers, which were renewed by five or six thousand voices as we drew alongside the wharf. A public breakfast was ready for us at Tattersall's Hotel and then the inevitable toasts, which in my opinion are carried to an extreme in Australia.*

The match on the Albert Ground produced the first encounter between Grace and young bowling hopeful Spofforth, but it was Coates, the professional from Huddersfield, who played havoc with the English batting, finishing with 6 for 29 in an innings of 92. Grace's cousin William Pocock, who was playing for the Warwick Club in Sydney, was one of several successful batsmen for Eighteen of New South Wales who scored 127 and 9 for 57 to defeat the tourists by eight wickets. There was tremendous jubilation each time W. G. was dismissed: spectators threw caps, hats, umbrellas and walking-sticks in the air as he departed. The *Sydney Morning Herald* commented that the win proved that "British blood has not yet been thinned by the heat of Australian summers".

Serious floods caused cancellation of the next scheduled match at Maitland and the Englishmen travelled instead over the Blue Mountains to Bathurst, a trip which enabled them to avoid further bouts of seasickness. The governor of New South Wales, Sir Hercules Robinson, was among those who travelled from Sydney for the event. But even the rail journey in those days needed a strong constitution. The train had to shunt back and forth to get over the mountains and the players were "painfully conscious that the snapping of a coupling could send us careering down the precipitous slope to certain death".

W. G. rode on the engine. Eight kilometres from Bathurst a cavalcade of horsemen met the train and the cricketers moved into the town accompanied by a brass band and hundreds of excited pedestrians. Numerous speeches, a lavish

and cardsharps who came on the ground "to ply their trade in complete disregard of the police".

W. G. and the amateurs in his team went shooting on the third day while the professionals were thrashed by a local eleven. The five English pros scored 26, the Eleven 172, including 88 before a wicket fell. W. G. Grace found kangaroo shooting highly exciting. "The way the stockmen ride when kangaroo hunting was a revelation," he wrote. "Some of us stood aghast at the recklessness with which they dashed through the bush."

The team experienced a wretched overnight sea trip in a tiny, smelly coastal steamer from Warrnambool to Melbourne, where W. G. rejoined his wife. Another rough voyage followed as they sailed up the coast to Sydney, with huge waves sending them to their cabins. W. G. recalled:

*As we steamed through the Heads we were enchanted by the beauty of Sydney Harbour, and no less delighted by the welcome we*

*Frank Allan, who travelled around strengthening local teams, played Grace's side, ready, according to Grace, "to represent any town on the Australian continent"*

the opposition for 98, the bowling of Southerton and Lillywhite proving too much for local batsmen Dave Gregory, Charles Bannerman, Nathaniel Thompson, Sam Cosstick, B. B. Cooper, and John Conway. The Combined Fifteen were left to score 309 runs in three hours. They chose to bat for a draw: one stonewaller scored only two runs in more than an hour.

Sydney spectators urged Cosstick, who had been given out, to return to the crease. He did so, maintaining that the wrong umpire had given the decision, and with three batsmen from the Combined Fifteen on the pitch, Grace led his team off the field. Cosstick finally abandoned his protest and play resumed. Wicket-keeper Bush distinguished himself when he and Gilbert ran what they believed were four byes only to discover Bush had been bowled. The crowd, who cheered the tourists enthusiastically, refused to disperse until each player came forward for a personal ovation.

After another nasty voyage back to Victoria England beat twenty-twos from Sandhurst and Castlemaine, despite abominable pitches and disputed umpires' decisions. Pace bowler Martin McIntyre took full advantage of the conditions at Castlemaine, said Grace, playing "merrily about the ribs of the Castlemaniacs, and enjoying himself in pure and innocent fashion". The match against Fifteen of Victoria ended early with another win to England, so Grace's players agreed to an exhibition against a Victorian XI. W. G. and Jupp scored 140 before they were parted and W. G. achieved 126 out of England's 5 for 250. At one point Sam Cosstick became so frustrated that he deliberately threw at W. G. Cosstick was immediately taken off.

The visitors were by now accustomed to rough sea trips so the 29 hours it took to steam across Bass Strait from Melbourne to Launceston came as no surprise. J. C. Lord, a former Hampshire player, scored 34 and 36 in dashing style, but it was not enough to save Twenty-Two of Tasmania from defeat by an innings and 32 runs at Launceston. G. F. Grace made a great 154

luncheon, and bets on whether W. G. could hit a ball out of the Bathurst ground were mixed with the cricket. England defeated Twenty-Two of Bathurst by eight wickets. W. G. hit a ball over the scorers' box but it fell inside the ground, so Mrs Grace missed out on a pair of gloves promised if her husband landed a shot outside. The next day W. G. went shooting again, this time for quail, and bagged "22 couples" in two hours.

Back in Sydney for a return meeting with a Combined Fifteen of Victoria and New South Wales, W. G. hit two shots over the fence in an innings of 73. England made 170 and dismissed

*Harry Boyle, the tough Bendigo miner whose medium-paced right-arm round-armers surprised Grace with their accuracy. They were destined to have many tense encounters over almost two decades*

against a Twenty-Two of Southern Tasmania at Hobart, where W. H. Walker hit W. G. out of the ground twice in an over. England won an eventful match by eight wickets.

With all their players now in splendid form, England returned to Melbourne for the decider against Victoria. In the nets a thirteen-year-old boy named Percy McDonnell made a big impression on the tourists. More than 5000 people watched Billy Midwinter open dramatically by clean-bowling his former Gloucester team-mates W. G. and G. F. Grace. Before a result was possible rain flooded the ground.

The night after the match the English professionals boycotted a farewell dinner, fed up with their second-class status. "Let the promoters send

us home first-class and we will at least have one kindly recollection of them," wrote James Lilly-white explaining their stand to the *Argus.*

The promoters had hoped to play the final match in Adelaide, where the South Australian Cricket Association considered The Oval was ready for big cricket. Unfortunately the association then decided that they could not meet the £800 guarantee required until they had worked out the match finances. They took so long over their sums that when they accepted the sponsors telegraphed back: "Too late. Kadina accepted yesterday. Any other match in South Australia can only be arranged with the consent of the English players."

The South Australian Cricket Association was badly shaken by this reply. An urgent meeting resolved to instruct all association members not to support any match involving the English team outside Adelaide. Meanwhile W. G. and his players had undertaken another wild sea voyage followed by a bone-shaking 161-kilometre trip down Yorke Peninsula to Kadina in a coach driven by J. H. Hill, whose renowned son Clem was born three years later. The Englishmen found Tom Wills in Kadina coaching the locals, who were strengthened by the inclusion of the leading Adelaide players J. E. Gooden, S. Morcom and J. Chittleborough. W. G. retained a vivid memory of Kadina, the one-horse town that outbid its State association:

*When we reached Kadina, we went out in search of the cricket ground; and a search it really proved. We came to an open space and asked to be directed to the cricket ground. 'This is it,' someone said and we whistled in astonishment. There was scarcely a blade of grass to be seen, while the whole area was covered with small stones. On the morning of the match a bushel of pebbles was swept up. Very naturally our men funked batting on a wicket like that and no one was expected to make a big score.*

The first six Kadina wickets fell for two runs before Gooden hit a four. Then it was 11 for 8 and thanks to sundries 19 for 25. Finally Mottle and Paqualin scored seven apiece in a brave stand to help the locals reach 42. McIntyre took 9 for 4, Southerton 11 for 29. England had replied with a first innings score of 64 by the end of the first day. Sixteen Kadina batsmen failed to score in their second innings, and only eight runs came from the bat in a total of 13. Lillywhite's figures were 13 for 7 from 84 deliveries. Wills, the former Rugby School and Cambridge University crack, tarnished his reputation by securing spectacles, both clean-bowled.

One of South Australian cricket's keenest supporters, Sir Edwin Smith, had offered a silver cup for the highest score by a local against the Englishmen. Mottle and Paqualin tied with seven runs, so the issue was decided with W. G. Grace bowling at each man with the England team fielding. The England players' sympathies lay more with one player who had been friendly to them. Both men were dismissed without scoring the first time round. Again each man batted, and again each was out for a duck. W. G. wrote:

*The contest was getting exciting and the destiny of the cup hung in the balance, when, for the third time, I dismissed the first man for a duck. Then we had the satisfaction of seeing our friend make a single off a very flukey hit and thus win the cup.*

The Kadina match ended England's tour arrangements with the Melbourne syndicate, but the South Australian Cricket Association sent emissaries to Kadina to invite England to play a supplementary match on the Adelaide Oval. W. G. Grace agreed to play for £110 and half the gate receipts "as we had been sent to Kadina in the interests of the promoters' pockets". His acceptance brought threats from the promoters, but W. G. pointed out that his tour schedule had been for 14 matches only. W. G. recalled later:

*This additional match necessitated an all-night journey from Kadina, which in turn led to uncomfortable adventures. In the dark we lost the track, and began driving about in the bush until at last, as we had taken seven hours to cover 35 miles [56 kilometres], we thought it wiser to wait until daylight before proceeding. Consequently we did not reach Adelaide until the afternoon, and after our night's exposure were so stiff and tired that to play cricket decently was beyond us. The Twenty-Two of South Australia did not, however, take full advantage of our incapacity and they lost eight wickets for 10 runs.*

This was the first major match on the Adelaide Oval. The South Australian Cricket Association used its influence to have a half-holiday declared for the second day of the match. Admission charge was two shillings and sixpence to the ground, an additional five shillings to the Reserve. The association made a profit of £300. When Kadina officials threatened to sue because they had exclusive rights to the English team's South Australian appearance, the association sent them £150 to help cover some of the £700 Kadina had lost on its match.

The South Australian *Register* recognised the importance of the Adelaide Oval's entry into international cricket:

*This game has never yet taken that position in the colony to which as a national sport it is entitled, but there is no reason why the advent of Mr Grace and his team should not be only the forerunner of many contests between our cricketers and those of England and of our sister colonies.*

The Twenty-Two made 63 and 82, England 108 and 3 for 73 to win easily. W. G. was out for six in England's first innings when a fieldsman named Alexander Crooks sprinted hard and caught a big hit in one hand before he fell over the boundary chains. Grace, naturally, objected and claimed that the ball had been caught over the chains. The umpire disagreed and W. G. departed. The catch brought overnight fame to Crooks, a bank clerk who had become a giant killer. The South Australian Cricket Association made him treasurer and he was promoted to general manager of the Commercial Bank of South Australia. When the bank lost £1,162,679, Crooks was sent to prison for eight months charged with fraud; he was more valuable on the field than as a financial manager.

The association's banquet for Grace and his players ended a tour on which the Englishmen had accepted hardships with unfailing good humour, attracted large, enthusiastic crowds, and fired young Australians with the ambition to emulate W. G. and his stars. Only the organisers' shabby treatment of the professionals soured a tour which consolidated cricket as Australia's major summer sport. The visit also renewed ties broken by migration, overcame doubt about Australian cricket standards, and generated enough interest for scores to be telegraphed to England for the first time. W. G.'s team played 15 matches, won ten, lost three, and had two draws. All matches were against the odds. The veteran Sam Cosstick summed up: "Bar W. G. we're as good as they are, and some day we'll lick 'em with eleven".

W. G.'s immense prestige had enabled the South Australian Cricket Association to set a valuable precedent by charging admission to the Adelaide Oval. Heartened by this breakthrough, the association staged the first intercolonial match on The Oval in December 1874, between South Australia and Victoria. This time admission charges were reduced to one shilling for the ground and two shillings and sixpence for the Reserve, which now boasted a pavilion. The association made £100 profit on the match.

The newly laid pitch favoured the bowlers and a fairly strong Victorian XI defeated Eighteen of South Australia by 15 runs. Sam Cosstick took 17 wickets for 73 runs for the match. South Australia led on the first innings by 16 runs but failed badly against the bowling of Cosstick and Paddy Horan (11 for 29) in the second innings. The pitch was so uneven that during lunch on the second day half a dozen spectators got between the shafts of the roller and, while six players pushed, rolled it.

After this unpromising start, South Australia made great improvement, and when the next England team visited Australia in 1876–77, under the captaincy of James Lillywhite, South Australia deservedly had a place in the itinerary. There were no South Australians, however, in the first Australian Test team which played against Lillywhite's team.

After Grace's team departed a curious letter in the name of W. G. Grace appeared in Australian newspapers. The writer launched a scathing attack on Australian conventions. He had refused to attend many official functions because

*I didn't want to fraternise with the tinkers, tailors and snobs who are the big guns in your cricket world. To take their money was a fair thing in return for work done, but to hobnob with a lot of scum was a different thing. Fancy the chance of a greasy butcher in his travels walking up to me some day at Lord's with 'How d'ye do, Mr Grace? I lunched with you in Australia.' My dear fellow, so far as I can see, colonial society is low, shockingly low. You have plenty of money, but your gentlemen are yet unborn.*

The letter was an obvious fraud, written by Richard Egan Lee, of Melbourne, in the satirical journalistic fashion of the period, and Grace denied all knowledge of it. But some believed it was by Grace and it did nothing to lessen what the *Sydney Mail* called "a disposition on the part of some of the rougher class to hoot and snarl at Grace".

# Anything will do for Australia

## The first Test matches 1877

When the National Club collapsed in Sydney in September 1867, Dave, Ned, Walter and Charles Gregory all joined the Warwicks, which then became one of the strongest clubs in the colony. Among those who attended the club's meetings in O'Brien's Hotel were J. R. (later Sir James) Fairfax, G. H. (later Sir George) Reid, Richard Driver, W. Hemming, A. L. Park, Charles and James Kellick, Charley Oliver, Billy Caffyn, Charles Bannerman, Bill, Jim, Bob and George Clark, James Oatley, John Tooher and Joe Seale, most of them state players.

Records of the Warwick Club show that Dave Gregory won the bowling trophy in 1871, taking his wickets at an average cost of 3.35 runs. Charley Bannerman won the batting trophy with an average of 16 runs per innings. The following year Dave Gregory carried off both trophies with a batting average of 25, his wickets costing 4.14 apiece. In 1873 he again won the batting trophy,

*The Albert Ground, Sydney's first fully enclosed ground and scene of the amazing single-wicket match in which the three Gregory brothers defeated the pride of Victoria after three exciting days' cricket. The Albert gave way to the Association Ground, later renamed the Sydney Cricket Ground*

averaging 20.2 runs an innings.

Ned, Dave and Charles Gregory played their famous single-wicket match against the Victorian trio, Wills, Conway and Cosstick, while they were with the Warwick Club. Single-wicket cricket was very popular at the time and many considered the three Victorians unbeatable. They had beaten the best five players of South Australia and twice defeated Caffyn, Lawrence and Nat Thompson, who were rated among the best New South Wales could produce. Sydney cricketers, piqued by the Victorian boasting, looked to the Gregorys to restore their honour.

After their challenge was issued, the Gregorys rose every morning at 5.00 a.m. and spent two hours practising hard at the Alliance Ground (now Sydney Cricket Ground No. 2), assisted by Hugh Massie, Charley Oliver and Charles Bannerman. The match was held at the Albert Ground on 8 April 1871, for £100 a side, with Dave Gregory captaining his family team and John Conway leading the Victorians, before more than 5000 people.

For three days the tension mounted, with Dave Gregory delivering 295 balls (some of them suspect) and Sam Cosstick 272. Umpire Nathaniel Thompson, who had already no-balled Dave Gregory three times for throwing, called him again, only to find that Gregory still had the ball in his hand. The delivery did not count, but Thompson, believing he had been tricked, was irked by the crowd's jeering and stalked off the field. Billy Caffyn replaced him and allowed Gregory to bowl as he liked. The Gregorys scored 24 and 30, the Victorians 21 and 28, and when Dave Gregory scattered Wills's stumps to seal victory by five runs, a wave of cheering swept across the ground. Dave reached the pavilion with a sharp sprint but Ned and Charles were carried off on supporters' shoulders.

The crowd and the players circled the table bearing the three silver cups. Most felt that if Dave Gregory threw, Wills was equally guilty. Conway stepped up onto the table to make the presentation and it was recorded in the *Referee*:

*Conway made an excellent speech, full of pith and point and free of unnecessary verbiage. Commencing with Ned he complimented him not only on his play, but also on the pluck with which he stood the knocking about he himself [Conway] had administered, and declared that he ... would not have taken such a pasting for anything. Ned having received his cup, Dave was next and without laying it on too thick the Melbourne captain gave his wiry opponent huge credit for his bowling and for the batting ability he showed in taking the cream off the bowling in each innings. Charley Gregory's fielding came in for a good allowance of praise; as did his bowling in the first innings when he sent down 64 balls for one run. Mr Conway concluded a very humorous speech by prophesying a very bright career on the cricket field for the third of the Gregorys, a trio he designated as 'very hot goods' at single wicket cricket.*

*And then a gentleman of Sydney, whose name was kept dark, requested to be allowed to call for champagne, which having been placed on the table by host Kettle, the cups were filled and healths were drunk in a manner which showed the good feeling of those who had just concluded such a hard tussle for mastery. This carouse being concluded, the players and a few friends then betook themselves to Kettle's hostelry, and here the cups were again filled with fizz. After treating the citizens along George and King Streets to 'Rule Britannia' and 'God Save the Queen', fortissimo, we arrived safely at The Oxford, from which headquarters of inter-Colonial cricket the brothers were allowed to depart after once more utilising the cups.*

*The Gregorys, Charles, Dave and "Ned", after their triumph over Tom Wills, John Conway and Sam Cosstick by five runs. The match attracted 5000 spectators each day and a stake of £100*

The Albert Ground, the scene of this Gregory clan triumph, was the nursery of many famous players, including the Bannermans, Frank Iredale, Hugh Massie, Harry Moses and Billy Murdoch. There, in 1873, not long after he turned 19, Fred Spofforth caused "near panic" among batsmen of the highly rated University Club when he took nine wickets, seven by knocking down the stumps. The batsman he did not dismiss was Edmund Barton, the future Prime Minister. At a time when the New South Wales Cricket Association was only able to continue because its treasurer, A. L. Park, guaranteed its overdraft, the Albert Ground provided urgently needed funds.

The Albert Ground had opened in 1864 with the issue of 300 £5 shares. Up to then artisans mixed with wharf labourers and gentlemen in all the Sydney clubs, and cricketers practised in ordinary clothes, flannels were unknown, cricket boots seldom worn, and if shoes became too slippery off they came. Even socks were discarded by those who found them uncomfortable. Few players owned bats or pads; all gear was kept in large canvas bags at the secretary's home. Boys used to think a great deal of a man who wore flannels and expected big things from him on the field. The Albert Ground's facilities changed all that, and cricketers started to buy their own equipment.

By charging admission to the Albert Ground, the NSWCA received income denied it at the Domain. The Albert Ground Company, which had converted boggy ground into a splendid fenced playing surface with a sheltered grandstand, retained 20 per cent of all takings for fixtures at their field. Already irked by the Albert Club's action in arranging a match with the Melbourne Cricket Club when the 1864 intercolonial game had been abandoned, the NSWCA considered this move a threat to its financial strength. As other grounds appeared at Newtown, Toxteth Park and Sydney University, the association resisted using the Albert Ground, although it was the best venue in Australia, and even intercolonial matches were played there only on sufferance.

In 1874, after the Albert Ground Company shareholders had received a 7 per cent dividend on their investment, the New South Wales Cricket Association found a promising field behind Victoria Barracks, known as the Garrison Ground. The *Sydney Morning Herald* contended that the ground, sometimes used for rifle practice, was too far from the centre of Sydney to attract crowds. Accessibility improved overnight, however, when the area known as Moore Park was drained, filled in and levelled, bringing footballers and cricketers onto the park and providing a pleasant approach to the Garrison Ground.

Despite his criticism over the treatment of professionals in W. G. Grace's touring team, James Lillywhite recognised the Australian desire for big cricket. He returned four summers later with his own team, an all professional outfit able to set their own conditions. John Conway, liaison officer for the tour, arranged suitable matches and grounds in advance. The Melbourne Cricket Club opened an impressive new grandstand for this 1877–78 season. Built for £4678, it had 2000 adjustable seats: they faced towards the cricket on the Melbourne Cricket Ground in the summer, but could be reversed to face Australian Rules football in Richmond Park in winter. The Melbourne Club would not tolerate footballers on their ground at the time, believing they would convert it into a sea of mud, impossible to repair for cricket. Tom Wills disagreed, and upset cricket purists by arguing that cricket grounds benefited from football activity. The design of the new stand showed that the Melbourne Cricket Club wanted none of this.

Wowserism was at its peak in Melbourne in the 1870s and the 1880s. There were complaints against the running of trains on Sundays, the National Gallery was only opened on Sundays after a long fight, and sport on Sundays was unheard of except in family backyards. When the nude painting "Chloe" by Lefebevre of Paris, was hung on the wall of Young and Jackson's saloon bar in Bourke Street, the puritans were outraged. But

*The English wicket-keeper Edward Pooley missed the first-ever Test because of a brawl in New Zealand. He was in prison when the game was played*

Melbourne cricketers switched from champagne luncheons to beer with no discernible deterioration in their play.

Lillywhite's team comprised seasoned cricketers from four strong English counties, Sussex, Yorkshire, Surrey and Nottinghamshire. Four of the team, Lillywhite, Greenwood, Jupp and Southerton, had toured Australia with the last England team. The great medium-pace bowler Alfred Shaw, whose bowling had a lovely fluid action, was in the side, along with Tom Emmett, the magnificent Yorkshire left-arm pace bowler,

and the gifted Yorkshire all-rounder George ("Happy Jack") Ulyett, who opened for England with W. G. Grace. Ulyett, a fun-loving craftsman, once claimed he was in the Yorkshire side for his whistling and in the England side just to give W. G. confidence.

These stars were supported by an outstanding wicket-keeper, Edward Pooley; a slow lob bowler and useful batsman in Tom Armitage; Allen Hill, a left-arm seam bowler, who had achieved a hat-trick and had clean-bowled 12 men for Yorkshire against Surrey in 1871 at The Oval; John Selby, of Nottingham, a right-hand batsman of rare skill on difficult pitches; and Henry Charlwood, the most talented of four Charlwoods who played for Sussex.

Despite its all-round strength, Lillywhite's team struggled from the start. Only in Adelaide, where good profits resulted from wins over twenty-twos of South Australia, could Lillywhite's players afford to relax. A New South Wales fifteen beat them by two wickets and later by 13 wickets, while Fifteen of Victoria won by 31 runs. At Goulburn, when England met a local twenty-two, play was held up twice when six hares and two young kangaroos raced on the field. Inspired by their earlier wins New South Wales met Lilly-white's team on level terms in January 1877, but had the worst of a drawn match: New South Wales still needed 48 runs to avoid an innings defeat with only four wickets left.

This success made Lillywhite's players confident that they could defeat Australia's best on level terms, and when an All Australia *v.* All England match was suggested Lillywhite agreed to add it to the tour schedule. While the English players went off to New Zealand for a few matches, John Conway made all the arrangements. He contacted leading players direct, ignoring the Victorian Cricketers' Association and the New South Wales Cricket Association. The latter was not impressed by this action and passed the following resolution just before the New South Wales players left for Melbourne:

*It has been publicly notified that a game is about to be played between the All England Eleven and a combined eleven of New South Wales and Victoria, this association desires to place on record that the same has been arranged without any reference to the association, and cannot be regarded as a match in which chosen representatives of New South Wales take part.*

Edwin Evans said he could not play because of his job as a government inspector of selections. Spofforth at first agreed to join Dave and Ned Gregory, Charles Bannerman, Nat Thompson and Tom Garrett, but withdrew when he found Billy Murdoch would not keep wicket. The *Australasian* was critical of this action.

*Spofforth, apparently believing his success was due to his wicket-keeper and not his own merit, and fearing he would be shorn of his lustre if*

*another 'who knew not Joseph' were behind the sticks, declined to play unless his own special wicket-keeper was selected. As this could not be arranged, this modest gentleman had to remain behind.*

Conway was adamant that John McCarthy Blackham, the black-bearded Fitzroy bank clerk

---

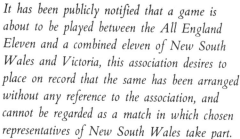

ABOVE LEFT: *Another of the withdrawals from the first Test was the distinguished medium-pace bowler Edwin Evans, who said he was too busy inspecting selections*
ABOVE RIGHT: *The great fast bowler Fred Spofforth rejected an invitation to play in the first Test because Billy Murdoch was not chosen as wicket-keeper. He changed his mind for the second Test*
RIGHT: *Australia's wicket-keeper for the first Test was John McCarthy Blackham, a fearless character whom no amount of heavy knocks could deter. He became known as "The Prince of Wicket-Keepers"*

MELBOURNE CRICKET GRO
1877

Scoreboard  Press and  Members' Pavilion
Scorers' Box

This picture shows the entire Ground Staff and the E
and the Ground at the date of the First Test Match
15ᵗʰ 16ᵗʰ and 19ᵗʰ March 1877

*The Melbourne Cricket Ground and its entire staff just before the start of the first Test on 15 March 1877. The press and scorers' box is at the rear (far left), the MCG Members' Stand is in the centre (rear) and the prized new grandstand runs along the back of the right-hand side of the ground*

with the glinting eyes and fast, competitive hands, should keep wicket. Blackham had earlier failed to win selection in Carlton firsts but had impressed Conway in a press match and eagerly accepted Conway's invitation to join South Melbourne.

Then lanky left-arm pace bowler Frank Allan, chosen to replace Spofforth, sent a telegram from his home in Allansford, Victoria, saying he could not spare the time. Allan, in fact, preferred to go to the Warrnambool Agricultural Show, held at the same time, and mingle with old friends. The Melbourne *Argus* attributed Allan's withdrawal to fear and Melbourne *Punch* awarded him a white feather.

England entered the match, now regarded as the first of all Tests, only a day after arriving from New Zealand with some players still seasick and

*Grandstand . "The Finest in the World"*

the Christchurch man realised that he had been outwitted.

On the morning of the first Test the combined Sydney and Melbourne Eleven, labelled "All Australia", elected Dave Gregory as captain, an honour handsome Dave cherished all his life, as Victorians outnumbered New South Welshmen in the side. Gregory had upset the New South Wales Cricket Association by playing in the match, lessening his chances of securing high office in the association. But he was proud of leading an Australian team, even if only five of the players were native born. The All England team appeared too powerful and an easy England win was unanimously forecast. Consequently only 1000 spectators turned up for the start of play on 15 March 1877.

Most observers were surprised that Bransby Beauchamp Cooper, by far the most experienced cricketer in the Australian lineup, had not been elected captain. All of them scoffed at the last-minute selection of John Hodges as replacement for Allan. Hodges, a fast-medium left-arm bowler, had been given a trial by Richmond but had not represented Victoria. Cooper, an accomplished batsman, could not be induced to practise.

Before he left England Lillywhite learned that G. F. Grace planned to bring a team to Australia. When he first arrived he found that Grace had booked the Melbourne Cricket Ground for the dates of the "first Test". Lillywhite booked the East Melbourne ground instead, but when Grace's team did not turn up the game was moved back to the MCG. When the East Melbourne Club threatened legal action, Lillywhite had to pay them £230 compensation and allow 500 East Melbourne members free admission to the MCG.

Statistician Bill Frindall has compiled biographical details of the players (see overleaf). Garrett was 18 years 232 days old when he played in the first Test, the youngest Australian ever to play in a Test against England (Ian Craig, 17 years 239 days old when he appeared for Australia against South Africa in 1953, is the youngest

without their only specialist wicket-keeper, Ted Pooley. He had been arrested in Christchurch on a charge of causing malicious damage after persuading a local to a bet in a pub on the Eighteen of Christchurch *v.* England match. Pooley said he could forecast every player's score and offered to pay a shilling for each wrong prediction providing he was paid £1 for each one he got right. Pooley wrote nought against each Christchurch name and since more than half the side were out for ducks, made a handsome profit. Pooley was held responsible for the disturbance that followed when

# The First Australian Test Cricketers

|  | Born | Died |
|---|---|---|
| BANNERMAN, Charles | Woolwich, England 3 July 1851 | Surry Hills, Sydney 20 August 1930 |
| BLACKHAM, John McCarthy | Fitzroy, Melbourne 11 May 1854 | Melbourne 28 December 1932 |
| COOPER, Bransby Beauchamp | India 15 March 1844 | Geelong, Victoria 7 August 1914 |
| GARRETT, Thomas William | Wollongong, N.S.W. 26 July 1858 | Warrawee, Sydney 6 August 1943 |
| GREGORY, David William | Wollongong, N.S.W. 15 April 1845 | Turramurra, Sydney 4 August 1919 |
| GREGORY, Edward James | Waverley, Sydney 29 May 1839 | S.C.G., Sydney 22 April 1922 |
| HODGES, John Henry | Collingwood, Victoria 31 July 1856 | Collingwood, Victoria 17 January 1933 |
| HORAN, Thomas Patrick | Middleton, Eire 3 March 1854 | Malvern, Melbourne 16 April 1916 |
| KENDALL, Thomas | Bedford, England 24 August 1851 | Hobart 17 August 1924 |
| MIDWINTER, William Evans | St Briavels, Glos. England 19 June 1851 | Melbourne 3 December 1890 |
| THOMPSON, Nathaniel | Birmingham, England 21 April 1838 | Burwood, Sydney 2 September 1896 |

Australian Test player against all countries).

Dave Gregory won the toss and decided to bat. Charles Bannerman, born in Kent 25 years earlier, faced the first ball in Test cricket from round-armer Alfred Shaw, which he blocked. Bannerman also scored the first run in Test cricket, off the second ball, and was missed by Armitage off Shaw before he reached 10. The ball lobbed up from the bat but the simple catch hit Armitage on the stomach without his getting a hand to it. Play began at varying times each day, this day at 1.00 p.m., but by the close at 5 p.m. Bannerman had scored 126 not out, the first Test century. He was particularly severe on Armitage, the lob bowler. After the dismissal of Thompson for one, Horan, and later Cooper, defended grimly to support Bannerman, who was not out at stumps with Australia 6 for 166.

Armitage became so frustrated with the brilliance of Bannerman's batting that he tried to lob the ball over his head in deliveries that one critic suggested could only have been reached with a clothes prop. Armitage then resorted to grubbers, a style not seen in Melbourne for 20 years. He was soon taken off.

On the second day Yorkshireman George Ulyett split Bannerman's thumb with a fast, rising delivery after Bannerman had scored 165 out of

# The First English Test Cricketers

| | | |
|---|---|---|
| ARMITAGE, Thomas | Sheffield, Yorkshire<br>25 April 1848 | Pullman, U.S.A.<br>21 September 1922 |
| CHARLWOOD, Henry Rupert James | Horsham, Sussex<br>19 December 1846 | Scarborough, Yorkshire<br>6 June 1888 |
| EMMETT, Thomas | Halifax, Yorkshire<br>3 September 1841 | Leicester<br>29 June 1904 |
| GREENWOOD, Andrew | Lepton, Yorkshire<br>20 August 1847 | Huddersfield, Yorkshire<br>12 February 1889 |
| HILL, Allen | Kirkheaton, Yorkshire<br>14 November 1845 | Leyland, Lancs<br>29 August 1910 |
| JUPP, Henry | Dorking, Surrey<br>19 November 1841 | Bermondsey, London<br>8 April 1889 |
| LILLYWHITE, James | West Hampnett, Sussex<br>23 February 1842 | Chichester, Sussex<br>25 October 1929 |
| SELBY, John | Nottingham<br>1 July 1849 | Nottingham<br>11 March 1894 |
| SHAW, Alfred | Burton Joyce, Notts<br>29 August 1842 | Gedling, Notts<br>16 January 1907 |
| SOUTHERTON, James | Petworth, Sussex<br>16 November 1827 | Mitcham, Surrey<br>16 June 1880 |
| ULYETT, George | Sheffield, Yorkshire<br>21 October 1851 | Sheffield, Yorkshire<br>18 June 1898 |

Australia's total of 245. Southerton, whose appearance in this match at 49 years 111 days made him the oldest-ever England Test player, took 3 for 61 off 37 four-ball overs, Shaw 3 for 51 off 55.3 overs. Blackham (17) and Garrett (18) helped Bannerman later in the innings.

Australia's bowling and wicket-keeping reached a high standard when England batted, but the fielding was scrappy. Despite splendid innings by Jupp and Charlwood, England's middle order failed and they finished 49 behind on the first innings. Only Horan (20), Midwinter (17), Ned Gregory (11) and Kendall (17) reached double figures in Australia's second innings of 104.

Bannerman batted with his finger heavily strapped, but was in obvious discomfort and made only 4 before he was bowled by Ulyett.

Left to score 154 to win, England appeared to have a good chance at 4 for 61, but after Selby and Ulyett had made 40 in a fine stand, the England batting was overwhelmed by Kendall's left-arm slows. Selby, who had kept wicket for England in Pooley's absence, topscored with 38, Charlwood made 13 and Ulyett 24, out of a total of 108. Australia won on the fourth day by 45 runs. Numerous authorities have acclaimed Bannerman's 165 retired hurt as the finest innings of Test cricket, for it was compiled on a rough

# Australia v. England—The First Test

*Played at Melbourne Cricket Ground on 15–19 March 1877*

## Australia

| First Innings | | |
|---|---|---|
| C. Bannerman, *retired hurt* | | 165 |
| N. Thompson, *b.* Hill | | 1 |
| T. P. Horan, *c.* Hill, *b.* Shaw | | 12 |
| D. W. Gregory, *run out* | | 1 |
| B. B. Cooper, *b.* Southerton | | 15 |
| W. E. Midwinter, *c.* Ulyett, *b.* Southerton | | 5 |
| E. J. Gregory, *c.* Greenwood, *b.* Lillywhite | | 0 |
| J. M. Blackham, *b.* Southerton | | 17 |
| T. W. Garrett, *not out* | | 18 |
| T. Kendall, *c.* Southerton, *b.* Shaw | | 3 |
| J. H. Hodges, *b.* Shaw | | 0 |
| *Extras* (B 4, LB 2, W 2) | | 8 |
| | Total | 245 |

| Second Innings | | |
|---|---|---|
| C. Bannerman, *b.* Ulyett | | 4 |
| N. Thompson, *c.* Emmett, *b.* Shaw | | 7 |
| T. P. Horan, *c.* Selby, *b.* Hill | | 20 |
| D. W. Gregory, *b.* Shaw | | 3 |
| B. B. Cooper, *b.* Shaw | | 3 |
| W. E. Midwinter, *c.* Southerton, *b.* Ulyett | | 17 |
| E. J. Gregory, *c.* Emmett, *b.* Ulyett | | 11 |
| J. M. Blackham, *lbw, b.* Shaw | | 6 |
| T. W. Garrett, *c.* Emmett, *b.* Shaw | | 0 |
| T. Kendall, *not out* | | 17 |
| J. H. Hodges, *b.* Lillywhite | | 8 |
| *Extras* (B 5, LB 3) | | 8 |
| | Total | 104 |

| Bowling | Overs | Maidens | Runs | Wickets |
|---|---|---|---|---|
| Shaw | 55.3 | 34 | 51 | 3 |
| Hill | 23 | 10 | 42 | 1 |
| Ulyett | 25 | 12 | 36 | 0 |
| Southerton | 37 | 17 | 61 | 3 |
| Armitage | 3 | 0 | 15 | 0 |
| Lillywhite | 14 | 5 | 19 | 1 |
| Emmett | 12 | 7 | 13 | 0 |

| Bowling | Overs | Maidens | Runs | Wickets |
|---|---|---|---|---|
| Shaw | 34 | 16 | 38 | 5 |
| Hill | 14 | 6 | 18 | 1 |
| Ulyett | 19 | 7 | 39 | 3 |
| Lillywhite | 1 | 0 | 1 | 1 |

### Fall of Wickets

| Wicket | Australia 1st | Australia 2nd | Wicket | Australia 1st | Australia 2nd |
|---|---|---|---|---|---|
| 1st | 2 | 7 | 6th | 143 | 58 |
| 2nd | 40 | 27 | 7th | 197 | 71 |
| 3rd | 41 | 31 | 8th | 243 | 75 |
| 4th | 118 | 31 | 9th | 245 | 75 |
| 5th | 142 | 35 | 10th | — | 104 |

# England

| First Innings | |
|---|---:|
| H. Jupp, *lbw, b.* Garrett | 63 |
| J. Selby, *c.* Cooper, *b.* Hodges | 7 |
| H. R. J. Charlwood, *c.* Blackham, *b.* Midwinter | 36 |
| G. Ulyett, *lbw, b.* Thompson | 10 |
| A. Greenwood, *c.* E. J. Gregory, *b.* Midwinter | 1 |
| T. Armitage, *c.* Blackham, *b.* Midwinter | 9 |
| A. Shaw, *b.* Midwinter | 10 |
| T. Emmett, *b.* Midwinter | 8 |
| A. Hill, *not out* | 35 |
| James Lillywhite, *c.* and *b.* Kendall | 10 |
| J. Southerton, *c.* Cooper, *b.* Garrett | 6 |
| *Extras* (LB 1) | 1 |
| Total | 196 |

| Second Innings | |
|---|---:|
| H. Jupp, *lbw, b.* Midwinter | 4 |
| J. Selby, *c.* Horan, *b.* Hodges | 38 |
| H. R. J. Charlwood, *b.* Kendall | 13 |
| G. Ulyett, *b.* Kendall | 24 |
| A. Greenwood, *c.* Midwinter, *b.* Kendall | 5 |
| T. Armitage, *c.* Blackham, *b.* Kendall | 3 |
| A. Shaw, *st.* Blackham, *b.* Kendall | 2 |
| T. Emmett, *b.* Kendall | 9 |
| A. Hill, *c.* Thompson, *b.* Kendall | 0 |
| James Lillywhite, *b.* Hodges | 4 |
| J. Southerton, *not out* | 1 |
| *Extras* (B 4, LB 1) | 5 |
| Total | 108 |

## Bowling

| | Overs | Maidens | Runs | Wickets |
|---|---|---|---|---|
| Hodges | 9 | 0 | 27 | 1 |
| Garrett | 18.1 | 10 | 22 | 2 |
| Kendall | 38 | 16 | 54 | 1 |
| Midwinter | 54 | 23 | 78 | 5 |
| Thompson | 17 | 10 | 14 | 1 |

## Bowling

| | Overs | Maidens | Runs | Wickets |
|---|---|---|---|---|
| Hodges | 7 | 5 | 7 | 2 |
| Garrett | 2 | 0 | 9 | 0 |
| Kendall | 33.1 | 12 | 55 | 7 |
| Midwinter | 19 | 7 | 23 | 1 |
| D. W. Gregory | 5 | 1 | 9 | 0 |

## Fall of Wickets

| Wicket | England 1st | England 2nd | Wicket | England 1st | England 2nd |
|---|---|---|---|---|---|
| 1st | 23 | 0 | 6th | 135 | 68 |
| 2nd | 79 | 7 | 7th | 145 | 92 |
| 3rd | 98 | 20 | 8th | 145 | 93 |
| 4th | 109 | 22 | 9th | 168 | 100 |
| 5th | 121 | 62 | 10th | 196 | 108 |

Umpires: C. A. Reid and R. B. Terry.

*Australia won by 45 runs*

*Australia's first cricket captain, David William Gregory, was elected by his team-mates in the dressing-room just before play began. He led his side with distinction*

epoch-making and a reminder to the leaders of the game at Lord's and The Oval that cricket was thriving in the colonies. "It may console them to note that the English race is not disintegrating in a distant land and on turf where lately the black-fellow hurled his boomerang," it said. Melbourne *Punch* produced a special celebratory poem, which ended with the lines:

> *When bowling cracks of little mind*
> *Prove beggars upon horses,*
> *Australia is compelled to find*
> *Fresh strength and new resources.*

> *For Allan, Evans, Spofforth*
> *She does not care a snuff,*
> *Since Kendall, Mid., and Hodges proved*
> *Themselves quite good enough.*

> *So patriotic A., E., S.,*
> *Next time, 'tis we will strike;*
> *Henceforth go play with babes,*
> *For like should mate with like.*

The return match on the Melbourne Cricket Ground a fortnight later was played for the benefit of the England tourists, since the takings for the first match had exceeded the organisers' predictions despite the poor crowd on the first day. The Australians' success in the first Test attracted bigger crowds the second time round. With Pooley still in New Zealand, England had only 11 fit players. Australia bolstered their side, including Spofforth for Ned Gregory, Murdoch for Horan and T. J. D. Kelly for B. B. Cooper.

The match lasted four days. The reversible stand was all but full and there was a sprinkling of women in the members' enclosure. A band played in the breaks during the afternoon. Nat Thompson and Charles Bannerman took Australia's score to 29, but with some awkward seam bowling by Yorkshireman Allen Hill, Australia slumped to 4 for 60 by lunch. After lunch Jupp relieved Selby as England's wicket-keeper but neither was particularly proficient. Midwinter topscored with 31 in Australia's 122.

track, and accounted for 67 per cent of the team total. Kendall's match figures of 8 for 109, including 7 for 55 in the second innings, were also crucial to Australia's success.

The Victorian Cricket Association gave each Australian player a gold medal; there was a slightly larger one for Dave Gregory, the winning captain. A subscription list for Bannerman realised £83 7s 6d and others for Blackham and Kendall £23 5s 0d each. Shaw, a master of accuracy, was unfortunate that his 89.3 overs, including 50 maidens, and match figures of 8 for 89, were not similarly recognised.

The Sydney *Daily News* acclaimed the win as

*Three players who accepted first Test invitations were: (top left) Bransby Beauchamp Cooper, (top right) John Hodges and (below) Tom Kendall. Cooper's great experience in England helped the Australians to success, and Kendall's bowling clinched the match for Australia. Hodges retained his place for the second Test but played badly*

Spofforth bowled extremely fast when England batted, but even so, Blackham took him standing up to the wicket. In the third over Blackham brilliantly stumped Shaw from a fast, rising delivery and at the close England were 2 for 7. Next day Australia's bowling reached a high standard, but seven catches were dropped. Greenwood started the England revival with 49, and Ulyett, 52, Emmett, 48, and Hill, 49, chimed in to lift England to 261, a lead of 139. Gregory appeared to lose control of the Australian fieldsmen as England's late order batsmen hammered his bowlers.

In the second innings an outstanding opening partnership of 88 by Dave Gregory and Thompson put Australia back in the match. Garrett, Blackham and Kelly all hit out lustily and Australia moved to 259. Set to score 121, England were 3 for 9 at lunch on the fourth day and 5 for 76 before tea, but a bold display of hitting by Ulyett took England to a notable win by six wickets. When Ulyett was out for 63 only nine runs were needed. He had topscored in each innings.

Although Australia had lost a tense, even contest, some critics rated Lillywhite's team the weakest to tour Australia, a judgment that seems harsh when the career performances of its members are considered. Shaw was the best bowler of his generation, Selby was England's leading batsman only one year later, and Ulyett scored 1000 runs in a season ten times. Had Armitage taken the simple chance from Bannerman in the first Test no doubt the rating of the team would have been higher.

The team played 23 matches — three against eleven and 20 against the odds. The results of the eleven-a-side matches were one win, one draw and one loss. Three of those against the odds were lost, 10 won and seven drawn. Australia produced exciting bowlers in Spofforth and Kendall, a great batsman in Charles Bannerman, and a wicket-keeper of revolutionary technique in Blackham. But their fielding was far below England's standard. "We would counsel whoever may enter into future speculation for importing an England XI to bear in mind the great improvements of colonial cricket, and not to imagine that anything will do for Australia," advised one critic.

Lillywhite's team each received £150 for the tour, plus the takings from the second international match. The tour organisers, Lillywhite and Conway, made substantially more than this. Lillywhite later assisted Australian cricket with wise counselling on his four Australian tours, and

*Colonel Richardson, commander of the Victoria Barracks troops, first developed Sydney Cricket Ground as the Garrison ground. His absence, due to the Sudan War, gave New South Wales Cricket Association supporters a chance to take over the ground*

also acted as an agent for Australian teams in England. Gregory's Australian players received only expenses, although Charles Bannerman, Jack Blackham and Tom Kendall benefited from collections. Neither the New South Wales Cricket Association nor the Victorian Cricketers' Association had any voice in the selection of the Australian team or in the promotion of the match.

Meanwhile in Sydney the search for a headquarters for New South Wales cricket had reached a crucial stage. A senior Lands Department official, Charles Oliver, who happened to be a former state cricketer, advocated that the New South Wales Government should allow the New South Wales Cricket Association to take over the Garrison Ground. Colonel Richardson, commander of Victoria Barracks, strongly opposed this, arguing that the army needed the ground for a rifle range.

*Phil Sheridan, one of the original trustees of the Sydney Cricket Ground. He feuded with the New South Wales Cricket Association for more than 30 years*

Finally, a deputation from the association led by Dick Driver junior had a long interview with the Minister for Lands, and on 3 November 1875 the government asked the association to nominate trustees to administer the 5-hectare site. The association nominated Driver, a prominent Mason, and Phillip Sheridan, a cricket-loving Irish Catholic, who had been in Australia since 1849 and had done valuable work for the Warwick Cricket Club. They proved an admirable combination. William Stephen, Under-Secretary for Lands, represented the government as the third trustee for the ground, which was formally dedicated by Governor Sir Hercules Robinson on 3 August 1877.

The great Anglo-Indian batsman Prince Ranjitsinhji described Phillip Sheridan as

*A small man, slightly built, but very active and vivacious, and always full of fun and spirits. One can always tell that Phillip Sheridan is in the room from the amount of talking and laughing that is going on. His ready wit is indeed astonishing; he always turns everything into a joke, and his puns at times are worthy of Charles Lamb. He is firm and a true friend.*

A stand at the Sydney Cricket Ground, built in 1909, honoured his name. It was pulled down in 1985.

The Albert Cricket Ground Company strongly objected to the association taking over the Garrison Ground, arguing that it was public parkland. A deputation from the company to Premier J. S. Farnell argued that he should stop the association charging for admission at what was then known as the Association Ground. The government believed that if the association was prepared to spend large sums improving the ground, it was entitled to charge an entrance fee.

Posters and handbills were distributed attacking the association, but on the day of the first match, Thursday, 25 October 1877, the expected demonstration outside the ground's gates did not eventuate. A German band entertained spectators, who paid one shilling to enter. It cost an extra shilling to enter the temporary stand. The match, the final of the Civil Service Challenge Cup, was notable for an innings of 169 not out by Alick Bannerman for the Government Printing Office against the Audit Department, which included Dave Gregory.

Seven months earlier Alick's brother Charles had been the hero of the first Test match. The New South Wales government was pleased that the state association were improving their ground, an essential development before Sydney could stage similar international matches.

Not long after the first match on the Association Ground, the Albert Ground, much admired by W. G. Grace and other notable visitors, was sold off for home sites, giving the shareholders a return of £12 for every £5 share. The chairman of the Albert Ground Company recommended that the site be sold because the New South Wales Cricket Association was spending profits from Albert Ground matches on upgrading the Garrison Ground. The association made these expensive improvements, however, in the mistaken belief that it had complete control of its new ground.

Hardworking John Conway considered the time was now right for an Australian team to visit England. He received unanimous support from Dave Gregory and all the leading players, but none at all from the youthful Victorian and New South Wales associations. The public was apathetic about the idea, and one newspaper declared that it was "a presumptuous adventure calculated to dampen the ardour of the most enterprising speculator". Ned Sheridan, no relation to Phillip, declined Conway's invitation because of the death of his mother. Dave Gregory urged Conway to check the availability of others who might be considered. Tasmanian John Arthur received this letter from Conway on 19 April 1877:

> It is intended if possible to send an Australian team to England, taking in India on route after playing a series of matches in the Australian colonies. Would you form one of the team if sufficient inducement is held out? It is intended to make all the colonies interested in order to ensure the economical working of the team. I may state that Charles Bannerman, Spofforth, the Gregorys, Thompson, Murdoch, Garrett and Coates have already promised their cooperation, and have sanctioned my actions in this matter. Would you favour me by asking Bailey (Launceston) if he would like to join the party?

Two days after this invitation arrived the 30-year-old Arthur died. His death, according to the Launceston *Examiner*, was due to "a short attack of brain fever", while the Hobart *Mercury* called it pleurisy, but his death certificate read "inflammation of the brain". Bailey thus became

the sole Tasmanian in the first white Australian team to tour England. Each member contributed £50, which was three times the cost of a voyage to Europe. Funds were raised with a 16-match preliminary junket round the colonies, and with games in America on the way home. All profits were to be shared equally by team members.

The players assembled in Sydney and on 3 November 1877, left for Brisbane. The Eagle Farm viceregal tent supplied the champagne, while Kendall and Allan added the curly or "Serpentine" slows, and Blackham was "as watchful as a Crimean Sergeant" adding pressure from behind the stumps. The Australians defeated Eighteen of Brisbane, scoring 149 against 58 and 68. Charles Bannerman hit the ball "in low parabolic curves", which the Queenslanders could not catch until he had made 74. Kendall wrecked Queensland's second innings with 13 for 35, bowling Just with one of his "spiral permeators".

An easy win over Toowoomba followed before the Australians returned to Sydney to play Fifteen of Sydney. A crowd of 12,000 was anticipated. But Sydney cricket fans lacked the *Brisbane Courier*'s enthusiasm, and only 200 turned up for the entire event. Publicity was poor and the crowds just as sparse for matches at Maitland and Newcastle. At Adelaide Spofforth took 17 for 125 in a nine-wicket win over Eighteen of South Australia. At Melbourne against a Combined Fifteen of Victoria and New South Wales the scores were tied when tour dropout, Edwin Evans, bowled the Australians' last man, Tom Kendall. Evans returned 7 for 44 and 4 for 42.

The pill box hats and bright sashes of the Australian team were next seen at Invercargill, New Zealand, where they defeated Twenty-Two of Invercargill. This was the first appearance of an Australian team in New Zealand and Charles Bannerman's 128 not out the first century by an Australian in New Zealand. Their only loss on this tour was to Canterbury, who refused to play if they had to field more than 15 players. Canterbury fielded 12 very tall players and dismissed

Australia for 46. A pace bowler named E. Fuller took 8 for 35 in Australia's second knock of 143. Canterbury lost eight wickets in scoring the 56 needed to win in the final innings. A crowd of more than 5000 attended the final day, and Canterbury were so encouraged by this win they sent a team to tour Victoria the next summer. But the trip was a box office disaster and money had to be sent to get the Canterbury players home.

Spofforth later recalled that when the Australians sailed along the New Zealand coast during a terrible storm he speculated, with expert swimmer Charles Bannerman, about whom he would save if they were shipwrecked. Bannerman replied that he would save the New South Welshmen and leave the Victorians to drown.

The hostility towards the English tour continued in Sydney when some of the players selected for Fifteen of New South Wales demanded more money. Ten thousand people attended, mainly to boo the tourists, who were criticised as money-hungry opportunists. Others contended that they did not constitute the best national team.

At two minutes to six, with time for only one over, the scores were level. Allan was at the crease but barely able to walk because of sciatica. He heard Ned Gregory remark: "Bring everyone in to save the single. He's too lame to hit, and will try for only one run". Evans bowled two fine deliveries and as he began his approach run for the third Allan moved down the crease. Evans failed to notice how far Allan had advanced up the pitch and what should have been a good length ball became a half volley, which Allan lifted over the fieldsmen for four. Allan stood watching the ball go to the chains but there was no applause, only an eerie silence from a hostile crowd. Allan limped from the ground without a single cheer.

The same enmity greeted the team in Melbourne where they played their last three games before leaving for England. Spectators wildly clapped the successes of their opponents but were unmoved by the Australians' triumphs. Allan, whose sciatica had forced him to miss the New

Zealand part of the preliminary tour, went back to Sale knowing that if he did not recover he would be dropped. When the SS *Chimboraso*, the ship on which the team was booked to sail via the Cape, broke down in Jervis Bay, manager Conway made last-minute arrangements for them to travel to London via America.

Meanwhile the management had decided to omit Kendall, hero of the first Test, from the touring party. They agreed that he was an outstanding bowler and perhaps the best of his type in the world. He had an easy left-arm action and could turn the ball sharply each way making it difficult to read. But his drinking was a problem. Left at home, Kendall grew steadily grosser and lost the suppleness that had made his 1877–78 season so memorable. He had taken 102 wickets at 6.26 in the Australian team's preliminary matches, a performance only bettered by Spofforth (281 at 4.1) and Garrett (103 at 3.2).

Nat Thompson was invited to replace Kendall but declined and 20-year-old Alick Bannerman, who had never played for his state, took his place. Allan made a hectic journey by coach and train to reach the wharf the day before the *City of Sydney* sailed for San Francisco, travelling at one stage for 18 hours in heavy rain, soaked to the skin. Billy Midwinter had agreed to join the team in England, where he was living, but the eleven players who left Australia knew Kendall's omission left the bowlers with an immense task. Less than a dozen people were at the wharf in Sydney to see them off and their departure was ignored by the newspapers. The Kendall decision was condemned by the critics and it hung heavily on the team. From San Francisco they took the train to New York, where they boarded the *City of Berlin* on 13 May 1878 for the voyage to Liverpool. Several members of the party took money with them to pay for their return fares in case the tour proved a flop; all agreed that they would be happy to break even. Understandably, in view of Kendall's experience, not one member let liquor get the better of him during their 13-month stint.

# Incessant rain and wild applause

## The first tour of England 1878

Australian captain Dave Gregory was 33, the father of three children, with 13 more to follow. Most of his players were under 25, Tom Garrett the youngest at 19 already sporting a luxuriant beard. But the men were mentally tough and physically prepared for a tour that would involve 37 matches, 15 of them first-class, in England alone. Their resilience was important, for apart from the nine early matches in which they had the help of Midwinter, the team had no replacements. They were lucky to be able to call on Melbourne medical student H. N. Tennant and their 37-year-old manager John Conway to enable some players to rest during minor matches.

The team had no baggage man, and drew lots before each trip to decide who would carry the huge canvas bag which held their gear. "Australian XI" was painted on its sides in large letters. Spofforth recalled that on one occasion in New Zealand he and Murdoch had dragged its great

*The first Australian team which toured England in 1878: (L to R) (back) J. Blackham, T. Horan, G. H. Bailey, J. Conway (manager), A. Bannerman, C. Bannerman, W. Murdoch; (front) F. R. Spofforth, F. E. Allan, D. W. Gregory (captain), W. Midwinter, T. W. Garrett, H. F. Boyle*

weight for two and a half kilometres over gates and fences. Players faced this onerous chore once a week on average until the team reached London. The bag was then lost, never to be seen again. This was a time when only an elite few owned bats or pads.

The team comprised D. W. Gregory, F. R. Spofforth, T. W. Garrett, W. L. Murdoch, C. Bannerman and A. C. Bannerman, from New South Wales; F. E. Allan, J. McC. Blackham, H. F. Boyle, and T. Horan, of Victoria; and G. H. Bailey from Tasmania. Midwinter, who had played for Victoria since the 1874–75 season and had been one of the heroes of Australia's first Test win in Melbourne, joined the team for its first match in Nottingham. During the past year he had lived in England, appearing in South of England teams with his teacher, W. G. Grace. When Gloucestershire upset England in a famous match at The Oval in 1877, Midwinter took 7 for 35 and 4 for 46.

Of the other Australians the heavily bearded round-arm bowler Harry Boyle was the player the crowds most wanted to see when the tour began. Boyle was born in Sydney, but spent most of his life in Victoria. He bowled his right-hand medium-pacers with machine-like accuracy, providing ideal support for the pace of hawk-nosed Fred Spofforth. Boyle was the inventor of the silly mid-on fielding position, known originally as "Boyley's mid-on". To team-mates his other idiosyncrasy was his insistence on always sitting out in the rain beside their coach drivers.

The team went straight from Liverpool by train to Nottingham, where a huge crowd, including the sheriff, local aldermen and noted cricketers, greeted them as they stepped onto the platform. Murdoch and Spofforth, who had been sleeping at the back of the train, slipped out unnoticed and mingled with the crowd. One burly bare-armed man wearing a blacksmith's leather apron exclaimed, "Well, I'm damned! They aren't black after all. If I'd knowed, I wunna come." Dave Gregory then alighted from the train and

the man studied his black beard and skin browned by the Australian sun. "Ah, 'ere's one's a 'arf caste any'ow," he commented. A band played as the Australians moved from the station, but cheering crowds in the streets made it difficult for them to reach their hotel. After the frosty farewells in Sydney nobody minded the crush.

James Lillywhite had drawn up a programme of matches. The players, remembering the itinerary the first England team had faced in Australia 14 years earlier, were amused to find so many games against fifteens and eighteens. Lillywhite had not been able to fill all the available dates and his schedule involved travelling repeatedly from one end of England to the other. The schedule proved so tiring that twice Frank Allan had to be shaken awake when it was his turn to bat. Lillywhite believed that the Australians could win half their matches if Victorian and New South Wales jealousies could be minimised.

In wet, depressing weather the Australians turned out in white silk shirts and white felt hats that would not stay on in the wind. Only Midwinter had experience of the sodden pitches and he advised Gregory to bat when Australia won the first toss. Midwinter was the only batsman to reach double figures in a miserable first innings of 63.

Gregory and Billy Murdoch were both out for ducks. "What on earth are we doing in this country? I wish I was back in Sydney with the sun on my back," a shivering Gregory exclaimed. Shaw, who had magical control of length, bowled unchanged with Morley in each innings. Notts scored 163, as the Australian bowlers slithered about in their approach runs, leaving Australia to score 90 to avoid an innings defeat. They were all out for 76. Shaw took 11 for 55, Morley 8 for 72.

Despite the efforts of Lillywhite and Conway, the Australians were denied a match against a full strength English team. This together with the dismal start at Nottingham and the unforeseen opposition of English professionals who regarded

*Billy Midwinter, lost to the Australian tourists after only nine of the thirty-one matches. W. G. Grace claimed him to play for Gloucestershire instead. Midwinter later regretted that he submitted to this*

the Australians as a threat to their earnings, threatened the tour.

English critics believed the team's strength was in its bowling, with Spofforth, Boyle, Allan and Garrett all capable of dismissing England's best batsmen cheaply. Blackham was a brilliant wicket-keeper of pioneering technique, and only the Cambridge amateur Alfred Lyttelton came close to his standard during the tour. The fielding was of the highest class, with Gregory manipulating alert, enthusiastic players with quite unexpected skill. The batting lacked depth, and missed the experience of Bransby Beauchamp Cooper familiar

with the vagaries of English pitches. Murdoch was not far behind Charles Bannerman in stroke play, Alick Bannerman could hold up any attack, and Tom Horan was ready to clump anything loose for boundaries. "The other seven are worth only 30 runs between them," wrote one critic.

The players all learned quickly, however, and few of them committed an indiscretion twice, either on the field or at receptions. By the end of a month they were all noticeably smarter in their dress than when they arrived.

From the start the team was pestered by people seeking news of relatives long lost in Australia. One man told Frank Allan he must know his brother, because he had only three toes on one foot. Jack Blackham was asked by an expensively dressed woman to take a parcel back to her sister in Adelaide. When Blackham said he lived in Melbourne, the woman replied that she would pay his return cab fare.

Grimly determined to revive their fortunes the Australians set out from the Tavistock Hotel, Covent Garden, on 27 May 1878, almost unnoticed. No fans met them at Lord's nor was there an official welcome. One Marylebone Cricket Club member grumbled that they could not be Australians because they were not black. He was privileged, however, to see one of the most astonishing cricket matches ever played.

The MCC batted first before only 500 spectators, who guffawed when W. G. Grace hit Allan's first ball for four, thinking there would be a lot more of the same. Then Midwinter, stealing round from fine leg, caught Grace at square leg off the second ball, his long experience of the doctor's repertoire crucial to this clever dismissal. Booth came in and Allan bowled him for a duck. The MCC captain Ridley joined Hornby, who was batting splendidly, and the score moved to 25. Then Gregory replaced Allan with Spofforth, who at once bowled Hornby for 19, including a hit into the crowd.

The notoriously stubborn Alexander Webbe followed, but Spofforth bowled him for a duck.

# MCC *v.* Australians

*Played at Lord's, 27 May 1878*

## Marylebone Club and Ground

| *First Innings* | |
|---|---|
| W. G. Grace, *c.* Midwinter, *b.* Allan | 4 |
| A. N. Hornby, *b.* Spofforth | 19 |
| C. Booth, *b.* Boyle | 0 |
| A. Ridley, *c.* A. Bannerman, *b.* Boyle | 7 |
| A. J. Webbe, *b.* Spofforth | 1 |
| F. Wild, *b.* Boyle | 0 |
| W. Flowers *c.* and *b.* Spofforth | 0 |
| G. G. Hearne, *b.* Spofforth | 0 |
| A. Shaw, *st.* Murdoch, *b.* Spofforth | 0 |
| G. F. Vernon, *st.* Murdoch, *b.* Spofforth | 0 |
| F. Morley, *not out* | 1 |
| *Extras* | 1 |
| Total | 33 |

| *Second Innings* | |
|---|---|
| W. G. Grace, *b.* Spofforth | 0 |
| A. N. Hornby, *b.* Boyle | 1 |
| C. Booth, *b.* Boyle | 0 |
| A. Ridley, *b.* Boyle | 0 |
| A. J. Webbe, *b.* Spofforth | 0 |
| F. Wild, *b.* Boyle | 5 |
| W. Flowers, *b.* Boyle | 11 |
| G. G. Hearne, *b.* Spofforth | 0 |
| A. Shaw, *not out* | 2 |
| G. F. Vernon, *b.* Spofforth | 0 |
| F. Morley, *c.* Horan, *b.* Boyle | 0 |
| *Extras* | 0 |
| Total | 19 |

| *Bowling* | Overs | Maidens | Runs | Wickets |
|---|---|---|---|---|
| Allan | 9 | 4 | 14 | 1 |
| Boyle | 14 | 7 | 14 | 3 |
| Spofforth | 5.3 | 3 | 4 | 6 |

| *Bowling* | Overs | Maidens | Runs | Wickets |
|---|---|---|---|---|
| Boyle | 8.1 | 6 | 3 | 6 |
| Spofforth | 9 | 2 | 16 | 4 |

Wild fell to Boyle for another duck and Ridley was beautifully caught by Alick Bannerman on the leg boundary after scoring seven. Spofforth clean-bowled Hearne for a duck, caught Flowers off his own bowling and then disposed of Vernon and Shaw with successive balls. Shaw was superbly stumped by Murdoch, who kept wicket for an unfit Blackham, Morley was out for one, and the final score was only 33.

The crowd, which had trebled as word of the dramatic cricket spread round London, clapped Spofforth and Boyle from the field, most of them believing that W. G. Grace and his colleagues would have their revenge in the second innings.

This optimism soon seemed justified. Hearne made a lot of ground to catch Charles Bannerman at short leg; Garrett got six before he, too, was caught. Midwinter, who was taken at short leg for 10, was the only bat to reach double figures. Gregory went first ball, Boyle scored two and Spofforth one. When Australia was 8 for 23 spectators wondered if they would reach England's miserable 33. Odds of 4 to 1 against it were offered in the pavilion. Allan later recalled that runs were like gold.

Murdoch batted dourly for what was later called a priceless nine before Shaw removed him. Allan managed six, and Bailey three not out. With

# Australians

|  | First Innings |  |
|---|---|---|
| C. Bannerman, | *c.* Hearne, *b.* Morley | 0 |
| W. E. Midwinter, | *c.* Wild, *b.* Shaw | 10 |
| T. P. Horan, | *c.* Grace, *b.* Morley | 4 |
| A. Bannerman, | *c.* Booth, *b.* Morley | 0 |
| T. W. Garrett, | *c.* Ridley, *b.* Morley | 6 |
| F. R. Spofforth, | *b.* Shaw | 1 |
| D. W. Gregory, | *b.* Shaw | 0 |
| H. F. Boyle, | *c.* Wild, *b.* Morley | 2 |
| W. L. Murdoch, | *b.* Shaw | 9 |
| F. E. Allan, | *c.* and *b.* Shaw | 6 |
| G. H. Bailey, | *not out* | 3 |
| Extras | | 0 |
| | Total | 41 |

|  | Second Innings |  |
|---|---|---|
| C. Bannerman, | *b.* Shaw | 1 |
| W. E. Midwinter, | *not out* | 4 |
| T. P. Horan, | *not out* | 7 |
| Extras | | 0 |
| | One wicket for | 12 |

### Bowling

|  | Overs | Maidens | Runs | Wickets |
|---|---|---|---|---|
| A. Shaw | 33.2 | 25 | 10 | 5 |
| F. Morley | 33 | 19 | 31 | 5 |

### Bowling

|  | Overs | Maidens | Runs | Wickets |
|---|---|---|---|---|
| A. Shaw | 8 | 6 | 4 | 1 |
| F. Morley | 8 | 4 | 8 | 0 |

*W. G. Grace won the toss from Dave Gregory and batted.*
*Australia won by nine wickets in 3 hours 40 minutes*

the tail adding these 18 invaluable runs Australia took an eight-run lead.

The ground kept filling up as Spofforth and Boyle set about the Marylebone Cricket Club batsmen in their second innings. Murdoch dropped Dr W. G. Grace off the first ball, then Spofforth bowled him with the second. Only Flowers reached double figures — 11 — in an MCC innings of 19. Left to score 12 runs to win Australia made them with the loss of one wicket.

Australia had taken three hours 40 minutes to defeat the elite of English cricket by nine wickets. By the finish 5000 people were present, although some saw only the last few deliveries. Spofforth's 4 for 16 in the second innings gave him 10 for 20 in the whole match and from this time he was known as "The Demon". Boyle's 6 for 3 in the second MCC innings gave him a match analysis of 9 for 17.

The win was more important to the Australian players than any Test victory, for it demonstrated clearly that Australia had the

*An artist's impression of the extraordinary scenes at the Oval in 1878, when Australia defeated the MCC in an afternoon. The team played seventeen first-class matches but no Tests*

cricketers to beat the best in the world on level terms. The *London Globe* commented:

> *Seldom in the annals of modern cricket has so small a score been made as by the Marylebone Club yesterday, and never was so severe a humiliation inflicted individually and collectively on the members of the Club. The Eleven was as good a one as could be found to represent London and England, and probably as good as the Club ever turned out. Yet its best batsmen were bowled out one after another as if they were novices.*

The statistic which astonished Englishmen most was that W. G. Grace was out second ball in each innings. Seven batsmen were out first ball, four to second balls. The last eight Marylebone wickets had fallen for eight runs in their first innings. Four wickets had fallen for one run at the beginning of their second innings and six wickets for four runs at the end of the innings. There was not a ball misfielded nor, apart from the first ball of England's second innings, a chance dropped by either side. No wickets were lost run out or leg-before. Nine men were clean-bowled in the MCC's second innings. Both teams were at full strength, apart from Murdoch wicket-keeping for Blackham.

The *Home News* admired Spofforth most. "His delivery is quite appalling; the balls thunder in like cannon shot; yet he has the guile when seemingly about to bowl his fastest to drop in a slow which is generally fatal to the batsman." The comment that endured, however, was expressed in verse by London *Punch*:

*The Australians came down like a wolf on the
    fold,
The Marylebone stars for a trifle were bowled.
Our Grace before dinner was very soon done,
And Grace after dinner did not get a run.*

Australia's display destroyed English complacency about their cricket superiority, enhanced international competition, and filled all the vacant dates for the rest of the visitors' tour. Large crowds attended all subsequent games, ensuring that all who had invested in the visit received a profit. The win also gave the Australians an unexpected day off and a chance to see the English Derby. They went to Epsom in a coach-and-four, and along the road bought pea-shooters from a hawker. They drove in to the races in a hail of peas conducting a "war" with other coaches.

Good wins followed over Yorkshire and Surrey. Spofforth took 4 for 30 and 5 for 31 in the Yorkshire innings of 72 and 73, Boyle 5 for 32 in the first innings, and Australia won by six wickets. Almost 40,000 people attended the two days of the Surrey match at The Oval, where only two gate keepers were on duty. Surging spectators finally burst through the fences and spilled out on the field. Conway grabbed a top hat and collected entrance money in it, but half the crowd still got in free. Midwinter topscored with 32 in Australia's first innings of 110. Surrey made 107 and 80, Spofforth taking 8 for 52 and 3 for 42. Australia then scored 5 for 78 to win by five wickets.

The matches against eighteens and twenty-twos, designed as social games, were full of shocks. Eighteen of Hastings including Lord Harris, the Hon. Ivo Bligh, F. Penn, and C. Absolom from the Kent county team, J. and H. Phillips of Sussex, and Noble of Surrey. The Eighteen scored 131 and 82, the Australians 260, with Bailey's 106 one of the two Australian centuries of the tour. The Eighteen of Yeadon and District included 17 professionals from Lancashire, Yorkshire and Derbyshire, England players Peate and Barlow among

them. The professional bowler A. Rylott played against the Australians eight times.

Boyle took 11 for 12 against Eighteen of Elland, seven of his wickets falling in eight deliveries. Allan commented that if three wickets in three balls was worth a hat, Boyle's effort was worth a whole suit of clothes. Wickets fell so swiftly that batsmen were not ready and the crowd grew impatient. "Send a man in," a spectator shouted. "Send three or four—one's no use," shouted another. Spofforth scattered the stumps eight times taking 10 wickets in the second innings.

The Eighteen of Longsight, a Manchester club, surprisingly included G. F. Grace and W. R. Gilbert. Spofforth took 8 for 38 and 5 for 28 in this match, Boyle 7 for 21 and 3 for 23, but Australia still lost! Australia scored 67 in each innings, the Eighteen of Longsight 63 and 15 for 72. G. F. Grace made the difference, scoring 23 and 42. The famous English players did not extend themselves in the matches against odds. They also found it difficult to avoid collisions with fellow fieldsmen. But these games did give them a chance to note the Australians' weaknesses.

The Eighteen of Hunslet included a bowler named Motley, who admitted he threw every ball, but had never been challenged. When a vicious delivery from Motley cannoned off Horan's chest on to his stumps, Dave Gregory threatened to cancel the match if Motley continued. Motley was taken off but the Australians later allowed him to bat.

One persistent cricket secretary followed the team around for a whole day trying to persuade them to give his club a game. He offered them all the takings, plus their expenses, but by then every possible date was filled. Eventually a three-day match against Trinity College, Dublin, fell through and the Australians were able to give him his day. The location was Burnley, Lancashire, but on the day a steady downpour of rain had set in. The Australians did not even bother to change, but the secretary, fearing a demonstration, insisted

that play should commence. Since there were 8000 people waiting under umbrellas or whatever cover they could find, his argument was sound. The Australians waded on to the field and played despite incessant rain. They were applauded wildly. Entrance to the field was only fourpence but the visitors received a cheque for £130 after they escaped with a draw. The players agreed that £100 was fine recompense for such an incredible day and returned £30 to the secretary for his pains.

One of the most bizarre events in cricket history occurred just before the eleventh match of the tour, against Middlesex at Lord's. Charles Bannerman and Midwinter were padded up when W. G. Grace burst into the dressing-room and grabbed Midwinter, who, he announced, was required across town to play for his native Gloucestershire against Surrey. Despite protests, W. G. bundled Midwinter into his carriage and departed for The Oval.

Dave Gregory, John Conway, and Midwinter's lifelong friend Harry Boyle hired another

*ABOVE: An oil painting by T. Bristow, hanging in the pavilion at Lord's, of the first Australian team in action against a combined Kent and Sussex XI in 1878 RIGHT: This photograph of the team appeared in the London newspapers after the extraordinary "kidnapping" of Billy Midwinter. It shows the touring team reduced to eleven players and manager Conway*

FIRST AUSTRALIAN ELEVEN TO VISIT ENGLAND
1878

coach and gave chase across London. Outside The Oval gates an unpleasant altercation erupted, Grace calling the Australians "a damn' lot of sneaks". The Australians pointed out that Midwinter had agreed to play the full tour before the tour began; otherwise they would have brought another player. W. G. was adamant that Gloucestershire had an agreement with Midwinter, and reluctantly Gregory and his colleagues let the kidnapper take his victim. They did not see Midwinter again on the tour. They returned to Lord's, and Allan, who replaced Midwinter, bowled them to victory, despite a brilliant 113 by the Honourable Edward Lyttelton, the only century scored against the tourists. Meanwhile at The Oval Midwinter severely injured his hand.

Gloucestershire's claim on Midwinter was based on the fact that he was born at St Briavels, Forest of Dean, Gloucestershire, even though he spent his early childhood at Cirencester in the Cotswolds, 80 kilometres to the east. His father, William John Midwinter, joined other unemployed workers from the Forest of Dean who opted to try their luck on the Australian goldfields in 1861, taking his wife Rebecca, William, 9, Jane, 7, and John, 5. Midwinter senior, then 38, tried his luck as a goldminer and then found work as a butcher at Sandhurst, where Billy began his long friendship with Harry Boyle. He helped him clear and level a pitch at Sydney Flat. Billy had no recollection of cricket in Gloucestershire when he returned to play for the county in 1877.

Rude, blunt letters were exchanged between the Australians and Gloucestershire club, which claimed that Grace's "stormy language" was justified because the Australians had induced Midwinter to break his contract by offering him more money than the county could afford. In truth, nobody knew at this stage how much the tour players would receive. After his injury Midwinter's form slumped. He later regretted that he had allowed W. G. to persuade him to leave the team.

Left without a twelfth man, the Australians proudly refused to borrow fieldsmen from opposing sides. Leicestershire, the only club to pay them a lump sum and the first to agree to a match, produced some sparkling cricket but were still beaten, thanks to a wonderful innings by Charles Bannerman. Leicestershire scored 113 before a wicket fell and at the end of the second day led by 192 runs with six second innings wickets left. On the third day they lost six wickets for 16 runs, leaving Australia to score 209 for victory.

Bannerman hit three fours in the first over and went on to a masterly 133, a chanceless knock that ended when he was run out. He hit 97 of his runs in boundaries: he scored 9 singles, 9 twos, 3 threes, 23 fours and 1 five. His innings, which did not include a false shot, was the first century by an Australian in England. Australia won by eight wickets with sixty-five minutes to spare — a feat that had seemed impossible at the start of the day.

It was during this summer that the Marylebone Cricket Club attempted to define a gentleman cricketer by passing a resolution

*That no gentleman ought to make a profit by his services in the cricket field, and that for the future, no cricketer who takes more than his expenses in any match shall be qualified to play for The Gentlemen against The Players at Lord's; but that if any Gentleman feels difficulty in joining in the match without pecuniary assistance, he shall not be barred from playing as a Gentleman by having his actual expenses defrayed.*

The Australians found it difficult to reconcile this definition with the payment of £60 each to W. G. Grace and W. Gilbert for playing with the Gentlemen XI, which defeated them at Prince's by an innings and one run. The Gentlemen scored 139, Australia 75 and 63. Boyle took 7 for 48, but

*Alick Bannerman won a place in the first Australian team although he had not played for New South Wales at the time. He became one of the game's most famous stonewallers*

Spofforth had one of his few bad matches. When Conway objected to the payment of £120 from the takings to Grace and Gilbert he was told that they were invariably paid these sums for appearing.

The ill-feeling of English professionals towards the Australians came to a head before the match at The Oval against a Professional XI. The Professionals, who normally played for £10 each, demanded £20. Conway refused this increase and his action was supported by the Surrey committee. Even though a second-string Professional XI replaced the original one, the subsequent game proved a thriller and was watched by large crowds.

When the Professionals needed 19 runs with their five remaining wickets, Spofforth took three wickets in an over to set up a win by eight runs. Gregory's men then agreed to pay each of their opponents £20, with an additional bonus of £5 for Edward Barratt, who took all 10 wickets in Australia's first innings with his tricky off breaks.

Grace did apologise for his language outside The Oval but excluded Conway. The tourists then insisted that they would not play Gloucestershire unless the apology included Conway. Grace was reluctant to make a further apology but when the Australians refused to budge he changed his mind. He sent the following letter to Dave Gregory:

*I am sorry that my former expression of regret to the Australian cricketers has not been considered satisfactory. Under the circumstances, and without going further into the matter, I wish to let bygones be bygones. I apologise again and express my extreme regret to Conway, Boyle and yourself, and through you to the Australian cricketers, that in the excitement of the moment I should have used such unparliamentary language to Mr Conway. I can do no more, but assure you that you will meet a hearty welcome and a good ground at Clifton. (Signed) Yours truly, W. G. Grace.*

Satisfied, the Australians set up a reunion at Clifton with "The Coroner", Dr E. M. Grace, a cricketer they liked more than any other, with the possible exception of "Monkey" Hornby. Australia won the match by 10 wickets on the second day, the first time Gloucestershire had been beaten on their own ground. Spofforth took 7 for 49 and 5 for 41. The two Bannermans gave Australia a great start, Charles hitting very hard for 33. Throughout the match E. M. Grace disdained the straight bat and hit across the line lustily; many of his shots were agricultural, but having a good eye and plenty of pluck he was hard to dismiss.

When the game finished early a return match was played on the last day and this time E. M. Grace played a stylish hand without blemish, surprising everybody with the correctness of his stroke play. He topscored with 55. "Why doctor, you batted like a cricketer—what came over you?" a team-mate asked. "Well," replied the good doctor, "I get such a lot of your rotten off theory stuff there is no necessity to play good cricket at it, but it's a different thing with these Australians. They bowl what I call bowling and force a man to play cricket if he wants to get runs."

At Old Trafford against Lancashire the Bannerman brothers were batting splendidly when Charles called his brother for a run. Alick failed to respond and remained in his crease. With both batsmen at one end it was obvious that one would be run out. Charles responded quickly, giving his brother a hefty push to force him out of the crease, and exclaiming: "I'm a better bat than you are; you go out". The bails were removed at the other end and the umpire gave Alick out, apparently ignoring the shove.

Frank Allan fielded in the slips at Scarborough when Spofforth took 6 for 19 off 52 balls against the Gentlemen. Allan later recalled:

*Spofforth had 'Monkey' Hornby on tenterhooks, beating him ball after ball. Presently, after Spoff shaved the wicket twice, Hornby walked round his stumps, vigorously swinging his bat, muttering to himself, 'The so-and-so wretch! I can't play him!' Then Spofforth knocked back his stumps with a beauty and as he passed me*

*Hornby commented, 'I knew he'd do it. He's too much for me.'*

There were few singers or instrumentalists amongst the tourists. Only Jack Blackham had any flair for music, excelling as a plaintive negro minstrel, but he was too shy to perform regularly despite many pleas. The Australians had to rely instead on the talents of Allan, whose sole accomplishment was a recitation of Marcus Clarke's "Bill Jinks". "All through England, America, Canada and Australia I had to trot out that old Ballarat ruffian until I wished Marcus Clarke had never been born," Allan later complained.

Authorities disagree on the number of matches the tourists played "in a summer when cricketers' boots were seldom dry", but there seems no reason to doubt Conway's figure of 41 since he had most to do with their arrangement. The discrepancies arose from additional scratch games played when four of the scheduled 37 matches ended within two days. According to Conway, the team played 17 first-class matches, two others against eleven-a-side, and 22 exhibition games or matches against the odds. They won 19, lost 7, and drew 15.

On the way home Conway took the Australians to America and Canada. Australia won four and drew two matches in the United States. One of the drawn matches was against a Philadelphian XI, who scored 196 including a knock of 84 by R. Newhall. Umpires, who clapped every run by Philadelphia, gave a series of laughable decisions. When they turned down a Blackham stumping appeal, with the batsman metres out of his crease, Dave Gregory led his team off the field. Philadelphian officials told the Australians that they would not be paid their share of the day's takings unless they returned to the field. Gregory took the Australians back and they played out time before the 10,000 strong crowd.

The Australians won their first match in Canada on 8 and 9 October 1878, against Twenty-Two of Ontario by 10 wickets. Ontario scored 100 and 54, Australia 123 and 0 for 31. Charles Bannerman created another record—the first century by an Australian in Canada. His 125 occurred in their second match, against the Twenty-Two of Montreal, in which they scored 319 in reply to Montreal's 91. Spofforth took 8 for 39 but was upstaged by Allan, who returned 9 for 24. While Gregory's men were on the field, a thief stole their cash and several presentation watches from their dressing room.

On the long train ride across America to California the Australians were befriended by a genial, grey-haired old man who called them "my boys" and regaled them with wonderful stories. He had the gift of the gab, possessed a fine wardrobe, and referred to himself as colonel. At one stop a policeman boarded the train and warned Conway that "The Colonel" was a well-known con-man who was after the team's money. At mealtimes "The Colonel" led the rush to the dining car, but always finished his meal quickly. Returning to the team's compartment, he would find two players sitting on the big black box in which Conway kept all the tour money. The team took turns guarding the cash and Conway slept with it padlocked to his arm. Halfway across America "The Colonel" saw a New York-bound train pull in at an opposite platform. Without a word he gathered his gear and changed trains. The players were quite sorry to see the old rogue go.

Their train was heavily guarded by soldiers, for train robberies were frequent, and they were the only passengers not carrying guns. Their conductor warned them not to "go runnin' about and picking up any bullets that might be flying round" when the train was attacked. The players joked that since Conway carried the money, he would be the robbers' main target—a fate, they added, that was all part of the manager's role.

One of the team's matches in California was constantly interrupted with the Americans calling for lemonade after every few runs. Indeed they called for refreshment so regularly that the

# Philadelphia *v.* Australia

*Played at Nicetown, 3, 4, 5 October 1878*

## Philadelphia

| First Innings | | |
|---|---|---|
| John Hargrave, *c.* and *b.* Spofforth | 10 |
| F. E. Brewster, *c.* Murdoch, *b.* Allan | 15 |
| C. A. Newhall, *b.* Allan | 3 |
| R. S. Newhall, *b.* Allan | 84 |
| G. M. Newhall, *c.* Spofforth, *b.* Horan | 13 |
| R. N. Caldwell, *st.* Blackham, *b.* Boyle | 22 |
| E. Hopkinson, *c.* Gregory, *b.* Bailey | 0 |
| D. S. Newhall, *not out* | 31 |
| T. Hargrave, *b.* Allan | 1 |
| E. T. Comfort, *b.* Allan | 3 |
| S. Meade, *b.* Allan | 0 |
| Byes 8, leg byes 6 | 14 |
| Total | 196 |

| Second Innings | | |
|---|---|---|
| John Hargrave, *st.* Blackham, *b.* Spofforth | 7 |
| F. E. Brewster, *c.* and *b.* Allan | 0 |
| C. A. Newhall, *lbw b.* Spofforth | 5 |
| R. S. Newhall, *c.* Bailey *b.* Spofforth | 0 |
| G. M. Newhall, *c.* Gregory, *b.* Allan | 2 |
| R. N. Caldwell, *b.* Allan | 8 |
| E. Hopkinson, *c.* Bailey, *b.* Spofforth | 5 |
| D. S. Newhall, *c.* Boyle, *b.* Spofforth | 7 |
| T. Hargrave, *st.* Blackham, *b.* Allan | 9 |
| E. T. Comfort, *b.* Allan | 4 |
| S. Meade, *not out* | 0 |
| Byes 6 | 6 |
| Total | 53 |

| Bowling | Overs | Maidens | Runs | Wickets |
|---|---|---|---|---|
| Spofforth | 24 | 8 | 51 | 1 |
| Allan | 20 | 4 | 27 | 6 |
| Boyle | 19 | 6 | 39 | 1 |
| Garrett | 13 | 5 | 26 | 0 |
| Horan | 10 | 2 | 24 | 1 |
| Murdoch | 10 | 2 | 10 | 0 |
| Bailey | 4 | 1 | 5 | 1 |

| Bowling | Overs | Maidens | Runs | Wickets |
|---|---|---|---|---|
| Spofforth | 18.3 | 7 | 24 | 5 |
| Allan | 18 | 6 | 23 | 5 |

Australians suggested they place a jug behind the stumps. When a new batsman came in and immediately ran a two, Charles Bannerman asked him, "Hadn't you better suck a lemon? Hot work you know." In San Francisco another "colonel" approached Conway and offered a substantial donation to the team funds if they could arrange to finish behind Eighteen of California on the first innings. Australia could still win the match outright, he explained, as his bets would be on the first innings. Conway threw him out. In San Francisco too, Charlie Bannerman found the beer hall run by Frank Gardiner, the bushranger, and the players had an interesting time discussing his spectacular hold ups in western New South Wales.

The team received a boisterous reception when they returned to Sydney in December 1878. Dozens of launches and small boats went out to meet their ship as it steamed up Sydney Harbour, cheering crowds lined the shores and there were hundreds of people and a band on the wharf. They were driven through streets decorated with flowers

# Australia

| *First Innings* | |
|---|---|
| C. Bannerman, *c.* G. Newhall, *b.* Meade | 0 |
| A. Bannerman, *c.* G. Newhall, *b.* C. Newhall | 46 |
| T. Horan, *run out* | 5 |
| F. R. Spofforth, *c.* R. Newhall, *b.* C. Newhall | 4 |
| D. W. Gregory, *b.* C. Newhall | 0 |
| W. L. Murdoch, *b.* D. Newhall | 37 |
| G. H. Bailey, *c.* Meade, *b.* C. Newhall | 0 |
| J. McC. Blackham, *b.* D. Newhall | 20 |
| T. W. Garrett, *b.* C. Newhall | 1 |
| H. F. Boyle, *c.* T. Hargrave, *b.* D. Newhall | 30 |
| F. E. Allan, *not out* | 4 |
| Byes 0, wides 3 | 3 |
| Total | 150 |

| *Second Innings* | |
|---|---|
| C. Bannerman, *b.* C. Newhall | 27 |
| A. Bannerman, *retired hurt* | 0 |
| T. Horan, *c.* R. Newhall, *b.* Meade | 0 |
| F. R. Spofforth, *b.* C. Newhall | 4 |
| W. L. Murdoch *not out* | 0 |
| G. H. Bailey, *b.* C. Newhall | 24 |
| J. McC. Blackham, *not out* | 0 |
| Bye 1 | 1 |
| Total (4 wickets) | 56 |

### Bowling

| | Overs | Maidens | Runs | Wickets | Wides |
|---|---|---|---|---|---|
| Newhall, C. A. | 52 | 28 | 67 | 5 | |
| Meade | 26 | 12 | 36 | 1 | 2 |
| Newhall, D. S. | 26.1 | 14 | 34 | 3 | |
| Comfort | 3 | 0 | 7 | 0 | |
| Caldwell | 2 | 0 | 3 | 0 | 1 |

### Bowling

| | Overs | Maidens | Runs | Wickets |
|---|---|---|---|---|
| Newhall, C. A. | 18 | 9 | 29 | 3 |
| Meade | 7 | 4 | 16 | 1 |
| Newhall, D. S. | 10 | 5 | 10 | 0 |

*The result was a draw*

and flags in a four-horse coach to the Town Hall, where the Lord Mayor greeted them. There were similar warm welcomes in Melbourne and Adelaide where the tourists played their last few matches.

Batting honours for the 13 month 965,600 kilometre trip went to Charles Bannerman, the first Australian to score centuries in three countries. He was the only batsman to exceed 1000 runs in England. Murdoch was slightly disappointing, with 755 runs and a top score of 73. Tasmanian George Bailey started badly, but

improved after Midwinter's departure. In the final match of the tour, against New South Wales in Sydney, he broke his arm while fielding; it snapped with a noise like a pistol shot as he threw a ball in to Blackham.

Spofforth had an amazing twenty-fourth year, bowling very fast most of the time, but quickly developing a style that combined alarming pace with subtle variations, all delivered with the same action but from different points of the crease. He had little use for leg traps and bowling for catches; he preferred a direct assault on the batsman's defences and he enjoyed working on opponents' nerves and exploiting his stark, sinuous, demoniacal demeanour. "A Mephistophelian cricketer" was how Gilbert Jessop described him.

He took 764 wickets during the tour at 6.08 each. He began with 281 wickets on the preliminary tour of Australia and took 326 wickets in England, 69 in America and Canada, and 88 in the final matches when the team returned home. He developed the art of variation to such an extent that batsmen often argued about whether he was a fast or medium-pace bowler. His best figures included 19 for 108 against Fifteen of New South Wales; 17 for 125 against Eighteen of South Australia; 22 wickets in the match at Hawkes Bay, New Zealand; and 20 for 64 at Auckland.

Spofforth wrote that he began by copying Tarrant, the 1864 opening bowler for England in Australia, who could not only cartwheel the stumps but sometimes smashed them to pieces. When Grace's team toured Australia in 1873–74 Spofforth interrupted a holiday in Tasmania to watch them in Melbourne. The skill and dexterity of Southerton and Shaw were a revelation to him. He modelled his style on the three Englishmen, trying to combine their best points with his own, natural action.

*In contrast to their unheralded send-off the first Australian team received a tumultuous welcome home. Their displays stirred the Sydney public to row out and meet their ship as it sailed up the Harbour*

Boyle was not far behind Spofforth. He was a bowler of unflagging accuracy who gave batsmen no respite after they got through one of Spofforth's overs. He took 197 wickets at 7.43 in England, 62 of them in eleven-a-side matches at 10 apiece. He was a master of direction, flight and leg spin; his figures included 7 for 48 against the Gentlemen, 12 for 19 against Eighteen of Dudley, 19 for 68 against Twenty-Two of Crewe. Boyle and Spofforth bowled unchanged against Eighteen of

*ABOVE: The formidable Fred Spofforth, a right-arm pace bowler of diabolical cunning, leaping high in his delivery stride*

*RIGHT: The first Australian touring team in action at Chilham Castle, Kent, in August 1878. This was a private affair against a side known as Willsher's Gentlemen. Lord Harris led the opposition*

Wales, Spofforth taking 17 for 75 and Boyle 15 for 75.

Allan was seldom fully healthy during the tour and failed to display the hostility that had earned him the tag, "the bowler of the century". But he still had days when he shocked the best English batsmen. Spofforth said that Allan got more swing in the air than any bowler he ever saw by bending his knees and releasing the ball well before he reached the crease, producing a pronounced upward curve. Allan took 106 wickets at 10.18 in England. Garrett, with his right-arm fast-medium deliveries, bowled straight and tirelessly, achieving surprising bounce, and when the pitch helped, spun the ball back sharply. Garrett took 146 wickets at 6.97 in England and also contributed some handy runs with the bat.

Dave Gregory, a relatively inexperienced captain, gave English cricket a lesson in enterprising field placements. At a time when most captains relegated their worst fieldsmen to square leg or mid-on, Gregory attacked with Boyle five to six metres from the bat at silly mid-on to catch defensive strokes to the off breaks of Spofforth and Garrett. Gregory's only lapse on the entire tour was to allow Edward Lyttelton to score some 70 runs, chiefly by cutting, before he positioned a deep third man.

This first white Australian team to visit England inspired cricketers across Australia with their excellent performances. Two years later South Australia met Victoria on level terms for the first time. The move for a better ground in Perth encouraged administrators to organise a team to take on the eastern states. Queenslanders consoled themselves with the thought that they had seen Charles Bannerman score 74 against Eighteen of Queensland just before the Australian side left for England. They requested more matches against southern teams.

Each Australian player and manager Conway received £750 from the tour according to generally accepted reports. It was more than enough in those times to build a luxurious home in the finest suburb. Years later, however, some of the players admitted to reporters that they had received £1040 each and that the team had paid Conway an extra 7.5 per cent because of his tireless negotiations. The New South Wales Cricket Association president, Richard Driver, who made the speech of welcome to the team on the Sydney Town Hall steps, helped Dave Gregory, Charles Bannerman and Tom Garrett apply for reimbursement of leave, at full pay, from the New South Wales government for their entire period of absence. These public servants claimed that they had brought prestige and future benefit to the colony. Driver persuaded 32 of his fellow MPs to endorse the application, but Colonial Secretary Henry Parkes, no cricket lover, rejected it out of hand.

The Australians returned home to find Tom Wills in an asylum, kept under restraint because of his drinking. Charles Lawrence, who had lived in Newcastle working for the Great Northern Railway since the return of the Aboriginal side from England, had a son playing for a team called the Young Alberts. This was the first junior venture developed by an Australian club. Sam Coststick, umpire in the second Test at Melbourne in 1877, had gone into virtual retirement, acting as curator of the Albion Ground at Maitland. He depended on friends to pay his fare to Sydney to watch big matches.

While the team was away, New South Wales had enjoyed a thrilling win over Victoria in the first intercolonial match on the Association Ground. The hero was Ned Sheridan, one of those who had declined the trip to England. A leathery, sun-bronzed right-hander, Sheridan had won the batting trophy for the Warwick Club two seasons in a row, 1873–75. He had gone out to bat with New South Wales 5 for 18, chasing 119 to win in the last innings, and had taken New South Wales to within 15 runs of victory. When the last pair won the match for New South Wales, spectators rushed the pavilion shouting for Sheridan. A collection raised him £40.

The Australians had discovered in London

that one of the most influential figures at Lord's was Lord Harris, a cricket missionary "unable to suffer fools gladly". Lord Harris was a free-hitting, stylish right-hand batsman of character and a handy round-arm bowler who had played for Eton, Oxford and Kent, where he revived the county's fortunes as secretary and president. Spofforth and Murdoch had great respect for him as a zealot who abhorred chucking, befriended professionals and violently opposed time-wasting off theory.

While the Australian team was still on its overseas tour, the Melbourne Cricket Club invited Isaac Donnithorne Walker, the youngest and best of the seven brothers from Southgate, London—a family record unsurpassed in English cricket, with six of the seven brothers playing for the Gentlemen—to bring an all amateur team to Australia in 1878–79. Isaac Walker was probably the most famous player in England at the time after W. G. Grace, but he had to decline the invitation when his brother Arthur died. The Walker brothers' frequent team-mate Lord Harris agreed to substitute when Isaac withdrew. When he gathered his side he found that amateur bowlers of quality were scarce, and was forced to include professionals George Ulyett and Tom Emmett. Nevertheless, his team was still advertised as "The Gentlemen of England".

They reached Adelaide, the fifth England side to tour Australia, just as the first Australian representative team arrived to that triumphant welcome home in Sydney.

# Sons of convicts

## The Sydney riot and Lord Harris 1878–79

Robert George Canning, the fourth Lord Harris, brought an England team to Australia in 1878–79 who, with two exceptions, were amateurs, gentlemen cricketers with public school and university backgrounds. They were used to refined and courteous behaviour. They arrived at a time when the pushes that prevailed in Australia between 1870 and 1900 were most active. Groups of larrikins with names like the Fitzroy Murderers, The Gibbies, Bantry Bay Devils, and Gore Hill Tigers wandered the streets at night with nothing to do but get themselves into mischief. At the cricket betting was widespread.

His Lordship's England team — chosen by Isaac Walker — were a pukka lot: Lord Harris' Kent team-mates Charles Alfred Absolom, formerly of Cambridge; Francis Alexander MacKinnon, a Highland chief educated at Cambridge; Frank Penn, well-connected enough to later assume the Kent Cricket Club presidency; Albert Neilson Hornby of Harrow and Lancashire; the Reverend Vernon Peter Fanshawe Royle of Oxford and Lancashire; Sandford Spence Schultz of Cambridge and

*Lord Harris's team, which toured Australia in 1878–79, included only two professionals—the bowlers George Ulyett and Tom Emmett. Lord Harris complained that his team was treated like a party of strolling players*

EMMETT

Webbe

Lord Harris

Lucas

Hone

Mackinnon

Lancashire, who later changed his name to Storey when he realised the German "Schultz" caused offence; Alexander Josiah Webbe, cricket missionary from Oxford and Middlesex; Henry Compton Maul of Warwickshire; Alfred Perry ("Bunny") Lucas of Cambridge, Surrey, Middlesex and Essex; Leland Hone of Rugby and Cambridge and one of a family of noted Irish cricketers; plus the tight-lipped Yorkshire professionals Emmett and Ulyett. Maul, who played for Warwickshire before it became a first-class county, and Hone, who played for Ireland, are the only England cricketers to tour Australia without having previously played a first-class game.

The team was far from balanced: it lacked a specialist wicket-keeper, and Lucas had long spells of bowling as he was the only man who could ease the workload of Emmett and Ulyett. These two hardened cricketers travelled second-class on the ship to Australia and stayed at inferior hotels to the amateurs. The tour organisers claimed that they preferred this, suggesting they did not enjoy dressing for dinner each night; Australians found this explanation difficult to accept.

The tour began in December 1878 with an easy win for England over Eighteen of South Australia at Adelaide, where the South Australian Cricket Association had finally overcome all opposition to charging admission to Adelaide Oval. Emmett took 9 for 45 and 5 for 58. One of the locals who lost was George Giffen, who had made his debut for his state in Melbourne two years earlier against East Melbourne at the age of 17. Giffen failed to take a wicket against Lord Harris's XI and did not score a run, the only occasion in his long career that he secured spectacles.

England struggled against Fifteen of Victoria in the next match — the last time Victoria fielded more than 11 men. They were puzzled by the peculiar South Melbourne round-arm leg-spinner William Cooper, who caused great amusement by bowling A. P. Lucas between his (Lucas's) legs. Donald Campbell scored a commendable 128 for

Victoria. This was one of the occasions when Thomas Joseph Dart Kelly created a stir by appearing in a red, white and blue coat, with sash to match, the first blazer of its type worn by an Australian.

Kelly, a magnificent fieldsman at point and a free-hitting batsman, was born in County Waterford, but his family moved to Bristol when he was a few weeks old. There on Durdham Downs he learned to play cricket with the Grace brothers. He migrated to Australia in 1863 aged 19, and two years later made his debut for Victoria in intercolonial cricket. At 35 he was picked to play for Australia, and again showed off his blazer, against Lord Harris's team in Melbourne in a match originally advertised as "Gentlemen of England versus Australian XI". This match on 3–4 January 1874 became accepted as the third Test match. Kelly was the only member of the Australian team who had not toured England the previous year. George Bailey had to watch the play from the stand, his arm in a sling.

In a sensational first morning Spofforth performed the first Test hat-trick, dismissing Royle, MacKinnon and Emmett, the first two bowled and the third caught by Horan. At 7 for 26, England were in disarray. Australia's belief that they could beat England on level terms appeared justified, but Lord Harris and Charles Absolom, "the Cambridge navvy" who trained on beer and haymaking, staged a magnificent recovery. Absolom hit "high, wide and handsome" in a partnership of 63, which ended when Garrett clean-bowled Lord Harris for 33. Absolom went on to 52 and England reached 113. Spofforth, with 6 for 48 off 25 overs, including nine maidens, took the last wicket when Blackham, in a remarkable piece of wicket-keeping, both caught and stumped

*The Bannerman brothers, Alick (left) and Charles. Alick had a long career in first-class cricket, while Charles dropped out of big cricket after a brief but spectacular career. He will always be remembered, however, for his century in the first Test*

Leland Hone. The ball, a fast yorker, passed between Hone's legs and the stumps.

When Australia lost the wickets of Charles Bannerman, Murdoch and Horan for 37, Spofforth was sent in as a nightwatchman. Spofforth and Alick Bannerman both gave chances but held out until stumps when Australia was 3 for 93. Next morning Spofforth was out for a useful 39, Garrett 26, Boyle 28, Kelly 10 and Dave Gregory 12. Alick Bannerman played a typically stubborn, strokeless innings—he was already known as the "Little Stonewaller"—for 73 and Australia secured a lead of 143. Emmett and Ulyett earned their keep by sending down 121 of the 160 overs bowled, Emmett taking 7 for 68 with his fast left-arm round-armers. He was a cheery man whose best ball was pitched on the batsman's legs and turned sharply to the off.

Lord Harris batted admirably in England's second innings but had no support. Spofforth, who dropped his pace and concentrated on his wide range of variations, was absolutely tireless as he took 7 for 62 to secure match figures of 13 for 110. England just escaped an innings defeat with their last pair at the crease, and Charles Bannerman and Billy Murdoch steadily hit off the 19 runs required for a ten-wicket victory. Spofforth's victims in both innings included F. A. Mac-Kinnon, 35th Chief of the Clan MacKinnon. He was a very handy batsman for Kent, having accumulated 2184 runs including two centuries, but could not prevent Spofforth scattering his stumps twice.

Charles Bannerman disappeared from international cricket after taking part in the first three Tests in 1877 and 1879. Ill health was given as the reason when selectors refused to persevere with him, despite his brilliant strokeplay and the fact that he was not yet 30. His friends suggested that

*Lord Harris, one of the most powerful figures in English cricket, helped establish the high standards of honour the game followed. He was a staunch believer in the amateur ethic*

he could not cope with celebrity status and that this was the reason for his gambling debts and why, like his co-star in the first of all Tests, Tom Kendall, he developed a fondness for the bottle. Careless with his cash and his choice of companions, he continued to appear at first-class matches, a striking contrast in stained, crumpled clothes and scruffy shoes to his dapper brother Alick. Cricket administrators gave him numerous handouts and coaching jobs in recognition of his past feats.

Lord Harris had engaged a young Victorian, George Coulthard, to accompany his side as an umpire. Coulthard, a ground bowler for Melbourne Cricket Club, was then 22 and a season away from his introduction to intercolonial cricket. In January 1879 he went to Sydney with Lord Harris's team, which played against a New South Wales XI and were beaten by five wickets. Evans, Tindall and the round-armer Coates were the outstanding bowlers, and Murdoch, vastly improved by the England tour, scored 70 and 49. Coulthard also accompanied the England players to Bathurst for a match against a local eighteen and stood in another against twenty-two at Victoria Barracks.

The Englishmen's record to that point was so poor that New South Wales were hot favourites with bookmakers for the return game on the Association Ground on 7 February. The *Sydney Morning Herald*'s report of the first day, on which England scored 267, criticised a blatant umpiring error in the visitors' favour by Coulthard. The paper also strongly objected to "the impunity with which open betting was transacted in the pavilion". The *Herald* said that betting was carried on with complete disdain for signs banning it, a characteristic of the fraternity that made gambling a trade. Next day feverish gambling continued as New South Wales were bundled out for 177 by mid-afternoon, despite a plucky 82 not out by Murdoch, who batted through the innings.

Forced to follow on, New South Wales were on 19 when Coulthard ruled Murdoch run out. Hooting erupted in the pavilion where the

from the field, received several heavy blows and lost all bar a few shreds of his shirt. Later it was found he had grabbed the wrong man.

In the midst of the demonstration an English sea captain in a tall hat pushed forward and remonstrated with the crowd. One of the spectators promptly "bonnetted" him, pulling his hat down over his ears and leaving him to contemplate his stance amid frantic efforts to remove his hat.

Trustees and members of the cricket association rushed to protect the English team from a mob intent on rescuing Hornby's prisoner. Some of the team received minor cuts and bruises but no serious injuries occurred. Umpire Coulthard came off unhurt, thanks to Hornby's prompt assistance, and after a lot of pushing and shoving the English team reached the safety of the dressing room.

Some reporters attributed the riot to intercolonial rivalry, emphasising that Coulthard was born in Victoria (at Boroondara in 1856), but A. B. "Banjo" Paterson gave a more innocent account of it.

*I was sitting by the picket fence, and couldn't tell if Murdoch was out or not, but we all started to hoot and a chap near me said, 'Come on, boys, we can't stand for this,' and he jumped over the fence. His feet had barely touched the ground when there were a thousand men over the fence, all running for the centre of the ground. The Englishmen thought they were going to be murdered and some of them got round the umpire, and others pulled stumps out of the ground to defend their lives. I remember seeing the big Yorkshireman, Ulyett, waving a stump at the crowd, so I sidestepped him. I was only a boy. When we got to the wicket we didn't know what to do. Everybody was hooting and arguing. Nobody really interfered with the English players. We just hooted them off the ground, and then it struck us that if we didn't get back to our seats we wouldn't see any more play. So back we went.*

*Lord Harris's greatest ally was the Lancashire captain, A. N. ("Monkey") Hornby who had the shirt torn from his back defending His Lordship from a larrikin's attack*

gamblers sat and a well-known bookmaker urged on the demonstrators. Spectators jumped the fence and rushed on to the pitch demanding that the decision be reversed. When Lord Harris attempted to protect Coulthard, as the intensity of the booing increased, an enraged spectator struck His Lordship a heavy blow across the back with a stick. "Monkey" Hornby, who then wrestled a man

The ground was cleared after half an hour, but Dave Gregory remained adamant that umpire Coulthard should be replaced. Lord Harris refused, arguing that both his point and cover fieldsmen, who had a good view of the run-out, believed the decision was fair. He later scoffed at allegations in the Sydney *Evening News* that Coulthard had money on the match.

Two attempts to resume play failed. Each time mobs rushed forward Lord Harris moved to the centre of the pitch to prevent New South Wales claiming the match on a forfeit.

After play was abandoned for the day the *Sydney Morning Herald* reported that two England players had provoked demonstrators by calling the first wave "sons of convicts". The second umpire, Edmund Barton, later Prime Minister of Australia, considered Coulthard's decision perfectly fair and defended the Englishmen's behaviour. Barton told the *Herald* that Emmett and Ulyett were incapable of making the "sons of convicts" comment, and their denials should be believed. Other *Herald* readers immediately wrote to say they had heard the comment and that it had "spread like wildfire around the ground".

The *Herald* also thought it was significant that the hooting had begun among persons known to be financially interested in the match.

> One wellknown betting man acted as a fugelman. The crowd, encouraged by his bad example, worked themselves into a state of violent excitement. A large number of larrikins sitting within the boundary fence made a rush for the centre of the ground and were quickly followed by hundreds of roughs who took possession of the wickets.

The *Australasian* noted that the only three policemen at the ground had remained on the safe side of the fence throughout the disturbance. Other papers stressed Dave Gregory's bad record of disputing umpires' decisions during the previous year in England and America. The cricket riot received more newspaper coverage than Ned

*Dave Gregory refused to allow the Sydney match to continue unless umpire Coulthard was replaced. Lord Harris had brought Coulthard from Melbourne for the game*

Kelly's gang, who on the same day raided the town of Jerilderie, New South Wales.

The rioters were back at work the following Monday when England won the game by an innings, but Lord Harris refused to keep his team in Sydney for the scheduled return bout against Australia, which would have been the fourth Test.

The Sydney Police Court fined two men who had struck Lord Harris and Hornby £2, plus 25 shillings costs. Dick Driver junior told the court a Victorian bookmaker had been evicted from the ground (his admission money was refunded) and instructions issued never to admit him again.

Unfortunately the riot overshadowed Ulyett's four wickets with four successive balls in New South Wales' second innings, as well as depriving Dave Gregory of a farewell Test before his home crowd. Gregory continued in intercolonial cricket until he was 37, and was secretary of the New South Wales Cricket Association and sole selector for five years.

Dave's first wife, Mary Ann Hutchings, mother of 13, died in 1890, and he was 47 when he married Lillis Leslie MacMillan in 1892. She bore him three children and saw him become paymaster of the state Treasury in 1897. After her death in 1911, he married Ellen Hillier, a cricketer's widow. When Federation took place he was offered a knighthood with the post of head of the Federal Treasury, but he refused both offers because the position would have entailed a move from Sydney to Melbourne. Until his death at 74, Australia's first cricket captain never wore dentures nor glasses, never stooped, played the flute, and was not once seen the worse for liquor. He was for many years a familiar figure, his vigorous beard jutting forth, as he took long walks in the bush near his home in Turramurra.

Ned Gregory, the groundsman who prepared the Sydney pitch and lived in a cottage at the ground, was a jolly character, full of chuckles, quite different from his bluff, dominant brother Dave, whose intransigence had led in part to the Sydney riot; he often took touring English cricketers fishing on Sydney Harbour. Ned, who had worked as a professional for the Bathurst Club in the 1860s, returned to Sydney as professional to the Military and Civil Club, and stayed on when the New South Wales Cricket Association made the ground its headquarters. He moved into the stone cottage built by soldiers from Victoria Barracks beside the ground, and his eldest son, Syd Gregory, was born there in April, 1870. The cottage was used as the dividing line when a fence was built between the No. 1 and No. 2 grounds in 1876.

According to Ned, a witty little man known as "Garden Honey" had a dismal time on the day of the riot. Honey sold pencils and scorecards to spectators before the big scoring boards were erected. He was one of the most bemused witnesses of the riot, which ruined his trade: he did not sell a single scorecard for the rest of the afternoon.

Lord Harris's team wound up their tour at the Melbourne Cricket Ground in March 1879 with a six-wickets win over Victoria, captained by Harry Boyle. The Victorians started this match without Allan, who had missed his train. In his place, Boyle reluctantly gave George Eugene ("Joey") Palmer a chance after England had collared the bowling. Palmer proceeded to clean-bowl nine of the 14 Englishmen dismissed in the match at a cost of 94 runs.

England won two eleven-a-side matches and lost three, including the Test. The 13 games against the odds resulted in 5 wins, 5 draws and 3 losses. Ulyett gave a grand all-round performance with 454 runs at 25.22 and 67 wickets at 11.80, although his captain felt he could have done better. Emmett's bowling was superlative with 137 wickets at 8.49 and Hornby headed the batting averages—574 runs at 33.76. Only the Melbourne Cricket Club provided a good pitch; in Sydney a parallelogram was marked out on the field and the captains chose a wicket within that area. *The Bulletin* said that the Melbourne Cricket Club had lost £6000 on the tour, the Englishmen's wine bill coming to more than that.

Critics agreed that the tour had proved that not only were Australia's bowlers superior to England's, but her batsmen were improving rapidly. Murdoch was the best of an emerging group of stroke players. Not long after the tour ended news came that Charles Absolom had died in agony when crushed by a load of sugar cane at Port of Spain, Trinidad. Absolom's taste for travel had been whetted by the Australian trip and he had taken a job as a ship's purser.

*The witty old man known as "Garden Honey" sold
scorecards and pencils at Sydney's intercolonial matches
before scoreboards were built*

*George Ulyett tried vainly to lift the performance of
Lord Harris's team in eleven-a-side matches. Spofforth's
hat-tricks, however, made England's defeat inevitable in
the only Test of the tour*

At the farewell dinner at Melbourne, Lord Harris had been affable and full of praise for the way in which Sydney officials had handled the riot. Back in London, however, he had some harsh things to say about the Australian press, which, like W. G. Grace before him, he found crude and aggressive. "Some of the press treated us as if we were strolling actors rather than a party of gentlemen," he complained. On 1 April 1879, Lord Harris claimed in a letter to the London *Daily Telegraph* that he had been "insulted and subjected to indignities it distresses us to look back upon on the Australian tour". His Lordship went on:

*I asked Gregory on what grounds his objections to umpire Coulthard were raised and Gregory said at first because of Coulthard's general incompetence, but afterwards admitted the objection was raised on account of the Murdoch decision. I implored Gregory as a friend, and for the sake of the New South Wales Cricket Association, which I warned him would be the sufferer by it, not to raise the objection, but he refused to take my view of the case.*

*Looking back on to the ground, I found that the pitch had been rushed by the mob and our team had been surrounded. I at once returned to the wickets, and in defending Coulthard from being attacked, was struck by a larrikin with a stick. Hornby immediately seized this fellow and in taking him to the pavilion was struck in the face by a would-be deliverer of the larrikin, and had his shirt nearly torn from his back. He however conveyed his prisoner to the pavilion in triumph.*

*For some thirty minutes or more I was surrounded by a howling mob, resisting the entreaties of partisans and friends to return to the pavilion until the field was cleared, on the ground that if our side left the field the other side could claim the match. I don't suppose they would have done so, but I was determined to obey the laws of cricket, and may add that for an hour and a half I never left the ground, surrounded during the whole time, except for two short intervals, by some hundreds of people. At about five o'clock the crowd was cleared. I then took the opinion of the Eleven as to changing the umpire, and it was decided . . . that we should decline to do so. I informed Gregory of this and he said, 'Then the game is at an end.'*

Lord Harris's letter added that when he asked umpire Barton if he could claim the match under the laws of cricket, Barton's reply was: "I will give it to you in two minutes if the batsmen don't return". Lord Harris then asked Barton to inform Gregory of his intentions. Before the batsmen could come out, the crowd covered the ground for the second time. It took a further 20 minutes to clear the ground and then Bannerman and Thompson came out. Before a ball could be bowled the crowd rushed on to the ground for a third time. There they stayed until stumps, Lord Harris standing erect and defiant amongst them, moustache bristling.

When the Australian newspapers reprinted Lord Harris's letter, a special meeting of the New South Wales Cricket Association drafted a reply, which was sent to the London *Daily Telegraph*. The letter stressed the association's strong disapproval of betting at cricket matches; it also pointed out that the Sydney press and the public had condemned the demonstrators, and added:

*Lord Harris, by what we feel to be a most ungenerous suppression of these facts, has led the British public to believe that in New South Wales, to quote his own words, 'a party of gentlemen travelling through these colonies for the purpose of playing a few friendly games of cricket should have been insulted and subjected to indignities,' while the Press and inhabitants of Sydney neither showed surprise, indignation nor regret.*

*We cannot let a libel on the people of New South Wales so unfounded as this to pass without challenge. The country upon which such a reproach could be fastened would be unworthy of a place among civilised communities, and the imputation is especially odious to Australians, who claim to have maintained the manly, generous, and hospitable character of the British race. The betting men to whom Lord Harris alludes were not members of this association at all, and it is completely unjust to assign the demonstration to any such agency.*

Betting had long been associated with cricket. As far back as the 1730s the Prince of Wales had played cricket for large bets. Wagers of £1000 were commonplace and one for £20,000 was recorded when an Old Etonian team played England in 1751. There was considerable betting, too, on the famous match at Blackheath in July 1766, between 11 one-armed men and 11 one-legged men, all pensioners, from Greenwich Hospital. English police, aware that big money attracted criminals, often found the villains they were seeking at cricket matches.

Cricket journals for years had included rules for betting, but now bookmakers were ejected from the grounds. The riot had brought home painfully to the New South Wales Cricket Association that it did not have exclusive rights to the Association Ground, which was used for a variety of sports. Some of these sports, such as cycling and professional running, had big stakes riding on the results. Unsavoury characters, who, the *Sydney Mail* said, had a flair for "impartial expectoration of tobacco juice", habitually defied ground betting bans.

In Brisbane, where the Queensland Cricket Association had bought a horse-drawn mower, which the Queen's Park curator believed would

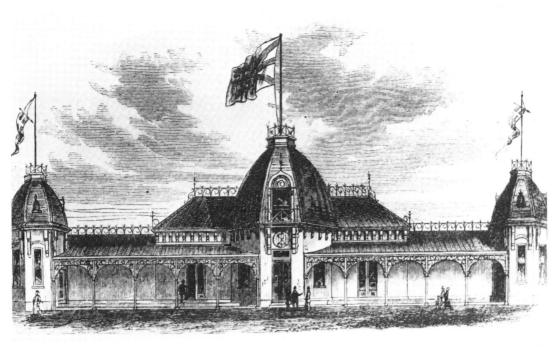

*An illustration in the* Sydney Mail, *16 February 1878, of the original Members' Stand at the Sydney Cricket Ground just before its inauguration during the Victoria–New South Wales match. The present Members' Stand replaced it in 1896*

produce a field "the equal of the croquet lawn at Government House", the Queensland association also had problems with gambling at its matches. In March 1879, the QCA passed a resolution decrying the practice and requesting "All clubs and individual members of the Queensland Cricket Association are to discourage betting at cricket in every possible way, as it is a practice that is gradually but surely debasing the game and robbing it of its nobility and purity".

Although many cricket followers believed a cooling off period was needed, Australia's cricketers decided to press ahead with a second tour to England in 1880.

The tour manager, George Alexander, and senior players from the previous tour, sifted carefully through the available talent before selecting a 13-man squad for what everyone hoped would be a peace-making trip. One of the matches Harry Boyle and his co-selectors considered before deciding on the team was the intercolonial contest between Victoria and New South Wales at Sydney on 22 February 1878. Since most of the best players from these states were away on the first English tour, some new talent was on display. The match provided the most exciting finish of all the intercolonials and produced several outstanding cricketers.

When New South Wales went in to bat a second time, they required 119 to win. The openers scored freely until engineer-turned-medical-student Herbert James ("Tup") Scott, a batsman of quality but a bowler of dubious merit, took 6 for 33, bringing New South Wales to the brink of defeat. Only brave hitting by the last pair, Jimmy Dummett and Edwin Tindall, enabled the locals to snatch victory in a tense finish. Seventeen-year-old Percy Stanislaus McDonnell, the Melbourne Jesuits' star pupil, failed to score in each innings of this match, his first for Victoria. When he next played for his state McDonnell

*South Australian Affie Jarvis was selected for the second Australian tour of England in 1880. He was a promising wicket-keeper and determined batsman*

made an impressive 48.

After losing seven successive matches to New South Wales, Victoria gave their Melbourne fans a fine all-round display of batting on 26 December 1879, by scoring 338 runs. Alexander, who top-scored with 75, helped Allan dismiss New South Wales twice to give Victoria a win by an innings and 96 runs, the biggest intercolonial margin to that time. Alexander's performance showed that the team for England had a manager who could substitute more than capably if needed.

The second Australian lineup included former tourists Alick Bannerman, Blackham, Boyle, Murdoch and Spofforth. Newcomers were McDonnell, the vigorous right-hand batsman with a strong defence, a product of Melbourne's St

Patrick's College; George John Bonnor, the bearded giant (1.9 metres, 107 kilograms) from Bathurst whose hitting was already spoken of with disbelief; Thomas Underwood Groube, a great cover-point fieldsman and right-hand batsman from East Melbourne, who replaced Charles Bannerman; James Slight, a wide-shouldered right-hand batsman who had scored heavily for South Melbourne; William Henry Moule, a successful right-hand batsman and accurate medium-pace change bowler; Arthur Haywood ("Affie") Jarvis, a wicket-keeper of promise as well as a dogged batsman, and the first South Australian to play for Australia; and Joey Palmer, the right-arm medium-pace spin bowler who had skittled Lord Harris's team in Melbourne.

Invited players subscribed to a new tour fund and agreed that, in the absence of Dave Gregory, who wanted to devote his attention to his family, the Melbourne warehouseman Harry Boyle should captain the side. Boyle was 33, but the average age of his team was only 23.

Without Charles Bannerman, Will Murdoch was the tourists' main batting hope. Murdoch was born at Sandhurst (later re-named Bendigo), Victoria, on 18 October 1854, of Tasmanian parents. Seven weeks later police and miners clashed at the Eureka Stockade at nearby Ballarat. The Murdochs moved to Sydney when Will was a child and he began playing cricket on a paddock at King Street, Balmain. Another boy who took part in these games was Fred Spofforth, who later refused to play in the first Test when Murdoch was not selected. Will graduated from Sydney University and followed his brother Gilbert into law.

The 1880 selections were more carefully considered than for the previous tour, the colonial associations this time supported the venture, and the preliminary arrangements undertaken by Harry Boyle were extremely thorough. The first tourists had gone away without a uniform, although some had worn the East Melbourne blazer in recognition of that club's help in raising funds. Team clothing varied until Scarborough, when Allan asked an opponent where he bought his handsome blazer. Securing the address of the tailor, he duly ordered one, plus a scarf in the same colours. Several Australians were so impressed that they ordered similar jackets, which turned out to be the uniform of a club called the Nondescripts, who had no objection sharing their colours with the Australians. For the 1880 tour, the Australians were fitted out in dark blue and white striped garments that looked more like smocks than blazers and reached to their thighs.

In the matches they played before leaving for England, the Australian XI lost to Fifteen of Victoria by 82 runs but had wins at Bendigo and against New South Wales at Sydney where Murdoch scored 99. Alick Bannerman, Dave Gregory and Tom Garrett played for the beaten New South Wales side. Big wins followed over Bathurst and Newcastle, where a local bowler named Tracey took eight wickets. At Daylesford, Victoria, the Australian XI lost by six runs to a local twenty-two after 62 wickets had fallen in a day. The Australian XI made 69 and 39, Daylesford 74 and 40.

In a return match Fifteen of Victoria defeated the Australians by one wicket in a match at Melbourne. The critics believed the tourists should have won: with several runs needed for victory, the Fifteen's last batsman, Tom Horan, could not be found, but the Australian XI sportingly did not penalise their opponents when he arrived several minutes later. The Australians won their last game, defeating Sixteen of South Australia in Adelaide by 69 runs.

Just before they sailed for England in the *Garonne* on 19 March 1880, the team received a telegram informing them that Lord Harris would refuse to meet them in England and that they would be regarded as professionals there. His Lordship, clearly still angry over the Sydney riot, was influential enough to have international matches involving Australia stopped. In Sydney the *Herald*'s reporter repeated the "sons of convicts" allegation. He claimed there was clear evidence that the comment had caused the riot and that spectators resented any suggestion that they were second-class citizens.

Phil Derriman, in his book *True to the Blue*, disclosed that George Ulyett was out in Sydney the night before the Sydney riot and laid a bet of £20 on England with a man who offered two to one on New South Wales. Ulyett shared the bet with Tom Emmett and they both won £5. "We may be sure they did not boast about it to Lord Harris," Derriman commented.

# Australia out-talked

## Test cricket in England and Australia 1880–82

At Suez, on the voyage to England, the Australians decided to depose Harry Boyle as captain and replaced him with Murdoch. This turned out to be a wise, if unhappily sudden move, for the friendly, good humoured style of Murdoch won over the team's critics. Boyle's taciturn demeanour might not have achieved this at a time when English antagonism to the Australians was so strong that the Australians had to advertise for matches.

When the team arrived on 13 May 1880, they were informed that the fixture lists had already been finalised—no matches had been arranged for them in London and most of their itinerary was confined to the industrial north. Lord Harris was critical of the lack of prior consultation about the tour, but he offered to try and arrange matches in London, providing the Australians declared they were touring solely for pleasure and accepted only their expenses. The Australians politely declined to give such an undertaking. W. G. Grace contended that there was growing prejudice in

*The second Australian team that toured England in 1880: (L to R) (standing) G. E. Palmer, W. H. Moule, G. J. Bonnor, G. Alexander (manager), T. Groube; (seated) F. R. Spofforth, H. Boyle, W. L. Murdoch (captain), P. S. McDonnell, A. C. Bannerman; (front) A. H. Jarvis, J. Slight, J. M. Blackham*

England against speculating tourists, which made the Australian venture problematic. "In consequence very few first-class games could be secured for the visitors, who did not make a single appearance at Lord's," he wrote later. "I made an attempt to get them a match there in July, but although the Marylebone Club granted use of the ground, it was found impossible."

London newspapers referred to the Australians as "commercial cricketers". Manager Alexander wrote to the *Sporting Life* newspaper challenging both the Gentlemen and the Players to a match, but without response. *London Society*, however, pointed out that English cricketers had reaped handsome benefits from Australian tours:

> *Few of the English professionals have a shilling left when winter has drained their store and the spring has come again with new engagements to public schools or county clubs. Some of the English Elevens who happily landed with money waiting for them in the bank, would but for the happy trip have been borrowing as many pounds to start with on some club engagement. Instead they had hundreds to their credit awaiting them.*

At the team's first practice on Mitcham Green, Bonnor hit a ball 135 metres. The English professional, James Southerton, who owned a Mitcham pub, could not believe it and personally measured the distance. Bonnor's best hit, however, was on the Melbourne Cricket Ground, where he was credited with a blow of 150 metres.

The tour began with a splendid win over Derbyshire by eight wickets. Australia did not bat well in the first innings of 129, but Derbyshire could only reply with 45 against hostile bowling by Spofforth and Palmer, who both turned the ball sharply. Following on, Derbyshire made 125, with Spofforth taking 8 for 8 to secure match figures of 13 for 65. The Australians lost only two wickets scoring 42 to win.

At Dewsbury, Australia beat Yorkshire by five wickets, Palmer taking 9 for 60, Spofforth

11 for 76 in the game. Needing 91 to win, Australia lost 2 for 13 before a fine stand by McDonnell (47) and Bannerman (18) secured victory. After an enjoyable trip to Ireland, the team played at Leicester, where Murdoch made a superb 73, and Huddersfield, where rain stopped play after Australia had scored 220 in reply to Yorkshire's 78.

Three brothers Grace played for Gloucestershire at Clifton, W. G., E. M. and G. F., but they could not prevent an Australian win by 68 runs. This was an impressive effort as the Australians were 81 runs behind on the first innings. McDonnell made 79 in Australia's second innings of 246 when Gloucestershire paid the penalty for dropping him five times. Spofforth was again in devastating form when Gloucestershire needed 166 to win. He took 7 for 54, including all three Graces, to finish with match figures of 11 for 130.

The geniality of Murdoch and his men made a deep impression on the Graces and W. G. agreed to try and organise a full international match in London. Of the seven new men, only Palmer and McDonnell performed well, but the Australians were not beaten until the twenty-seventh match.

Off they went to Rochdale, where the mayor bought them all a drink because his son had top-scored in Eighteen of Rochdale's first innings. The mayor boasted that his son could handle Spofforth but found Boyle difficult. "Very unkind since I let the lad get a few," retorted Spofforth. "Next innings I'll get him for a goose egg." The mayor offered to put up £10 against this happening, and Spofforth accepted. Next day Spofforth kept asking the name of each incoming batsman. When the mayor's son finally appeared he went back to his long run and knocked the boy's stump from the ground. The mayor paid up, commenting that his

*Australia's second tour strengthened the close friendship between Murdoch (left) and W. G. Grace, seen here together at Sheffield Park. Murdoch wore the gold sovereign presented to him for his Test score of 153 on his watch chain until the day he died*

son had not seen the ball that got him.

Restricted to only 11 first-class matches, the Australians were not amused to learn that counties which had previously said they could not alter their schedules were readily doing so to accommodate a Canadian team that had arrived weeks after them. Murdoch offered to play All England for the benefit of the Cricketers' Benevolent Fund but was turned down. Finally, late in the season, manager Alexander went to Lord's to argue Australia's case for an international match. Pressed by W. G. Grace and Surrey secretary C. W. Alcock, Lord Harris at first protested that the best amateurs were all "out on the moors", but finally relented and agreed to organise an All England side to play Australia at The Oval, in what was the first Test in England. The Australians were badly weakened by the absence of Spofforth, who had injured a finger at Scarborough. Some of the touring team joked that the match was only held to settle a bet between W. G. and Murdoch as to who would topscore.

The roofs of surrounding houses were crammed with people, The Oval's accommodation unable to cope, when W. G. and E. M. Grace opened for England before 20,814 paying fans on 6 September 1880. Murdoch suggested that Palmer try a yorker first ball before W. G. was set. "It might get through," Murdoch whispered. Palmer pitched the first delivery right in the block hole and it passed under W. G.'s bat grazing the stumps, but the bails did not fall. Watched by their proud mother, the Graces continued a running conversation which could be heard on the boundary. They added 91 runs, interspersed with wisecracks and comments on almost every ball bowled at them, often continuing their commentary while running between the wickets.

W. G. and Alfred Lucas added 120 for the second wicket, and Lord Harris contributed 52. When W. G. was out for 152, the first Test century by an Englishman, England were 4 for 281. They were 8 for 410 at stumps. Francis Thompson's inspired lines could well have captured

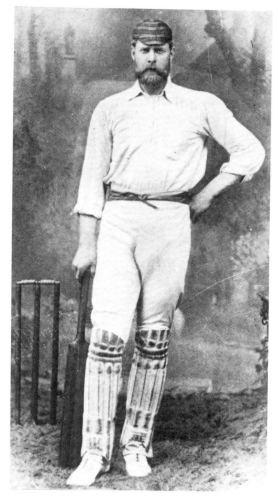

*A shot that shows why Bonnor, to whom a bat was like a match-stick, was described as the "Colonial Hercules". At 198 cm and 102 kg, he was the smallest of three brothers from Bathurst, New South Wales*

the mood of the Australians coming off the field:

> The long-whiskered Doctor, that laughest rules scorn,
> While the bowler, pitched against him,
> bans the day that he was born,
> And G. F. with his science makes the
> fairest look forlorn.

After England were out next day for 420, Australia made only 149 on a pitch deadened by overnight rain before 19,863 people. Following on with a 271-run deficit, Australia lost 3 for 14. McDonnell joined Murdoch and they began to bat with unexpected freedom, hitting the ball to all parts of the ground. At stumps Australia were 6 for 170, still 101 behind, with Murdoch 79 not out in 150 minutes.

Going in at No. 7, Bonnor awed the crowd with his sheer physical presence, a golden-haired god from another planet whom W. G. Grace called a "model of physical beauty". Bonnor was also a sensitive individual—singing Irish ballads brought tears to his eyes. From the start W. G. taunted him with suggestions that he was just a slogger who could not bat. For a time Bonnor kept his head down, but after he had scored 16 he swung in under a ball, lifting it higher than anyone could remember a ball being hit. He and Murdoch had run two and were on their third run when George Grace caught it in a remote part of the outfield, about 110 metres from the bat. When team-mates commiserated with Bonnor for falling victim to G. F.'s tremendous athleticism, Bonnor said: "Hard luck nothing! I should have hit the perisher."

Murdoch, who had made a duck in the first innings, was supported first by team manager Alexander, the Melbourne Cricket Club all-rounder who had been forced to play because of his team's injuries, and then by barrister William Moule. Alexander made 33, and Moule 34 in a last wicket stand of 88 with Murdoch. When the innings closed at 327, Murdoch was 153 not out, one run ahead of W. G. and winner of their bet. The gold sovereign he won from Grace hung on his watch chain until his dying day. Murdoch's faultless knock was the only century on the second tour, but did not prevent England winning by five wickets. The English players needed only 57 but Boyle and Palmer made them earn every run. At 5 for 31, with G. F. Grace out for a duck (securing a pair for the match) and E. M. Grace clean-bowled for nought, W. G. Grace strode to the crease. How Murdoch must have sighed then for injured Spofforth's talents! England did not lose another wicket.

Bonnor hit the ball out of the ground 26 times during that tour. Murdoch, who preferred Bonnor to play his natural game as a hitter rather than attempt more orthodox play, dropped him down the order. When Bonnor complained, Murdoch replied, "What's the good of putting you in early—you're only a plodder". Bonnor would beg for a chance to bat early and then bombard neighbouring buildings with his big hits. Asked to name the best batsmen in the world, Bonnor considered carefully. "W. G. must be the first and Murdoch second," was his reply. "After that I would prefer not to comment."

The Australians found that it was the custom to allow umpires to keep the ball after an important cricket match. Sometimes when a successful Australian bowler tried to claim the ball with which he had taken a great number of victims he would find the umpires had already sold it. They learned to rush round to the umpires' rooms and offer more than the going rate of £2 when play ended.

Despite their defeat in the international match, the Australians were offered six more games in the last month of their trip. They drew with Sussex at Brighton, where Palmer had 7 for 44 in Sussex's first innings; defeated the Gentlemen of Scotland by six wickets (Palmer 10 for 100); drew at Bradford with the Players (Palmer 8 for 93); playing with only ten men, lost a thriller to Nottinghamshire by one wicket when Arthur Shrewsbury made a brilliant 66 not out; and finally scored an exciting two-wicket win over the Players at Crystal Palace. Spofforth reappeared in the last match, contributing a valuable 25 in Australia's first innings, but he did not bowl.

Murdoch needed all his tact handling the enthusiastic "Joey" Palmer on this tour. Palmer grabbed his chance when Spofforth was injured and bowled as if his life depended on each delivery, but he became quite emotional when he was not given first use of the ball. Murdoch explained that

*"Joey" Palmer took 80 wickets on his first tour of England in 1880, a total he was to lift to 138 in 1882*

his priority was to win and while he considered Palmer the best on hard wickets, he preferred Boyle to open when the pitch was wet.

While on tour the Australians received the news that Tom Wills had eluded asylum attendants and had stabbed himself to death with a pair of scissors. Meanwhile, Tom Kendall had taken a coaching job in Tasmania, where his pupils later demonstrated how needlessly that state had given mainland states an edge by not appointing professional instructors. Kendall worked for 45 years as a compositor for the Hobart *Mercury* and was noted for his latter-day sobriety.

The first Test on English soil proved to be George Grace's last game of cricket. After holding that fabulous catch to dismiss Bonnor he caught a cold after sleeping on a damp bed and developed pneumonia. He died within a few days. He was the youngest of the brothers, the fifth son, and appeared to have a brilliant future. He had more charm than his brothers and did not talk constantly during play. His 6910 runs included eight first-class centuries. The Australians were shocked by his death and wore black armbands when they met the Players.

The Australians recognised that they were only able to play 37 matches because of the generosity of Lord Harris, who had been won over by the kindly Murdoch and the forthright stance of Spofforth who shared Lord Harris's intense distaste for throwing and time-wasting off theory. After the abuse and wounds of the Sydney riot, his change of heart was a noble gesture. Ironically he had to endure harsh criticism for changing England's batting order in the second innings of the Test.

Lord Harris's change of mind was characteristic of the man who, in a letter to *The Times*, expressed his feelings about cricket in this way:

> *You do well to love it, for it is more free from anything sordid, anything dishonourable, than any game in the world. To play it keenly, honourably, generously, self-sacrificingly, is a moral lesson in itself, and the classroom is God's air and sunshine. Foster it, my brothers, so that it may attract all who can find the time to play it; protect it from anything that would sully it, so that it may be in favour with all men.*

Australia won 21 matches, lost 4 and drew 12. The four losses all occurred when Spofforth was unavailable. Eleven of the Australian matches were on level terms, 26 against the odds. The team had to use countrymen W. A. Giles in one game and J. Macdonald in another. They lost the one that counted most, against England, but fought so hard that they enhanced the growing public fondness for international cricket. The Australians received £1100 as the team's share of the Test receipts and each player also received a handsome tour dividend when they arrived home. The tour also healed old wounds. When they were

*The belt buckles awarded to each of the players in the first Test played in England gave the batsmen's scores. Murdoch topscored with 153 not out, one more than W. G. Grace*

honoured by London's Lord Mayor at a farewell banquet at Mansion House, Murdoch paid tribute to all their English cricketing cronies and especially the late lamented G. F. Grace.

On the way home the Australians played ten matches in New Zealand, winning 6, losing 1, and playing 3 draws. They were so keen to avenge their defeat three years earlier by Canterbury that Murdoch successfully backed himself to score more than the entire Canterbury side. Australia scored 323 and won by an innings and 100 runs. The sole loss was to Twenty-Two of Wanganui, who

wisely picked a lineup who could field well. Spofforth took 148 wickets at 3.70 and Palmer 141 at 3.30 in this final segment of the tour.

Expert opinion differed over whether Spofforth was faster or slower on this tour than he had been two years earlier, but he was at the peak of his powers the second time round and had mastered the art of deception. He remained an almost ghoulish figure whose face frightened some opponents, but he could still uproot the stumps of batsmen like W. G. who could not be intimidated. He took 763 wickets at 5.49 apiece on the entire tour, 391 of his victims in England. Boyle, who had vastly improved his batting, took 411 wickets on the tour, and the nineteen-year-old Palmer took 533. Between them they dismissed 909 of the 967 batsmen Australia faced in England.

*Murdoch's famous "draw" shot, a leg-glance played behind an uplifted front leg. Recommended only for batsmen in form*

authority, and running cheekily between wickets.

Murdoch and McDonnell were the only batsmen to score 1000 runs in England. Murdoch scored 1218 at 22.14 and McDonnell 1020 at 21.25. Nobody else made a century, but Alick Bannerman furthered his reputation as an unsurpassed stonewaller. Bonnor's 782 runs included some tremendous blows, but the stalwart of the team was wicket-keeper Jack Blackham, whose hands became scarred and disfigured but who was still unmatched by any English keeper.

Blackham devoted himself to the art of dismissing batsmen. Highly strung and moody, he started to brood in the dressing room when games were close. He was a swarthy, intrepid figure with a flourishing beard and fast hands, and wore a cricket cap that looked too small for his head. He spread his feet far wider than future wicket-keepers. He objected strenuously when his captain placed a long stop. "Put him out where he can do some good," was his admonition. When Blackham caught the ball and whipped off the bails in the same motion, spectators invariably roared with delight. Most of his front teeth were knocked out and for much of his life he had a cavity in his chest where a ball had smashed his ribs. But he always insisted on standing a beard's length from the stumps, even when Spofforth bowled at his fastest.

Deputy wicket-keeper "Affie" Jarvis proved a brave, talented batsman but had few chances to get behind the stumps. Because of his absence with the Australian team he missed the very first 11-a-side match between South Australia and Victoria, which was played on the East Melbourne Ground in November 1880. The South Australians had improved enormously under the coaching of Jesse Hide. Victoria batted first and piled up 329, with Tom Horan scoring 113 and Fred Baker 83. The South Australians collapsed for only 77 in their first innings, with the wide leg breaks of the remarkable William Cooper defeating batsman after batsman. Cooper had not taken up cricket until 27 when his doctor advised him to get more

Palmer secured many wickets with off breaks pitched on the leg stump, which batsmen touched to short leg.

The decision of the players to change captains proved justified. The gamin-like Murdoch delighted all he met. With his exhilarating stroke play, he advanced to greatness as a batsman, perfecting his draw shot (the leg glance played through his legs), driving and cutting with exercise. From the time he first played for Victoria in 1878–79, against Lord Harris's England team, he took a host of wickets dismissing batsmen who were taken by surprise by the extent of his spin.

Following on, South Australia made a commendable 314. Will Slight, brother of Australian team member James Slight who had also begun his cricket with South Melbourne, topscored with 70 run out, George Giffen scored 63, H. Gooden 49 and Hide 48. A seven-wicket defeat was, nevertheless, a creditable start in intercolonial cricket by the South Australians, who thereafter met Victoria annually.

Meanwhile Billy Midwinter, who had played for Gloucestershire against the Australians, rejoined the Victorian team, which defeated New South Wales twice in the summer of 1880–81, despite outstanding displays by Evans and Massie. Midwinter scored 76 in the first match, 42 not out in the second. Frank Allan and the fast-improving Cooper puzzled all the New South Wales batsmen. Victoria won the first match by two wickets, the second by 30 runs.

Midwinter commuted between Australia and England with surprising regularity given the slow transport of the time. He had a spell with Lord's ground staff in 1880. He played a superlative knock in one of his last matches there against Leicestershire; he helped the Marylebone Cricket Club recover from 2 for 19 to reach 3 for 473 in five and a-half hours. Midwinter scored 187, Barnes 266. Despite his mixed loyalties, Midwinter was an accomplished cricketer, a hard-hitting right-hand batsman, medium-pace round-arm break bowler, and outstanding outfielder with a wonderful throwing arm.

When Alfred Shaw arrived in Australia with the sixth English touring team in 1881–82 Midwinter joined them. Shaw's team, all professionals, included James Lillywhite, John Selby, Tom Emmett, George Ulyett and Shaw returning after earlier visits. Among the interesting newcomers were the brilliant and artistic Arthur Shrewsbury, who was also a talented Rugby player; William

Scotton, a left-handed batsman who earned a *Wisden* comment that "He carries caution to such extremes it was often impossible to take any pleasure from seeing him play"; Richard Pilling, the best professional wicket-keeper of his period; and Edmund Peate, one of a long line of outstanding Yorkshire left-arm bowlers. This Australian tour was the first of three organised by Shaw, Lillywhite and Shrewsbury in the 1880s, and 18 matches were played. Midwinter appeared for England in all four Tests.

The Englishmen played five matches in America on their way to Australia—although they declined an offer of £300 from King Kalakaua, of the Sandwich Islands, to play a match against his tribesmen—where they reported that the outspokenness of the critics was still equalled only by their ignorance.

In Australia the tour began with a series against twenty-twos in Maitland, Newcastle, Orange and Bathurst, where a local boy named Charles Thomas Biass Turner took 17 England wickets for 69 runs. The captains had the right to select a fresh batting strip for the main tour matches, an arrangement that provided some unexpected results.

In December 1881 more than 30,000 people saw England beat New South Wales by 68 runs at Sydney, where the Saturday crowd of 20,000 was a record for the Association Ground. Shaw's team began by scoring 5 for 235. Barlow scored 75 in four hours; when he came off a spectator handed him a belt for stonewalling excellence. (During his career, Barlow carried his bat through an innings more than 50 times.) The last five English wickets added only 37 runs on the second day. By stumps New South Wales were 3 for 164, which included a belligerent 56 by Massie. Only Murdoch, 58, offered further resistance and New South Wales were out for 210. Midwinter topscored in England's second innings of 162. Massie completed a splendid double with 76 in New South Wales's second innings of 156.

At the Melbourne Cricket Ground a fortnight

*Hugh Hamon Massie continued his brilliant first-class career during the 1881–82 season when the sixth English team toured Australia*

later Palmer, benefiting from the experience gained on tour, forced Shaw's men to follow on after they scored just half Victoria's first innings of 210. On a damp pitch, Shrewsbury was at his best on a wicket others found difficult, and he made 80 not out, leaving Victoria 94 to win. Shaw was so confident his bowlers could do the job that he backed his own side to win—a practice he rarely followed. Peate and his Yorkshire team-mate Billy Bates dismissed McDonnell, Groube, Horan, Blackham, Bonnor and Edwards for only seven runs before Boyle hit a lusty 43 to take Victoria close to victory, but the Englishmen eventually won by 18 runs. Peate took 6 for 30 in this innings, Palmer

11 for 99 in the match. The captain of the ship taking the Englishmen to Adelaide delayed departure so that play could be finished and Shaw could collect his wager.

Bookmakers had offered 30 to 1 against an English win when Victoria wanted 94 to win. Some of the Englishmen bet £1 on the result and won £30. This was unsavoury enough, but local newspapers alleged that two English players accepted £100 each to throw the match. The two players tried to get Midwinter to join them. Midwinter refused and reported the approach to Shaw. The conspirators later beat Midwinter up. Shaw held an enquiry into charges that the two players deliberately dropped catches, but perhaps diplomatically, found no evidence to support the claim. The enquiry overshadowed a draw against Fifteen of South Australia in Adelaide, where betting had by then been banned.

The first Test at Melbourne—from 31 December 1881 to 4 January 1882—ended in a draw. Ulyett, 87, Selby, 55, and Bates, 58, batted soundly to lift England to a first innings total of 294. Midwinter had Massie stumped by Pilling at nine, but Alick Bannerman and Murdoch began a recovery which Horan sustained with a display of powerful straight driving. Giffen assisted as Horan moved to 124. Australia finished 26 ahead with 320. Cooper perplexed all England's batsmen with his big leg breaks, but Australia were handicapped when Murdoch had to replace the injured Blackham. England's 308 gave them a lead of 283, but Australia only had time to score 3 for 127 before the Englishmen had to join their ship to New Zealand. Cooper had 9 for 200 in his first test.

Between the first and second Tests, 27-year-old Murdoch became the first Australian to score more than 300 in a first-class match when he batted for two days for 321 against Victoria in Sydney. He gave only one chance, at 120, and scored 38 fours, 9 threes, 41 twos and 60 singles off ten Victorian bowlers. His score remained the highest on the Sydney Cricket Ground until Bradman made 340 not out against Victoria, at the age of 20, and 452 not out against Queensland, at 21. The match was originally scheduled for three days but was extended by agreement. Murdoch missed the fourth day because of a court hearing in Cootamundra, but returned on the milk train for the fifth day when New South Wales won by an innings and 138 runs despite another plucky century by Horan.

## Highest Innings
## in Intercolonial Cricket
## New South Wales *v.* Victoria,
## played at Sydney, 1881

*New South Wales*

| | | |
|---|---|--:|
| A. C. Bannerman *c.* Palmer *b.* Turner | | 30 |
| H. H. Massie *b.* Palmer | | 17 |
| W. L. Murdoch *c.* Bannerman (sub.) | | |
| | *b.* Horan | 321 |
| C. Bannerman *lbw b.* Baker | | 3 |
| S. P. Jones *c.* Boyle *b.* Baker | | 109 |
| J. Davis *c.* Boyle *b.* Baker | | 4 |
| T. W. Garrett *b.* McShane | | 163 |
| D. W. Gregory *c.* McDonnell *b.* Palmer | | 28 |
| H. C. Hiddlestone *std.* Blackham | | |
| | *b.* Cooper | 27 |
| F. R. Spofforth *b.* McShane | | 8 |
| E. Evans *not out* | | 2 |
| *Extras* | | 63 |
| | Total | 775 |

*Bowling*

| | Balls | Maidens | Runs | Wickets |
|---|--:|--:|--:|--:|
| Palmer | 320 | 28 | 161 | 2 |
| McShane | 172 | 13 | 91 | 2 |
| Cooper | 280 | 26 | 120 | 1 |
| Boyle | 268 | 31 | 115 | 0 |
| Baker | 276 | 25 | 109 | 3 |
| Turner | 120 | 10 | 66 | 1 |
| Horan | 92 | 15 | 23 | 1 |
| Slight | 8 | 0 | 8 | 0 |
| Blackham | 48 | 8 | 11 | 0 |
| Bonnor | 8 | 0 | 8 | 0 |

After five wins and two draws in New Zealand, England returned to the Sydney Cricket Ground for the second Test in February. Murdoch kept wicket for the injured Blackham, who fielded marvellously at mid-off and opened the batting with Massie. The match see-sawed for three days, at the end of which Australia were 2 for 35, chasing 169 to win. Copybook batting on the fourth morning by Horan, Jones, McDonnell and Murdoch brought victory by five wickets. Shaw tried seven bowlers but none emulated the accuracy of Palmer, Garrett and Evans.

At the end of play the New South Wales Cricket Association presented Maltese Crosses to Murdoch, Barlow and Ulyett; Murdoch for his 321, and Barlow and Ulyett for the first century opening stand (122) in Tests in a second innings. Blackham received a silver plate for his contribution to international cricket. A fortnight later in the third Test Alick Bannerman and Percy McDonnell put on 199, a record fourth wicket partnership, which set up an Australian win. They were not rewarded with silverware. McDonnell's 147, his initial first-class century, included a massive six into the northern stand.

With Australia leading two–nil, the teams left by the overnight train for the fourth Test at Melbourne. This was the accepted form of travel at the time but it necessitated a change of trains at the border because of the different gauge lines in each colony. Batsmen dominated this Test. Ulyett's 149 was the first century for England in Australia and Alick Bannerman and Murdoch had an opening stand of 110 when Australia replied to England's 309 with 300. England were 2 for 234 in their second innings when the match was abandoned on 14 March to permit the Australians to catch their ship to England.

The series demonstrated that the Australians were at last combining sound technique and grace with their natural hitting style. The two drawn Tests, both caused by sailing schedules, were the last draws in Australia till 1946–47.

Shaw's sixth English touring team won eight

minor matches, lost three and drew three. They lost two and drew two of the four Tests. The tour was a financial success, but not as profitable as Australia's English tours. Ulyett topped England's batting with 1424 runs at 33.11. Peate was the leading wicket taker with 264 wickets at 5.84. Another bowler Emmett often pushed off theory to absurdity. Pilling kept wicket skilfully and the energetic Midwinter played in all four Tests for England. The tour did a great deal for Shrewsbury, who previously was an insomniac away from his own bed. He returned to England sturdier in frame and with his reputation enhanced. In domestic cricket, Victoria erred by sending a weak team to play South Australia at Adelaide in March 1882. Norwood left-arm bowler Jack Quilty hit the stumps six times, returning match figures of 9 for 55. Jack Noel's 61 in South Australia's second innings paved the way for a 31-run win, and convinced many South Australians that Noel should have been in the Australian team that toured England that year.

The loss caused Victoria to field her strongest team when these states met a year later in Melbourne. Sent in to bat on a mud heap, the South Australians were helpless against Palmer and Boyle, who had the whole side out for 23, the lowest score ever in intercolonial matches. Noel was the only batsman to play authentic shots. Crowds gathered outside the *Register* office in Adelaide could not believe the figures shown on a large board.

| | |
|---|---|
| J. Noel *b.* Boyle | 18 |
| G. Giffen *b.* Palmer | 1 |
| A. H. Jarvis *b.* Palmer | 0 |
| T. O. Richards *b.* Palmer | 0 |
| J. Hide *b.* Palmer | 0 |
| W. F. Giffen *c.* Palmer *b.* Boyle | 0 |

*Arthur Shrewsbury was a newcomer to the English side that toured in 1881–82. He developed into one of the greatest English batsmen—a thorough professional who quickly won Australians' respect*

| | |
|---|---|
| F. King *run out* | 0 |
| J. E. Gooden *b.* Boyle | 0 |
| W. Knill *b.* Palmer | 1 |
| G. Watsford *c. and b.* Boyle | 2 |
| J. Quilty *not out* | 0 |
| *Extras* | 1 |
| | Total 23 |

*Bowling*

| | Balls | Maidens | Runs | Wickets |
|---|---|---|---|---|
| Boyle | 85 | 16 | 6 | 4 |
| Palmer | 84 | 16 | 16 | 5 |

Victoria only scored 200 but it was enough to win the match by an innings and 98 runs. Even at that early stage it was obvious that South Australia relied on George Giffen to perform heroically in order to extend the eastern states. Giffen was absent on the fourth English tour when the teams met again in February 1884 at Adelaide on a beautiful wicket. South Australia scored 334 and 319 but lost by four wickets, Victoria scoring 285 and 6 for 369. A versatile personality named Norrie Claxton made 72 and 73 for South Australia, batting at No. 10 in the first innings. (Claxton, an Adelaide stockbroker, was a fine hockey player, Australian Rules footballer, state champion athlete, winner of major bicycle races, and later donor of the Claxton Shield, Australia's premier trophy for baseball, a game at which he also excelled.) James Trinnick made 109 for Victoria.

New South Wales and Victoria carried on as they had begun, with each side struggling fiercely for supremacy. The year after New South Wales had staggered Victoria with a total of 775 at Sydney in February 1882, the Victorians returned to dismiss them for 49 and 66 and win by an innings and 166 runs, the biggest winning margin ever in intercolonial cricket. The teams were usually evenly matched, with the bowling of Spofforth and Garrett opposing that of Boyle and Palmer, and Horan scoring as heavily, if not as stylishly, with the bat as Murdoch. Massie was a more scientific hitter than Bonnor, who had joined the Melbourne Cricket Club, but both

*Four of the leading players from the South Australian team: (L to R) George Giffen, Affie Jarvis, John Lyons and Walter Giffen. The team was all out for 23 against Victoria in 1883—the lowest score ever in intercolonial cricket*

could turn a match in a few overs. The patience of Alick Bannerman was just as troublesome as McDonnell's strokeplay.

Despite jealousies between states, poor pitches, the Sydney riot, a handful of greedy international players, and the lack of a national control authority, the first 60 years of Australian cricket had produced sustained growth. By the 1880s even small bush towns boasted cricket clubs. Six England teams had played before large, enthusiastic audiences and Australian teams had attracted big crowds in England. Australia had produced a steady stream of top-class bowlers, though not as many batsmen, from a relatively small cricketing population. But poor match scheduling and the use of off-theory bowling threatened to erode the game's popularity.

The 1881–82 season yielded some outstanding

achievements in club cricket, including the first double century by a coloured cricketer — 280 by Sam Morris for Richmond against St Kilda. (Morris was not an Aborigine, but had West Indian parents who had been lured to Australia by the goldrushes.) In Adelaide, George Giffen made 158 for Norwood against the Kent Club in dramatic style. In Sydney, Alick Bannerman made a century in each innings, 111 and 104 not out, for Carlton against the Albert Club. Fred Spofforth had gone off to a life in the bush, but on one occasion, after recovering from a nasty fall from a horse, he took all 20 wickets in a club match at Bendigo, clean-bowling every batsman.

For all cricketers, the lure of a tour of England remained supreme. Percy McDonnell was still suffering sunstroke when he was carried aboard the steamer *Assam* for the fourth Australian team's trip to England. Nobody would have guessed the Australians had a hard job ahead if they had watched Murdoch and his manager Charles Beal perform their hilarious black-and-white-minstrel act for passengers on that voyage. Nor did George Bonnor appear apprehensive when he bet a punter on board that he could throw a cricket ball 105 metres with his first throw in England.

# An unrivalled victory

## The Ashes story 1882–83

The 1882 Australians took only two matches to convince English cricket fans they were an outstanding team who would worry the best England side. They hammered respected bowlers in a spectacular orgy of runs, while their bowlers and fieldsmen performed heroically. Australia won both matches decisively with time to spare.

In the opening game at Christ Church ground, Oxford, on 15 May, Hugh Massie scored 100 before lunch and 200 before tea against the university. His first century came out of Australia's lunch score of 145, his second while his team-mates made 12. Sammy Jones, who was reckoned a free-hitting batsman, made five. Massie was a last minute selection replacing Horan, whose form was disappointing.

Massie's 206 took 180 minutes. His off drives were so severe that Oxford had four men on the boundary between point and mid-off but he still pierced the field. When he was out, some of the Oxford players discussed recalling him, as they believed he had been caught beyond the chains. Massie simply said he had had enough and it was a good catch, and kept walking.

At Brighton in the next match Murdoch took

*Five of the players who established Australia's international cricket reputation: (L to R) Dave Gregory, Fred Spofforth, Hugh Massie, Alick Bannerman and Tom Garrett*

over as Australia's match winner, with 268 not out in a total of 643, the largest score in English first-class cricket to that time. Murdoch hit 39 fours and a five. Australia had passed Sussex's first innings total of 95 before a wicket fell. They dismissed Sussex for 193 in the second innings to win by an innings and 355. Palmer took 8 for 48 and 6 for 62. Sussex officials then determined to sign Murdoch, whom they rated a superior batsman to W. G. Grace. Massie broke his bat before the Sussex match and was unhappy with the replacement. He still hit eight fours with it in a 20-minute stay for 45, some of his blows drawing gasps from the crowd.

One of the most enjoyable matches of the tour was the third against an Orleans Cricket Club side led by renowned big-hitter C. I. Thornton at Twickenham. Bonnor, who had won the bet he had made on the way to England by throwing a ball just a few millimetres short of 110 metres at Raglan Barracks, Plymouth, when the Australians landed, was out for a duck in Australia's innings of 75, after the Orleans club made 271. Following on, Australia was rescued by a superb knock of 107 not out from Murdoch. Wicket-keeper Pilling dropped the ball with Murdoch's run out apparently certain. Apart from this Murdoch's innings was chanceless.

In the duel of the big hitters, fieldsmen got as far away from the pitch as they could without climbing fences when Thornton and Bonnor appeared. Thornton made some massive hits in his 25, but Bonnor made the biggest of all when he on-drove a ball over the top of a house next to the ground before being bowled by W. G. Grace. Australia were 44 runs ahead at 9 for 240 when time ran out.

Bonnor was a born demoraliser of bowlers and fieldsmen, and embarrassed team-mates with his quest for orthodoxy. "When he was exerting all the strength in that Herculean frame, it was a sight for the Gods as he smote the bowling," Giffen wrote. Banjo Paterson recalled that when George walked down the main street of Orange

with his two brothers, both of them two metres in height, the locals would watch them and ask, "Who's that little bloke with the Bonnors?"—meaning George, who was only 1.95 metres tall.

Unlike the previous Australian team, the 1882 tourists did not have to advertise for matches or play a surfeit of cricket against local eighteens. Their itinerary was arranged for the first time by the Marylebone Cricket Club, whose secretary H. Perkins filled their schedule from May 15 until the middle of September. The team had held an election on board the *Assam*, formally confirming Murdoch as captain and appointing Murdoch, Blackham and Bannerman as selectors. They adopted red, black and yellow as their colours, wearing them for the first time in the fourth tour match against Surrey.

The Australians went 10 weeks without defeat, despite a worrying lack of form by Spofforth. Cambridge University ended their winning run, thanks largely to the three brothers Studd, known as "The Shirt Front". C. T. Studd (who later became a missionary in China) scored 118 in Cambridge's first innings of 266 with 14 boundaries, and G. B. Studd 42; in the second the Studds contributed 131 out of 165—J. E. K. Studd 66, G. B. 48, and C. T. 17 not out. The Australians were dismissed for 139 in the first innings because of the splendid bowling of Robert Christian Ramsay, who was known as "Twisting Tommy" because of his "curly leg breaks". Ramsay took 12 for 179 in the match, Cambridge winning by six wickets. Ramsay was one of four brothers brought up on a Queensland sheep farm; he had returned to England to attend Harrow and Cambridge and to play cricket. The defeat demonstrated Murdoch's limitations as a substitute wicket-keeper, for he missed vital chances.

The tourists questioned the action of Lancashire bowler Crossland, having no doubts that he threw. But Lancashire's captain, "Monkey" Hornby, was such a pleasant man that Murdoch did not argue the point that Crossland cheated two or three times an over. The Lancashire professionals, Dick Barlow and Dick Pilling, told the Australians how a customer once came into the store they ran in Manchester. "Let me have three penn'orth of court plaster, two yards of bandaging lint, and a bottle of liniment for bruises," said the man, "I'm playing against Jack Crossland."

Australia played five times against Yorkshire on the tour, including three successive games. They won three of the five and drew two. At the end of the series *Bell's Life* commented that Yorkshire were over-matched.

At Nottingham there was a problem when it was discovered too late that the Australians were expected to bring their own lunch and eat it on the ground with the opposing professionals, who usually resorted to bread and cheese and beer during the interval. When manager Beal remonstrated with the Notts secretary, Captain Holden, he was informed that there was no agreement to provide lunch. Holden, known locally as Hellfire Jack then went into a ten-minute harangue, arguing that it was sufficient honour to play at Trent Bridge without being fed. "Say no more about it! I will positively hear no more," he added. Beal merely smiled and said, "But you have had all the say yourself." Holden ignored him and produced a cigar. "Will some *Englishman* give me a light?" he asked. Bonnor overheard him and exploded. "I am such an Englishman as you are! You or any *gentleman* present. I can trace my family back for six generations, and I wonder if you can do the same."

Rain interrupted the match, which was drawn, but the Australians still made £238 from it. The county committee apologised for the incident at lunch and the Australians showed there was no ill-feeling by returning for a benefit match for William Oscroft, a professional who had toured Australia with W. G. Grace in 1873–74. This time Australia won by 159 runs, dismissing Nottingham for 48 in their second innings.

Australia gave one of their finest displays to beat the Gentlemen by an innings at Lord's, where Giffen, then only 23 years old, distinguished himself by taking 8 for 47 in the first innings and 3 for 60 in the second. Bonnor hit the bowling to the far corners of the field, with three mighty sixes in his 74. Australia scored 334, the Gentlemen 182 and 157. The sherry importer and author John Ruskin could not take his eyes off Bonnor. "I thank God that England has colonies capable of producing such splendid young giants as Bonnor, who looked as amiable as he was grand," he wrote.

At Chichester against a United Eleven Australia scored 501, Tom Horan topscoring with 112. Only two of the Australians failed to top 30 runs. A man short because of the absence of Midwinter, the United XI managed only 166 and 72, and lost by an innings and 263 runs. Although Maurice Read scored 90 in their first innings, the locals struggled from the time Spofforth dismissed both W. G. and E. M. Grace for only seven runs. Bonnor kept wicket in the second innings in place of Blackham.

Horan scored his second century of the tour against Gloucestershire at Clifton, where he made 141 out of a total of 450. W. G. Grace was out for 12 in Gloucestershire's first innings of 108 and was most indignant when he was given out leg before wicket for 77 in the second. Gloucestershire were out the second time for 183, giving Australia victory by an innings and 159 runs.

Australia's worst defeat was at Derby, against a strong Players side. With Spofforth unavailable because of a foot injury, the Players mastered the Australian bowling to score 322. The tourists replied with 150, and, following on, were out for 138. Morley did the damage with 4 for 39 and 3 for 31. A further defeat was inflicted by Cambridge Past and Present. The Australians, handicapped by the absence of Palmer and Giffen who were both injured, needed to score 208 to win in the fourth innings. When Bonnor hit 4 sixes, 6 fours, 3 threes, and a two in half an hour's batting, victory seemed likely. But after Bonnor's dismissal for 66 when Australia was 79, wickets fell steadily. Bonnor was cheered boisterously all the way to the pavilion and Cambridge fielded superbly to win by 20 runs.

The Australians reached The Oval late in August 1882, for the only international match of the tour, with an impressive record; they were worried only over Spofforth, whose bowling had been a mixture of brilliant and mediocre. Palmer was unfit and McDonnell was omitted. Hornby had done so badly against Australia's bowlers that there was criticism of his appointment as captain of an England team that lacked Lord Harris and Arthur Shrewsbury. There was also widespread regret over the decision to play only one match between two such fine teams, when three or five would have been a fairer test.

The visitors went into the match bearing nicknames dreamed up by vocal spectators or taken from the advertising posters round the field. Spofforth was "The Demon"; Bonnor, "Jumbo"; Bannerman, "Little Jumbo"; Massie, "The Deer"; Garrett, "Shoofly"; Murdoch, "Eaglewings"; Horan, "Features"; and Blackham, "Black Jack." Two of their opponents had been honoured by the Lancashire poet, Francis Thompson:

> And a ghostly batsman plays to the bowling
> of a ghost,
> And I look through my tears on a
> soundless-clapping host,
> As the run-stealers flicker to and fro,
> To and fro:
> O my Hornby and my Barlow long ago!

Australia began badly in front of a capacity crowd when Ulyett uprooted Massie's leg stump with the third ball of his second over amid wild applause. This dramatic success, so early, lifted the English fielding. There were five excellent saves, with W. G. at point excelling. With the score at 1 for 20, England sent down 14 consecutive maidens. Despite the slow scoring, every ball, every stroke and every clean pick-up was warmly applauded. At 13 Murdoch played on. Bonnor was bowled for one, Bannerman was cleverly caught at point by W. G., and Horan and Giffen were both bowled after tame, stroke-

*In 1882 the third Australian team to tour England won the Test that established the Ashes legend. Excitement was so intense spectators fainted*

less innings. At 6 for 30, Garrett and Blackham put on 18 before Garrett was caught at long-off. The other wickets fell cheaply and Australia was

all out for 63, their lowest score in all 30 matches of the tour so far. Barlow took 5 for 19, Peate 4 for 31.

Grace and Barlow opened for England, but at 15 Spofforth hit W. G.'s leg stump with a yorker. Three runs later Spofforth had Barlow caught at point. Ulyett and Lucas then took the score to 50 before Ulyett rashly stepped down the pitch to drive Spofforth and was stumped. Lucas was caught at the wicket and at 4 for 59 England slumped disastrously. C. T. Studd was bowled without scoring, and, with the scores level, Lyttelton was caught off the glove. Spofforth bowled at his best on a wicket that suited him

*Sammy Jones, whose run-out by W. G. Grace angered the Australians and made them more determined to win the 1882 Test*

scored 55 out of 66 in better than even time, a magnificent knock in such a low-scoring game, and something no other player in either side could have done. He hit without hesitation or nervousness, and with authority. His 55 included 9 fours.

Massie's success inspired Murdoch to send in Bonnor, but he added only four before his middle stump was sent flying. Murdoch needed all his skill to survive, playing patiently as Horan and Giffen were dismissed. Joined by Jones after Blackham was out, Murdoch hit a flukey shot to leg. After completing a run, Jones wandered out of his crease. Lyttelton, who was not quick enough to catch Murdoch's risky shot, picked up the ball and threw it to W. G. He whipped off the bails and appealed for a run-out.

Jones later claimed that he was merely "gardening"—patting down a bump in the pitch—when W. G. appealed. Umpire George Thoms gave Jones out, but later the Australians contended that they distinctly heard Thoms say: "As you claim it, sir, Out!" Murdoch reacted immediately, questioning the ethics of Jones' dismissal. *Bell's Life* disapproved of Grace's action: "It was strict cricket but it was taking advantage of a young player's thoughtlessness".

Further disaster overtook Australia at 8 for 122. Hornby threw rapidly from the outfield, Studd took the ball and relayed it to Lyttelton, who knocked off the bails with Murdoch out of his ground. Had either Hornby or Studd hesitated Murdoch would have been safe. Australia's innings ended at 122 when Steel bowled Boyle. More than half the runs had been scored in the first 55 minutes when the ball and pitch had been wet. None of the last nine batsmen displayed the confidence of Massie or Murdoch, who scored 29 of the last 56 runs. Peate's 4 for 40 gave him 8 for 71 for the match.

England's chase for the 85 runs required began with Spofforth encouraging all his team-mates. "It can be done," he kept saying loudly. The 20,000 people at the ground concentrated on every ball. *Bell's Life* later claimed that the mixture of

ideally, finishing with 7 for 46. England were out for 101. Maurice Read's 19 not out was cheered enthusiastically.

Heavy rain fell during the night and improved Australian prospects. The experts forecast that the pitch would play easily for a while and then become difficult as it dried out in the afternoon. Here Massie took what proved to be a match-winning opportunity, hitting with power and authority from the start of the Australian innings despite occasional awkward bounce. Lucas got his hands to a catch when Massie was 38 but could not hold this vigorously struck blow. At 66 England's sixth bowler, Peate, bowled Massie to the delight of another capacity crowd. Massie

silence and wild cheering of runs helped unnerve the batsmen. W. G. Grace and Hornby opened with seven singles, each applauded as if they had been hits into the street. Spofforth hit Hornby's off stump at 15, and his next delivery turned sharply from the off to scatter Barlow's stumps. W. G. and Ulyett then took the score to 50 with some glorious batting. With only 35 needed and eight capable batsmen still to come England seemed certain of victory.

Blackham then caught Ulyett low on the leg side at 51. Two runs later W. G. hit an off-drive straight into Bannerman's hands at mid-off. W. G.'s score of 32, on a turning pitch, was superb batting. Horan observed that the incoming batsmen had ashen faces and parched lips. At 4 for 64, 20 short of a win, Lyttelton and Lucas began a long period of careful, scoreless defence. Not one Australian had lost confidence or betrayed the slightest hesitation, fielding safely as Boyle and Spofforth bowled with needlepoint accuracy.

After 12 maidens in succession Spofforth whispered to Murdoch, who then had Bannerman deliberately allow a single to give Spofforth a chance at Lyttelton. Four maidens later Spofforth bowled him. England was 5 for 66. Though needing only 19 to win, the batsmen had completely lost the ability to get the ball past the fieldsmen. Spofforth now bowled his break-backs at awesome speed, with Boyle sustaining a perfect length. Blackham took every ball that passed the bat with inspiring skill, standing right up on the stumps. The tenseness of the struggle infected the crowd, who cheered Lucas to the echo when he hit Boyle for four. Spofforth struck back immediately by dismissing Steel and Read in one over.

At 7 for 75 with 10 runs needed, Lucas played Spofforth onto his stumps and was replaced by the in form C. T. Studd, who had hit two centuries against Australia earlier that summer. Murdoch caught Barnes off his glove at point from the first ball of Boyle's nineteenth over. Last man Edmund Peate swung wildly at his first ball and took a lucky two. He swiped at the next and was

*Spy's famous cartoon in* Vanity Fair *of Spofforth, "the demon bowler", who did so much to achieve Australia's victory in the Ashes match. He bowled ten maidens in his last eleven overs, and took four wickets for two runs off his last seven balls*

almost bowled, then swung again at the last ball of the over and was bowled. Australia had won by seven runs.

The stunned crowd sat voiceless for an instant and then let out a huge roar, jumping the fence to applaud the men who had won. Spofforth was carried shoulder-high to the pavilion. Studd, who had not faced a ball, trudged behind. In the dressing-room Spofforth danced and jigged, singing "I'm a demon! I'm a demon!" A spectator had died in the excitement, several had fainted, and one man had gnawed away part of the handle of his umbrella. One unsteady scorer had written what looked like "Geese" instead of "Peate" in his book.

Spofforth had bowled 10 maidens in his last 11 overs, and taken 4 wickets for two runs off his last seven balls. This gave him 7 for 44 and 14 for 90 in the match, figures that were not bettered by an Australian at Lord's for 90 years, until Bob Massie took 16 for 137 in 1972. Criticised for not giving Studd the strike, Peate quipped, "Mr Studd was so nervous I did not feel I could trust him to score a run". Surrey secretary C. W. Alcock commented, "Men noted for their coolness in a crisis trembled, some shivering as if from cold". Amid the excitement Blackham quietly pocketed the ball that had bowled Peate.

Four days later London's *Sporting Times* printed a mock obituary, written by Reginald Brooks, son of the *Punch* editor:

*In Affectionate Remembrance of English Cricket Which Died at The Oval on 29 August 1882*

*Deeply lamented by a large circle of sorrowing friends and acquaintances.*
*R.I.P.*
*N.B. The body will be cremated and the ashes taken to Australia.*

Murdoch's magnificent generalship, Blackham's wicket-keeping, Boyle's steady bowling, and the brilliant fielding of Bannerman and the rest of the Australians had given Australia a victory unrivalled in the history of cricket. Massie was the man who, with his fierce hitting on the final morning, gave his team a chance to win, but Spofforth was the man who took that chance. In the dressing-room just after Australia had won, with both teams sharing champagne, Spofforth said he could not have had a pitch that suited him better. "Though England for the first time had to lower her colours to Australia at home, we were beaten by a magnificent eleven, before whose

prowess it was no disgrace to fail," reflected *Bell's Life.*

After the drama at The Oval the remaining eight matches of the Australians' tour proved an anticlimax, although large crowds continued to attend. Bonnor provided one of the tour highlights with a memorable display of hitting against I Zingari at Scarborough, scoring 122 not out in 105 minutes. He hit 4 sixes and 16 fours.

Four Australians—Murdoch, Horan, Massie and Bannerman—scored more than 1000 runs on the 38-match tour. Murdoch topped the averages with 1711 runs at 30.55, a performance critics acknowledged as unrivalled by the world's great batsmen. Sydney Pardon stated in *Wisden* that W. G. Grace had planned to retire to medical practice until the success of the Australians revived his ambitions as a cricketer. W. G. wrote in his memoirs:

*The 1882 Australians were the best Australia has ever sent to the Mother Country. So brilliant were their achievements, and so completely did they captivate the British public, county cricket suffered complete eclipse. They were foemen worthy of our steel, plucky, resolute, and resourceful, and they proved their ability to meet, and in most cases beat, the best teams we could set against them.*

The Australians' triumph was all the more praiseworthy because of the wet English summer. Only 10 or 12 of the 38 games were played on hard pitches, many were seriously affected by rain, and seven whole days were lost through bad weather. They still won 23 games, drew 11 and lost only 4, and all this despite an injury to one of their best bowlers, Joey Palmer, who missed the last 13 matches.

Palmer still managed to take 138 wickets at

*Ivo Bligh's team, which toured Australia in 1883. England and Australia both won two Tests, but Bligh claimed the Ashes as the fourth Test was not on the original tour programme*

*A remarkably clear photograph of four outstanding early Australian players watching Bligh's side in action: (L to R) Fred Spofforth, Tom Horan, John Blackham and Harry Boyle*

12.54. Three other Australians took more than 100 wickets: Garrett 128 at 13.74, Boyle 144 at 11.68, and Spofforth 188 at 12.13. Spofforth confirmed his place as the greatest of living bowlers. The sole disappointment was young Sam Jones, who scored only 370 runs in 32 innings at an average of 11.93.

The seventh England team to tour Australia, captained by the Honourable Ivo Bligh, left England in October 1882 on the *Peshawar*, as guests of the Melbourne Cricket Club, well before Murdoch and his men returned home. The team consisted of amateurs A. G. Steel, C. T. Studd, W. W. Read, E. F. S. Tylecote, G. F. H. Leslie, G. B. Studd and G. F. Vernon, and professionals Billy Bates, Richard Barlow, Fred Morley and William Barnes.

At night on a moonlit deck Ivo Bligh often spent time talking to another passenger, Florence Rose Morphy. Some 563 kilometres after leaving Colombo, Barlow noticed a full-rigged barque, later identified as the *Glenroy*, bearing down on the *Peshawar*. "She's coming too close to be pleasant and if they're not careful there'll be an accident," said Barlow, who had barely finished speaking when the *Glenroy* crashed into their vessel and ripped a huge hole amidship. The captain gave orders to lower the lifeboats but fortunately the sea was calm and the *Peshawar* did not sink. Fred Morley was knocked out and cracked one of his ribs; Bligh injured a hand. The *Peshawar* limped back to Colombo with a gaping hole just 610 millimetres above the water line. Barlow noted the sharks in the sea below.

Even with this detour the Englishmen still arrived in Australia early in November before Murdoch and his team, who returned to a heroes' welcome. The *Bulletin* commented that it "rained dinners" for the triumphant side in capital cities. Melbourne's special reception committee added a torchlight procession and awarded each player a medal.

The *South Australian Register* reported on 10 November 1882 that "The gentlemen members of the England team have been elected honorary members of the Adelaide Club and will stay at the South Australian Hotel, while quarters have been found at the Prince Alfred for the professionals". Bligh's hand injury forced him to miss the first six matches and wicket-keeper Tylecote captained England. The Adelaide match was drawn, England scoring 153, South Australia 7 for 128. England then defeated Victoria, whose six tourists had not returned, by 10 wickets. Cooper took 5 for 89 with his leg-breaks in an England score of 273; Victoria made 104 and 169.

Midwinter had returned to the Victorian team after playing 30 matches for the fourth Australian side in England. Prudent mining investments now enabled him to change his status from professional cricketer to amateur while he ran his Melbourne pub. The *Sydney Mail*, however, was critical. "Are we to have another season of vagueness from this very slippery cricketer? One day he is an Australian, the next day an Englishman." Midwinter objected to being called an Anglo-Australian and claimed he was "Australian to the core".

By the time the Englishmen reached Sydney at the beginning of December to play New South Wales, Murdoch and his tourists were in Adelaide playing against South Australia. Bligh's handsome team, which had abandoned the pith helmets of previous years for wide-brimmed bush hats, made 461 against New South Wales, including 146 by C. F. H. Leslie; the home side replied with 152 and 165. Matches at Maitland, Newcastle and Ballarat followed before England went back to

*The amazing Billy Midwinter bobbed up in the Victorian side during the Australian tour by Bligh's team. He was in and out of both the Australian and England Test teams so often that the* Sydney Mail *called him "a slippery cricketer"*

Melbourne for the first Test on 30 December.

George Alexander was persuaded to manage the English team after the Melbourne Cricket Club had advertised the job without response. Bligh resumed the captaincy but England were still without their only fast bowler, Morley. With Australia 5 for 162, Bonnor twice hit the ball into the crowd. Then, after clubbing Bates up into the elm trees, he hit a huge skier which Read dropped in front of the pavilion. Australia reached 291 on the second morning, Bonnor contributing 85. England struggled on a pitch affected by overnight rain that allowed Palmer to turn the ball sharply and take 7 for 65. Following on 114 behind, England again found Australia's bowling hostile. Australia needed 56 to win and they lost only one wicket in the chase.

Despite this defeat Bligh still hoped to regain the "revered ashes of cricket". Murdoch replied: "Ivo, I've only to add that you have simply waxed up that little urn a trifle tighter". Three weeks later in Melbourne England shook Australian complacency.

After Palmer dismissed Barlow and C. T. Studd cheaply, England scored 294; Walter Read made 75, Barnes 72, Bates 55. On a rain-sodden pitch round-armer Bates, the fifth bowler tried, discovered a spot cut up by the Australians. Bates hit it with such consistency that he took 7 for 28, including the wickets of McDonnell, Giffen and Bonnor with successive balls—the first Test hat-trick by an England bowler. Bates bowled five of his victims. Scoring only 114, Australia were forced to follow-on and Bates took a further 7 for 74 to clinch victory for England by an innings and 27 runs.

The teams moved to Sydney for the deciding Test on 26 January 1883. Mrs Annie Fletcher, wife of the Paddington Cricket Club secretary, offered to provide Bligh with a bag in which he could take home the ashes. When Bligh enjoyed the joke, Mrs Fletcher requested artist Blamire Young to sketch a design and made the velvet bag herself.

England won the third Test by 69 runs. The turning point came in England's first innings when Tylecote joined Read with the score at 5 for 75. They attacked the bowling with bravado, adding 118, each man scoring 66, so that England made 247. Australia appeared to have that total within reach at 1 for 133 but heavy rain transformed the outlook. Only a deplorable display in the field by England allowed Australia to make 218, 94 of which were scored by little Alick Bannerman. The game next swung Australia's way when Spofforth took 7 for 44 to have England all out for 123.

Needing 153 to win Australia were out for

*The Ashes bag and urn. Mrs Fletcher of Sydney designed and embroidered the bag, but some Melbourne ladies did not like it and burned a stump to fill the urn with ashes. Ivo Bligh accepted both*

83 on a strip made more treacherous by further rain. Barlow took 7 for 40, bowling on a pitch the Australians claimed he cut up with his spikes. Bligh would have none of their protests and said Spofforth did the same when he bowled.

Mrs Fletcher presented her embroidered "Ashes" bag to Bligh, who at the dinner which followed challenged the "All Australia" team to a match. The Englishmen went off to Queensland where the professionals again stayed in inferior hotels, a procedure which perplexed their Australian hosts. Ivo Bligh assured the organisers that the arrangement was normal English practice. The voyage to Brisbane from Sydney took three days in a small coastal ship, which tested the fortitude of amateurs and professionals alike.

England defeated Eighteen of Queensland by an innings. Walter Read scored 84 of England's total of 265. The Queensland Eighteen's first innings yielded 62. Steel took 10 for 28, C. T. Studd 6 for 22. The second innings was even worse, Steel taking 9 for 16 and Barlow 8 for 49 in a score of 49. At Maryborough an admirer of Read's innings of 66 gave him a block of land.

The disappointing performances of Queenslanders in these matches persuaded Brisbane cricket officials that they badly needed more expert coaching for their players and in 1883 Ned Sheridan was engaged as coach by the Stanleys Club. Sheridan, one of the most diligent instructors in batting, opened a barber-tobacconist shop in Queen Street, Brisbane, where he set aside a special reading room for cricketers. He used to show customers marks on his shins he had collected in encounters with Spofforth.

With the Ashes mission accomplished, the England team agreed to play a fourth international match against "All Australia" on Sydney's Association Ground in February. Bligh and Murdoch experimented by using a different pitch for each innings. All Australia won by four wickets despite a substantial knock from A. G. Steel, who was dropped four times in his first 45 runs. Steel went on to 135 not out on the second morning, when

*Ivo Bligh not only won the Ashes but also won a bride. The Countess of Darnley, as she was later known, was a Melbourne girl. She helped Bligh restore his rundown country estate in England*

England were out for 263. Murdoch took a long time selecting a strip on which to bat and when the openers finally appeared roars of laughter greeted the sight of Bonnor at 1.95 metres completely dwarfing Alick Bannerman, 1.55 metres. Bonnor responded with some huge blows in an innings of 87, taking Australia to 262, just one run behind.

His cherished wish to be regarded as a stylist rather than a slogger had finally been granted, but Bonnor was unimpressed by his luck. "Catch me goin' in first with Alick again!" he bellowed. "First it's 'Come on Bon, are you asleep?' Then it's 'Go back, you fool!' And when you've done everything he's called for, he'll come halfway down the pitch and read the Riot Act at you."

After England scored 197 in their second

innings, Australia lost six wickets scoring the 199 needed to win. Bonnor and Bannerman began the chase with a stand of 44, Bannerman hitting crisply for 63. Blackham made 58 not out after two wickets fell for two runs. Midwinter in his last Test—four for England, four for Australia—hit Australia's winning runs. Bonnor left the ground with a wealthy widow who had pursued him from England; somehow he "escaped", for he never married.

England's tour ended at Melbourne where Midwinter's 92 out of Victoria's 284 brought decisive victory for the locals. Palmer led the rout of England (dismissed for 52 and 156) with match figures of 11 for 86. Bligh's team won four and lost three of the matches on level terms. They won five and drew five of those against the odds. The popularity of Bligh's side produced a cash surplus that enabled the Melbourne Cricket Club to reduce its debts on two stands by £2100.

When the handsome, tall, 23-year-old Bligh hurt his hand while batting, bandages were taken on to the field and were secured by a lady's handkerchief. Later he insisted on thanking the lady and was reintroduced to Florence Morphy, a daughter of a Beechworth magistrate, whose early death had left her living in "genteel poverty". Melbourne ladies in Florence's circle thought the velvet Ashes bag inappropriate and purchased an urn for them. Arguments over whether they burned a stump or a pair of bails to fill the urn remain unresolved. But ashes have been part of the mythology of cricket since Oliver Cromwell banned cricket in Ireland in 1656 and had all stumps, bats and bails burned. Australian newspapers claimed that since Bligh's team had won only two of four Tests, the Ashes should stay in Australia, but Bligh reasoned that only three Tests had been set down in England's original programme.

The Ashes were reported to have been in his luggage, his private property, when he returned to England, but as he had to inform a grumpy father who had allowed the Darnley estate to run down that he was returning to Australia to marry Florence Morphy, it is more likely he left them with her in Melbourne. Bligh returned the following year to find her the guardian of the Clarke family children. The Blighs' first child was born in Melbourne before they went back to England and revitalised the Cobham Park family estate.

When Bligh died, as the eighth Lord Darnley, in 1927, his will made no mention of the Ashes, but his Australian widow presented them to the Marylebone Cricket Club, who have retained them at Lord's. There are two urns, one of pottery and one of gold. Many replicas have been made but the originals have not left Lord's. In 1953 the Ashes urns were moved from the Long Room at Lord's to the Imperial Cricket Museum nearby, along with Annie Fletcher's velvet bag and the score card of the match Australia won in 1882 that started it all. The mystery of whether the Melbourne ladies burned a stump or a bail, and where they did it, has not been solved. A 1982 article in the *Cricketer*, edited by Christopher Martin-Jenkins, suggested that Lord Darnley's servants had upset the urn whilst cleaning and, with the Ashes scattered all over the carpet, had burned twigs to replace them. The Marylebone Cricket Club refuses to comment on the authenticity of the contents of the urns.

Fred Morley's injuries from the collision near Colombo troubled him throughout the tour. Right near the end he was found to have a broken rib, an injury he had concealed, never worrying team-mates over the pain bowling gave him. The seriousness of his injury would have had more chance of discovery and proper treatment had he and his fellow professionals not been segregated from the rest of Bligh's team. Morley died of congestion and dropsy within 18 months of their return to England.

# Gate money cricketers
### England and Australia 1884–85

Throughout the Victorian era a large number of women attended Australian cricket matches, converting intercolonial and international cricket into minor fashion parades. At Melbourne and Sydney crowds of 20,000 were common for intercolonial matches and Adelaide was not far behind. A new stand opened at Adelaide in November 1882, at a cost of £3100, was repeatedly filled by women eager to be seen in the latest fashions. Women's cricket, which had begun at Bendigo in 1874, spread through all the colonies. But the big development in the 1880s was the expansion of junior cricket.

Boyle and Scott's *Cricketers' Guide* for 1882–83 reported that crowds of 10,000 or 11,000 people were not unusual at Melbourne junior matches. Similar enthusiasm left the organiser of junior cricket in Sydney, F. J. Ironside, hard-pressed to find enough pitches for all who wanted to play. Competition for the juniors' Gardiner's Cup was as keen as for the seniors' Holdsworth Cup, with a new club called the Belvidere prominent in the junior competition.

The *Referee* gave Ironside credit for introducing matting pitches. "The ground on Moore

*The professionals waited on the field for the amateurs to emerge from another gate during the Gentlemen v. Players match at Lord's. Some noted Australians were amongst the crowd*

Park was so uneven, it was dangerous to batsmen," recalled Ironside, explaining how the first matting came to be made from coconut fibre by prisoners in Darlinghurst Jail at £6 each. Matting revolutionised the preparation of junior and social match pitches and was later improved with the development of concrete wickets over which matting could be laid. Soon every country town had its matting pitch.

Country cricket in New South Wales had never been in such a flourishing condition. In Wagga Wagga and Cootamundra, the Cox Challenge Shield created widespread interest, with Wagga emerging triumphant over teams from Hay, Adelong, Tumut and other smaller towns. At the hub of bush cricket the Bathurst Cup produced still-discussed feats with bat and ball in Bathurst, Blayney and Orange. Sydney teams that visited Kiama, Wollongong and Broughton's Creek were surprised to find the country sides too strong for them.

The one discouraging feature in Australian cricket was the stagnant Sydney club movement. Critics attributed this to the habit of deferring all club cricket when big matches were played on the Association Ground. The *Cricketers' Guide* pronounced:

*To put club cricket on its legs, the first step is to decline for a couple of seasons a visit from English cricketers, and to resolutely oppose our men going to England in that period. It is bad for club cricket that other matches are suspended at the best part of the season to accommodate mammother events; but it is an excellent arrangement for the trustees of the Association Ground, with no other enclosed ground in Sydney.*

Rugby football was first played on the Association Ground in 1881 and the following year the Rugby Union sought representation on the ground committees. The NSWCA found Phillip Sheridan, who had originally been appointed to represent it on the trust, increasingly unsympathetic. In a letter to the NSWCA on 3 March 1883, Sheridan pointed out: "It is a mistake to conclude that the ground is under the direction of the Cricket Association . . . The ground may, upon proper authority being obtained, be used for any other public amusement". A hundred years of bickering between the association and the Cricket Ground Trust ensued.

Devoid of funds and without its own ground, the NSWCA had no means of preventing players from continually touring England. The *Cricketers' Guide* urged administrators to "let leading players recover from their labours," for "Murdoch is getting too portly and aldermanic for cricket, the ever reliable Garrett is showing unmistakable signs of staleness, Massie, the most brilliant of batsmen, is fast degenerating into a slogger."

The criticism was not confined to Sydney. The *Guide*'s South Australian representative said of the Norwood player T. A. Reeves: "If ever he could bat, he doesn't do it now". The same critic reprimanded North Adelaide's A. M. Pettinger for "shirking practice", and said J. C. Sands, of College Park, was "a very soft batsman, seems afraid of breaking the ball. Poor field; excellent club secretary". Mount Gambier's Jack Medhust was judged "a light of other days. Cricket has advanced too much for him".

Almost unanimously, Australia's growing band of cricket writers decided that there was too much international cricket and urged the associations to keep the best players at home for a season or two. The associations were not strong enough to do so, for by then Australian tourists were fast becoming an exclusive group who guarded their own interests zealously.

One player who managed to join this elite in the 1883–84 season was Dr Henry James Herbert ("Tup") Scott, who when still a schoolboy had impressed Sam Cosstick as a potential champion. Scott had the backing of the powerful Melbourne Cricket Club. At Melbourne in December 1883, Scott helped Victoria recover from an apparently losing position with a splendid

*Dr Henry ("Tup") Scott's skills forced him into the Australian team in 1884, even though the Australian team looked like a "closed shop"*

Unlike Sydney club cricket, which was controlled by lengthy committee meetings, Melbourne cricket was run by the Victorian Cricketers' Association, a less cumbersome body with players in key jobs. When E. D. Heather became honorary secretary of the VCA in 1882, with control over all clubs, he received £20 for his annual expenses. For the 1882–83 season, the VCA appointed William Cooper, the remarkable leg-spin bowler, sole selector of state teams. Cooper's teams beat New South Wales, England, and South Australia in successive matches, all by an innings.

After the Melbourne Cricket Club, East Melbourne, founded by Tom and Charlie Dight with Fred and Joseph Moody, was the most powerful club in Victoria. It was based at a number of grounds, including one at Clarendon Street and East Melbourne. It had originally been known as the Abbotsford Club in 1860, when permission was granted to construct a cricket field on what was known as Captain Lonsdale's Paddock.

One of the most remarkable clubs was formed at Walhalla, a rich goldmining town in the mountains of Gippsland. The terrain at Walhalla was so steep that bodies in the cemetery were placed vertically in their graves. A huge amount of explosives was used to blow the top off a mountain to provide space for a cricket ground. The approach to the ground involved a very strenuous half-hour climb, and Walhalla used to win matches by making the opposing team field as soon as they got there; the Walhalla team went up the night before and slept in the pavilion. Teams from Moe and Erica travelled for hours to get to Walhalla, part of a network of fascinating goldfields cricket centres that included California Gully and Lambing Flats.

Clubs in all major centres had begun to depend more on local schools for recruits rather than rely on new settlers. The King's School, founded at Parramatta in 1831, was strong enough to play first grade opposition right through the second half of the nineteenth century. Sydney Grammar School, established in 1859, played the

114 not out. Murdoch's 158 had taken New South Wales to a first innings of 412. Horan batted bravely for 126, and with Scott's score this enabled Victoria to lead by eight runs. On a worn pitch Midwinter then took 7 for 54. With New South Wales out for 143, Victoria lost seven wickets in scoring the 136 needed for a win.

The first visit by an Australian colony to New Zealand came in that season. A Tasmanian team, which included Tom Kendall, Ken Burn, John George Davies, E. H. Butler and Harold Hale, spent five weeks there. Kendall forsook a Test trial in Australia that might have seen his return to international cricket to take part in this tour. Playing on level terms Canterbury twice beat Tasmania on rain-affected grounds in close finishes, and Otago beat them by six runs. Kendall's bowling was the feature of the tour and Tasmania were captained by his employer, *Hobart Mercury* proprietor, John Davies.

J. ALLEE

H. MUSGROVE

J. HEALEY

W. R. ROBERTSON

W. BROWN

V. TRAPP

W. MIDWINTER

P. G. McSHANE

H. BOYLE

T. HORAN

E. P. HASTINGS

T. U. CROUSE

H. J. H. SCOTT

C. ALLEE

G. GORDON

W. CAMPBELL

P. LEWIS

McLEAN
CHALLENGE CUP
1882-3-4
WON BY E.M.C.C. WITHOUT A DEFEAT

first inter-schools match in Sydney in 1875 against King's, and the first interstate school match against Melbourne Grammar in 1876. The first school match in Victoria was played in 1858 between Scotch College, founded in 1851, and Geelong Grammar, established 1855. "Tup" Scott became the first of a long line of players from Melbourne's Wesley College to appear for his country when he was picked in the 1884 team to England.

All the members of the 1884 team followed the same procedure as earlier teams, entering into a legal agreement with their team-mates and their manager George Alexander. Under this agreement, which is given in full in the appendix, the players each put up an agreed sum to fund the tour and shared all profits or losses. No control body or state cricket association was involved.

Before the 1884 tourists left they played Fifteen of New South Wales at Sydney. Harry Moses, born at Windsor and educated at Dr Sly's School, Calder House, Sydney, scored a dashing 149 for the State Fifteen. A left-hander with a sound defence that was seldom beaten, he hit powerfully all round the wicket and was brutally efficient in despatching short-pitched deliveries. He was then 26, at the peak of his considerable powers, but refused all offers to join this and later Australian tours of England. He could have challenged Murdoch as Australia's No. 1 batsman had he toured, but he preferred to concentrate on his job as a Sydney wine merchant. He was also a dog-breeder and was a president of the New South Wales Kennel Club at one time.

One of the main hopes of the 1884 Australian side was the bald-headed Cooper, who had puzzled all the best batsmen in three English touring teams. Before the Australians left he took 15 for 194 against Fifteen of South Australia. On the voyage

*William Henry Cooper, the Melbourne-based player who took up cricket at 27 when advised by his doctor to exercise more. He was a main hope of the Australian side during the 1884 tour of England but was only able to bowl in six matches after he severely tore ligaments in his bowling hand during the voyage*

to England Cooper collided with Alick Bannerman in a game of shinty and was thrown against the engine-room skylight. He suffered a severe strain of the third finger—his spinning finger—of his bowling hand. The ship's surgeon failed to cure it, and in London Queen Victoria's surgeon, Sir James Paget, said it would have been easier to mend if he had broken a bone. A long rest was the only cure for the torn ligaments. Cooper bowled in only six matches in England, leaving unanswered the question of whether his sharp spin would have made him virtually unplayable in England. He retired from cricket, but 18 years later won an Australian lawn bowls championship.

In one of Cooper's few appearances he seemed to have W. G. Grace in trouble at Lord's. W. G.

*Some of the players from the East Melbourne Club, the most powerful club in Victoria after the Melbourne Cricket Club. It was originally known as the Abbotsford Club and was based at several grounds*

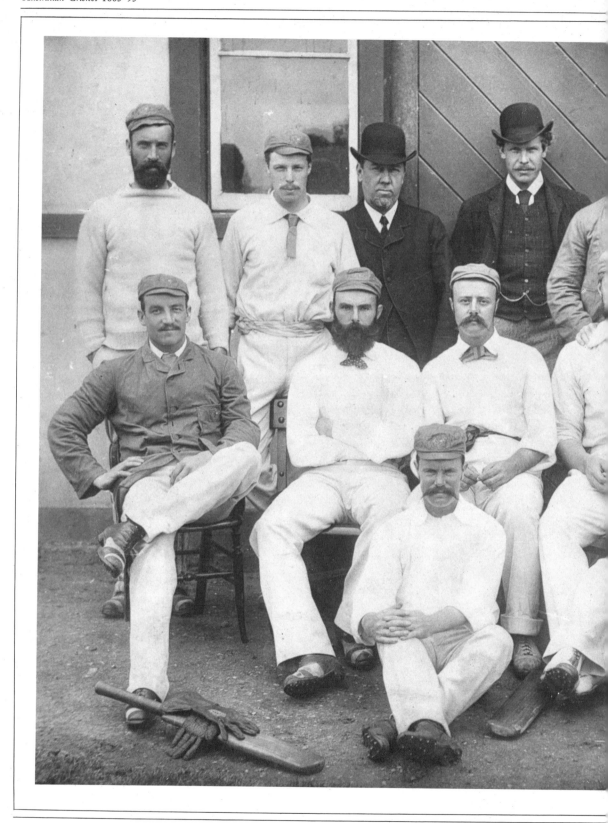

went down the pitch, missed, and Blackham had the bails off in a twinkling. W. G. waited for the appeal but none was made. At the change of ends, Cooper asked Blackham why he had not appealed. "I was in such a hurry to get him out I snatched the ball in *front* of the wicket," replied Blackham, who never appealed unless he believed it justified. Blackham's sportsmanship contrasted with that of W. G. Grace, who in a social match at Sheffield Park insisted on having the bats used by Alick Bannerman and Percy McDonnell measured. McDonnell's bat was found to be a little too wide and had to be shaved, but it was a petty objection for a friendly outing in such a majestic setting.

Despite the absence of Massie, Horan, Garrett and Moses, the 1884 team undertook the most ambitious programme to that time. George Alexander, who kept the team's accounts in co-operation with Cooper and Blackham, arranged three Tests. There was no adequate substitute for Blackham as Murdoch had allowed his "keeping" to fall away, and Cooper's injury left the team with only 11 fit men. Alexander filled in five times to rest weary players, while Cooper rested as a guest of Lord Harris at Brighton.

The first Test was played on 10–12 July 1884 at Manchester, the first time an international had been staged outside London. When the England team was announced three days before the game, it included Lord Harris. His Lordship announced that he could not play in a team that included the "chucker", fast bowler John Crossland. When the selectors stuck with their team, he was replaced by T. C. O'Brien, later Sir Timothy Carew O'Brien, third baronet. Rain washed out the first day and when England batted on the second day, Crossland was no longer in the side. Lord Harris returned to the side for the second Test, in which

*The 1884 Australian team which went to England still ranks among the finest we have ever fielded. They were a superb team physically, well disciplined and brilliantly led*

Crossland did not play.

"Monkey" Hornby and W. G. Grace faced Spofforth and Boyle. Hornby was stumped off the third ball he received, W. G. soon followed, and despite a stubborn 43 from Shrewsbury England were out for 95. "After the retirement of Shrewsbury, wickets fell with ridiculous rapidity," said the *Manchester Guardian*. Australia lost only four wickets passing England's score, and after Bonnor was given out hit wicket—he remained at the crease for 30 seconds before walking—Australia reached 183. Hornby was stumped again and, at 6 for 114, England were in real danger. A dogged 20 by O'Brien saved the game and England were on 9 for 180 when time ran out.

The second Test, just over a week later, was Australia's first at Lord's. Australia lost 4 for 46, all to Peate, but a last wicket stand of 69 by Scott and Boyle took them to 229. With England 5 for 135 next morning, the match was in the balance until A. G. Steel hit out for 148, the first Test century on the ground and still one of the best. England led by 150, but Australia appeared safe. Then Ulyett dismissed Bannerman, Murdoch and Giffen in failing light, and topped his effort by holding a remarkable catch to get rid of Bonnor. Bonnor hit the ball so hard that spectators behind the bowler stood aside, expecting the shot to clear the boundary. Ulyett luckily grasped the ball with his fingers—the players agreed it would have broken his wrist had it struck him a fraction higher.

Ulyett clinched victory for England next morning, bowling into a patch created by Spofforth's follow-through. Blackham, batting without gloves, retired when he was struck by a spiteful kicker from Ulyett, who finished with 7 for 36.

The Australians, beaten by an innings and five runs, suffered further humiliation when British newspapers learned they had been paid the entire proceeds from the Lord's Test—£1334. For the rest of the tour, they were referred to as the "gate money" cricketers. One cartoonist portrayed a British Lion, bat in hand, saying to a kangaroo with a face like Spofforth's and a pouch full of money: "Well, you don't mind a good licking so long as you get the gate-money do you?"

The Australians depended on the Lord's Test to cover the costs of the tour. For all other matches, they received only a share of the gate money, an arrangement appreciated by the county clubs, who benefited from the Australians' popularity. But the sniping continued. The Melbourne *Sportsman* expressed the hope that this would be the last "gate money team" to tour England.

Antagonism towards the Australians increased when Murdoch, mindful of the Sheffield Park protest, objected to the bat used by A. G. Steel in the Lord's Test. The bat was found to be perfectly legal when measured. The *Standard* then published scores of Australia's matches without the customary "Mr" before players' names. Only *The Times* did not follow suit. The Gentlemen of Philadelphia, who were also touring England at the time all received "Esquire" after their names in the *London Globe*. When London newspapers invited Murdoch to comment on the Americans' willingness to play the United Services at Portsmouth without receiving gate money, he said, "The Gentlemen of Philadelphia apparently know how much it is worth to see them play".

On the last day of the match against the Players at The Oval in June, Australia needed 11 runs to win, with nine wickets in hand, when lunch was taken. Infuriated spectators rushed on to the field as the players walked off, blaming the Australians for what they regarded as an attempt to secure an afternoon "gate". *Punch* had a different view, publishing a couplet headed "To the Surrey Crowd":

*Shame, sirs! When victory fails to crown*
*our banners,*
*Bad cricket is not mended by bad manners.*

The press campaign against the Australians had not the slightest affect on their crowd appeal or their play. They continued to be a big drawcard among those who paid sixpence to watch them, and gate takings in the third Test at The Oval in August were £1445. London newspapers noted sourly that this sum was shared equally with the Surrey Club, which staged the match.

On a very hot first day Murdoch, McDonnell and Scott all made centuries, a feat unprecedented in big cricket at the time. McDonnell hit very hard for 103 and as punishment of the England bowlers continued, wicket-keeper Lyttelton took off his pads to bowl high lobs. Scott was out at 102. Murdoch carried on to 211, the first double century in Test cricket, on the second day, when Lyttelton again bowled to rest his exhausted bowlers. When Shrewsbury, amid laughter, began to bowl, the entire England eleven had had a turn with the ball. In an Australian total of 551, keeper Lyttelton was the best bowler with 4 for 19 off 12 overs of lobs.

England tried only to save the match, Scotton batting for five hours 45 minutes for 90. Walter Read, with 117 in two hours, was alone in attacking the bowling. England reached 346 and were 2 for 85 in the second innings when time ran out.

Most newspapers agreed England were lucky to take the series and that Australia had the best of the two drawn Tests. They were unanimous in declaring Spofforth and Palmer better bowlers and Blackham a superior wicket-keeper to any in England. Only the English batting had saved the series. The tour generally was acclaimed an outstanding success. The Australians, who played 32 games with only 11 fit players, were widely praised. The *World* reflected on the tour:

*The Australians' visit has made all other matches seem tame and insipid, for it has introduced a bloodthirsty spirit . . .*

*The Australians make their own terms, insist on them, not always very gracefully, and play too obviously for the money's sake. They arrogate to themselves the rank of gentlemen.*

*It should be made clear to them that if they visit England to make money, they must rank, with others in the same condition, as paid professionals.*

*English professionals are sore at this point, and it is for the Australians to decide between their pride and their pocket. That they should decide for the latter would be best, perhaps, for all.*

*They would continue to gather their golden harvest and we would then be in a position to put a stop to certain little practices they are so fond of. At any rate a decision should be made before their next visit.*

Australian cricketers remained steadfastly free of a status label when they joined the national team, favouring neither the amateur nor the professional tag. None of these distinctions appealed to them and they preferred to be regarded simply as "cricketers".

Despite their failure to regain the Ashes, the 1884 Australians provided rare entertainment. At Birmingham against an England XI the pitch was so poor that the match finished in six hours, Australia winning by four wickets. Spofforth took 14 for 37, including 7 for 3 in the second innings when England were out for 26. Giffen, the carpenter's son, took a hat-trick and scored 113 before the game against Lancashire was washed out. Needing 188, the Gentlemen had an opening stand of 60 by W. G. Grace and C. T. Studd. Spofforth then took seven wickets to restrict the score to 141, Australia posting a fine win by 47 runs. Umpire F. H. Farrands upset Spofforth in this match when he disallowed a slips catch, which caused Spofforth to bowl at his fastest with Blackham standing back and six men in the slips.

The Australians won 18 of their 32 matches, lost 7, and drew 7. For the first time the programme involved only eleven-a-side matches. The tour ended with a highly successful contest between Smokers and Non-Smokers in which erstwhile rivals became team-mates. Bonnor made 124 out of 156, while he was at the crease, for the Non-Smokers. He hit 14 boundaries and even hit Spofforth for six. All proceeds of the match went to the Cricketers' Fund Friendly Society, a charity for destitute players. The Smokers made 111 and 152, the Non-Smokers 250.

This visit showed how evenly matched the two countries were. Spofforth again headed the wicket-takers with 216 victims at 12.23, followed by Palmer with 132 dismissals at 16.14. Between them they enabled Australia to overcome the loss of Cooper. Murdoch, McDonnell and Giffen all topped 1000 runs and Scott had his stumps disturbed only 10 times in 51 innings to score 973 runs. The lack of one more quality batsman, such as Moses, or the fast rising Billy Bruce, hurt the Australian cause.

The Australians were joined on the voyage home in September by the eighth England team, which was captained by Arthur Shrewsbury and managed by Alfred Shaw. An all-professional outfit recruited by James Lillywhite, the team consisted of Billy Bates, dashing Yorkshire all-rounder, whose singing enlivened tour social functions; effervescent Lancashire all purpose player Johnny Briggs, on the first of his six trips to Australia; tireless George Ulyett, one of the few cricketers with a century in America to his credit; left-handed Nottinghamshire batsman William Scotton, a noted outfield; H. H. Stephenson's nephew, John Maurice Read, a right-hand Surrey batsman and fast-medium change bowler; Nottinghamshire off-break bowler Wilfred Flowers, later a first-class umpire; Yorkshire wicket-keeper Joseph Hunter; deadly accurate medium-pace bowler William Attewell, for 16 years a vital part of Nottinghamshire's attack; the knockabout Yorkshire left-arm spinner Bobby Peel; the tour organisers, Lillywhite, Shaw and Shrewsbury; and right-hand batsman William Barnes, who was more than once warned by the Notts committee not to attend matches the worse for liquor. After one reprimand Barnes retorted: "How many of

*The English team that accompanied the 1884 Australian side on the voyage home to Australia was captained by Shrewsbury (back row, second from left) and managed by Alfred Shaw (seated, second from left). Johnny Briggs (front row) enlivened the tour with his singing*

you gentlemen could make a hundred, drunk or sober?" Billy made 21 centuries and later was to become an innkeeper.

The Englishmen toured South Australia, Victoria, New South Wales and southern Queensland, playing at towns like Windsor, Parramatta, Wollongong, the two Maryboroughs, Gympie and Benalla, places which later seldom saw an

England eleven. Disputes over management and match fees resulted in Australia's fielding scratch Test sides and this probably cost Australia the series, as well as lowering public respect for the leading players.

Only McDonnell, Blackham and Giffen arrived in time for serious practice before the Test in Adelaide, the first ever played on that ground, on 12–16 December 1884. The Australians demanded half the gate takings and threatened not to play when they were offered 30 per cent. They then offered to play for 40 per cent, but to pay their own expenses and hand the extra 10 per cent to charity. This was also rejected and finally the South Australian Cricket Association took over financial responsibility for the match and paid each team £450, much to the disgust of the Englishmen who believed their higher expenses entitled them to more than the Australians.

To add to the trouble, several Australian players, Spofforth among them, disagreed with their team-mates' demands. Murdoch, as impish as ever, refused to allow Lillywhite to umpire despite his long experience. Lacking time to get seasoned umpires from Sydney, the South Australian Association used locals I. Fisher and J. Travers. Some of their decisions upset the players. Spofforth dropped out, owing to a family bereavement, and Midwinter was ill. Only players from the 1884 touring team were considered, an absurd policy that arose because there was no national control body.

McDonnell scored his second successive Test century, 124, and at 4 for 220 Australia were in a strong position. Billy Bates then finished off the innings for the addition of only 23 more runs by taking 5 for 31. England replied with 369, Barnes surviving thunder storms in the morning and dust storms in the afternoon (which forced players to lie down on the pitch to avoid suffocation) to score 134, his only Test century. Scotton batted 535 minutes for 82.

McDonnell rushed to 83 with another fluent display and seemed certain to score his second hundred in the match when Giffen, troubled by lumbago, ran him out. Giffen struggled to 47 but with Bannerman absent, hurt, Australia were all out for 197. England lost two batsmen scoring the 66 required to win.

The second Test at Melbourne in January 1885 threatened the very foundations of Australian cricket when the entire 1884 team refused to play unless they got 50 per cent of the gate. The Victorian Cricketers' Association, which was staging the contest, refused, and disqualified all the Victorians involved. Jack Blackham joined his tour team-mates and withdrew, ending his unique record of having played in all of the first 17 Tests. With a completely new side, the association's

hopes rested on show business promoter Harry Musgrove, who had scored 109 against England at Ballarat, and Jack Worrall, who had shared a 151-run stand with Musgrove. Five of those who boycotted this match never played Test cricket again, reflecting how strongly players felt that they deserved a share of the gate money; they were ready to give up their careers if they did not get what they believed was a just reward. The *Bulletin* reported that when news of the Australian players' demands for half the gate money reached London, the Marylebone Cricket Club decided that if any of the offenders took part in the scheduled 1886 tour of England they would not be admitted to Lord's or The Oval. The threat was never carried out.

Shaw's team inflicted a heavy defeat on the new Australian team, which included Sam Morris, the first black man to play Test cricket for Australia, a right-hand opening batsman of West Indian parents born in Hobart; Dr Rowley Pope, the nomadic Tasmanian medico; John Trumble, elder brother of the noted off spinner; Sam Jones and Paddy Horan from the 1882 team to England; and "Affie" Jarvis, Blackham's perennial deputy. Horan, as captain of Australia, allowed James Lillywhite to umpire.

Australia began promisingly, scoring 279 in reply to England's 401. But when a draw looked probable they folded to the bowling of Billy Barnes (6 for 31) and Bobby Peel (2 for 45) in a second innings of 126 and England won by 10 wickets.

By the middle of February the tourists had forgotten their money woes and appeared at Wagga Wagga, Candelo, Nowra, Yass and Moss Vale, where Bates hit the ball over the fence 11 times scoring 111 and Scotton plodded for 500 minutes for 123 out of England's 432. Peel took 18 wickets for seven runs in Twenty-Two of Moss

*Sam Morris, born in Hobart of West Indian parents, became the first coloured man to play for Australia during the second Test at Melbourne of the 1884–85 England tour*

*The famous quartet who found themselves at the centre of the row over higher pay for Test players during the 1884–85 season: (L to R) Murdoch, Spofforth, Boyle and Alick Bannerman*

Vale's innings of 14.

Murdoch, Bannerman and Bonnor refused to play for New South Wales against England and Spofforth dropped out with a sprained ankle. The second-string batsmen were no match for Peel (7 for 27) and New South Wales were out for 60 and 108 chasing England's 205. The Queensland section of the tour proved a picnic for the English bowlers. Peel took 11 for 29 and 12 for 42 at Maryborough. At Gympie Peel returned 9 for 41, Attewell 12 for 27, and Bates 13 for 40. The big winner, however, was Scotton, who was given some mining shares by an admirer for being the top-scorer.

Socialite Hugh Massie took over the Australian captaincy for the third Test, played at

*Jack Blackham refused to appeal for a stumping against W. G. Grace because he took the ball in front of the stumps*

*John Trumble, elder of the Trumble brothers, also made his debut in a completely new Australian team for the 1884–85 Melbourne Test*

Sydney in mid-February, after Murdoch returned to his law practice at Cootamundra—a sad day for Australian cricket, which lost the man who had led his country on three triumphant English tours. Jarvis again kept wicket, Blackham still being under suspension. The match turned on a last wicket stand of 80 by Garrett (51) and Evans (33) in Australia's first innings of 181. England replied with 133, Spofforth taking the first three wickets in four balls. Left to score 214 to win in the final innings, England failed in a thrilling finish by only seven runs, one of the smallest margins on record. Spofforth took 10 for 144 in the match.

Blackham became Australia's fourth captain in four Tests when all the rebels except Murdoch returned to Sydney for the fourth Test of the series

on 14 March. Australia levelled the series after Bonnor hit 128, the first 100 in even time, in Australia's first innings. Bonnor's only chance, on a wicket badly cut up at one end, was the stroke through slips with which he brought up his century. England had a choice of pitches for the last innings but chose to bat on the strip Australia had used and were all out for 77.

Australia's team for the deciding fifth Test at Melbourne on 21–25 March was again disrupted by argument and suspensions; England retained the same side throughout the series. Australian newcomers were Victorians Frank Walters and Pat McShane, who had been an umpire in the previous Test.

Australia batted first on a pitch that had not dried after heavy watering and lost 6 for 45 by lunch. John Trumble and Spofforth gave substance to the innings with a last wicket stand of 64, which ended when Spofforth "tried to play a puzzling ball several different ways". Bates was dropped so many times when England batted that the crowd became derisive. He stayed long enough to help Shrewsbury score 105 not out, the first century in Test cricket by an English captain. England made 386.

Horan, who had resumed the Australian captaincy, decided not to roll the pitch in case it crumbled. At tea on the third day, with Australia in desperate trouble at 3 for 26, umpire John Hodges refused to return because of complaints about his decisions from English players. Tom Garrett took his place. James Phillips was one of the umpires for the first two days, but was replaced by J. C. Allen on the third and fourth days. England won by an innings and 98 runs on the fourth morning when Australia were out for 125 to end one of the most controversial series on record.

One London newspaper hailed England's success as proof that "Professionals were at all times better to rely on than gentlemen". Australian critics disagreed that status made the difference and one wrote that Ulyett had placed England at a disadvantage after his 68 in Adelaide because of his "bibulous activities". Ulyett's last six innings in the Tests yielded 0, 2, 4, 10, 2 and 1. "Ulyett was far from being the first player, English or Australian, fond of his beer," said the *Bulletin*. Alick Bannerman, when asked the difference between W. G. Grace and Ulyett, retorted, "Nothing—up to the shoulders".

The Australian tour by Shaw and Lillywhite's professionals indicated that while the frequent excursions had vastly improved England's fielding, they had done little to lift Australian umpiring standards. The Englishmen were sharp and reliable in the field; the Australian umpires—eight were used in the five Tests—were habitually prone to error. One Australian newspaper blamed their lack

of confidence on the "dreadful going-over they received years ago from W. G. Grace".

On 3 March 1885 a contingent of 770 Australians marched out of Victoria Barracks under the command of Colonel John Richardson. After parading through Sydney streets they boarded two troopships at Circular Quay. They were headed for the Sudan, to do battle with the forces of the messianic rebel, the Mahdi, who had killed the English hero General Gordon at Khartoum earlier that year. This force, the first Australia ever sent to war, was involved only in minor skirmishes before the British government abandoned the campaign. But the absence of Colonel Richardson, guardian of the Garrison Ground, gave the New South Wales Cricket Association the chance to take over the ground virtually without opposition.

*Cricket* magazine's Charles Alcock reported "on the best authority" that both Murdoch and Spofforth were engaged to two of Derbyshire's fair daughters. He was half right, as Spofforth did later marry Derbyshire socialite Phyllis Cadman, but Murdoch's ardour for his fair English rose had weakened on the long voyage home. Before he made his stand for the appearance money he thought players deserved, Murdoch married instead Jemima Watson, an amateur actress he met travelling on the ship back to Australia. Bonnor was his best man and George Alexander gave the bride away at the Adelaide wedding soon after the *Mirzapore* docked. Murdoch's father-in-law, Bendigo mining magnate John Boyd Watson, was said to have been shocked by the marriage.

While the players lost their fight for more match pay, a wife and a well-paid career in law recompensed Murdoch. His retirement proved a far bigger problem than acquiring umpires of calibre. Umpiring was soon to be given a significant boost by the likes of the decisive "Dimboola Jim" Phillips. The quest for a captain to match Dave Gregory and Billy Murdoch was to haunt Australian cricket for far longer.

# A period of decadence

## Australia's captaincy dilemma 1886–90

For a variety of reasons, all five players tried as Australia's captain immediately after Murdoch departed were failures. They were all admired for their courage and skill and had impressive backgrounds, but somehow lacked the flair that had characterised Gregory's and Murdoch's handling of the job and made it the most prestigious in Australian sport.

Thomas Patrick Horan, the only Irishman to captain Australia, played 15 times for his adopted country against England, wearing black pads and sporting a beard. He was the son of a building contractor (who reckoned Melbourne was a better place to bring up children than the Blarney Castle region), and a one-time playmate of Jack Blackham at Bell Street school, Fitzroy. A solid right-hand batsman and round-arm medium-pace bowler with enormous shoulders and forearms, Horan was the best cricketer in Victoria for several seasons — in 1879–80, he played an innings of 250 not out for

*The 1886 Australian team which toured England: (L to R) (back) G. Giffen, F. R. Spofforth, Ben Wardill (manager); (centre) Farrand (umpire), Bates (scorer), W. Bruce, J. McIlwraith, T. W. Garrett, E. Evans, J. W. Trumble, Salter (scorer), Thoms (umpire); (front) G. J. Bonnor, J. M. Blackham, H. J. H. Scott (captain), S. P. Jones, G. E. Palmer, A. H. Jarvis*

East Melbourne (742) against Tasmania—and had successful tours of England in 1878 and 1882 behind him. But the luck of the Irish ran out in the 1884–85 Tests, when the two Australian teams he captained were thrashed.

He declined to go to England in 1884 because of family responsibilities—his marriage to Kate Pennefather, a police sergeant's daughter, five years earlier produced nine children. He was deposed as Australia's captain, but kept playing for Victoria until 1891, arranging his vacations from the Victorian Audit Office to coincide with inter-colonial games. Under the pen-name "Felix", he wrote famous weekly articles on cricket for the *Australasian.* Two of his four sons played for Victoria: James Francis, who made 820 runs at 24.11 from 1903, and Thomas Ignatius Bernard, who averaged 21.00 whilst scoring 210 runs in five matches from 1906.

Horan scored eight first-class centuries, with a top score 141 not out against Gloucestershire in 1882. Five of his centuries were for Victoria, for whom he scored 2,101 runs.

Horan was again unavailable for the 1886 tour to England organised by the Melbourne Cricket Club, which had invited Lord Harris's side in 1878–79; all four Australian teams that had toured previously were sponsored by the players. The Melbourne Club opted for an all-amateur party, which meant excluding cricketers who coached professionally, such as Alick Bannerman. Murdoch was in retirement, McDonnell could not get leave from the Victorian Education Department and Boyle wanted a rest to concentrate on business.

Another major loss to the 1886 team was Hugh Massie, who had decided to concentrate on his career in banking. He was a genial, companion-able man with an intellect suited to leadership, who had been born on a property near Port Fairy, Victoria, where Rolf Boldrewood wrote *Robbery Under Arms.* The year after the tour Massie married Agnes Dibbs, eldest of the seven daughters of Sir Thomas Dibbs, general manager of the Commercial Banking Company of Sydney. The Massies

lived in Marilbah, a house on the hill at North Sydney, in the grounds of Agnes Massie's parents' stone mansion Graythwaite. Hugh continued to play club cricket in Sydney as he worked his way up in the bank to the position of general manager, his father-in-law's old job.

The Melbourne Cricket Club bypassed the more experienced Jack Blackham to appoint Henry ("Tup") Scott captain. The 1886 side included nine players from previous touring teams and four new-

*ABOVE: Tom Horan, the only Irishman to captain Australia. He wore brown pads long before Kerry Packer introduced coloured clothing to the game, but had no luck with his captaincy*
*RIGHT: Melbourne left-hander Billy Bruce, whose first tour of England in 1886 produced one century*

comers, William Bruce, Edwin Evans, John Trumble and John McIlwraith. Scott was the first Victorian to take an Australian team to England, and earned his nickname there, because of a liking for twopenny bus rides around London. The other tourists were Spofforth, Jones, Palmer, Bonnor, Jarvis, Blackham, Garrett and Giffen—who shovelled coal in the ship's stokehold on the voyage to get fit. The team was managed by Major Ben Wardill, secretary of the Melbourne club, who announced that while he was in England he would sign up players for an Australian tour in 1887–88 to be sponsored by the Melbourne Cricket Club.

Friction developed among the players before a match was played and Scott and Wardill spent much of their time adjudicating quarrels. "The cares of leadership affected Scott's run-getting, for disputes among his players were many, and he did not have the strength of character to cope with this situation," wrote cricket historian Arthur Haygarth.

The Australians began badly, losing their first match to Lord Sheffield's XI and the third to Surrey. They then beat the Gentlemen in the sixth match despite a grievous setback when Spofforth dislocated the middle finger of his left hand fielding a hard drive from Lord Harris. He was never the same bowler again. Palmer's skill had declined, Evans at 37 years of age was only a shadow of the great bowler he had once been, Bonnor was lost after an injury in July and Giffen took a month to find his batting form. Manager Wardill and Dr Rowland Pope, who travelled with the side, filled in occasionally.

All three Tests were lost. The first at Manchester on 5–7 July 1886 was close (Australia 205 and 123; England 223 and 6 for 107), but the second at Lord's a fortnight later and the third at The Oval in August provided one-sided wins for England. At Lord's England scored 353 when Shrewsbury batted for seven hours on three types of pitches—fiery, slow and sticky—to win acclaim as the greatest of all batsmen on difficult wickets, showing unsurpassed expertise in dead-bat play.

He was probably the pioneer of pad play, a man of inexhaustible patience, whose 164 in this match has been called one of the best of all Test knocks. At The Oval W. G. Grace recaptured the record for the highest Test innings from Shrewsbury by scoring 170 in a total of 434. Australia made 68 and 149. Sam Jones scored 87 at Manchester, but no Australian approached that in the other Tests.

Little Johnny Briggs, the popular Lancashire left-arm spinner, took 5 for 29 and 6 for 45 in the second Test and in the third Test made 53 and took six good wickets. The South Australians Giffen and Jarvis were impressive—Giffen headed the batting and bowling averages. In the first fortnight of June he took 6 for 71 against the Gentlemen, 7 for 41 and 9 for 60 against Derbyshire, 8 for 56 against Cambridge, and 8 for 23 and 8 for 42 against Lancashire. W. G. Grace batted 19 times against the Australians for 812 runs.

The editor of *Wisden*, Sydney Pardon, criticised the Australian captain for his lack of authority and experience in handling men.

*Scott led the team with the best of intentions and greatest sincerity, but he was no Murdoch. It is exceedingly doubtful whether even an ideal captain would have pulled the team through its engagements unless, indeed, he had been backed by that confidence and energy which we so seldom see in any teams.*

Although Scott's side won only nine of their 38 matches, the tour was a financial triumph. More than 33,000 people watched the three days of the Lord's Test, for example, and once again the Australians' contests completely outdrew county cricket. The team lost 7 matches and drew 22; the sole game against the odds was lost. Test fielding lapses cost the team dearly—W. G. Grace was dropped four times in his first 100 runs while scoring 170 and Shrewsbury was missed in the slips and should have been stumped in his knock of 164.

Scott remained in London to become a

member of the Royal College of Surgeons when the rest of the Australians went home. He played only a few more matches for Victoria before retiring to become a pioneer country doctor who appeared regularly in bush cricket. He practised at Bathurst and at Scone, where he became mayor and chief magistrate. He never charged patients who he knew could not pay, and Scone's Scott Memorial Hospital was named after him. He included four centuries among his 2863 first-class runs.

McDonnell and Bonnor, disgusted by the treatment meted out to them by the Victorian Cricketers' Association, transferred to New South Wales for the 1886–87 season. Murdoch had by then gone to live in Melbourne, but refused to play against his old New South Wales team-mates. Spofforth, who had also made his home in Melbourne, had no such qualms and joined Midwinter in the Victorian XI. In the opening match of the 1886–87 season of intercolonial games in December McDonnell gave a thrilling exhibition of hitting combined with stylish stroke play to score 239 out of New South Wales' 363 in Melbourne. Charles Turner supported this dazzling batting by taking 6 for 42, vindicating those who believed he had been allowed to languish too long in bush cricket—five seasons earlier he had dismissed all ten batsmen playing against Shaw's team. Turner's analysis included a hat-trick in which Palmer, Horan and Trumble were all cleanbowled by similar deliveries. At the other end a twenty-year-old left-arm bowler from the Belvidere Club in Sydney, John Ferris, took 4 for 42 in his first intercolonial game. In January 1887 Turner and Ferris began a wonderful Test partnership when they opened the bowling together in the first Test of the season on the Sydney Association Ground.

Shaw's third team to Australia included 13 players. Shaw and James Lillywhite themselves seldom played, leaving the captaincy to Shrewsbury. When William Barnes was disabled the team had only 10 fit regulars and called on Reginald Wood, a left-hand batsman and left-arm medium-pace bowler who had migrated from his birthplace in Cheshire to Melbourne, where he played for the state team.

The tour was badly promoted—some of England's games clashed with intercolonial matches and attendances were disappointing—despite the organisers' experience. This was Lillywhite's fifth visit to Australia, the fourth for Bates and Shaw, the third for Barnes, Barlow, Scotton and Shrewsbury, and the second for Briggs, Flowers and Read. All were agreeably surprised they no longer had to endure rough sea trips to and from Adelaide, but could travel on the Melbourne–Adelaide railway, although this included a six-hour wait at Bordertown and two hours at Dimboola.

The new men were William Gunn, perhaps the first of the classic stylists; George Lohmann, a lower order right-hand batsman, brilliant slips fielder and often devastating fast-medium bowler; and Mordecai Sherwin, a jocular, powerfully framed wicket-keeper who forsook a winter as Notts County's soccer goalie to tour Australia.

Lohmann proved a marvel of agility and energy. A handsome man with fair skin and bright blue eyes, he had suffered from tuberculosis since his teens and had come to Australia hoping the warm climate might effect a cure. Sadly the disease had advanced too far, but he was able to make two more tours before his death in South Africa at the age of 36.

After missing a place in Scott's 1886 team to England, Percy "Greatheart" McDonnell found himself captain in both Tests of a team hampered by dissension. The players quarrelled among themselves, with their state associations, and unhappily with their English opponents. Ray Robinson wrote that McDonnell was the only Australian captain who could read Greek philosophers and playwrights in their own language. He appreciated Aristotle's logic and chuckled at *Lysistrata*. His barrister father, Morgan McDonnell, was attorney-general in two Victorian governments.

*The 1888 tour of England brought together one of Australia's greatest bowling partnerships for the first time. John James Ferris (left), the Sydney left-arm spinner, and Charles Thomas Biass Turner (right), the right-arm off-spinner from Bathurst*

McDonnell was the first Test captain to win the toss and invite the opposition to bat, which at the rain-affected Association Ground suited the new boys Turner and Ferris well. England were all out for 45, one of the lowest Test totals in England–Australia competition. Turner took 6 for 15, Ferris 4 for 27, but the low score was as much due to some astonishing catching as it was to the bowling. Spofforth, in what turned out to be the last of his 18 Tests, excelled himself catching Barnes at point. Then McShane, who had replaced the sick Palmer, held a very difficult high chance at square leg to dispose of Shrewsbury. At 3 for

13, Turner bowled Barlow and Gunn. Spofforth took another remarkable catch to dismiss Read, diving wide to intercept a powerful cut with his left hand. Lohmann (17), the only batsman to reach double figures, was then caught off a skier by Garrett in a display of breathtaking agility.

Australia lost 2 wickets for 18, but passed England's score without further loss. Harry Moses, in his first Test, batted soundly while Sam Jones mixed good strokes with bad. Starting the second day at 4 for 76, Australia lost six wickets for 43.

England was only 29 runs ahead with three wickets in hand at the start of the third day but all these wickets added valuable runs. Although the pitch was helpful to bowlers, Australia seemed certain to win with only 111 needed. Moses and Midwinter took the score to 80 before the seventh wicket fell, but shrewd handling of the bowling by Shrewsbury got England home by 13 runs.

Between the first and second Tests McDonnell had an argument with England's Billy Barnes. Barnes threw a punch, missed, and hit a brick wall, injuring his hand so badly he could not play in the second Test. Honours for fisticuffs were about even: Spofforth also missed when he threw a haymaker at Barlow, who was an experienced boxer and tough enough not to miss a single match on three Australian tours.

Spofforth was dropped from the Australian XI after the first Test, at the age of 34. He had taken 853 first-class wickets at 14.95, and was only six short of 100 wickets at 18.41 in Tests. It was a curious fate for the first great modern bowler, but typical of a madcap summer. He retired from Australian cricket and returned to England where he married his Derbyshire girl and became a director of the Star Tea Company, a business owned by her father. Between 1889 and 1891 he turned out occasionally for Derbyshire, and in 1889 took 15 for 81 against Yorkshire. He took 11 for 100 for Wembley Park against the 1896 Australians. He became managing director of his company and continued to top the bowling averages for Hampstead Club, London. He died in 1926 at Long Ditton, Surrey, at 73, leaving £164,000—a fortune then.

Turner, in superb form, compensated for Spofforth's loss. He took 8 for 32 and 6 for 27 for New South Wales against England, but England won by 122 runs. England also won the second and last Test of that series late in February 1887. Turner and Ferris took nine wickets each in the match and removed England for 151 and 154 but Australia, with five newcomers, managed only 84 and 150. Burton replaced Blackham behind the stumps. The other new men, R. C. Allen, J. T. Cottam, J. J. Lyons, and Walter Giffen, could not handle Lohmann, who hit the stumps six times in his first innings bag of 8 for 35. Moses was Australia's best batsman in both Tests, the second of which provided the unusual spectacle of William Gunn both playing and umpiring.

*Fred Spofforth's reputation was so great that it was said that he had only to glare at batsmen to get them out but, curiously, he was dropped from the Australian XI after the first Test in 1886*

The tour ended at the East Melbourne Ground in March when Non-Smokers scored 803, then the highest total in first-class cricket. Shrewsbury made 236, Gunn 150, and of the Australians Billy Bruce reached 131, Jack Worrall 78 and Harry Musgrove 62. The Smokers responded with 356 and 5 for 135, Joey Palmer scoring 113 and 24. In the final moments of the game Scotton—on the last of his three trips—played a ball a metre in front of the crease, picked it up and put it in his pocket. Amid uproarious laughter he was given out for handling the ball, the last wicket to fall in a drawn match.

England played 29 matches in all, winning six of those rated first-class, with two losses and two draws. The big bonus for Australia was that the team played in 19 country towns, winning 6 and drawing 13 matches against the odds.

Turner took 55 English wickets during the season at an average of 7.7 runs, an achievement that established him as Spofforth's replacement.

*Harry Trott, the Melbourne postman whose first tour of England in 1888 revealed his talents as a leg-spinner. He was the only bowler who could give Ferris and Turner a spell without weakening the attack*

He had huge hands, and bowled right-arm medium-paced off breaks with a front-on action. At Bathurst Grammar School he had been unable to win selection in the First XI. He took a job servicing Cobb & Co. coaches, getting up at 4.00 a.m. to harness the horses, so that he could devote the rest of the day to bowling at a single stump.

A Victoria youth of 20, George Henry Stevens Trott, who was usually called Harry, was also making an impact, turning leg breaks sharply and batting confidently against the colony's best bowlers. John Trumble's young brother Hugh, who had just entered intercolonial cricket, was a gawky, long-fingered all-rounder who leapt high to deliver his off breaks. Like Spofforth and Turner, Trumble usually wore half a necktie when bowling.

In February 1887 in his last big match, Midwinter bowled Victoria to victory over South Australia by taking 5 for 22 while Sam Morris captured 5 for 21 at the other end. Midwinter then retired, at 36, to enjoy his pub and his family. A year later his daughter Elsie died, and in 1889 his wife, followed three months later by their son Albert. Midwinter broke down soon after and was committed to Kew Asylum. In one of his rare moments of lucidity he spoke with Harry Boyle. He died in 1890, aged 39.

Australian cricket was in such disarray that none of the players, unhappy with their prospects for better financial rewards, wanted a sixth English tour in 1887. The Melbourne Cricket Club, unhappy over the team's behaviour on the 1886 excursion, felt the same way, and the state associations lacked both the support and the funds to promote a tour.

Some strange cricket teams formed in those years. Kalgoorlie Miners XI was an enthusiastic outfit whose umpire always carried a rifle, an accessory today's umpires would no doubt envy. Some of the players had left the ships that had brought them from England at Melbourne or Geelong, and then pushed wheelbarrows carrying all their belongings to the goldfields. While the Western Australian Cricket Association president, J. C. H. James, was calling for subscriptions to send a team east, Kalgoorlie cricketers played before audiences consisting of prospectors, camel drivers, con men and prostitutes. Their captain was usually the only man in town who owned cricket whites.

New South Wales had humiliated Victoria in January 1887, by dismissing them in Sydney for 61 and 68 to grab a six-wicket win, which Victorians blamed on the pitch. Worse followed in December in Melbourne when Victoria were out for 35. Victoria made a brave recovery to score 266 in the second innings, but still lost by two wickets. In January 1888 Harry Moses played the innings of his life, 297 not out in a New South Wales total of 576. He was in such dominant form only a lack of partners prevented his threatening Murdoch's record of 321. New South Wales won this time by an innings and 35 runs. Victorians always expected similar heroics from Frank Walters, but he could not repeat his intercolonial form — 106 and 112 in successive summers — playing for his country.

Two England teams toured simultaneously in 1887–88, and both suffered heavy financial loss. One side, sponsored by the Melbourne Cricket Club, was captained initially by the Honourable Martin Bladen, a friend of Lord Harris, who played for Eton and Cambridge and had captained Yorkshire since 1883. After five matches his father died and he returned to England to become the seventh Lord Hawke. The Middlesex right-hand batsman George Frederick Vernon, who had represented England at rugby five times, took over the captaincy. Vernon had injured his head when he fell down a companionway on the voyage out and had only just recovered. His team was the tenth England team to tour Australia.

Vernon's men suffered a tragic loss during net practice in Melbourne when the popular Yorkshire round-arm spinner Billy Bates, received a fierce blow on the face that permanently affected his sight. At Adelaide there was further drama when somebody flooded the pitch and cut out chunks of turf during the night, when England was leading South Australia by 239 runs. After the pitch was repaired George Giffen scored 203 to force an amazing draw.

All the colonies had by then achieved a degree of sophistication in the preparation of pitches, using the best soil available. Soil from Merri Creek in Victoria was exported to Sydney after its success at the Melbourne Cricket Ground, but it was found to behave badly after rain. In the era of uncovered pitches, "Merri Creek stickies" presented immense problems for batsmen. Later Bulli soil, which came from a hillside at Bellambi in southern New South Wales, was found to have all the necessary adhesive and water-resistant properties.

Vernon's team played 26 matches, 8 on level terms and 18 against the odds. They won 6 eleven-a-side games, lost 1 and drew 1 and they won 3 and drew 13 of the matches against the odds. Andrew Stoddart scored 285 in six hours batting against Eighteen of Melbourne on a matting wicket, and topped the tour batting averages with 1188 runs at 38.32. Bobby Peel made 1011 runs at 33.70 and headed the bowling averages with 213 wickets at 7.53.

The other England side in Australia that summer was captained by C. A. Smith (later Sir Aubrey Smith, the film actor) and was organised by the old partnership of Lillywhite, Shaw and Shrewsbury for the New South Wales Cricket Association. This group, the eleventh England side to Australia, played 22 matches, 7 against elevens and 15 against the odds. They won 5 and lost 2 on level terms and won 7 and lost 8 against the odds. C. A. Smith's side twice defeated a Combined Australia XI, which the following year became the nucleus of the sixth Australian team to England.

In between writing impassioned love letters to a girlfriend back in England, Shrewsbury was the top batsman in Smith's side, scoring 1113 runs at 37.10, including 232 against Victoria. He always wore a cap on the field, a bowler hat off it, and a nightcap in bed. Inside that cunning bald head he knew he had the Melbourne Cricket Club's English tour checkmated because he had exclusive rights to Sydney Cricket Ground.

Australians produced some excellent performances against both touring teams. McDonnell blasted his way to 112 for New South Wales against Vernon's XI, who were defeated by nine wickets. Ken Burn scored 99 out of a Tasmanian total of 405 against Vernon's men. Sam Jones made 134 for the sixth Australian team, but the season belonged to Charles Turner, labelled "The Terror"

*The sixth Australian team to tour England kept secret the fact that Sam Jones had smallpox. Jones is the only player missing from this team photograph: (L to R) (back) J. J. Ferris, A. H. Jarvis, J. Worrall, C. W. Beal (manager), J. M. Blackham, H. F. Boyle, J. D. Edwards; (front) G. J. Bonnor, C. T. B. Turner, P. S. McDonnell (captain), H. Trott, A. C. Bannerman*

in newspapers. Turner set a record for an Australian season that has never been equalled by taking 106 wickets at 13.59 in first-class matches. His victims were 91 English batsmen, 15 Victorians.

Towards the end of the summer the England teams combined to play the only recognised international of their tour. February rains had drenched the Sydney pitch when Stoddart appeared in his first Test, opening with Shrewsbury. The ball turned so sharply that some deliveries from Ferris were fielded by the slips. Blackham could not reach several balls that offered stumping chances. Shrewsbury's craftsmanlike 44 enabled England to reach 113. Batting in poor light, Australia were

8 for 36 at stumps.

Two days' play was lost to rain and when the match resumed on the Tuesday all public interest had gone. Australia were out for 42, their lowest in a Test until they were out for 36 at Birmingham in 1902. England batted shrewdly on a spiteful pitch to score 137, Maurice Read hitting an exciting 39. Australia's task of scoring 209 on such a pitch was hopeless and England won by 126 runs. Turner had match figures of 12 for 87, Peel 10 for 58, Lohmann 9 for 52. At the end of the tour Stoddart remained to play for the British rugby tourists, taking over as captain after R. L. Seddon drowned.

According to Alfred Shaw, the Melbourne Cricket Club lost £4000 on Vernon's tour, which left the club with an overdraft of more than £500. "Shrewsbury and I dropped about £2700, and we had every penny of it to pay between us because Lillywhite could not meet his share of the loss," said Shaw. "On our previous trips we had made in all about £1500, so we lost all and had a good round sum to pay on top of it." Shrewsbury was adamant this fourth tour in which he had been involved would not have occurred had he or Shaw known that Lillywhite was broke. To reduce their losses, Shaw and Shrewsbury asked the NSWCA for a 2.5 per cent rebate on ground rental (which was 20 per cent of the gate takings). From this time on Shaw strongly urged the Marylebone Cricket Club to organise all tours to Australia; 16 years later his suggestion was accepted.

When 28-year-old Percy McDonnell returned to his birthplace, London, in 1888, his captaincy record in Tests was three losses. Harry Boyle, the sole survivor of the first Australian team, was way past his best. Apart from Alick Bannerman, Bonnor, Jones and McDonnell, none of the batsmen had experience of English conditions. George Giffen declined to go because his brother Walter was not picked and Moses again declined. Turner and Ferris were the only bowlers who could get good players out, although Trott's leg breaks occasionally surprised even brilliant shot-makers. Harry Altham rated Turner and Ferris cricket's most successful bowling partnership.

*To those who regard 1000 overs in a season as more than flesh and blood can stand, the record of Turner and Ferris in 1888 will come as a revelation. They knew that unless they got the enemy out, they would continue to field. Bowl they had to, and bowl they did. Together they took 534 wickets or just 405 more than the rest of the team put together, and this against the flower of English batting with hardly a rest for close on 20 weeks.*

Altham, in his *History of Cricket*, ranked Turner with Spofforth among the greatest Australian bowlers. The 1888 statistics of Turner and Ferris were:

|  | Balls | Maidens | Runs | Wkts. | Av. |
|---|---|---|---|---|---|
| C. T. B. Turner | 10,359 | 1,222 | 3,492 | 314 | 11.38 |
| J. J. Ferris | 8,890 | 998 | 3,103 | 220 | 14.23 |

Altham commented that Turner had extraordinary nip from the pitch; his length was splendid and his break-back so deadly that on sticky wickets he was virtually unplayable. Turner ignored body turn, bowling at medium pace, never wasting time between deliveries or overs. Ferris, then only 21, bowled his left-arm swingers at a lively pace, moving the ball either way and sustaining his accuracy for hours on end. Later, when the ball was worn, he turned his spinners disconcertingly. In the opening match of the tour on 7 May 1888 only two of the Australian batsmen passed 20, but they won easily, Turner and Ferris taking all 20 wickets for 161 runs. Two weeks later at Old Trafford against Lancashire, Ferris took 8 for 41 in the first innings, and against an England XI at Stoke, Turner in July had 9 for 15 in the first innings.

The tour was promoted and managed by C. W. Beal, who carefully kept secret the nature of Sam Jones' illness when Jones became sick shortly after the trip began. Had it become known that he had smallpox the entire tour could have been ruined. Jones, educated at Sydney Grammar School and Sydney University, was on the dangerously ill list for weeks, but his splendid physique helped him recover and take the field by the end of the tour. He was a watchful right-hand batsman with a strong defence and a magnificent field. He bounced back to health to take part in his fourth English tour in 1890.

Beal and McDonnell erred in not developing more support for Turner and Ferris and in conscripting Cambridge Blue Sammy Woods only for the Tests. On muddy pitches the limited attack was adequate, but on hard pitches Australia's weaknesses were exposed. The team did well to reach the third Test one-all.

Sam Woods was a colourful, incredibly versatile sportsman born at Glenfield, near Sydney, who had attended Sydney Grammar School. He travelled to school on the Manly ferry and sparred with deckhand Peter Jackson, later world heavyweight champion. When he went to England to

*The remarkable all-round sportsman, Sammy Woods, who also played Rugby and cricket for England, was taken into the sixth Australian Test team when Jones became ill*

finish his education, he played soccer and billiards, went beagling and fox-hunting, and became a legendary rugby forward. He played for England and Australia at cricket, and captained Cambridge, Somerset and the Gentlemen. His wit was as admired as his style. When he clean-bowled W. G. Grace he watched the famous gamesman depart and quipped: "I shouldn't go, doctor— there's still one stump standing".

Woods bowled only four overs of his right-arm pace in the first Test at Lord's on 16–19 July,

where Australia had the best of a wet pitch and won by 61 runs. Australia made only 116 in the first innings but England managed only 53 in reply. Twenty-seven wickets fell on the second day. Set to score 124 to win, England were out for 62 in the final innings. Turner took 5 for 27 and 5 for 36, Ferris 3 for 19 and 5 for 26. Blackham made four stumpings in a match that yielded only 291 runs, the lowest aggregate in England–Australia Tests.

Spectacular catches by Lohmann set Australia on the road to defeat a month later in the second Test at The Oval. He caught McDonnell low down in one hand before a run had been scored and an hour later, after Bannerman had defended dourly, jumped to his right and fell to the turf to take a dazzling catch from a powerful cut. Australia never recovered, scoring 80 and 100, England winning by an innings and 137 runs after scoring 317. Abel was run out for 70 and Barnes and Lohmann both scored 62.

The Australians suffered five defeats in a row before the deciding Test on 30–31 August at Old Trafford, where Woods at last had a long bowl. England batted first in dismal conditions, with W. G. Grace losing two partners for six runs. Grace then hit out freely for 38 and on a damp pitch England reached 172. Lyons, in his first Test in England, tried gamely to prevent the follow-on, but Australia fell 11 short under the 80-run rule of the time. All out for 81, they were soon 7 for 6 in their second innings as hot sun affected the strip. Last out, for 32, Lyons had the satisfaction of topscoring in each innings. Australia scored 70, failing by 21 runs to make England bat again. This was the shortest Test match in which there has been a result, the game ending at 1.55 p.m. on the second day.

McDonnell moved to Queensland soon after his 1888 team returned home, having lost 14 of their 40 eleven-a-side matches, won 19 and drawn 7. They had been no match for the best English counties on hard pitches, but had been fortunate that their virtual two-man attack had encountered a wet summer. McDonnell (1393 at 22.83), Bonnor (1204 at 19.73) and Harry Trott (1212 at 19.23) had been the only batsmen to score 1000 runs while Turner had produced an innings of 103 to go with his impressive 314 wickets. McDonnell had played the innings of the tour, a marvellous 82 against the North of England at Old Trafford, but was not seen again in Test cricket. Australia lost five of the six Tests in which he was their captain. His three matches for Queensland in 1894–95 brought his first-class run tally to 6470 at 23.52. A four-time English tourist, he had extensive experience on uncovered English wickets and was one of Australia's most accomplished batsmen on wet pitches. He died of a heart attack when he was only 35.

The Victorian Cricketers' Association decided in 1889–90 that it could not afford two matches against New South Wales and asked for just one. The New South Wales Cricket Association would not agree and intercolonial arrangements were in disarray. Fortunately the Melbourne Cricket Club helped to stage the games. Early in January 1889, New South Wales won the first at Melbourne by six wickets to stretch their winning sequence over Victoria to six, but three weeks later at Sydney they suffered a reversal. Set to score only 76 to win, New South Wales could not handle clever bowling by big Hugh Trumble (6 for 43) and Jack Worrall (4 for 19) and failed by 12 runs. Harry Trott's batting for 44 and 36 had provided Trumble and Worrall with just enough runs.

Trumble repeated this effort in December 1889 at Melbourne when he bowled Victoria to a fine win. Dr John Barrett, a left-hand batsman of rare patience scored 69, Blackham 63 and the left-handed Billy Bruce 61, to leave New South Wales to score 251 for a win. Trumble bowled superbly to take 6 for 40 and have New South Wales out for 109. Following on, New South Wales revived with a typically stubborn 115 in six hours from Alick Bannerman, but no one else supported him sufficiently. Harry Trott was 71

not out when Victoria reached the 121 required, for the loss of only two wickets.

On Anniversary Day 1890, a few days after this Victorian success, Sam Jones scored a century out of a New South Wales total of 349. New South Wales then dismissed Victoria for 216 and 237 to win by four wickets. Some critics had suggested that Blackham was finished, but he kept superlatively in this match and scored 66 and 46. Harry Moses also had a fine match, with some splendid strokes in his 48 and 52 not out.

The biggest improvements in standards towards the end of the 1880s came in South Australia. In 1888–89 the former miner Ernie Jones scored 70 out of 80 for North Adelaide in 35 minutes, the first 50 in 20 minutes. Adelaide officials were convinced that if Jones's action could be improved, and hints of a throw eliminated, he would prove the ideal bowler to open an innings before Giffen came on with his off spinners. Jones, a man of boundless energy, with heavily muscled shoulders changed considerably from the day when, playing in an Adelaide club match, 48 byes came off his bowling.

South Australia's match winner was George Giffen, a letter sorter with stevedore's muscles, who conditioned his legs for hard labour by deliberately walking to and from Adelaide club games. After four-hour practice workouts he ran 100 metre sprints. Giffen completed the unique double, a century and ten wickets, on nine occasions. He took 16 wickets in a match five times, and scored four double centuries and 14 centuries. His most unusual match, however, was against Victoria at Adelaide in 1889 when he defied the umpire.

Giffen received one of his severest hammerings, 1 for 108, when Victoria scored 320. South Australia lost two wickets cheaply before Giffen came in. Before he scored, a confident appeal for leg before wicket was dismissed. At nine Giffen fell over as another ball rapped his pads. The Victorians appealed for leg before wicket and, after a bail fell off, for hit wicket. The umpire at the

*This portrait of South Australia's first great player, George Giffen, hangs in the Adelaide Oval Committee rooms. Some of his achievements as an all-rounder have never been equalled*

bowler's end disallowed the leg before appeal but gave him out hit wicket. Giffen refused to leave, claiming the ball was dead and that the second appeal could not be made. Every Victorian and most of the South Australians disagreed with him, but he refused to go. Finally the Victorians played on under protest. Giffen was at last bowled out by Hugh Trumble for 85. Fortunately Victoria won by 18 runs, despite a swashbuckling 134 from Lyons, who played Trumble's alarming break-backs with ease. Trumble returned 15 for 189 in the match. Giffen later admitted he had been wrong and should have walked.

The persistently impressive form of Giffen, the thrilling hitting of Lyons, reminiscent of Bonnor at his best, and reports that J. C. "Dinny" Reedman was a rare crowd pleaser, finally persuaded the New South Wales Cricket Association to inaugurate regular matches against South Australia. The teams met in February 1890, with the agreement that if the South Australians did well in Sydney the New South Wales team would play in Adelaide the following season. Matches between these two colonies involved a nine-day trip, with two consecutive nights on trains each way.

South Australia dismissed New South Wales for 240 on a soft Sydney pitch but they managed only 155 and 148 and lost by nine wickets. Only Lyons, 19 and 63, and Giffen, 52 and 32, were comfortable against Percy Charlton's right-arm fast-medium pacers. Charlton, a stalwart of I Zingari who had begun his career with the Belvidere Club, took 7 for 44 in the second innings. At Adelaide in the second match Ferris had match figures of 14 for 192. Moses and Iredale both scored 67 in New South Wales's first innings of 406. South Australia scored 241 and 191 and New South Wales won by six wickets.

Australia was then in the midst of what Horan called "a period of decadence". Test crowds had fallen dramatically since 1882–83, when Shaw's team had attracted 169,729 people to four Tests, an average of 42,432 per match. Crowds had dropped to 94,134 for the five Tests in 1884–85; 17,528 for two Tests in 1886–87; and only 1971 at the one Test in 1887–88. Compiling these figures, Richard Cashman established that the 1888 Test, staged to celebrate Sydney's and Australia's centenary, was the worst attended in Australian cricket history.

Poor promotion, the major cause of falling attendances at international matches, stemmed from the continual bickering between state associations. The Victorian Cricketers' Association was so incensed with the Melbourne Cricket Club for staging the 1889–90 Victoria–New South Wales matches that it stopped members playing against the club, which then quit the association. This

*The remarkable Billy Murdoch bounced back as captain of the Australian team that toured England in 1890: (L to R) (back) H. Trumble, J. M. Blackham, K. E. Burn, Dr J. E. Barrett, H. F. Boyle (manager); (seated) F. H. Walters, G. H. S. Trott, W. L. Murdoch, J. J. Lyons, C. T. B. Turner; (front) S. E. Gregory, J. J. Ferris, P. C. Charlton, S. P. Jones*

club, second only to the Marylebone Cricket Club among the world's cricket clubs, was later re-admitted when it relinquished control of inter-colonial games.

The slump in public support for Tests was accompanied by scornful press treatment of players and officials alike. When Murdoch returned after missing 15 Tests and two tours of England, he was not spared. One paper denigrated his "succession of bad strokes" for New South Wales against Victoria, another observed that he would not have dared return had his father-in-law been alive.

Only George Bonnor, who had returned to Australia after three years in London, pleased the critics. "There are only two real cricketers in Australia," he boasted in the Sydney Cricket Ground members' pavilion. "Who's the other one?" someone asked, amid laughter. Most people guessed Bonnor meant Giffen. At 35 Bonnor was over 114 kilos, but in April 1890 he proved that the extra weight had not diminished his powers by scoring 297 not out in a total of 9 for 423 for Bathurst against the Oriental Cricket Club of Sydney. Bonnor was not picked for the 1890 team to England by the sole selector, Harry Boyle.

Giffen was selected but declined the trip, saying he was disgusted by the bickering during the 1886 tour. Giffen was about to be married, but critics said the real reason he pulled out was that once again his brother Walter was not in-

cluded in the team. The biggest shock in the selections, however, was the choice of Ken Burn ahead of the talented Sid Deane as the second wicket-keeper. Burn admitted to his team-mates when he joined their ship in Adelaide that he had never kept wicket in his life. Boyle and his adviser,

*ABOVE: Syd Gregory (left) was also chosen for the 1890 touring team to England. He was a sound fielder and batsman. Frank Walters (right) was selected for his strong batting and medium-paced bowling*

*LEFT: Ken Burn was a surprise selection for the 1890 Australian team to tour England. He had never kept wicket in his life. He did, however, prove himself to be a fine batsman*

Jack Blackham, had mistaken him for another Tasmanian, John Burn, who had kept wicket against Victoria in 1869. Deane, from a prominent Sydney musical family, had the consolation of securing a role in the Nellie Stewart Opera Company.

Apart from Burn, who was destined to score 42 centuries at various levels of cricket, other new men in the team were John Edward Barrett, an all-rounder who batted and bowled left-handed and saw the trip as a chance to further his medical studies; Percy Chater Charlton, a right-hand batsman and medium-pace bowler who was also studying medicine; Sydney Edward Gregory, son of the Sydney Association Ground curator, already renowned for his dashing fielding and sound right-hand batting; Hugh Trumble, the gangling, long-necked brother of the 1886 tourist; and Francis Henry Walters, a right-hand batsman and medium-pace bowler with a fine record in inter-colonial cricket. The rest were Murdoch, Trott, Lyons, Blackham, Turner, Ferris and Jones.

# Lord Sheffield's shield

### Australia's major domestic competition 1892–93

Wild, intemperate newspaper criticism became part of the Australian cricket scene as it entered the 1890s, and gaffes like the selection of Burn for the 1890 touring team simply provoked the critics. The players wanted to pick their own teams and captains and have the main say in administration; overseas tours remained largely money-grabbing jaunts; state associations all went their own way and were frequently in disagreement; and noisy, uninhibited spectators had assumed the right to vulgar and loud comment. Most of these ills were to be curbed eventually, but the barrackers who provided Australian cricket with such an unsophisticated image were to reappear regularly.

Murdoch's team arrived in England at the end of April 1890, with condemnation of Burn's selection heavy upon them, to learn the intriguing news of the first visit to South Africa by an English team. The Australians had tried to organise a

*W. G. Grace (seated cross-legged on the steps) at Government House, Sydney, with some of his Australian rivals: (L to R) K. E. Burn, H. F. Boyle, J. J. Lyons, W. L. Murdoch, J. J. Ferris (with gun and dog) and C. T. B. Turner (with umbrella). The women are unknown*

10-match tour there on their way home from England but failed. They discovered that an English team captained by C. Aubrey Smith had won both big games against South Africa, with Bobby Abel scoring the initial first-class century.

Australia defeated Lord Sheffield's Eleven at Sheffield Park, Sussex, by an innings in their opening match on 8 May, thanks to Turner and Ferris, who had the opposition out for 27 and 130. Ferris took 12 for 88 and followed with 7 for 42 in the second match against Warwickshire, where he and Turner bowled unchanged. Turner took 12 for 34. Australia's dependence on Turner and Ferris continued throughout a trip on which her batsmen failed to score well on wet pitches.

The newcomers had little chance to settle in on unprotected batting strips, and the 36-year-old Murdoch lacked his former agility. Barrett had no charm or style but he proved plucky and patient, filling Alick Bannerman's barn door role with honour. Syd Gregory had some exciting matches and Burn improved as they progressed. Lyons's improvement, with both the bat and the ball, was even more striking. Most disappointing were the team's recurring fielding lapses, and with the advent of Scottish Rugby international and now England wicket-keeper Gregor McGregor, Australia no longer enjoyed a big advantage behind the stumps. Like Blackham, McGregor stood up to the stumps to take fast bowlers.

Johnny Briggs's left arm slows brought him 11 for 92 and defeat for Australia in the third tour match against W. H. Laverton's XI. Conditions were drier at Oxford, where Australia won by an innings. Australia's hopes rose as they defeated Surrey by eight wickets, but immediately afterwards they lost to Yorkshire by eight wickets on a treacherous pitch. Peel took 12 for 69 for Yorkshire. Warmer weather at Manchester helped them beat Lancashire by an innings and 155 runs when 18 Lancashire wickets fell for 109 runs on the second day. Turner took 11 wickets for 63 runs.

The match against Marylebone Cricket Club in the first few days of July seemed headed for a draw until the club scored 111 in 70 minutes to pull off a narrow win. Nottinghamshire, the South of England and the Players (twice) all defeated Australia before the first Test, by which time it seemed unlikely that the visiting batsmen could score enough runs to give Turner and Ferris a chance to win the big matches. Nonetheless they kept taking heaps of wickets. Against Staffordshire Turner had 9 for 49 and Ferris 10 for 33, and against Leicestershire Ferris had 6 for 19 in the second innings.

The public ignored forecasts of a one-sided England win in the Lord's Test on 21–23 July 1890, packing the ground for an absorbing tussle as Australia lifted their game. Murdoch provided a surprise by opening with the hitter John Lyons, and Australia got off to a fine start with Lyons scoring 55 out of 66 in 45 minutes. Turner, who also opened with Lyons, made 24, the only other Australians to reach 20, and the side were out for 132. Turner caught and bowled W. G. Grace with his second ball and England were 4 for 20 in just over half an hour. Ulyett and Maurice Read then took the score to 92 in the best stand of the series, but fine bowling held England to a lead of 41.

Barrett, playing in his first Test, became the first batsman to bat through a Test innings, scoring 67 not out in Australia's second knock. Lyons made 33, but Australia's lead of 136 proved too small. England had the best batting conditions of the game to win by seven wickets. W. G. Grace, missed at 44, scored 75 not out. Not a single bye was conceded in a Test of memorable wicket-keeping that boasted Jack Blackham and Gregor McGregor at their best.

The Australians encountered far sterner opposition from county cricket than on any of the six earlier tours. The county championship, which had been conducted haphazardly since 1873, had built up enormously and for the first time county matches challenged the Australians' fixtures for public support. Lord Harris and his colleagues at

Lord's had successfully nurtured an overwhelming ambition in amateur cricketers to play for their counties. Simultaneously they had helped the best professionals improve their image and their standards. More batsmen started to combat dreary off-side theory by cutting, pulling or hitting across the ball.

The English lineup for the second Test at The Oval in August lacked Stoddart, who preferred to play for Middlesex, and Peel and Ulyett, who had been claimed for a Yorkshire county match. Briggs and Attewell were unfit. Patched up, England were still good enough to win a thriller by two wickets once rain drenched the pitch. Trott batted cleverly for 39 in Australia's first innings of 92. England were rescued by William Gunn, whose 32 enabled them to lead by eight runs on the first innings. By stumps Australia had lost 2 for 5, 22 wickets having fallen on the first day.

Trott and Charlton added 36 priceless runs while their team-mates floundered on the second day. Left to score 95 to win, England opened with W. G. Grace, who hit the first ball straight into Trott's hands and out again. W. G. struggled to 16. At 4 for 32, England put on 51 for the fifth wicket, Maurice Read hitting boldly for 35. Three wickets then fell for three runs. The memory of Australia plucking a win from a similar position at The Oval in 1882 was in the minds of the English batsmen, who showed clear signs of panic. With two wickets left and two runs to make, both England batsmen were stranded in mid-pitch and an Australian win was still possible. But Barrett threw wildly when he had time to aim carefully at either end and the two overthrows gave England the match and the Ashes. Trott's failure to catch W. G. for a "golden pair" and Barrett's error proved a sorry end to Murdoch's career for Australia in Tests, as the third Test scheduled for 25 August at Old Trafford was washed out without a ball being bowled.

At the end of the tour in September the Australians said goodbye to their captain, who, according to those at home, was too old for big

*Dr Percy Charlton, of whom it was said "he touches nothing he does not adorn", played only one Shield match after his tour of England in 1890, preferring to devote himself to his medical practice and the affairs of I Zingari*

cricket. Murdoch joined Sussex and confounded critics by piling up a series of huge scores. An unrivalled clubman with a tremendous appetite for food and drink, he was "a man who could enjoy a Klondike or a Mansion House dinner," wrote C. B. Fry. He had a vocabulary all his own, which charmed the Sussex players he captained, as it had outback Australians. He would not say it looked like rain. Instead it was "The sparrows will be washed out, boys." Instead of telling his men that the umpires were waiting, it was always "The white coats are out, boys."

Ferris also left Australian cricket, joining W. G. Grace in the Gloucestershire side, and at the end of their first season of county cricket both Murdoch and Ferris toured South Africa with the second England team to visit that country. At Newlands in the only Test of the trip Ferris took 6 for 54 and 7 for 37. Murdoch kept wicket for England in the second innings but scored only 12 with the bat in a total of 369. England won by an innings and 89 runs. Murdoch continued as Sussex captain from 1893 to 1899 and played for W. G. Grace's London County XI for six seasons until 1904. Ferris had three good seasons with Gloucestershire before his bowling magic deserted him and he began to rely on his batting. He went off to the Boer War and died at Durban in 1900 of enteric fever, while serving with the Imperial Light Horse.

Murdoch's seventh Australian team—the fourth he had led to England—played 38 matches, all on level terms and won 13, lost 16 and drew nine. Of the new men, only Barrett succeeded, but Gregory, Burn, Charlton and Trumble all had distinguished careers later, which suggests they needed the experience of the tour. Ferris and Turner both took 215 tour wickets, Ferris at 13.20, Turner at 12.67. Murdoch headed the batting averages on 23.53, but Harry Trott had the highest score, 186. Walters's contribution was negligible.

The Melbourne Cricket Ground Museum includes a display of the cheques paid the seventh Australian team on 22 September 1890. It shows that at least 15 players were paid for their services to the side. Dr Rowley Pope received £4, Walters £5, Charlton £28 and Trumble £77 in what were regarded for some reason as payments to the team's amateurs. Burn got £389, the highest remuneration of all. These were probably interim settlements and not full payment for a tour that incurred heavy losses.

The 1890 team took a fearful hammering from Australian newspapers for losing more matches than they won, but English spectators and pressmen loved them. There were, for example, 30,729 "bob" patrons at the Lord's

Test—attendances of members were never counted in those days—and Australia's share of the gate was £750. For the fourth time Murdoch made most runs and had the best average, a feat that has never been matched. One sour Sydney sniper said: "Our team have quarrelled among themselves as usual, and we learn by cable that the wiry Boyle has taken a severe fall out of the burly Lyons". The *Bulletin* could not resist a jibe at the Australians' high living:

*The Australian cricketer in England, batting the day after a banquet, sees at least two balls approaching. One is dead on the wicket. He smites at the other and then sees four bails flying about, two wicket-keepers looking the other way, two prostrate and two erect stumps. Then he retires to two pavilions, makes 22 excuses, and another cable about bad luck and wet wickets is dispatched. The Australians always bat on a wet pitch after a banquet.*

There had been no England teams in Australia in 1889 and 1890 and this gave Australia a chance to develop a group of talented young players. Surprisingly, support for intercolonial cricket had not fallen away as it had for international matches, which averaged an attendance of 13,344 per match and 3431 per day from 1882 to 1890. Ten seasons of New South Wales versus Victoria at the Sydney Cricket Ground—1890–91 to 1900–01—attracted an average of 26,340 per match and 5853 per day. Large crowds continued, too, at club cricket, which provided some breathtaking displays. In 1890–91 for instance, Syd Gregory, 235, and Monty Noble's brother, Ted, 227, put on 442 for the eighth wicket for Sydney *v.* Warwick, while in 1891–92 Melbourne scored 828 playing Essendon.

Bob McLeod, the first of three brothers to play for Victoria, took 7 for 107 and scored 87 when Victoria surprised in the 1891–92 season by defeating the favoured New South Wales XI by six wickets at Melbourne. A month later Walters repeated the form that had given him a fine 106 the previous summer by scoring 112 at Sydney, where Victoria won again, this time by an innings and 115 runs. Turner, without Ferris to support him, found Syd Callaway an inadequate replacement and could not stop a steady flow of Victorian runs.

Victoria's claims to colonial cricket superiority were soon shattered by some outstanding performances by the South Australian side. In January 1891 South Australia scored 472 in defeating Victoria, 220 and 190, by an innings and 62 runs at Melbourne, George Giffen scoring 237 and taking 12 wickets on a perfect pitch. This astounding double earned Giffen a civic reception on his return to Adelaide, at which he was presented with a purse full of sovereigns.

John James Lyons, who had taken over from Bonnor as the most powerful hitter in Australian cricket, made 104 in the next match at Adelaide in November 1891, but was again upstaged by Giffen, who took 16 wickets for 166 (9 for 96 and 7 for 70) and scored 271. This has been widely acclaimed as the greatest all-round performance in the history of cricket. One of George's drives in this match crushed his brother Walter's fingers against the bat handle; Walter retired hurt for 65.

South Australia's most significant display came at Sydney in the third match against New South Wales in January 1892. New South Wales struggled through the first day to make 215 against fine bowling by Giffen. When a slight drizzle began the next day, Lyons and Giffen lashed out. Under heavy punishment, the New South Wales players induced the umpires to stop play, but the crowd objected. After a mid-field discussion play continued, as did the battering of the bowling. Sydney had never seen hitting of the ferocity Lyons produced that day: the ball left his bat like cannon shot. Syd Gregory was loudly clapped when he stopped one. One fieldsman had a chance to catch Lyons but realised the ball was travelling at frightening velocity and pulled his hands away. The ball flashed past him and smashed one of the pickets in front of the pavilion like a piece of

*Syd Gregory set a record by playing in 58 Tests. His father was the Sydney Association Ground curator. Gregory was selected for the 1890 tour of England and had some exciting matches*

matchwood. Lyons was out for 145 and at stumps Giffen was 95 not out, South Australia being 2 for 249. When play resumed after rain had held up play for two days, Giffen went to 120, South Australia to 330. New South Wales were then routed for 62, giving South Australia the match by an innings and 53 runs.

Queensland played intercolonial matches against New South Wales in 1884, 1889 and 1890, had a game against northern New South Wales in 1891, and received a visit from a Victorian side in 1889. A Queensland team went south for matches at Sydney and Melbourne in 1890. But the highlights of this period for Queensland cricket lovers were the games in 1884 and 1889 against Australian elevens and the visits by England touring teams to Queensland. The fondness for cricket waned somewhat when it got down to club level, but it was the clubs that undertook frequent trips into remote areas and spread the game, covering enormous distances under such difficult conditions it makes modern players appear dilettantes. Fear of the intense heat was forgotten and even in the most remote settlement people supported their cricketers, firing the ambition of young boys to get into the Queensland team and one day, perhaps, "go home" to thrash the Englishmen.

Cricket heroes in Queensland were fewer in number than in the south and as a result were more warmly feted and were made part of a select group. When the eccentric Arthur Coningham started to display his special brand of mayhem at Brisbane in the 1890s he was talked about in awe. Coningham was to become the first player chosen from Queensland to play for Australia. (He was not a Queenslander, however, having been born in South Melbourne in 1866.) He was a left-arm fast-medium bowler of strength and vicious bounce and a daring right-hand batsman. In January 1891 he had the unusual experience of scoring 26 runs for the Stanleys against the Alberts in Brisbane, those runs comprising his side's entire total in an innings that produced no extras. Coningham's shots brought him 6, 4, 5, 5, 3, 2, 1. In 1890, when Coningham made 43 for Queensland out of a total of 116 against the Melbourne Cricket Club at Melbourne, it was hailed in Brisbane as if he had made a century. His knock gave some respectability to a Queensland first innings loss.

Meanwhile Tasmanian cricket was alive and well. A fine batting display against Vernon's touring England team in 1888, when Fourteen of Tasmania scored 405, encouraged Tasmania to resume matches against Victoria on level terms. On New Year's Day 1889 Victoria fielded their strongest side and went on to win by nine wickets. Tasmania had to bat the first time on a soft pitch and were out for 67 but scored 195 in the second innings—Claude Rock, the former Cambridge University star, contributing 102. Rock, Ken

Burn, Gatehouse, the Savignys and the big-hitting Charles Eady all batted well enough to suggest that given two or three first-class bowlers, Tasmania could beat the best teams from other states.

The Victorian cricket scene was enlivened at that time by the remarkable James "Dimboola Jim" Phillips, a skilful right-hand batsman and right-arm medium-pace bowler for the Melbourne Cricket Club. Phillips, born at Pleasant Creek near Adelaide in 1851, lived in the town that gave him his nickname until an age when most cricketers think of retiring. He first played for Victoria in 1885–86 and in 1893 made 165 for Players of Melbourne against Melbourne. For a number of years he travelled between England and Australia, following the cricket seasons, playing for the Marylebone Cricket club from 1888 to 1893 and for Middlesex from 1890 for nine seasons. He had 17 matches for Victoria, usually contributing wickets or runs, and coached for a time at Christchurch, New Zealand.

New Zealand cricket offered satisfying tours for Australians once the hardships of sea travel had been endured, and in 1890 J. C. Davis, the editor of the Sydney sports paper, the *Referee*, took an unofficial New South Wales side over for a seven match trip. New South Wales won six and drew the other. Sydney Callaway exploited the soft pitches to take 40 wickets at 9.2 apiece, and 31 wickets at 15.2 each went to the inimitable Walter McGlinchy, who made two later tours to New Zealand with Queensland teams and spent his old age as the dressing-room attendant to Australian Test teams. At one stage against Otago, Callaway's figures were four for none.

Davis, who had always been highly critical of captains who disputed umpiring decisions, found himself at the centre of just such a wrangle in the match against Wellington. The New South Wales umpire displeased Wellington players, who asked that he be replaced. Davis at first refused, but when the Wellington president informed him that if the deadlock interfered further with the game New South Wales would not be paid their share of the gate money the umpire was changed. Davis, who played for the Alberts in Sydney, headed the New Zealand tour batting averages with 272 runs and was dismissed eight times.

The Melbourne Cricket Club had succeeded with a daring move by allowing footballers to use their ground for the first time for the August 1890 grand final, which a staggering 32,595 people attended. The following November Carbine won the Melbourne Cup from a field of 39 before 89,000 spectators. In June 1891 the divine Sarah Bernhardt was in Melbourne for a fee of £20,000. Tickets were so scarce they were sold at auction and on opening night women fainted, had hysterics, and had their expensive gowns torn. Into this euphoric city came a fat, stumpy little man dressed like an overfed farmer, his hair long and straggly, his face roughly shaven, with a tuft of beard on his pudgy chin; the sort of man who would make an ideal landlord for a bush pub.

This was Henry Holroyd North, the third Earl of Sheffield, Viscount Pevensey, Baron Sheffield of Dunsmore, Meath, Baron Sheffield of Rosscommon, Ireland, and Baron Sheffield of Sheffield Park in East Sussex, where he had lavishly entertained most of the first seven Australian touring teams. Lord Sheffield, born in London on 18 January 1832 and educated at Eton, had worked in the British diplomatic service before winning a seat in Parliament as the member for East Sussex. Lord Sheffield was already a legend in England because of his generosity to his tenants, his Christmas and New Year spending for the poor, and his lavish staging of cricket matches at Sheffield Park, where he thought nothing of inviting 300 people to lunch. He had taken over from his father as president of the Sussex Cricket Club in 1879, although he had no great aptitude for the game and had achieved spectacles in his sole first-class game for the Gentlemen of Sussex against the Gentlemen of Kent in 1856.

The cricket historian Ric Finlay has argued that Lord Sheffield came to Australia at the urging

*The Earl of Sheffield, donor of Australia's most prestigious domestic cricket trophy, was a camera-shy, carelessly dressed character of great generosity*

of friends in the diplomatic corps anxious about their investments in the colonies and after strong persuasion from his friends Lord Harris and the Earl of Darnley. Both these gentlemen were concerned at the decline in Australia's cricket standards and the long delays by the colonies in achieving federation, events they felt would be corrected by a visit by an English cricket team.

When he was first invited to tour by the Melbourne Cricket Club, Lord Sheffield sought the advice of two hard-headed professionals, Alfred Shaw and Arthur Shrewsbury. Shaw was on his Lordship's personal staff and often accompanied him on trips abroad. It was Shaw who suggested that Lord Sheffield's entourage play a match against the crew of their ship, the *Lusitania*, under the midnight sun at Spitzbergen on 12 August 1894. Shrewsbury pointedly stressed the unbusinesslike behaviour of James Lillywhite and the losses of the 1887–88 visit to Australia, and drew up a theoretical income and expenditure account for the proposed tour.

For 21 weeks in the colonies, Shrewsbury estimated the total expenses for a party of 13 men at £6632, his detailed account even covering items like tips for stewards on board ship, weekly laundry bills, payments to bandmasters at the team's matches and advertising for the team's eight big matches. Shrewsbury estimated the average cost per player at £250, but cautioned his Lordship against the inclusion of amateurs.

*I was told when in Australia that the expenses of each amateur member of Lord Harris's team was more than double that of the professionals. Should W. G. Grace go out, I should imagine looking at the matter in a purely pecuniary point of view, that his presence would at the very least make a difference of £1500 or £2000 in the takings.*

On the basis that four matches in Melbourne would each bring in £500, four Sydney matches £600 each, two in Adelaide £300 each and 18 country matches £100 each, Shrewsbury estimated the takings at £6800.

Shrewsbury had built up a lucrative business selling cricket equipment to Australia and New Zealand, largely through the hard work of his Melbourne agent Frank Illingworth and he now generously loaned Lord Sheffield the services of Illingworth, who conducted all the preliminary negotiations in Australia for the tour. The New South Wales Cricket Association granted the tour its patronage immediately, but the Victorian Cricketers' Association did so only after securing a promise that Lord Sheffield himself would promote the tour. The VCA's hesitancy stemmed from concern that the losses of the 1887–88 English teams in Australia would be repeated if the English team comprised only money-hungry professionals.

When Lord Sheffield wrote to W. G. Grace inviting him to captain the touring team, Grace thanked him but refused on the ground that his fee would be too high. Grace would turn 43 in July 1891, and understandably wanted to consolidate his medical practice. But Lord Sheffield invited Grace to Sheffield Park and when they met in March 1891 Grace quickly agreed to tour. Lord Sheffield outlayed more than £5000 to get him, paying Grace a fee of £3000, plus all expenses for Grace, his wife and two children, Bessie, 13, and Charles, 9, plus the cost of employing a locum to look after Grace's practice while he was away.

Lord Sheffield's team was without Gunn and Shrewsbury, who both refused the terms offered. He agreed when Frank Illingworth visited him at Sheffield Park to finalise an itinerary to add matches in Tasmania, Queensland and New Zealand. Illingworth assured his Lordship that the presence of W. G. Grace would more than compensate for the absence of Gunn and Shrewsbury, who had each been offered £300, plus expenses, "exclusive of wine and cigars". William Attewell, George Lohmann, Johnny Briggs and Robert Peel all accepted these terms.

To this hard core of professionals, Lord Sheffield added Gregor McGregor, Octavius Goldney Radcliffe, Andrew Stoddart, Bobby Abel, George Bean, John Sharpe and Hylton Philipson, a former Oxford Blue who replaced William Chatterton at the last minute. (Chatterton elected to tour South Africa with a rival English tour.) In a letter to Illingworth that was tabled at a meeting of the NSWCA, Lord Sheffield emphasised that no amateur member of the team, the strongest ever to leave England, had a financial interest in the tour. He had budgeted for expenses of £11,000; any profits above that figure would be divided among the professional members of his side.

Lord Sheffield hired a band to play at London's Albert Dock as his team boarded the *Arcadia* in October 1891 for the voyage to

*Andrew Stoddart, a player in Lord Sheffield's team that toured Australia during the 1891–92 season. There were reports that he came to blows with W. G. Grace during the third Test in Adelaide*

Australia. He was accompanied by his aide-de-camp, Major Dorien, and his nephew, Aubrey Harcourt. A fellow passenger was H. M. Stanley, the famous African explorer, who was off on a four-month lecture tour of Australia. At Colombo in a match against a local twenty-two, W. G. found the heat so unbearable he tipped off a bail and walked off after scoring 14 despite the protestations of the umpire, who gave him not out.

When the team reached Albany in November, Lord Sheffield said it was his wish to avoid publicity and to quietly see as much as possible of Australia while he recovered his health. He was irked by an injury to Frank Illingworth, which prevented Illingworth from sharing management of the team with Shaw, but he readily agreed that Ben Wardill should take over Illingworth's duties.

Lord Sheffield said he hated making speeches and when he discovered he would have to make twenty on the tour he handed the job to W. G.

Ben Wardill returned from his first meeting with Lord Sheffield and immediately sent a letter to the NSWCA secretary John Portus, in Sydney, saying that his Lordship had offered a trophy to the value of £150 for a competition between New South Wales, Victoria and South Australia. Wardill asked Portus to suggest regulations for the competition and make any recommendations he thought appropriate for its conduct.

England began well on 20 November by defeating South Australia at Adelaide by an innings and 62 runs, with Attewell taking 11 wickets and Briggs, Read and Stoddart all scoring half centuries. The team arrived at Melbourne's Spencer Street Station on the Adelaide Express without Lord Sheffield, who preferred to travel by sea. There was what one paper called "a storm of cheering when the heavily bearded face of the old warrior Grace appeared on the platform". The Englishmen toured the city in coaches decorated in Lord Sheffield's colours and pulled by horses in matching harness. At the Melbourne Cricket Ground the band played "That Fine Old English Gentleman" as W. G. arrived with his players, his wife and his children.

W. G., already annoyed by the realisation that Lord Sheffield intended to remain in the background, was disappointed by the renovations to the MCG. "Where are the grape vines that climbed over the wall and the wooden pavilion, that provided the players with luscious grapes?" he asked. "And where is that famous well into which a bucket was lowered and players drank copious draughts of icy cold water?" The *Bulletin* was amazed at W. G.'s huge feet: "He could get £2 a week and tucker merely to walk about in the grasshopper districts and kill off the pest".

The amateurs and professionals in the England team stayed in different hotels throughout the tour. In Melbourne the amateurs went to the posh Oriental while the professionals resided at the staid

Treasury Hotel. They assembled for a reception at the Town Hall, where Grace expressed regret at the absence of Lord Sheffield and was humorously installed as "Cricket Mayor" of Melbourne, complete with chain of office.

Lord Sheffield had asked his players to provide bright, entertaining cricket, and they did their best to oblige. W. G. told newspapers too much time was wasted in Australian cricket and demonstrated what he meant by continuing to bat through the tea interval against Victoria. When the players started to leave the field, W. G. refused to go and everybody was in such awe of the man that the match continued. W. G. went on to 159 not out and England won by an innings and 117 runs. Lord Sheffield arrived midway through W. G.'s innings and then went off to his hotel to escape the heat.

Before he went, Melbourne officials persuaded Lord Sheffield to go out and inspect the MCG pitch between innings. The 6000 spectators cheered him all the way to the wicket. The *Australasian* said:

*His Lordship is genial, jovial, hearty and a thorough sportsman, cricket being his special hobby. He cares little for the vanity of wearing apparel, but dresses himself for comfort in a style all his own. He wore an Alpine hat with the colours of his eleven (yellow, red and dark violet) as a band, a dark-blue shooting coat, and roomy nankeen trousers. He chatted heartily with all and sundry who were presented to him, and when he toured the ground the crowd recognised a true sportsman who had always been the first to welcome 'our boys' on English soil.*

In Sydney the amateurs stayed at the Australia Hotel, the professionals at the Oxford, but they arrived together for a reception at the Town Hall. The governor Lord Jervis entertained the amateurs on the first night at Government House, although the entire team were guests at a dinner for 150 people after the second day's play against New

*John Creswell, as South Australian Cricket Association representative, upset Lord Sheffield when he threatened to withdraw Giffen and Lyons from the first two Tests unless Adelaide was granted the third*

South Wales, with the NSWCA president George Reid in the chair. On the first day the game started late because Harry Moses objected to Denis Cotter, whom the Englishmen had recruited in Melbourne, acting as an umpire. Set to score 153 to win, England were in danger at 6 for 88 in the last innings with Charles Turner bowling, but then Lohmann and Peel knocked off the required runs without further loss.

Lord Sheffield remained in Sydney while his team made a short country tour, defeating in turn Twenty of Cumberland, Twenty-Two of Camden, Twenty-Four of Bowral and Twenty-Two of Goulburn. The Bowral team included a player named Richard Whatman, whose sister

Emily married George Bradman two years later and produced a son whose fame was to rival even that of W. G. Grace.

The Australian team for the Tests was selected for the first time by a panel of selectors (one from each colony) — George Giffen, Jack Blackham and C. T. B. Turner; previously the colony staging the big games had picked the teams. The South Australian Cricket Association secretary John Creswell upset Lord Sheffield when he threatened to withdraw Giffen and Jack Lyons from the first two Tests unless Adelaide was granted the third Test. Lord Sheffield would have nothing further to do with Creswell and wrote to the SACA asking them to appoint somebody to deputise for Creswell. Fortunately, his Lordship got on well with Ben Wardill, who secured his agreement on major tour issues and kept him interested in a trophy for the three-state competition.

England lost two of the three major matches against Combined Australia, but in January 1892 they put on marvellous entertainment in the first Test at Melbourne, where in eight hours 20 minutes batting they made only 54 runs fewer than Australia scored in 13 hours. Left to score 213 in 150 minutes to win, England went for the runs instead of settling for a draw. At a time when Victoria faced the worst depression in its history, 75,000 people paid for admission, the highest number recorded up to then for a match anywhere in world cricket, although the highest daily total of 25,000 had been exceeded in England.

The Melbourne Cricket Club granted free use of the MCG in appreciation of Lord Sheffield's warm hospitality at Sheffield Park to so many Australian cricketers. The first day's takings were £1110 and the second day's £1172, which made nonsense of Shrewsbury's forecast that his Lordship would receive only £500 for each of these matches. Bob McLeod, in his Test debut, took 5 for 55 in England's first innings and Turner had 5 for 51 in the second innings. Bannerman batted for 435 minutes while scoring 45 and 41, and was at the crease for 15 hours in all during the first

two Tests. While the first Test was in progress a prominent Melbourne businessman, victim of the financial crisis, shot himself in Nicholson Street.

At Sydney in the second Test at the end of January, Australia made 145 and 391, England 307 and 156, Australia winning by 72 runs. Bold punter Jack Lyons backed himself at 20 to 1 with two £50 notes to score 200 runs in this match, but failed by 25 when he was out for 41 and 134. He had covered his wager however, with another bet of £100 to £10 that he would beat Bobby Abel's first innings score of 132 not out. Lord Sheffield gave Abel £50 for becoming the first Englishman to bat through a Test innings.

The New South Wales governor, Lord Jervis, was again widely condemned for inviting the amateurs in Lord Sheffield's team to Government House during this match and ignoring the professionals. W. G. Grace was also embarrassed when Lohmann shouted at him in the hearing of a number of Australians: "Not for a thousand a week would I join another team captained by you!" There were reports, too, that Stoddart and Grace came to blows at Adelaide, in March, where England won the third Test by an innings and 230 runs.

Having lost the Test series by two matches to one, the English team was embarrassed by comments made on their performance back home. Lord Hawke went on record as saying that Australia could not field a side to extend any of the leading counties and bitterly opposed Australian tours, which he labelled money-making ventures that disrupted the county programme. *Blackwood's Magazine* claimed Australian cricket was so contaminated by gambling that higher class Australians had severed connections with the game. Lord Sheffield was moved to deny that any of his team concurred.

Grace made 50, 15, 26, 5 and 28 in the three Tests and in the eleven-a-side matches on the tour scored 445 runs at 44.5, well ahead of the next best England batsman, Abel, on 38.8. The

Australians elected excitable Jack Blackham their captain for this series, the first to feature six-ball overs. Blackham seldom slept during a Test and often in tense situations hid in the dressing-room, hiding his head in a towel. He got most support from Billy Bruce, Australia's most consistent batsman in the series, who was not as sound as Moses, but just as stylish. Bruce scored 57, 40, 15, 72, and, on a wet Adelaide strip, 5 and 37. Briggs took 6 for 49 and 6 for 87 at Adelaide.

Meanwhile there were reports from Tasmania that Lord Sheffield spent his days talking to derelicts in the streets near his Hobart hotel. When one of his players was served with a £500 writ for allegedly assaulting a Sydney barmaid, his Lordship settled the affair for £90. Throughout the tour newspapers took up their old feud with W. G. Grace, with honours even. Much fun was had with his expanding girth. The *Bulletin* said he lumbered up to bowl "like a Clydesdale".

The *Australasian* said Grace was an unpopular captain with his team and claimed he deserved more money for all the speech making. "W. G. is admittedly a bad loser, and when he lost two Tests in succession he lost his temper, too, and kept losing it to the finish," the paper went on. "He has developed a condition of capriciousness, fussiness, and nastiness strongly to be deprecated." Blackham strongly defended Grace against these jibes, asserting that he was a model of sportsmanship.

Events during the Sydney Test were typical of the great man's problems. Moses had injured a leg so badly in the first Test he was not expected to play. When Australia decided to risk him and make Syd Gregory twelfth man, Grace warned Blackham that he could not expect a substitute if Moses broke down. Moses began to hobble after scoring 20 runs. Grace generously offered him a runner but in view of his earlier warning Blackham

*Harry Donnan, dropped after the first Test, replaced Bob McLeod, whose brother had died, during the Sydney Test*

*W. G. Grace walking out to bat was a formidable sight despite his waistline. He enjoyed a fame matched by no other Englishman*

refused to accept. Out for 29, Moses limped painfully to the slips after each over when Australia fielded, while the crowd shouted abuse at Grace. Next morning Grace persuaded Blackham to accept a replacement fieldsman for Moses.

On the Tuesday morning Bob McLeod learned that his brother Norman had died in Melbourne. The Australians wore black armbands and after scoring 18 runs in Australia's second innings McLeod left in the Melbourne Express. Forced to ask Grace for another substitute, Blackham suggested that he use Ernest Hutton, a Melbourne University student.

"Is he a better field than McLeod?" asked Grace.

"Yes," replied Blackham.

"Then get someone else," came the reply.

Harry Donnan, who had been dropped after playing his first Test in Melbourne, went onto the field for McLeod. Just to round off the fun Briggs took a hat-trick to end Australia's second innings at 391, dismissing Callaway, Blackham and Walter Giffen. When George Giffen caught and bowled Attewell to complete the England innings at 156 and regain the Ashes after 10 years, there were unprecedented scenes at the Sydney Cricket Ground. The *Argus* reported that "Straw hats, a popular summer wear in Sydney, were thrown in the air a thousand at a time. The ladies who crowded the reserve smashed their parasols on the seats and battered umbrellas were kicked about the lawn."

Despite his irascibility it was Grace who drew the record crowds and brought a revival in Australian cricket. He did not see much of Lord Sheffield during the tour, but he fully earned his fee, as the tour organisers worked him incessantly. When an official farewell on Sydney Harbour and a farewell dinner for the Englishmen had to be cancelled at Grace's request, Lord Sheffield was still absent in Hobart.

In the match against New South Wales, umpire Briscoe walked off when W. G. abused him for disallowing a catch. W. G. apologised but Briscoe refused to return and after a long delay Charles Bannerman took Briscoe's place. At Adelaide when rain interrupted play during the third Test, Grace upset the umpires by demanding that they inspect the pitch every 15 minutes. Lord Sheffield helped patch up these irritations by making donations to the hospital where Billy Midwinter's crippled son was a patient and to a fund to buy a tombstone for the Aboriginal cricketer, Johnny Mullagh.

Although Ben Wardill had kept a tight rein on expenses throughout the summer, the tour expenses blew out to £16,000 compared with the

*Sydney club cricketer E. J. Briscoe claimed he was insulted by W. G. Grace while umpiring one of England's matches in Sydney. Despite apologies, Briscoe refused to return to the field*

original estimate of £11,000. Receipts failed to cover this by £2700, but Lord Sheffield considered £2700 a fair price to pay for the impetus the tour gave to Australian cricket. Officials presented Mrs Grace with a floral tribute after the last Test at Adelaide. The following week, when Lord Sheffield arrived in Melbourne aboard the *Arcadia*, bound for London, he took the trouble to recognise Ben Wardill's efforts by presenting him with five silver dessert pieces of the choicest design and workmanship.

The Englishmen departed for home early in April 1892, with W. G. insistent that something would have to be done to improve umpiring in big matches. He also said, "If I'd known I had to make so many speeches I would have stayed at home." To his credit, W. G. had played in every match and adjusted his batting order so that he always batted when most people would see him. Nonetheless, by the last Test even his friend "Felix", Tom Horan's pseudonym for his articles in the *Australasian*, had turned against him.

The decisive defeat of Lord Sheffield's team in the first two Tests changed England's attitude towards Australian cricket overnight. Vic Cohen, who was to manage Australia's tour to England in 1893, had no difficulty securing matches. English officials, keen to avenge the defeats, welcomed Cohen's requests for a game, regardless of any disruption to county fixtures. Lord Hawke's condemnation of Australia's cricket standards was quickly forgotten by county secretaries eagerly anticipating the takings the Australians' next matches in England would draw.

Lord Sheffield was delighted by the warmth of his reception in Australia and he sent a letter to Ben Wardill from Naples renewing his offer of 150 guineas to be "spent on the advancement of Australian cricket". Wardill had tried all the summer to secure some agreement about how the money should be spent. He now found the states still undecided. Victoria was keen to split the money with South Australia and New South Wales; the difficulty was that New South Wales played Victoria twice each summer but both New South Wales and Victoria had only one match a season against South Australia. Wardill himself preferred three trophies, for which clubs within the states would compete.

Meanwhile the formation of the Australasian Cricket Council at a meeting at the Oxford Hotel in Sydney on 13 September 1892 distracted attention from Lord Sheffield's 150 guineas. New South Wales and Victoria each had four delegates at this meeting and South Australia two, while Queensland and Tasmania sent letters regretting their inability to attend. Richard Teece and John Portus, of New South Wales, were elected chairman and secretary respectively, with Victor Cohen and J. M. Gibson also representing New South Wales. The Victorian representatives were R. W. Best, H. H. Budd, D. A. Madden and W. Kelleher. The South Australian delegates were G.

Mostyn Evans and A. Robinson, who was based in Sydney. Evans held proxy votes for G. O. Whitridge and John Creswell, SACA secretary.

Most of that first meeting was occupied with the 1893 tour of England and how the players should be selected, and it was not until late in the afternoon that the meeting addressed itself to Lord Sheffield's 150 guineas. When Victoria moved to split the money between the three states, a fiery discussion developed, which ended when Robinson moved an amendment that the money "be devoted to a premiership shield, to be held by the premier colony for the year, and that a subcommittee consisting of Messrs Cohen, Robinson and Kelleher be appointed to draft the necessary rules". Further heated discussion followed before the amendment was carried by one vote, with the four Victorians plus Evans outvoted by Robinson, Cohen, Portus, Gibson and the two absentee delegates, Whitridge and Creswell.

This slender margin saw the creation of the Sheffield Shield. The subcommittee met that evening and drafted rules for the new competition for the full committee to approve next morning during a meeting on the steamer *Dawn* as it cruised round Sydney Harbour. South Australia's strong performance in January 1892, when they defeated a full strength New South Wales team in Sydney by an innings and 53 runs, had undoubtedly swayed delegates and paved the way for Australia's most important domestic cricket competition. On board the *Dawn* the rules were agreed on:

1. That Lord Sheffield's donation be devoted to the purchase of a silver shield to be called the Sheffield Shield and to be given for competition between the three colonies named.
2. That the competition be confined to inter-Colonial matches.
3. That the first competition for possession of the Shield be held on the occasion of the next meeting between two of the three participating colonies and that the colony winning the match hold the Shield until it suffers a defeat

*The ill-fated Australasian Cricket Council tried to take control of the administration of all Australian cricket. Its failure to win recognition stemmed partly from the lack of prominent players among its members. George Giffen (front, third from left) is the only Test player included in this photograph taken at the March 1893 meeting in Adelaide*

in an inter-Colonial match, upon the happening of which event the Shield shall pass into the possession of the colony inflicting the defeat; similarly for all succeeding contests.

4. In the event of a tie, the Shield shall remain in the possession of the colony holding it at the date of the commencement of the match resulting in the tie.

5. The representatives of the colony holding the

As Ric Finlay has established, these rules meant that one colony could hold the Shield for several seasons even if it lost most of its matches, or that the Shield could even change hands several times a season. They also meant that some matches would be irrelevant to the fate of the Shield, but the delegates flatly refused to change the practice whereby New South Wales and Victoria met twice, and only played South Australia once.

On 25 March 1893 a meeting of delegates from the colonies of New South Wales, Victoria and South Australia at the Club Hotel, Adelaide, defined the following objects of the Australasian Cricket Council:

1. The regulation of the visits of England and other teams to Australia.
2. The regulation of Australasian teams to England or elsewhere, in conjunction with the governing bodies of the places visited.
3. The appointment of umpires for international and inter-Colonial matches played in Australasia.
4. The settlement of disputes or differences between associations represented on the council.
5. The alteration or amendment of, or the addition to, the Laws of Cricket in Australasia.

Each colony paid two guineas to join the council, which even at a time of economic recession was an absurdly low amount, but indicative of the council's ineffectual bid to gain control of all cricket in Australia and New Zealand. The use of the word Australasian in the council's name became increasingly sad as the months went by with New Zealand ignoring all requests to join.

The council ignored all the real problems it faced, but allowed the first Sheffield Shield matches to proceed on an absurd basis. By sheer luck the Shield competition became its only lasting monument. South Australia defeated New South Wales at Adelaide in December 1892, and, as Ric Finlay has shown, under the existing rules became the first holders of the Shield. The next match between New South Wales and Victoria had no bearing on the Shield as neither held it, but when

Shield (providing they have played in not less than two matches in any season) shall each be awarded a badge to be worn on coat or cap, such badge to be of a suitable design. Subject to the permission of Lord Sheffield, it is suggested that the design shall be the Sheffield Coronet and the figures representing the year to which the badge is applicable.

South Australia travelled to Melbourne and lost to Victoria on 4 January 1893, they also lost the Shield they had held for only 14 days. By the middle of January, when it became obvious Victoria would have the best playing record for the current season, delegates agreed to alter the rules so that the colony with the best performance each season in intercolonial matches took the trophy. Victoria, which had voted against using Lord Sheffield's 150 guineas for a shield, thus became the first summer's holders. But neither South Australia, the first holders, nor Victoria had a shield to show for their efforts, as the 150 guineas had still not arrived from England.

When it did, Ben Wardill, as custodian of Lord Sheffield's affairs in Australia, did not feel obliged to hand it over to council secretary John Portus as he was not confident about the council's future. Finally Wardill sent the draft for 150 guineas to Phillip Sheridan, and he handed it to John Portus. As secretary of the council, Portus then advertised for tenders from jewellers for a shield worth £150 sterling. Originally it was intended to have a figure of Lord Sheffield on top, but when the council accepted the bid by Melbourne jeweller Phillip Blashki from 21 tenders it was decided to replace the unathletic frame of his Lordship with the bosomy figure of Victory, a symbol of success in Greek mythology.

Blashki was born a Jew in the village of Blaszki, near Kalisz, 190 kilometres south-west of Warsaw, on 21 February 1836. His real name was Uri Wanczewski, and he was the son of a tanner. When he arrived in Manchester in 1854, he found employment with a tassel-maker, who had problems with his name, and so he changed it to Blashki, after his home village. Blashki intended to settle in America but when he and his bride, a Polish widow, arrived at the docks they found their boat had already gone, so they opted instead to take ship to Australia where travel agents said there was "gold in the streets". Blashki became an outstanding craftsman and the head of a profitable business. Apart from the Sheffield

*The Sheffield Shield. The States disagreed about whether to divide Lord Sheffield's £150, and finally decided to spend it on this trophy designed by Melbourne jeweller Phillip Blashki*

Shield he also made the Hordern Shield, for Sydney's first-grade cricket premiers.

The Australasian Cricket Council aimed to control overseas tours and draw its main income from them, but it was in difficulty from the start with players who reserved the right to pick their own teams, to finance and share tour profits, and to elect their own captains. George Giffen wrote in *With Bat and Ball* that the captains of seven of the first eight Australian teams to England were selected by the players. The exception was "Tup" Scott whom the 1886 team accepted as the nominee of the tour sponsors, the Melbourne Cricket Club. Thus it was significant that the council refused to tackle this issue at its first meetings, a weakness that enabled the players to retain their close-knit establishment.

Jack Blackham went on all the first eight tours. Harry Boyle, Bonnor, Spofforth and Alick Bannerman went on five of the first six, and Joey Palmer toured four times in succession.

Blessed with some remarkably talented players, Australia had made a marvellous start in international cricket, losing only two of the first ten Tests against England. Faced with opponents intent on making money, England had recovered dramatically to win 19 of the next 30 Tests.

According to George Giffen, the Australasian Cricket Council upset all Australia's leading players by instructing selectors of the 1893 Australian team to England — Giffen, Blackham, Turner, Alick Bannerman, Lyons and Harry Trott — to include Arthur Coningham, the former Queensland all-rounder who was then playing for New South Wales. The players believed that as the council had no money with which to finance tours they could not dictate to anybody. Coningham still toured.

The miraculous thing was that although Australian cricket had no effective control body, its Test team being run as a virtual fiefdom, the regular tours improved playing skills and established the international reputation of Australian cricket. From the humble beginning in Sydney's Hyde Park some fine grounds had appeared, with facilities, playing surfaces and crowd control superior to anything in England. Indeed it had become a frequent joke among Australian tourists that "half the English grounds don't even have a shower bath".

The leading players had gone too far on their return home in 1884 when they demanded half the gate-money from all international matches, and there had been generations of bickering between intercolonial associations. But Australians' passion for cricket had intensified, thanks mainly to the achievements of players who lined their pockets on the way round England but still refused to take the field through the professionals' gate. And in the years before Federation, the feats of Australian cricketers did as much to unite the colonies into a nation as her politicians, soldiers and public servants.

# Appendix

## The Players' Agreement of 1884

This Indenture made the first day of January in the year of our Lord one thousand eight hundred and eighty four Between George Alexander of Melbourne in the Colony of Victoria of the first part Henry Frederick Boyle of the same place of the second part George Eugene Palmer of the same place of the third part John McCarthy Blackham of the same place of the fourth part William Midwinter of the same place of the fifth part George John Bonnor of the same place of the sixth part William Henry Cooper of the same place of the seventh part Percy Stanislaus McDonnell of the same place of the eighth part George Giffen of Adelaide in the Colony of South Australia of the ninth part William Lloyd Murdoch of Sydney in the Colony of New South Wales of the tenth part Alexander Chambers Bannerman of the same place of the eleventh part Henry James Herbert Scott of Melbourne aforesaid of the twelfth part and Frederick Robert Spofforth of Sydney aforesaid of the thirteenth part Whereas the said parties hereto have agreed to enter into a partnership for the purpose of playing a series of matches at Cricket in the Australian Colonies, the Colonies of Tasmania and New Zealand and in Great Britain and Ireland and such other places as may be mutually agreed upon. Now this Indenture witnesseth that each of them the said George Alexander, Henry Frederick Boyle, George Eugene Palmer, John McCarthy Blackham, William Midwinter, George John Bonnor, William Henry

Cooper, Percy Stanislaus McDonnell, George Giffen, William Lloyd Murdoch, Alexander Chambers Bannerman, Henry James Herbert Scott, Frederick Robert Spofforth, so far as the stipulations and provisions hereinafter contained are to be observed and performed by him his executors or administrators doth hereby himself his heirs executors and administrators covenant with the others of them their executors and administrators and as a separate covenant with each of the others his executors and administrators that they the said George Alexander, Henry Frederick Boyle, George Eugene Palmer, John McCarthy Blackham, William Midwinter, George John Bonnor, William Henry Cooper, Percy Stanislaus McDonnell, George Giffen, William Lloyd Murdoch, Alexander Chambers Bannerman, Henry James Herbert Scott, and Frederick Robert Spofforth will become and remain partners for the purpose and period and under subject to the stipulations and provisions hereinafter expressed and contained that is to say—

I. The object of the partnership shall be the playing of a series of matches of cricket at such times and places within the Colonies and in the United Kingdom aforesaid and such other places as may be mutually agreed upon by a majority of the partners aforesaid.

II. The partnership shall commence on the first day of January one thousand eight hundred and eighty four.

III. The partnership shall be carried on under the style or firm of "The Australian Team."

IV. The capital of the partnership shall be the sum which a majority of the said partners shall at their first meeting agree upon and shall be contributed by the partners in such proportions and at such times as may then be agreed upon by such majority and each partner shall prior to such meeting of the partners deposit with the said George Alexander the sum of fifty pounds to be applied to partnership purposes.

V. If it shall be found requisite according to the resolution of the majority of the partners to increase the capital for the time being so much additional capital as shall be fixed by such resolution shall be brought into and contributed by the partners respectively in the proportions fixed by such resolutions.

VI. The capital for the time being shall (subject as hereinafter mentioned) be used and employed in the partnership business and no part of such capital shall be withdrawn or made use of for any other purpose by any partner except by special agreement in writing under the hands of a majority of the partners for the time being.

VII. The bankers of the partnership shall be the Commercial Bank of Australia Collingwood or such other Bank as the Executive Committee hereinafter appointed shall from time to time agree upon and all monies brought into the said partnership and all monies or negotiable securities received for or on account of the partnership (except for current expenses) shall be paid into such Bank and on payment of any Bills, Notes, Drafts or Cheques into any such Bank such two or more of the partners as the said Executive Committee shall from time to time appoint for that purpose may make and sign all such indorsements and instruments as are usual or may be requisite or necessary on that behalf and for the purposes of the partnership (and for no other purpose) may draw and accept any Bill Draft Note or Cheque in the name or on account of the firm.

VIII. All outgoings in respect of the said partnership and the salaries wages travelling expenses and remuneration of all persons employed in or about the partnership and all debts and other monies to become payable on account of the said partnership and all losses which shall happen in or to the same shall be borne and paid out of the gains and profits of the partnership if sufficient for that purpose but if insufficient then out of the partnership capital and funds for the time being or if the same shall be deficient by the partners in the shares and proportions in which they shall be respectively interested in the said partnership.

IX. The majority of the partners for the time being shall have the power of appointing and removing three partners to be called the Executive Committee and such Committee (one of whom shall be the Manager) shall have the management conduct and superintendance of the business and affairs of the said partnership and such powers and duties as are hereinafter set forth and the said George Alexander shall be the first Manager and in all questions and differences which may arise between the partners concerning the partnership or the management conduct or regulation thereof the decision of such Executive Committee shall be final and conclusive upon the other partner or partners.

X. The partners shall meet at the Oriental Hotel Collins Street East in the City of Melbourne in the Colony of Victoria on the twelfth day of January next for the purpose of appointing the first Executive Committee and for other business and thereafter at such place and time and as often as the Executive Committee for the time being may from time to time by writing signed by them appoint for the purpose of mutual information and consultation relating to the affairs of the partnership.

XI. Proper books of account shall be kept by the Manager for the time being in which all transactions relating to the partnership business shall be duly entered and such books together with the several agreements securities letters documents and vouchers of and belonging to the partnership shall be kept at the Manager's Office or such other place as shall from time to time be fixed or agreed upon by the Executive Committee and be there subject to the free inspection of every partner or his Agents or Solicitor at all reasonable time for the purpose of perusing or examining the same or taking extracts or copies from or out of the same.

XII. The partners shall be entitled to the net profits arising from the said partnership after making the payments hereinbefore directed and providing for all liabilities and contemplated outlay and the division of the balance shall be made among them in proportion to their respective shares in the capital.

XIII. If any partner shall die the partnership shall thereupon determine as to him and his executors or administrators shall have no interest in common with the other or surviving partners or partner in the property of the partnership. But an account shall thereupon be taken of the share in the said partnership of the partner so dying and the amount thereby appearing to the credit of such deceased partner, after deducting thereout all monies (if any) previously advanced to him on account of such share, shall as soon as it can be conveniently done, be paid to his executors or administrators by the surviving partners or partner.

XIV. The Executive Committee shall as soon as conveniently may be after each match furnish a written financial statement of the receipts and disbursements of each such match.

XV. Any partner seceding from such partnership on any account whatsoever shall pay to the other partners a sum to be decided on and by way of liquidated and ascertained damages and not by way of penalty.

XVI. Any partner guilty of any act of inebriety misconduct or nonobservance of these presents (of which the Executive Committee shall be the sole judges) shall forfeit and pay to the other partners for each offence a sum to be fixed by the Executive Committee at their discretion not exceeding the sum of twenty-five pounds with power

to the Executive Committee in case of repeated acts of inebriety, misconduct or nonobservance by any partner and if the majority in number of such partners other than such offending partner or partners shall think proper to forfeit for the benefit of the other partners the interest of such offending partner.

XVII. The said partners shall immediately after the first meeting go into strict practice under the direction and control of the Executive Committee and for such period as they shall order and direct.

XVIII. The said partners shall and will during the continuance of this partnership give their exclusive services to the said partnership concern and will during all that period faithfully cheerfully punctually and to the best of their ability perform fulfil and carry out all matches engagements and arrangements which the Executive Committee shall make or enter into for them and shall and will act on the premises under the direction of the said Executive Committee and obey all their lawful orders in relation thereto.

XIX. Whenever any doubt difference or dispute shall hereafter arise between the partners or between the representatives of any deceased partner and the surviving partners touching these presents or the construction hereof or any clause or thing herein contained or any account valuation or division of assets debts or liabilities to be made as hereinbefore is mentioned or any other matter in anywise relating to or concerning the partnership business or the affairs thereof or the rights duties or liabilities of any of the partners in connection therewith the matter in difference shall be referred to the Executive Committee whose decision shall be final and conclusive.

# Bibliography

Altham, H. S., *A history of cricket*, vol. I, Allen & Unwin, London, 1926

Arlott, John, *The great allrounders*, Pelham, London, 1968
  *The great bowlers*, Pelham, London, 1969
  *A word from John Arlott*, Pelham, London, 1983
  *Arlott on cricket*, William Collins, London, 1984

Ashley-Cooper, Frederick Samuel, *Cricket and cricketers*, Edmund Seale, London, 1901

Australian Society of Cricket Statisticians (ed. Roger Page), *Victorian cricketers 1850–1978; Queensland cricketers 1892–1979; New South Wales cricketers 1855–1981; Tasmanian cricketers 1850–1982; Western Australian cricketers 1892–1983; South Australian cricketers 1877–1984*, Association of Cricket Statisticians, Retford, Notts, 1979–85

Bachelor, Denzil, *The book of cricket*, Collins, London, 1952

Barker, Ralph, *The great bowlers*, Chatto & Windus, London, 1967

Bettesworth, W. A., *The Walkers of Southgate*, Methuen, London, 1900

Bowen, Rowland, *Cricket: A history*, Eyre & Spottiswoode, London, 1970

Brodbribb, Gerald, *Hit for six*, Heinemann, London, 1960
  *Felix on the bat*, Eyre & Spottiswoode, London, 1962

Caffyn, William, *Seventy-one not out*, Blackwood, London, 1899

Cardus, Neville, *Cricket*, Longmans Green, London, 1930
  *Autobiography*, Collins, London, 1947
  *Second innings*, Collins, London, 1950
  *Cricket all the year*, Collins, London, 1952
  *Full score*, Cassell, London, 1970
  *Cardus on cricket*, Souvenir, London, 1977

Cashman, Richard, *'Ave a go, yer mug!*, Collins, Sydney, 1985

Cumes, J. W. C., *Their chastity was not too rigid*, Longmans, Melbourne, 1979

Darling, D. K., *Test tussles on and off the field*, privately published, Hobart, 1970

Derriman, Philip, *The grand old ground*, Cassell, Sydney, 1981
  *True to the Blue*, Richard Smart, Sydney, 1985

Downer, Sidney, *100 not out*, Rigby, Adelaide, 1972

Dunstan, Keith, *The paddock that grew*, Cassell, Melbourne, 1962

Egan, Pierce, *Pierce Egan's book of sports*, Tegg, London, 1832

Ferguson, W. H., *Mr Cricket*, Nicholas Kaye, London, 1957

Fingleton, J. H. W., *Cricket crisis*, Cassell, London, 1947
  *Masters of cricket*, Heinemann, London, 1959
Frindall, Bill, *The Wisden book of Test cricket*, MacDonald & Jane, London, 1978
  *The Wisden book of cricket records*, Queen Anne Press, London, 1981
Frith, David, *"My dear victorious Stod"*, Lutterworth Press, London, 1977
  *The fast men*, Van Rostrand Reinhold, London, 1977
  *The golden age of cricket*, Angus & Robertson, Sydney, 1978
  *England versus Australia*, Richard Smart, Sydney, 1980
  *The slow men*, Horwitz Grahame, Sydney, 1984
Fry, C. B., *Giants of the game*, Ward Lock & E. P. Publishing, London, 1910
Garnsey, George, *Cricket: Its origin and development*, Australian Broadcasting Commission, Sydney, 1935
Giffen, George, *With bat and ball*, Ward Lock, London, 1898
Grace, Dr Edward Mills, *The trip to Australia*, W. H. Knight, London, 1864
Grace, Radcliffe, "The Australasian Cricket Council", *Hill Chatter*, Journal of the Australian Cricket Society (Sydney Branch), 1983
Grace, Dr William Gilbert, *"W. G.": Cricketing reminiscences*, Bowden, London, 1899
Green, Benny, *Cricket archives*, Pavilion, London, 1985
Harris, Lord, *A few short runs*, Murray, London, 1921
Harte, Chris, *A history of the Sheffield Shield*, with research by Ric Finlay, Allen & Unwin, Sydney, 1986
Hawke, Lord, *Recollections and reminiscences*, Williams & Norgate, London, 1924
Haygarth, Arthur, Ashley-Cooper, F. S., and Lillywhite, Frederick, *M.C.C. cricket scores and biographies*, Longmans, London, vols I–XV
Hayter, Reg. (ed.), *The cricketer international*, Cassell, London, 1981
Hill, Clement, Twenty articles of reminiscences, *Argus*, Melbourne, 1922
Hopper, Peter, *A history of the Western Australian Cricket Association*, unpublished thesis, Perth, 1974
Horan, Thomas Patrick (under the pseudonym "Felix"), "Under the elms", weekly cricket column in the *Australasian*
Hutcheon, E. H., *A history of Queensland cricket*, Queensland Cricket Association, Brisbane, 1947
Iredale, Frank, *33 years of cricket*, Beatty Richardson, Sydney, 1920
Ironside, Frederick James, *Australasian cricketing handbook*, Ironside, Sydney, 1880
Jessop, Gilbert, *A cricketer's log*, Hodder & Stoughton, London, 1922
Laver, Frank, *An Australian cricketer on tour*, Bell & Sons, London, 1907
Lyttelton, Robert Henry, *Cricket*, Duckworth, London, 1898
*McMahon's Cricket & Sports Manual* (ed. P. C. Curtis), Sydney, 1910
Mandle, W. F., "Cricket and Australian nationalism in the nineteenth century", *Journal of the Royal Australian Historical Society*, 1973
  "Games people played: cricket and football in the late nineteenth century", *Historical Studies*, 1973
Martin-Jenkins, Christopher, *The complete who's who of Test cricketers*, Orbis, London, 1980
Millbank, Susan, *Cricket and South Australia 1871–1914*, unpublished thesis, Flinders University, 1981
Monfries, John Elliott, *Not Test cricket*, Gillingham, Adelaide, 1950

Moody, Clarence P., *Australian cricket and cricketers 1856–1894*, Thomson, Melbourne, 1894
  *Album of noted Australian cricketers*, Hussey & Gillingham, 1898
  *South Australian cricket: reminiscences of fifty years*, W. K. Thomas, Adelaide, 1898

Moyes, A. G., *A century of cricketers*, Angus & Robertson, Sydney, 1950
  *Australian bowlers from Spofforth to Lindwall*, Angus & Robertson, Sydney, 1953
  *Australian batsmen from Charles Bannerman to Neil Harvey*, Angus & Robertson, Sydney, 1954
  *Australian cricket: a history*, Angus & Robertson, Sydney, 1959
  *The changing face of cricket*, Angus & Robertson, Sydney, 1963

Mullins, Patrick J., *Cricket in the tropics*, privately published, Brisbane, 1975
  *Cricket memorabilia in Australia*, privately published, Brisbane, 1985

Mulvaney, D. J., *Cricket walkabout*, Melbourne University Press, Melbourne, 1967

Noble, M. A., *The game's the thing*, Cassell, London, 1928

Pace, Jack, *The City & Suburban Cricket Association: a history*, Annual Reports of the CSCA, Sydney, 1982–83 and 1983–84

Page, Roger, *A history of Tasmanian cricket*, Roger Page, Hobart, 1957

Piesse, Ken, *The Prahran Cricket Club's Centenary History*, Prahran Cricket Club, Melbourne, 1979
  *Cricketer*, Newspress, Melbourne
  *The great book of Australian cricket stories*, Currey O'Neil, Melbourne, 1982

Pollard, Jack, *Bumpers, boseys and brickbats*, Murray, Sydney, 1962
  *Cricket: the Australian way*, Lansdowne Press, Melbourne, 1961
  *Six and out*, enlarged 6th ed., Pollard Publishing, Sydney, 1980
  *Australian cricket: the game and the players*, Hodder & Stoughton, Sydney, 1982
  *The pictorial history of Australian cricket*, Dent, Melbourne, 1983

Pullin, A. W. ("Old Ebor"), *Talks with old English cricketers*, Blackwood, London, 1900

Raiji, Vasant (ed.), *Victor Trumper*, Vivek Publications, Bombay, 1964

Ranjitsinhji, Kumar Sri, *The jubilee book of cricket*, Blackwood, London, 1897
  *With Stoddart's team in Australia*, Bowden, London, 1898

Robertson-Glasgow, R. C., *Cricket prints*, Werner Laurie, London, 1946
  *More cricket prints*, Werner Laurie, London, 1948
  *Crusoe on cricket*, Alan Ross, London, 1966

Robinson, Ray, *Between wickets*, Collins, London, 1946
  *From the boundary*, Collins, London, 1951
  *On top down under*, Cassell, Melbourne, 1975

Rosenwater, Irving, and Ralph Barker, *England v. Australia*, Heinemann, London, 1969

Ross, Gordon, *A history of cricket*, Barker, London, 1972

Samuels, Cyril, *The big game in Australia*, Publicity Press, Sydney, 1925

Smith, Sydney, *History of the Tests*, Australasian Publishing Co, Sydney, 1947

Sparks, William P. H., *Test cricket: a record of Australia–England matches*, 1877–1922, Ouseley, London, 1925

Sporting Globe, *Test cricket book* (ed. E. M. Baillie), Sporting Globe, Melbourne, 1930

Standing, Percy Cross, *Anglo–Australian cricket 1862–1926*, Faber & Gwyer, London, 1926

Swanton, E. W., and John Woodcock, *Barclay's world of cricket*, Collins, London, 1980

Swanton, E. W., *The world of cricket*, Michael Joseph, London, 1966

Taylor, Percy, *The story of the Carlton Cricket Club*, Carlton Cricket Club, Melbourne, 1956

Thomson, A. A., *Odd men in: a gallery of cricket eccentrics*, Pavilion, London, 1985
    *Cricket: the golden ages*, Phoenix House, London, 1961
    *Cricket my pleasure*, Museum Press, London, 1953
    *Cricket: the great captains*, Stanley Paul, London, 1965

Toms, Stanley T. (ed.), *England v. Australia Tests 1878–1908*, Sports Publications, London, 1909

Torrens, Warwick, *Queensland cricket and cricketers*, Brisbane, privately published, 1981

Tresidder, Phil (ed.), *Australian cricket*, Modern Magazines, Sydney

Trumble, Robert, *The golden age of cricket*, privately published, Melbourne, 1968

Turner, C. T. B., *The quest for bowlers*, Cornstalk Publishing, Sydney, 1926

Wakeley, Bertram Joseph, *Classic centuries in Tests between England and Australia*, Kaye, London, 1964

Warner, Pelham Francis, *How we recovered the Ashes*, Chapman & Hall, London, 1904
    *Cricketing reminiscences*, Richards, London, 1920
    *My cricketing life*, Hodder & Stoughton, London, 1921
    *Long innings*, Harrap, London, 1951

Webber, Roy, *The Playfair book of cricket records*, Playfair, London, 1951

Whitington, Richard Smallpeice, *An illustrated history of Australian cricket*, Lansdowne Press, Melbourne, 1972

Whitridge, W. O., *The South Australian cricketer's guide*, E. S. Wigg, Adelaide, 1877

Williams, Marcus (ed.), *Double century: 200 years of cricket in* The Times, Willow Collins, London, 1985

Wills, Thomas Wentworth, *The Australian cricketer's guide*, McKinley, Melbourne, 1870 and 1871

*Wisden's cricket almanack*, Sporting Handbooks and MacDonald & Jane, London, 1863–1986

Woods, Samuel Joseph James, *My reminiscences*, Chapman & Hall, London, 1925

Wrigley, Arthur, *The book of Test cricket*, Epworth Press, London, 1965

Wynne-Thomas, Peter, Philip Bailey and Philip Thorn, *Who's who of cricketers*, Newnes Books and the Association of Cricket Statisticians, London, 1984

Wynne-Thomas, Peter, *"Give me Arthur"*, Arthur Barker, London, 1985

# Picture credits

The author and publishers gratefully acknowledge the following people and organisations who gave permission to reproduce photographs and illustrations on the pages noted. Every effort has been made to trace copyright holders and apology is made for any unintended infringement. Pictures not listed come from the author's collection.

*Age*, 277

Philip Derriman, 229

Ric Finlay, 31, 34–5, 280–1, 296

Albert Gregory Collection (Mitchell Library), 72, 106, 134–5, 179, 182 (left), 191, 207, 221, 248–9, 269, 311

Mrs P. Harrison, 30

Herald & Weekly Times, 239, 278 (left)

Hobart City Corporation, 32

La Trobe Library, State Library of Victoria, 44, 125, 134, 167

Library Board of Western Australia, 78–9

Marylebone Cricket Club Collection, 2–3, 4, 5, 9, 13, 14, 15, 18–19, 36, 114–15, 136, 157, 168, 169, 181, 196–7, 204, 205, 214, 222, 224, 227, 235, 236, 252–3, 262, 264–5, 290, 307

Mechanics Institute, Harrow, 160

Melbourne Cricket Ground Museum, 38–9, 41, 46–7, 48, 50, 94–5, 99, 106–7, 117, 118–19, 128–9, 138, 152, 154–5, 162–3, 164–5, 173, 182 (right), 183, 184–5, 202, 258, 268, 278 (right), 282, 295

Mitchell Library, State Library of New South Wales, 6–7, 20, 49, 70–1, 91, 112–13, 130, 141, 145, 148–9, 176–7, 212–13, 232–3, 287, 305

Mortlock Library, State Library of South Australia, 52–3, 57, 60, 62

Pat Mullins Collection, 80–1, 108–9

National Library of Australia (Rex Nan Kivell Collection), 214–15

New South Wales Cricket Association, 100, 110, 192, 193, 242, 303, 316 (photo Vivienne Cray)

Roger Page, 22–3

Queensland Cricket Association, 91, 92 (left)

South Australian Cricket Association, 54–5, 58, 64, 294, 308

Victorian Cricket Association, 288

Western Australian Cricket Association, 75

Western Australian Newspapers Ltd, 76–7

Peter Wynne-Thomas, 244

# Index

*ANGUS & ROBERTSON PUBLISHERS*

*Unit 4, Eden Park, 31 Waterloo Road,*
*North Ryde, NSW, Australia 2113, and*
*16 Golden Square, London W1R 4BN,*
*United Kingdom*

*First published in Australia*
*by Angus & Robertson Publishers in 1987*
*First published in the United Kingdom*
*by Angus & Robertson UK in 1987*

*Copyright © Jack Pollard 1987*

*National Library of Australia*
*Cataloguing-in-publication data.*

*Pollard, Jack, 1926-*
   *The formative years of Australian cricket, 1803–1893.*

   *Bibliography.*
   *Includes index.*
   *ISBN 0 207 15490 2.*

   *1. Cricket — Australia — History — 19th century.*
   *2. Cricket — Australia — Societies, etc. — History —*
   *19th century. 3. Cricket — Australia — Tournaments —*
   *History — 19th century. 4. Test matches (Cricket) —*
   *History — 19th century. I. Title.*

*796.35 '8 '0994*

*Typeset in 11 pt Bem by Midland Typesetters*
*Printed in Australia by Globe Press*